Total Productive Maintenance

Total Productive Maintenance

Bikash Bhadury

Department of Industrial Engineering and Management
Indian Institute of Technology
Kharagpur — 723 102

ALLIED PUBLISHERS LIMITED

New Delhi • Mumbai • Calcutta • Lucknow • Chennai
Nagpur • Bangalore • Hyderabad • Ahmedabad

ALLIED PUBLISHERS LIMITED

Regd. Off.: 15. J.N. Heredia Marg, Ballard Estate, Mumbai — 400038
Prarthna Flats (2nd Floor), Navrangpura, Ahmedabad — 380009
3-5-1114/1 Kachiguda Cross Road, Hyderabad — 500027
16A Ashok Marg, Patiala House, Lucknow — 226001
5th Main Road, Gandhinagar, Bangalore — 560009
17 Chittaranjan Avenue, Calcutta — 700072
81 Hill Road, Ramnagar, Nagpur — 440010
13/14, Asaf Ali Road, New Delhi — 110002
751 Anna Salai, Chennai — 600002

ISBN 81-7023-805-6

ASSOCIATE EDITOR	:	JYOTI MEHROTRA
PRODUCTION MANAGER	:	B.K. DAS
COVER	:	KAM STUDIO

Published by Sunil Sachdev and printed by Ravi Sachdev at Allied Publishers Limited (Printing Division), A-104 Mayapuri, Phase II, New Delhi — 110 064. Typeset by ***Printo Graphic Systems,*** M-66, Sriniwas Puri, New Delhi — 110 065

Dedication

"Dedicated to the memory of my Father whom I lost in 1979.
He has been the inspiration in everything I have done."

PREFACE

When we graduated (in 1962) and armed with an honours degree in mechanical engineering joined industry as young professionals, we were advised to forget all the theory that we had learnt. Learning theory was only necessary to get a degree and once we had a degree and a job, theory seemed redundant. Moreover, theory and practice seemed to have no connection (or, so it seemed at that time). As time passed and a number of practical problems came up, slowly it dawned on us that some of these problems could probably be better tackled with the theory we had learnt (and forgotten by then). To some of us, it also seemed that it would be better if we went back to the colleges and universities to get more theoretical knowledge. Now it seems that theory is not only very relevant but also that theory and practice are so interdependent that it is very difficult to distinguish between the two. Practice is the real test of knowledge but there cannot be any practice without a theoretical base. Also, theory that is developed from practice is probably the most relevant of all. Total productive maintenance (TPM) has evolved entirely out of the shop-floor practice of maintenance of equipment and machines - the overall aim of maintenance, its immediate objectives and the constraints that the maintenance department has to work with. At the same time, it has very strong conceptual underpinnings and a thorough understanding of these basic concepts is necessary for the proper implementation of TPM. All this drove me to learn TPM and later to share what I had learnt with others.

My first encounter with TPM was sometime in 1982 when I read the guest editorial written by the then Chairman of the Japan Institute of Plant Engineers, A. Tamaki. This guest editorial was entitled 'TPM and Its Impact on Japanese Industry' and it had been published in the January 1981 issue of Terotechnica (the earlier incarnation of Maintenance Management International). Later, a number of papers were published in Terotechnica and Maintenance Management International and the most notable among them were the two papers by Nakajima (1982 and 1986), Takahashi (May, 1981) and Kelly (1984). Nakajima's "Introduction to TPM" was brought out by the Productivity Press, Cambridge, Massachusetts (U.S.A.) in 1988 and this was probably the first book on TPM. This was closely followed by two books in close succession, namely on implementation of TPM edited by Nakajima in 1989 published also by the Productivity Press and by Takahashi and Osada published by the Asian Productivity Organization, Tokyo in

1990. In early 1991, a fantastic opportunity came my way. A large tyre manufacturing company located in Western India sent a letter to us noting therein that they were interested in implementing TPM and that they were prepared to offer a part of this activity as an M. Tech project for one of our M. Tech students. We sent a student to work on the project and he spent nearly six months in the tyre manufacturing factory working on various aspects in the implementation of TPM. Moreover, on his return from the factory, the student told me that the company was interested in implementing TPM because they felt that the implementation of TPM would facilitate the introduction of standard maintenance and operating procedures as part of the implementation of the ISO9000 clauses. This way, through TPM, they wanted to get ISO9000 certification and subsequently implement TQM. This showed the interdependence and inter-relationship between TPM and TQM. This M. Tech project, carried out under my guidance, was the spark that ignited my interest in TPM. I read all that I could on the subject and I even started teaching it as part of the reliability and maintenance course. Another opportunity of implementation came my way in 1995 again in a tyre manufacturing company located in Eastern India. Although this was a much smaller application, it was very useful since it brought out the need for the implementation of TPM.

TPM was developed in Japan and accordingly, all the available books, except the one by Wireman (Industrial Press, Inc., 1991), have been writen by Japanese authors. These books suffer from the following shortcomings:

1. The Japanese authors have tended to write only for the grassroots and because of this, they have tended to gloss over the theoretical and conceptual backgrounds. This makes these books unsuitable for classroom instruction of undergraduate and postgraduate students in colleges and universities as well as practising engineers and managers in executive development and continuing education programmes.

2. These books contain certain misrepresentations and confusing statements. As an example, even a renowned expert such as Nakajima has taken preventive maintenance to include only routine maintenance and periodic inspections. This is not true any more and serious students and practitioners know that preventive maintenance also includes condition-based, or predictive maintenance and designing-out-of-maintenance activities.

3. Students and practitioners generally find it difficult to fully comprehend and appreciate cases and illustrative examples from Japanese industries.

I noticed these shortcomings during my study of the subject and felt the need for a book which removes these shortcomings and presents and explains the subject in today's perspective with appropriate cases and examples from Indian industries. This prompted me to take up the task of writing a book on TPM.

The book has primarily been written for practising engineers and managers in industry. It will be of interest not only to the maintenance engineers, planners and managers in the manufacturing and continuous process industries, but also to industrial engineers, production planners and production/operations executives and managers. The purpose of the book is to present to the practitioners (in the language they understand and in the form they will accept) the basic ideas, principles and also the steps of implementation so that they may, with confidence, implement this down-to-earth and useful practice. This book can also be used as a textbook as and when TPM is offered as an elective subject at the senior undergraduate and postgraduate levels in engineering colleges/institutes and in management schools. In the meantime, it can be used as a textbook for executive development/training programs and as a companion text, or reference book for courses on maintenance management, reliability and maintenance, and terotechnology and life-cycle costing.

There are eight chapters in all. The book develops the subject right from the basic principles of preventive maintenance. Productive maintenance is an uncommon term and therefore, the reader is initially taken from a basic understanding of preventive maintenance to productive maintenance. The first two chapters are, therefore, devoted to the explanation of the need for TPM and the difference of maintenance, as it is commonly known and understood, and productive maintenance. Moreover, since TPM is based on the concepts of terotechnology and total quality management (TQM), in the third chapter, the conceptual foundations of TPM are explained through a comparison of terotechnology, TQM and TPM. These three chapters provide the basic understanding of the subject and form the basis for what is given in the later chapters. Simple block-diagrams and easy-to-understand cause-and-effect diagrams are used to explain the basic elements of the practice of TPM presented in Chapters 4, 5 and 6. Chapter 7 is devoted to the measurement of maintenance effectiveness. In this chapter, all known indices and methods have been presented and discussed. Two real life case studies are discussed in the last chapter. Herein as well, care has been taken to develop the subject matter of TPM. The first case study helps to bring out the need for the application of TPM, whereas a much larger and more involved application is described in the second case study. These case studies will not only help students and practitioners appreciate the need for TPM and quickly identify situations calling for its application, but also to take up its application in an industrial setting with conviction and confidence.

There are many persons whose help was both sought and received during the writing of a book. It is not possible to acknowledge the contribution of each and every one of them. My students have been my inspiration and some of them have also contributed directly in this task. I must acknowledge the contributions of Lt. Sanjay Singh of the Indian Navy (he must be a Lt. Comdr. now) and Mr. P.V. Prakash. I must also thank the reviewer for having read the manuscript closely and critically, and for making many useful suggestions. Thanks are also due to the editorial staff of Allied Publishers Limited, New Delhi, without whose help and cooperation, this book would not have been published. Lastly, thanks are due to my wife, Malyasree, and son, Shubhayu. Without their patient understanding and trust and confidence in me, I could not have taken up and completed this task.

Bikash Bhadury
April, 1998.

CONTENTS

Total Productive Maintenance

1

What and Why of TPM

The Japanese are very fond of abbreviations, [7]- QC circles and TQC stand for *quality control circles* and *total quality control*, ZD group and TPM for *zero defect* group and *total productive maintenance*, and JIT is the acronym for *just-in-time* production system. However, there is a little bit of a confusion with PM, since it is used both for *preventive maintenance* and *productive maintenance* by the Japanese. This book is on total productive maintenance, and in the context of TPM, PM stands for productive maintenance, which, as we shall see later, includes preventive maintenance as well. We shall take up the discussion of maintenance, preventive maintenance and productive maintenance in the subsequent chapter and for the time being let us come back to QC circles (we shall call them quality circles), TPM and JIT. All the three are Japanese innovations,[1] and all of them are manifestations of the Japanese obsession with losses — or what they call wastes.[2] Defective products, in the form of scrap, rejects, yield losses, and rework are wastes, machine breakdowns and losses of capacity due to inadequate maintenance of machines and equipment result in waste, and inventory is a waste since it ties up scarce resources which could be effectively utilised for producing saleable goods and thus implies a loss of opportunity. TQC is directed at elimination of defective products/components and thus its objective is zero defects; TPM has the objective of zero breakdowns and zero defects; and JIT has the objective of zero inventory. Moreover, the elimination or more correctly the minimisation of inventory cannot be achieved without the minimisation of defective products and the minimisation of machine breakdowns and loss of productive capacity. The central principle of just-in-time production system is that inventory reflects waste and minimising this form of waste results in a reduction in inventory and this, in turn, results in an increase of productivity. Now if the product, or component, quality is poor, then one must have extra parts on hand to replace the defective parts. Thus, if quality is improved then the extra inventory required to be held as a cushion can be eliminated. Similarly, work in process inventory is often held to provide components for the next operation/ process in case a machine breaks down, and therefore, if the machine/equipment availability is improved, then this additional inventory can be eliminated. Thus, we see that these three Japanese innovations are complementary and as a matter of fact, one drives the other.

Before we take up the definition and identifying characteristics of TPM, let us briefly discuss the history of TPM, and through this discussion, trace the origin and motives for the adoption of TPM in Japan.

History of TPM

After World War II, the entire Japanese effort was directed at industrialising itself in order to raise the gross national product. Consequently, Japanese companies took up the task of achieving the fullest possible utilisation of their industrial equipment. The origin of TPM can be traced back to 1951, when preventive maintenance was first introduced in Japan. The Japanese took the concepts and techniques of preventive maintenance from the USA. The induction of preventive maintenance heralded the modernisation of plant maintenance in Japan. The Nippondenso Company Limited, which belongs to the Toyota Group of companies and is the largest manufacturer of automotive electrical parts in Japan, first introduced plant-wide preventive maintenance in 1960. This was the usual form of preventive maintenance, wherein operators devoted themselves only to production jobs and the maintenance personnel were responsible for the maintenance of plant and equipment. In the mid 1960s, Nippondenso undertook automation of its production, with the result that the manufacturing and assembly operations became largely automated. This brought in a new problem — the maintenance of automated equipment. It was found that the maintenance crew, only by itself, could not effectively maintain the greatly increased number of automated equipment. Accordingly, the management of the company decided to change the allotment of duties of the operators of automated equipment in as much as each operator was made responsible for routine maintenance of the equipment. This was the origin of the first important feature of TPM, which is autonomous maintenance by the production operators.

In the meantime, the idea of small group voluntary activity originated in Japan in 1962 under the name of 'QC circles,' and it was soon recognized as an effective tool for employee involvement, motivation and quality and productivity improvement. In the same year, a new movement called the zero defect program (ZD program) originated in the USA. The zero defect program was introduced in Japan in 1965, and since quality circles were already active in some of the Japanese corporations by that time, the zero defect program was combined with quality circles to give birth to voluntary small groups, unique to Japan, called the 'ZD groups.'[3] The activities of the ZD groups are primarily aimed at the assurance of the quality of products and production processes. Nippondenso had already recognized the importance of preventive maintenance in improving equipment availability and had also by then introduced autonomous maintenance by the production operators, thereby freeing the maintenance personnel from routine maintenance tasks and making it possible for the maintenance department to take up the essential tasks of maintenance planning based on equipment performance, plant and equipment modifications for improved reliability and maintainability, development of reliability and maintainability specifications for new equipment and designing-out-of-maintenance. These tasks are aimed at maintenance prevention (MP). Thus, preventive maintenance together with MP and maintainability improvement (MI) activities gave birth to productive maintenance (PM). The aim of productive maintenance is, therefore, the maximisation of plant and equipment effectiveness in the pursuit of economic effectiveness and achievement of optimum life cycle costs of the production equipment. This was the origin of the second important feature of TPM which involves activities for maximising equipment effectiveness. Moreover, Nippondenso, by then, had already developed quality circle activity with all the employees participating in it. It recognized the utility of small group voluntary activity for promoting the absorption of PM and for getting the total involvement of plant personnel in productive maintenance of plant and equipment. Based on this, Nippondenso decided to evolve PM with the total participation of all employees — through small group voluntary activity. This essentially was the origin of the third important feature of TPM which is the use of company-led small group activity.

Based on these developments, Nippondenso evolved TPM between 1969 and 1971, and was awarded the 1971 Distinguished Plant Prize (PM Prize) for the development and effective implementation of TPM by the Japanese Institute of Plant Engineers (JIPE). Thereafter, the formal definition of TPM was enunciated by JIPE in 1971. TPM gained early recognition in Japan as is evident from the fact that by 1976, ten per cent of all industrial firms in Japan had introduced TPM and by

1979-80, this figure had risen to 25 per cent[7]. In the 1980's, TPM crossed the shores of Japan, and the developed nations of the West realized that TPM is not merely a concept but a practical and down-to-the-earth technique for achieving significant savings and corresponding improvement in productivity, revenues and profits. Indian companies have also now shown active interest in TPM. In the last chapter of this book, we will discuss a case study which describes the implementation of TPM in one of the units of a large tyre manufacturing company in India.

Motivations, Definition and Identifying Characteristics of TPM

Having discussed in chronological sequence the origin of the three important features of TPM, we now take up the basic motivations, definition and identifying characteristics of TPM, one after another. Takahashi has identified three specific motives for advocating and subsequent adoption of TPM in Japan [6]. These three motives are as follows:

1. Adoption of the life cycle approach for improving the overall performance of production equipment.
2. Improving productivity through a highly motivated workforce which can be achieved through job enlargement in which all workers are given a range of challenging jobs, in order to develop their skills in different crafts/production functions.
3. The use of voluntary small group activity for identifying the likely cause and frequency of failure of critical equipment, possible plant and equipment modifications which will result in significant savings, and efforts required to fully utilize existing equipment through improved availability.

Let us now take up these three motives one by one, and examine the need for TPM and underlying motivations for its implementation by manufacturing organisations.

Manufacturing organisations use equipment and machinery and employ labour to convert raw materials of relatively low value into finished products of higher value with the objective of earning an adequate return on investment. In recent years, the combination of economic trends — rising inflation resulting in increased costs of production and the continuing reduction in buying power, resulting in budget limitations have made it extremely important to ensure that the useful working life, or the life cycle of industrial plant, equipment and machinery is increased and at the same time, the availability of plant and equipment is maximised. Further, it is becoming increasingly clear that industrial equipment and machinery are going to become more automated and very much more expensive to own than ever before. This situation is compounded by the fact that the cost of maintaining equipment and machinery is very high, and in fact, the maintenance costs associated with an industrial plant or equipment frequently exceeds its total acquisition cost. Added to this is the fact that when the plant, equipment or machine is under maintenance, the manufacturing organisation loses heavily due to the loss of production capacity. Thus the objective should be the pursuit of economic life cycle cost of plant, equipment and machinery[4] by building in reliability and maintainability features, either through their incorporation as a part of the design of the equipment or through plant modifications after its acquisition and during its use, and by effective maintenance during its life cycle.

The extension of the life cycle and the attainment of optimum life cycle costs of plant and machinery ensures effective utilisation of available productive capacity and this is the primary goal of productive maintenance. However, this, by itself, does not ensure an improvement in overall performance of equipment and machinery. The improvement in overall performance of plant and machinery in a manufacturing organisation comes not only from ensuring the minimisation of loss of capacity due to breakdowns but also from activities directed at ensuring the minimisation of losses due to poor quality — defective products/components and yield losses, set up, adjustments, idling and minor stoppages of equipment and due to equipment operating at reduced speeds giving rise to lower productivity. In manufacturing organisations, the loss of capacity due to breakdowns is recognized as a major cause for poor performance of equipment. What is not so clearly evident, however, is the loss of performance due to defective products and/or yield losses. In most manufacturing organisations, this is also a major contributor and accordingly the ultimate aim of TPM is zero breakdowns and zero defects. Moreover, TPM recognizes that the four other kinds of losses, namely, losses due to set up, adjustment, idling and minor stoppages, and the speed losses together also have a significant effect on the overall equipment performance and one of the identifying characteristics of TPM is the emphasis on the elimination of these 'six big losses.'

There are, thus, two specific parts of the first motive, namely the adoption of the life cycle approach for improving the overall performance of the production equipment, and these are as follows:

(i) Pursuit of economic life cycle costs of physical assets, which must include building in of reliability and maintainability features and an extension of the useful life of the assets, and since TPM deals primarily with production equipment and is used in manufacturing industries, such assets are plant and machinery.

(ii) Improving the overall performance of plant and machinery, which should also take into account the effective use of such production equipment through the minimisation of losses not only due to breakdowns, but also due to poor quality and losses due to set-up, adjustment, idling and minor stoppages of equipment and equipment operating at reduced speeds.

Although the contribution of the last four causes, namely set-up, adjustments, idling and minor stoppages, and operation at reduced speeds, may seem small as compared to breakdowns and defective products, in actual practice, they add up to a significant loss of the productive capacity. This recognition differentiates productive maintenance (PM) from preventive maintenance. Whereas the practical application of preventive maintenance nowadays[5] covers much more than just 'routine,' or periodic preventive maintenance, and includes condition-based maintenance, or predictive preventive maintenance, plant modifications and designing-out-of-maintenance, activities aimed at the minimisation of quality losses and set-up, adjustment, idling and minor stoppages, and speed losses do not come under the purview of preventive maintenance.

This brings us to the second motive, namely one of improving productivity through a highly motivated workforce, which incidentally includes both the production operators and the maintenance tradesmen. With increasing competition, manufacturing organisations have to cope with the need of reducing manufacturing costs on the one hand and improving deliveries, that is, reducing manufacturing leadtimes on the other. These requirements are essential and inevitable because production equipment today is capable of much higher production rates and is necessarily becoming increasingly sophisticated, and therefore, much more expensive to own and operate. This results in a situation wherein the price paid by a manufacturing organisation for the loss of one hour of production on an equipment, or a machine, is much greater today than it was ever before, since the machine hour rate is much higher and the loss of production capacity, or the loss of opportunity, is also much greater. Moreover, one must realize that this loss is going to be more in future than it is now. Thus to be able to stay in business, manufacturing organisations have to ensure much higher levels of equipment availability. Such high levels of equipment availability cannot be achieved with the 'I operate, you fix' attitude wherein production operators only run the machines and the maintenance department attends to all maintenance activates, including routine activities which are carried out to keep the machines in good running order, such as cleaning of the machines, periodic lubrication, periodic checks and inspections and minor adjustments and repair. The maintenance departments are finding it difficult to attend to such routine tasks. Moreover, attending to such routine tasks is resulting in a situation wherein the necessary preventive maintenance activities, such as preventive replacement of critical components, equipment overhauls and necessary plant modifications, are getting backlogged for lack of available manpower, and this, in turn, is resulting in greater incidence of failures and loss of equipment availability.

As against this backdrop, let us consider a situation wherein the production operators perform basic maintenance activities on their own machines. They not only maintain their own machines in good running order but also are capable of detecting potential problems before a major breakdown occurs (at which time, if considered necessary, the maintenance department is called in to take the necessary preventive action to avoid a long shutdown). This will not only leave the maintenance department free to attend to more pressing tasks which require higher levels of skills, but also bring back in the production operators, the pride of craftsmanship. Thus, the integration of simpler and routine maintenance tasks with production work not only enlarges the production job and makes it more interesting but also fosters in the production operators a commitment to the plant [3]. Moreover, with this the maintenance tradesmen are also able to carry out their tasks properly and in a more congenial atmosphere and this brings with it a feeling of job satisfaction in them. This, as we had noted earlier, is what is meant by autonomous maintenance and a key ingredient of TPM is that the production operators perform basic maintenance tasks on their own equipment, thereby enlarging their jobs.

Now we can discuss the third motive, which is the use of voluntary small group activity for the promotion, implementation and absorption of PM in an organisation. The objectives of maximisation of equipment availability, minimisation of quality loss, and minimisation of set-up, adjustment, idling and minor stoppages and speed losses are major challenges to any manufacturing organisation. These challenges call for reforms and improvements in standards, processes, methods and procedures. Such reforms and/or improvements cannot be carried out by a few technical people working in the production and maintenance departments; they require the active participation and involvement of all employees in an organisation.

In the preceding paragraphs we have discussed the need for having a highly motivated workforce, the persons who carry out the essential tasks, or activities, whether they are production operators, maintenance tradesmen, or quality control inspectors. After all, in the final analysis, they perform the important tasks which directly affect equipment availability, product quality and productivity. These persons must not only do their allotted task to the best of their capability, but should also forever attempt to reach higher levels of performance. Higher levels of performance require commitment to the job, motivation and a sense of belonging to an organisation. This sense of belonging to an organisation also inculcates in the employee a sense of belonging to the larger group, wherein the maintenance fitter not only identifies with the plant/equipment, but also identifies with the production operators and the quality control inspectors, who are also a part of the same group. Thus, innovative ideas and suggestions for reforms and improvements must be preceded by an attitudinal change in the workmen leading to involvement, which, in turn, comes from a conscious effort through a synchronization of the hand, head and heart and from creative work which is beneficial to the larger group. One of the practical and time-tested ways of inducing involvement and a sense of belonging in the workman is through active participation, wherein he voluntarily joins a group of people who discuss their problems and suggest better ways of doing their work; a small group of volunteers who meet to discuss problems of housekeeping, quality, equipment availability and productivity and to suggest reforms and improvements. This is active participation and quality circles and ZD groups are its different forms. In the context of TPM, we call these PM circles (and PM sub-circles). Through such active participation, the production operator, for example, develops an appreciation of the problems faced by the maintenance tradesmen and quality control inspectors, and only such appreciation and identification with the larger group can bring about reforms and real improvements, in the form of improved work methods, processes and procedures through the implementation of which the objective of minimisation of losses, or the 'elimination of wastes,' can be achieved.

To effectively deal with these challenges, an organisation has to ensure the involvement of all functions in an organisation, namely marketing/sales, design/ engineering, materials management/purchasing, production, maintenance and quality control. Thus, the promotion and absorption of TPM requires the development of the TPM Promotion System which links the various PM sub-circles and PM circles to the Departmental PM Committees and the Departmental PM Committees, in turn, are linked upwards to the Corporate PM Committee. The Corporate PM Committee establishes the company PM policies and objectives and oversees the activities of the various Divisional/Departmental PM Committees. Similarly, Divisional/Departmental PM Committees establish the PM policies and objectives for the division/department and oversee the activities of the PM circles which come under them. There is an overlap and the shop manager/foreman who is a member of the Divisional/Departmental PM Committee is the PM circle leader. The PM sub-circles come under the overall direction and guidance of a PM circle and consist of volunteers who may be operators, maintenance tradesmen etc. and is headed by a leader, who is typically also a volunteer.

Since we are discussing the possible motivations for implementation of TPM by manufacturing organisations, let us for a moment return to our discussion of TQC, TPM and JIT. We had noted that the ultimate goal of TQC, or TQM, is zero defects, or defect-free production, whereas the ultimate goals of TPM are zero breakdowns and zero defects. Thus, it must be noted that TQC is an essential prerequisite of TPM. Next, the ultimate goals of JIT are zero defects, zero breakdowns, zero set-up times, zero lead times (both procurement and manufacturing lead times), zero inventories, and a lot, or batch, size of one. From this, we can see that JIT requires as a primary prerequisite the implementation of TPM. It must also be noted here that TPM not only aims at the minimisation of losses due to breakdowns and defective products, but also tries to minimise losses due to set-ups, adjustments, idling and minor stoppages, and operation at reduced speeds. Thus, TPM, through its stress on reduction of loss due to set-ups, has the same ultimate goal of zero set-up times. In addition to this, TPM also attacks other seemingly minor losses which also contribute to an increase in manufacturing lead times. Thus, we see that one of primary steps that an organisation has to take to enable the implementation of JIT is the implementation of TPM, since productive maintenance not only concentrates on the maximisation of equipment availability, but also aims at the maximisation of the overall effectiveness of the equipment, which, as we have noted, comes from overall performance of the equipment. TQC, TPM and JIT are the secrets of the Japanese success in the areas of quality and productivity, and one of the key constituents of the JIT production system is TPM. Manufacturing organisations all over the world are being increasingly driven to the JIT production system since only through the implementation of JIT can they effectively cope with increasing competition coupled with the requirements of increasing product variety and decreasing production volume (i.e., batch sizes).

We can now take up for discussion the definition of TPM [5]. The definition of TPM was developed by the Japan Institute of Plant Engineers (JIPE) [the predecessor of the Japan Institute of Plant Maintenance (JIPM)] in 1971 and it remains unchanged till date. The definition of TPM is as follows:

TPM:

1. is aimed at maximising equipment effectiveness (improvement of overall effectiveness).
2. establishes a total system of PM covering the entire life-cycle of the equipment.
3. covers all departments, such as equipment planning department, equipment usage department[6], maintenance department, and so on.
4. all employees participate, from top management down to shop-floor workers.
5. promotes PM through motivation management, that is, small group autonomous activities.

Nakajima explains that TPM has become widely known throughout Japanese industry as an abbreviation for 'PM with all employees participating in it through small group activities' [5]. Tamaki also echoes the same thought by saying that 'TPM is a blend of what is understood by the Japanese as productive maintenance, or PM, with particles of Japanese autonomous small groups, who are promoting its absorption' [7]. The use of autonomous small group activity for TPM promotion and absorption came about naturally because 'autonomous small group activity has become overwhelmingly popular in Japanese industry to the extent that almost all companies, regardless of their scale, are practising it' [7]. Moreover, from our earlier discussion, it is obvious that T in TPM stands for total equipment effectiveness, total maintenance and total participation, and participation of all-employees can only be obtained through motivation, involvement and a sense of belonging. Also, the best known method of inducing motivation, involvement and a sense of belonging in the employees is through the use of small group autonomous activity, and such small autonomous groups may take the form of quality circles, ZD groups/JK groups, or PM circles and committees depending on the objectives/goals of the groups and the organisation — its products, structure, concerns/weaknesses and past experience in the use of participative approaches for quality and productivity improvement.

Productive maintenance is directed at using the production equipment to the maximum for manufacturing the desired quality of products efficiently. The causes of equipment failure and poor product quality are interdisciplinary in nature and for maximum equipment effectiveness, it is necessary to have maintenance-oriented plant management and a plant-oriented management structure to support it. Thus, 'total' in TPM stands for the following:

(i) total effectiveness aimed at the pursuit of economic efficiency and improvement of productivity and profitability;

(ii) total maintenance, and this must include not only periodic, or routine, preventive maintenance activities but also condition-based maintenance of plant and machinery, building in of reliability and maintainability features, plant modifications and other activities aimed at maintenance prevention and designing-out-of-maintenance; and

(iii) total participation, which is achieved through a motivated workforce, job enlargement of production operators, maintenance skills training of maintenance tradesmen and small group activity in every department and shop and at every level of the organisation.

Thus, we see that TPM is a practical method of achieving the aim of maintenance-oriented plant management, through a positive investment in human resources in order to fully utilize existing equipment, through improved plant and equipment availability, through more assured product quality and through reduced maintenance costs and saving in labour as a result of plant modifications [6]. The implementation of TPM requires dedication and effort but the gains are very substantial. The implementation of TPM results in the following tangible benefits:

(i) a very large reduction in the number of unexpected equipment failures,

(ii) a large reduction in the direct costs of maintenance,

(iii) a significant reduction in quality costs - both internal failure costs due to defective products and defects in production processes and external failure costs in the form of a significant reduction in customer complaints and adjustment claims,

(iv) a very large reduction in work-in-process inventory, and

(v) a significant increase in labour productivity, that is, the value added per worker.

TPM is not only profitable; it also creates a more pleasant working environment, a workplace full of vitality [5].

As noted earlier, one of the identifying characteristics of TPM is the stress it places on the elimination of the 'six big losses' namely:

(i) due to breakdowns of production equipment,

(ii) due to defects and defective products and components,

(iii) due to set-up,

(iv) due to adjustments of equipment,

(v) due to idling and minor stoppages of equipment, and

(vi) resulting from equipment operating at lower speeds which, in turn, results in lower productivity and yield losses.

This characteristic is based on the realization that the most appropriate measure of equipment effectiveness is value added by manufacturing/production, since it is a process of value addition and it uses equipment for this purpose. The value added or created in a product by the manufacturing/production process is the difference between the sales revenue earned and the cost of materials, supplies and services purchased by the company to produce the product. This value addition is significantly reduced by waste of material and labour and also by the six major equipment-related losses mentioned earlier. On the other hand, value addition increases as equipment availability and productivity go up and defects, defective components and products and rework come down.

The stress on the elimination of the 'six big losses' is very closely connected with, and compliments, the two fundamental bases of TPM, which are:

1. enunciation of the term 'productive maintenance' and the stress on it as opposed to preventive maintenance, and
2. adoption of the life cycle approach for improving overall performance of the production equipment.

These two bases are very closely connected with each other (and also compliment each other), and both are in a way 'an application of terotechnology by the Japanese in their own unique way' [7]. We have already noted that the Japanese view that preventive maintenance only consists of routine maintenance and periodic inspections is essentially wrong, and nowadays, the practical application of preventive maintenance covers much more than just `routine' or periodic preventive maintenance. The reason behind the enunciation of a new term and calling it productive maintenance is to differentiate it from the common man's concept of preventive maintenance and to stress the fact that maintenance is carried out to keep an equipment in good running order and to take all necessary actions directed at the prevention of unforeseen failures so that the plant, equipment and machinery are available for production of saleable products and services. Thus, effective maintenance must not only include periodic preventive maintenance, in the form of routine activities and periodic inspections, but also must include essential condition-based maintenance of critical equipment, plant and equipment modifications and designing-out-of-maintenance activities. Such activities will not only improve plant and equipment availability but will also help in prolonging the useful life of plant, equipment and machinery. The pursuit of economic life cycle costs is the objective of terotechnology and this entails improvement of plant and equipment availability and extension of their useful lives. As a matter of fact, TPM has the same objective as terotechnology, but in its approach it is different [7]. We shall discuss the definition and objectives of maintenance, types of maintenance, preventive maintenance and productive maintenance in Chapter 2. Thereafter, we shall discuss terotechnology, TQM and TPM in Chapter 3.

The remaining two identifying characteristics of TPM are the following:

(i) autonomous maintenance by production operators, and

(ii) use of small group activity for the promotion and absorption of TPM.

There are, thus, two fundamental bases and three identifying characteristics of TPM, and the latter provide the framework for the development of a TPM programme for a manufacturing organisation. After discussing the two bases in Chapters 2 and 3, we shall discuss in detail, the three identifying characteristics in Chapters 4, 5 and 6. In Chapter 4, we shall discuss the methods used for eliminating the six big losses. We have already discussed the motivation for the integration of simpler and routine maintenance tasks with production work and have also noted that with this, the maintenance tradesmen can attend to the essential jobs of plant modifications and designing-out-of-maintenance and also carry out the necessary maintenance tasks adequately and in a more congenial atmosphere. For effective use of the maintenance personnel, it is necessary to have a programme of maintenance skills training to update knowledge and skills of the maintenance tradesmen. In Chapter 5, we will discuss in detail, autonomous maintenance by production operators and maintenance skills training of maintenance tradesmen. Thereafter, in Chapter 6, we will discuss the use of small group activity and methods of TPM promotion in a manufacturing organisation.

The management of the maintenance function requires measurement of maintenance performance. Without proper evaluation of the effectiveness of maintenance, realistic target setting and planning of improvement programmes cannot be carried out. Accordingly, in Chapter 7, we will discuss models and techniques used for measuring maintenance effectiveness. In this chapter, in addition to the older and classical models, we will also discuss concepts of productivity, the difference between production and productivity, and productivity measures to be able to develop effective measures of productive maintenance as applied to a manufacturing organisation. Finally, in Chapter 8, we will discuss the basic steps and methods of implementing TPM and we will do this through two real-life case studies of implementation of TPM in a large tyre manufacturing unit in India.

TPM is neither an enigma nor an utopia. TPM is implementable and as opposed to terotechnology, which is essentially a concept, TPM is a practical and down-to-earth technique developed specifically for manufacturing organisations. However, the implementation of TPM requires will and determination, a clear statement of goals, attitudinal change and dedicated efforts by people in various departments and at different levels in an organisation. Let us start with the objectives of zero breakdowns and zero defects. Although approaching zero is difficult, believing that zero defects and zero breakdowns can be achieved is, by itself, an important prerequisite for the success of TPM. One has to begin by cultivating new attitudes, that is, changing the way people look at breakdowns and defects. Instead of believing that (i) it is not the operator's responsibility to perform routine maintenance activities and periodic equipment inspections, (ii) all equipment eventually break down, and (iii) all equipment breakdowns can be fixed, production operators and maintenance tradesmen must believe that equipment should never break down and they can be maintained so that the loss due to breakdowns can be minimised, if not totally eliminated. The implementation of TPM requires a motivated and disciplined workforce, and coordinated action by different departments and by different levels directed at the same set of goals. Accordingly TPM promotion has to be an organised group effort and for this purpose, it needs a formal TPM promotion system. In essence, TPM programmes call for the following types of activities:

1. Group activities to eliminate the six major equipment - related losses.
2. The involvement of production operators in periodic (daily, weekly etc.) autonomous maintenance activities, which include daily inspection, cleaning, lubrication and bolt tightening, to maintain basic equipment condition.
3. Restoration of all equipment to optimal operating conditions and elimination of accelerated deterioration of equipment.
4. Activities directed at improvement of maintainability of all existing equipment.

5. Increased efficiency and cost-effectiveness of maintenance work through better planning, scheduling and control.

References

1. Abegglen, J.C. and Stalk, George Jr., Kaisha: *The Japanese Corporation*, Charles E. Tuttle Company, Tokyo, Japan, 1985 (Basic Books, Inc., New York, 1987).
2. Hewgill, J.C. and Parkes, D., 'Terotechnology—Philosophy and Concept, *Terotechnica*, Vol. 1, No. 1, May, 1979, pp. 3-8.
3. Kelly, A., 'Topics in Terotechnology: An Instructional Series - 10, Motivation of Maintenance Tradeforce,' *Maintenance Management International*, Vol. 4, No. 2, January, 1984, pp. 71-81.
4. Nakajima, S., 'The Organisation of Maintenance in Japanese Industry,' *Maintenance Management International*, Vol. 3, No. 2, August, 1982, pp. 83-88.
5. Nakajima S., 'TPM - Challenge to the Improvement of Productivity by Small Group Activity,' *Maintenance Management International* Vol. 6, 1986, pp. 73-83.
6. Takahashi, Y., 'Maintenance-Oriented Management Via Total Participation — Total Productive Maintenance, A New Task for Plant Managers in Japan,' *Terotechnica*, Vol. 2, No. 2, May, 1981, pp. 79-88.
7. Tamaki, A. (The Chairman, Japan Institute of Plant Engineers), 'Total Productive Maintenance and Its Impact on Japanese Industry', *Terotechnica*, Vol. 2, No. 1, January, 1981, pp. 3-4, [Guest Editorial (on Total Productive Maintenance)].

Endnotes

1. They are really adaptations and not innovations in the true sense. However, the adaptations are so different from the originating concepts/techniques that calling them innovations is more appropriate.
2. This obsession with waste, or the instinctive drive to minimise waste in any form, is derived from the strong bias towards growth that is characteristic of successful Japanese corporations [1]. Growth comes from higher productivity and waste in any form impedes productivity growth.
3. In the iron and steel industry of Japan, a similar small-group activity is carried out under the name of `JK activity.' JK is an abbreviation of `Jishu Kanri,' the literal translation of which is self management. JK activity is also derived from a combination of quality circles and zero-defect programs.
4. The pursuit of economic life cycle costs of physical assets is the objective of terotechnology. Terotechnology involves `the specification and design for reliability and maintainability of plant, machinery and equipment with their installation, com-

missioning, maintenance, modification and replacement, and with feedback of information, performance and costs'[2].

5. Nakajima [4] has taken preventive maintenance to include routine maintenance and periodic inspections, whereas productive maintenance (PM) must include not only routine or periodic preventive maintenance activities but also the concept of maintenance prevention (MP) and designing-out-of-maintenance.

6. This is essentially an effect of translation from Japanese. We read it as production/manufacturing planning department and production department, or shops. Moreover, although the definition explicitly identifies these two departments in addition to the maintenance department, the reader will appreciate that other departments such as materials management/purchasing and quality control, should also be included.

From Maintenance to Productive Maintenance

To maintain, as per Webster's Third New International Dictionary, is to keep in a state of repair and efficiency, and accordingly, the dictionary defines maintenance as the labour (job, act, or set of activities) of keeping something, such as buildings or equipment, in a state of repair and efficiency. To repair is essentially to fix, or to mend, since equipment (or any physical asset for that matter) does break down. Failures are inevitable and the asset has to be restored to its working state after the failure and this act of restoration is repair. But the word 'efficiency' has also been included in the definition of maintenance and accordingly, the dictionary points out that to maintain is also to preserve an equipment, or a physical asset, from failure or decline. Thus, maintenance is essentially an act of care or upkeep and this not only includes fixing or mending broken parts and machines but also ensuring that the acts of repair must renew or revive the equipment, that is, restore it to a sound or healthy state; and at the same time, maintenance must include all activities taken to ensure the prevention of failure and also the prevention of decline of the equipment to the extent possible. This stresses two essential facts, which are the following:

1. Maintenance must not only restore an equipment to its working state so that it can be used to produce goods and services but also must preserve it and extend its useful working life.
2. There are two kinds of maintenance activities, namely, restorative or corrective, and preventive.

The manager of the maintenance function, therefore, has two distinct roles, namely, as a manager of physical assets and also as a provider of service to his customers, who are his colleagues in the production and other departments of a manufacturing organisation. His first role requires him to take proper care of the physical assets and to take actions which will extend, or prolong, their useful working life. The second role is quite different and demands the provision of fast and prompt reaction to his customers needs. This role, therefore, has the objective of maximisation of plant and equipment availability. The two roles are seemingly contradictory but are in reality, complimentary since timely and efficient customer service can only be provided if plant and equipment are managed properly. The overall objectives of the maintenance function are the following:

1. Achieving and maintaining the desired, or the planned, level of output and productivity, and also producing products of an acceptable quality consistently.
2. Maximising the utilisation of resources through the minimisation of losses, such as, losses due to leakage, energy losses, etc.
3. Providing the required level of safety since, in many cases, industrial accidents are caused by the poor condition of technical installations.

These objectives should be obtained at a minimum cost since maintenance, whether it is in the form of repairs, replacements of components, plant and equipment modifications and overhaul of equipment and machines does not directly add to the value of products produced by the industry;[1] on the other hand, it adds considerably to the overall production costs. Added to this is the fact that when the plant, equipment, or machine is under maintenance, the manufacturing organisation loses heavily due to the loss in production capacity. In this context, it should be noted that the direct cost of maintenance in various industries averages at four per cent of the cost of fixed assets, varying from 2.6 per cent for the oil industry to 8.6 per cent for the steel industry, and in the manufacturing industry, the cost of lost production due to breakdowns is as much as, and often more than, the direct cost of maintenance. Thus, through proper maintenance, one can save quite substantially. Thus, we may conclude that the objectives of maintenance are the maximisation of plant and equipment availability at minimum cost and the proper care and upkeep of physical assets to ensure that their useful working life is also extended.

Why Has Maintenance Become So Important Today?

In the continuous process industries, such as the steel, fertilizer and pharmaceutical industries and thermal power plants, maintenance should logically be a very important function. The reasons for this are (i) continuous process industries very often use plants of single-stream series design, and the failure of a machine may result in the shutdown of a line or even the entire plant, and (ii) unlike manufacturing industry, in the continuous process industry, production jobs cannot be subcontracted, and the plant produces product/products only as long as the machines are working.[2] However, maintenance has been, and in many cases, still is, a thankless job. The maintenance function is generally neglected as long as the plant and equipment are running satisfactorily. The top management suddenly realizes its importance and need when an equipment, or a machine, breaks down and the production is stopped or otherwise hampered in any way. Add to this the fact that this realization goes away (or so it seems) as soon as the equipment, or plant, is restarted and production resumes. Thus, maintenance is considered as a necessary evil by management and does not get the attention it deserves. However, there is an awareness now of the pressing need for effective maintenance of plant and machinery.

Maintenance has come of age but this awareness has taken around thrity-five years of hard work by maintenance professionals to come together in various industrialized nations and share their knowledge and experiences and spread the message of the pressing need for effective maintenance of plant and machinery. In the United Kingdom, a national maintenance conference was organised for the first time in 1961. This was followed up by the initiation of local maintenance associations, which in 1967, got merged through the formation of the British Council of Maintenance Associations. Around this time, a number of conferences and seminars were held across the United Kingdom, creating the realization that though maintenance had come of age, it was still not being taken seriously by managements. As a result, in 1968, an United Kingdom Government Working Party on Maintenance Engineering was set up to focus attention on the problems being faced by plant engineers and to find out the reasons for the general inadequacy of industrial maintenance. The Working Party surveyed 515 companies and the survey revealed that the efficiency of industrial maintenance was unsatisfactory and considerable savings (through a reduction of the cost of maintenance) and earnings (through an improvement in availability) could result from more effective maintenance of plant and machinery. This finally led to the formation of the Committee for Terotechnology in 1970, and this Committee took two years to come up with a clear and concise definition of terotechnology. We shall discuss terotechnology in the context of TPM in the next chapter but the above discussion shows that the work of spreading the message of proper care and upkeep of physical assets started in the 1960s in Britain which gave the world the concept of terotechnology. Japan gave the world TPM in the 1960s similarly resulting in the formation of the Japanese Institute of Plant Engineers and finally in the definition of TPM in 1971.

The realization of the pressing need for effective maintenance of plant and machinery came through conferences and seminars but the scale was turned by two basic economic reasons which are as follows:

1. Availability is increasingly being recognized as an essential factor having an important effect on process plant operation [10]. Moreover, with the increasing use of automation, availability has turned out to be an important factor in the manufacturing industry as well.
2. Industrial plant and equipment are becoming increasingly complex and their costs also growing rapidly [5]. Moreover, this complexity coupled with higher costs of acquisition has brought about significantly higher costs of maintenance and the 1980s have seen heavy expenditure on replacement of plant and equipment and also on acquisition of spare parts [25].

We shall discuss these two reasons in detail in the following paragraph to bring out clearly the pressing, and ever growing, need for proper maintenance of industrial plant and machinery.

Maintenance affects the company profits and profitability and this is primarily due to the effect of equipment availability, cost of maintenance and the useful life of the equipment on production costs, profits and profitability. The ways in which maintenance affects costs, profits and profitability are as follows:

(i) through its relationship with availability, maintenance gives rise to the indirect cost of maintenance, namely the cost of lost production, which occurs when the equipment, or the plant, is either under scheduled maintenance, or under repair (or, waiting for repair);

(ii) through its relationship with the direct costs of maintenance, which includes the cost of maintenance manpower, spares and incidental materials, and also tools and instruments required to carry out the maintenance job; and

(iii) through its relationship with the useful life of the equipment, or the plant.[3]

Thus, in most industrial situations, the objective of maintenance should be the minimisation of the sum of the direct and indirect costs of maintenance, always taking into due consideration the long-term effect of any maintenance decision taken on the useful life, or the life cycle, of the equipment. This objective is becoming all the more critical in recent years due to rising inflation and the continuing reduction in buying power resulting in budget limitations. Inflation results in increased costs of production and maintenance manpower and also in higher prices of essential spare parts and replacement equipment. Together with this, budget limitation sometimes results in the postponement of essential repairs, replacement of components and equipment modifications, which, in turn, has a deleterious effect on equipment availability and also the equipment life cycle. Add to this the fact that industrial plant and equipment are being designed for higher productivity and the loss of one hour of production, that is, the indirect cost of maintenance, is much more than it was ever before. Such plants and equipment are also becoming larger and more complex, employing higher levels of automation bringing about higher incidences of failure. They also employ processes which involve severe operating conditions and are also of single stream series design incorporating minimal amounts of unit redundancy thus requiring higher unit reliability and maintainability, if they are to realize the economic advantages expected from them [10]. Moreover, it is becoming increasingly clear that industrial plant and equipment are going to become more automated and much more expensive to own than ever before. We may conclude by noting that industrial equipment and plant are becoming increasingly complex and the costs associated with their acquisition and use are also growing rapidly. This situation is further compounded by the increasing competition which brings into focus the production costs and the fact that increases in the indirect and direct costs of maintenance have a corresponding effect on the production costs.

Types of Maintenance

Maintenance was, till recently, synonymous with repairs and consisted of breakdown maintenance. Breakdown maintenance refers to a maintenance activity which is necessitated by a breakdown. Moreover, if it is brought about by an unforeseen breakdown, then it should more correctly be called an emergency repair, since as per the B.S. glossary of maintenance management terms (B.S. 3811:1984),[4] emergency maintenance has been defined as `maintenance work necessitated by unforeseen breakdown or damage.' The advantages of this system of maintenance are that in this system (i) no unnecessary maintenance is carried out, and (ii) the administration and record keeping is reduced to a minimum. As opposed to this, however, the limitations of this system of maintenance are many and are as follows:

(i) There is a great risk of unexpected failures with consequent losses of production. Moreover, some of these failures may be catastrophic and may result in long shutdowns of critical equipment, and even the entire plant.

(ii) There is a high risk of secondary and/or consequential damage to plant and machinery.

(iii) The use of only breakdown maintenance (without any kind of preventive actions) results in lower life of components and machines.

(iv) This system of maintenance may result in production of nonconforming products/items, possible rejections, or generally a drop in the quality of the product.

(v) This system may result in higher consumption of fuel, raw materials or energy as the machine wears, or the lubricant becomes contaminated etc.

Thus breakdown maintenance, by itself, not only results in higher costs of maintenance, lower availability, and possibly also higher costs of use and lower product quality, but also goes against the basic objective of care and upkeep of plant and equipment, since there always exists the possibility of consequential damage and accelerated degradation resulting in a reduction of the useful life of the equipment. This is essentially a justification for the use of preventive maintenance which, by definition, should consist of all activities directed at prevention of failures or decline in the useful life of the equipment. Preventive maintenance came to be used together with breakdown maintenance and for a long time, people conceived of two types of maintenance jobs — breakdown and preventive. This resulted in a classification of maintenance under two main heads — breakdown maintenance or emergency repairs, and preventive maintenance. This classification of maintenance is shown in Fig.2.1. This classification is the simplest and also removes all possible confusion in the use of various terms since anything that is not an 'emergency' job falls under preventive maintenance.

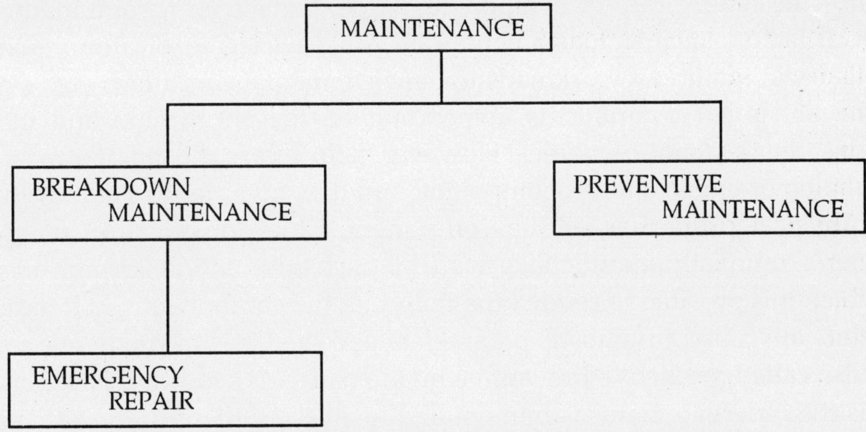

Fig. 2.1. Types of Maintenance (Most Basic Classification)

In the early days, preventive maintenance took the forms of (i) routine activities like oiling/greasing, cleaning of the machine, the internals and the working surfaces, (ii) periodic replacements of wearing parts, which are not capital items, (iii) programmed replacements of bearings and other items with pre-determined lives, and (iv) periodic overhauls. Such routine maintenance, which should more correctly be termed as periodic preventive maintenance, is based on the assumption that mechanical failures and process of deterioration of components depend only on the running time of the machine. The limitations of periodic preventive maintenance are as follows:

(i) It does not give full protection against breakdowns. This is particularly applicable to random failures and if random failures are predominant, then periodic preventive maintenance has no effect on equipment availability [24].

(ii) Some of the maintenance actions are unnecessary and sometimes the plant, or equipment, is maintained too frequently resulting in a corresponding loss of production capacity [9].

(iii) The components are, in many cases, not allowed to run till the end of their mechanical life and are replaced, at times, too early.

(iv) Increased number of running-in failures may be caused by periodic overhauls. Incorrect assembly has been found to be a critical cause of failure for mechanical equipment, and incorrect assembly may occur during servicing [4]. In a study conducted on a 110 MW thermal power unit, it was observed that there is a period of running-in after a capital maintenance shutdown [4].

Since the failure rate of components is dependent on a combination of a number of factors such as load fluctuations, duty cycles, lubrication, quality of materials used, quality of workmanship, environmental conditions etc., even for the same or similar components, depending on the application and working conditions, the resultant life varies. However, failures are caused by processes of accumulation of damage to the component and they give rise to gradual changes in the physical properties of the component. Thus, observation of specific parameter(s) rationally should make available such information through an analysis of which it is possible to predict the failure of the component. Such indicative parameters are called prognostic parameters and the basis of predictive maintenance, also called predictive preventive maintenance or condition-based maintenance, is the observation, measurement and analysis of these prognostic parameters. The possible maintenance actions for random failures and also time-dependent wear-out failures, based on whether the prognostic parameter(s) is observable or not, are given in Table 2.1. Since the monitoring of such prognostic parameters is carried out to assess the condition, or health, of the component and the equipment (since the failure of the component may result in the failure of the equipment), such monitoring is called condition monitoring. Condition monitoring can be dynamic, also called on-line, or static, which is done by stopping the machine, or during shutdowns. The monitoring methods generally used are visual, performance monitoring, vibration monitoring, noise or sound-level monitoring, and wear-debris monitoring. In the last fifteen years, vibration monitoring has become an important technique, particularly on rotating machines [27].

Table 2.1. Type of Prognostic Parameter and Recommended Maintenance Action

Type of Failure	*Random Failures (Not dependent on time)*		*Wear-out Failures (Time dependent)*	
Prognostic Parameter	Not Observable	Observable	Observable	Not Observable
Possible Basis of Maintenance Action	No condition monitoring possible	Condition Monitoring possible		Past failure data can be analyzed
Recommendation	Accept breakdown repairs	Predictive preventive maintenance, or condition-based maintenance		Programmed (planned) replacements

The need to carry out checks/inspections of the equipment from time-to-time had been felt earlier and preventive maintenance, in its early form, that is, before the advent of condition monitoring techniques, did include periodic inspections.[5] Such periodic inspections are also carried out so that wear/deterioration of components can be detected and timely action taken to prevent catastrophic failures and long-duration shutdowns of the equipment. However, these inspections were mainly of the shutdown, or stop-job, variety. Moreover, many periodic preventive maintenance activities also call for the stopping of the equipment since they cannot be carried out when the machine is running. Now consider the fact that in a process plant, in particular, the stoppage of an equipment results in a loss of productive capacity with resultant loss of revenue. At the same time, unexpected failures resulting in losses of production and revenue may take place if the necessary preventive maintenance activities are not carried out. This consideration has also given rise to the increasing use of condition-based maintenance, and economic pressures have also created a trend from 'planned preventive maintenance' to breakdown maintenance since the use of techniques of on-line condition monitoring make it possible to achieve the advantages of a breakdown maintenance policy without the attendant loss of revenue resulting from catastrophic failures and long-duration shutdowns of the equipment [8]. Many people tend to think of preventive maintenance as planned maintenance since most often preventive maintenance jobs are scheduled, and thus planned in advance. As a matter of fact, most of the scheduled maintenance jobs in a process plant consist essentially of periodic preventive maintenance activities. This feeling is further strengthened by the fact that equipment overhauls are planned well in advance. Although overhauls are usually classified under preventive maintenance, one should realize that overhauls are very special kind of jobs which not only consist of servicing kind of activities, such as cleaning, lubrication, replacement of wearing parts and programmed replacement of some capital items, but also include minor repairs, adjustments and equipment modifications, which are carried out to reduce the incidence of failures. Because of this, in Indian process plants, equipment overhauls are generally referred to as capital maintenance. So we notice that there are two types of preventive maintenance activities, namely periodic preventive maintenance and predictive preventive maintenance. Moreover, predictive preventive maintenance can either be dynamic, or on-line, or static, that is, one requiring the stopping or shutdown of the equipment.

Wiegel first talked of planning in maintenance and stressed the need to identify critical equipment centres and weak spots in a plant and through planned maintenance reduce the costs of maintenance and also increase the equipment and plant availability [26]. His cyclic model of 'functional maintenance' defined a built-in system of feedback from the maintenance department to the design office[6] through the costing department, and the design office, after evaluation and identification of the weak points, fed forward to the maintenance department suggestions for modifications to the plant and machinery. McBrady and Kier have also stressed the need to 'study all equipment failures and breakdowns to determine what action is needed to prevent recurrences' [16]. They also suggest that after due analysis of breakdowns, a review should be carried out with regard to the following possible changes:

(i) Changing the process;

(ii) Redesign of the component/item that failed;

(iii) Replacement of the failed item with an improved item or an entirely new machine;

(iv) Changing the preventive maintenance procedure; as for example, performing lubrication as per schedule, and readjusting the frequency and content of equipment inspection; and

(v) Changing the operational variables; as for example, training of the operators in the proper operation of the equipment and changing the load on the particular machine.

We shall return to Wiegel and his cyclic model of functional maintenance in the next chapter when we discuss terotechnology, but let it suffice here to say that planned maintenance refers to analysis of past failures and condition monitoring data from critical equipment and planning of plant and equipment modifications and designing-out-of-maintenance jobs. Moreover, 'planning in maintenance and setting up of tasks in order of priority' has been differentiated from preventive maintenance [7]. This differentiation is necessary to stress the fact that not only such maintenance jobs are important for the prevention of recurrent failures, improvement of plant and equipment availability and reduction of costs of maintenance, but also that planned maintenance includes the identification of necessary tasks, deciding their priority, and also other planning functions of these tasks such as estimating the time, skill levels, and number of maintenance tradesmen required, provisioning of spares etc.

The formal definition of planned maintenance is as follows [6]:

> "that maintenance which is organised and carried out with forethought, control and records."

This definition implies that planned maintenance should also include planned breakdown maintenance, since in a plant there are certain equipment which can be allowed to run, without any danger of subsequent/consequential damages, till they fail. However, even in these cases, advance planning helps to ensure that the equipment is restored to its working state quickly. B.S. 3811:1984 defines such activities of planned breakdown maintenance as follows:

> "maintenance work which is carried out after a failure, but for which advance provision has been made in the form of spares, materials, labour and equipment."

So planned maintenance should be further subdivided under two heads, namely, planned breakdown maintenance and planned corrective maintenance, and the latter includes activities which correct weak points, or situations, or designs by modifications to plant and equipment and other designing-out-of-maintenance activities which may also include changing the process, or the operational variables, as discussed earlier. Herein it must be noted that planned corrective maintenance is differentiated from programmed replacements, which, as we have noted earlier, must more appropriately, come under periodic preventive maintenance. With the separation of planned maintenance from preventive maintenance, maintenance can now be classified under three main heads, namely, breakdown maintenance, planned maintenance, and preventive maintenance. In this classification, only emergency repairs come under breakdown maintenance, whereas planned breakdown maintenance comes under planned maintenance, as noted above. This new classification of maintenance is shown in Fig. 2.2.

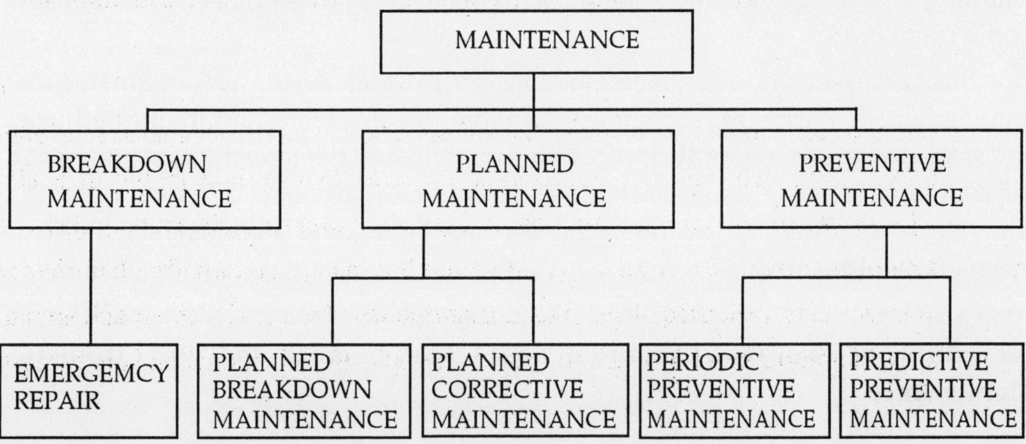

Fig. 2.2. Types of Maintenance (An Intermediate Classification)

There is a third possible method of classifying maintenance. This classification is based on the formal definitions of maintenance, corrective maintenance and preventive maintenance, which are as follows [9] [19]:

Maintenance: All work undertaken to keep in or restore every facility to a specified acceptable condition.

Corrective Maintenance: That maintenance which is performed to restore an item to a satisfactory condition after a failure.

Note: *In this context, a substandard performance is also a failure as it necessitates action(s) to restore satisfactory performance.*

Preventive maintenance: That maintenance which is performed to keep or retain an item in a satisfactory operational condition. This includes periodic lubrication, calibration, replacement and overhaul, equipment inspection, and detection and prevention of incipient or random failures.

Corrective maintenance actions can either be taken after a breakdown to restore an equipment to a satisfactory condition, or as noted earlier, they can be planned actions emanating from an analysis of past failure data, or resulting from an analysis of condition monitoring data and observations from periodic equipment inspections. Therefore, under this classification, planned breakdown maintenance should come under breakdown maintenance in place of planned maintenance. This classification is shown in Fig.2.3. This method of classification is the most appropriate, since it brings out an essential difference between the two basic types of maintenance, based on the acceptable definitions taking care to include planning in maintenance and essential activities of designing-out-of-maintenance in the framework.

Such a classification of maintenance is useful in structuring and organising the maintenance department, particularly of large process plant and integrated iron and steel-works, since the education, training, skills and personal traits required for the job of maintenance analyst/condition monitoring specialist differ very greatly from those required for planners on the one hand and maintenance fitters/ mechanics on the other.

Prevention of Failures—Condition Based Maintenance and Opportunistic Maintenance

Preventive maintenance is the total of all functions which are aimed at maintaining and improving, if possible, the reliability performance characteristics of assets in

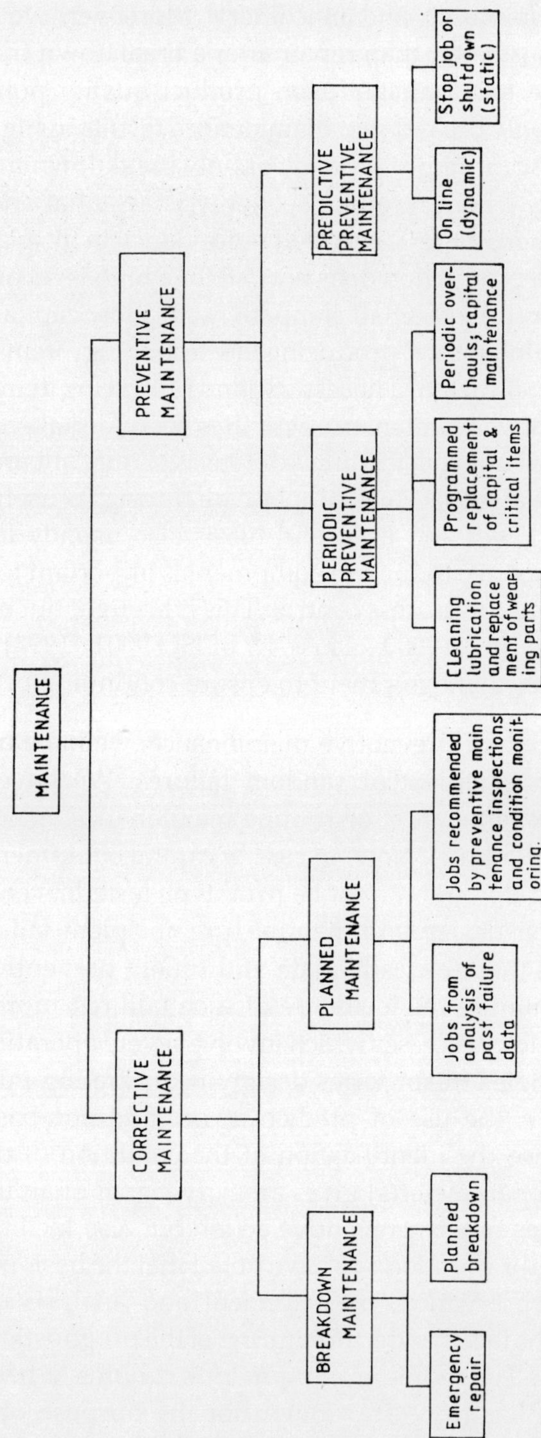

Fig. 2.3 Tyeps of maintenance (modern and detailed classification)

the form of plant, equipment and machinery. Moreover, we have noted that prevention of failures is better than repair after a breakdown from the economic, safety, equipment life and possibly even product quality points of view, and following a policy of only breakdown maintenance results in higher consumption of resources as well. Accordingly, a policy of only breakdown maintenance is not desirable in situations where resource economy is essential and may at best be justified (i) in cases where there is a built-in redundancy in the plant or equipment, (ii) where the required production does not call for a high level of utilisation of the specific equipment, or (iii) in a small company with a low capital investment (i.e., low indirect cost of maintenance) producing low technology items (and production of which may be sub-contracted, if necessary) and producing items where the value added is small. Preventive maintenance activities are undertaken because the costs of lost production from unexpected breakdowns is significant and also because of the fact that when the asset receives proper care during its useful life, the cost of owning it is usually lower and its useful life is also usually longer. Moreover, preventive maintenance of production equipment is important for product quality and is an essential input for process control. This is brought out by the fact that the process control clause of ISO 9000 (clause 4.9 of ISO 9001 : 1994) stresses the need for 'suitable maintenance of equipment to ensure continuing process capability.'

From the definition of preventive maintenance, we have noted that it must include prevention of incipient or random failures. We have also noted that periodic preventive maintenance, or routine maintenance, is not effective in the prevention of random failures. Now, in case of capital equipment used in process plants, which are 'one-off' and cannot be prototype tested, even with all possible care taken during their design and manufacture, incipient failures will, and do, occur. In these cases, therefore, adequate and timely preventive actions are required which will minimise the incidence of such failures, more so because very often such plants employ processes which involve severe operating conditions and these plants are of single stream series design incorporating minimal redundancies [10]. Accordingly, the use of predictive, or condition-based, maintenance becomes essential since the identification of the condition of the equipment by monitoring of certain parameter(s) gives an early signal of an impending failure which not only enables timely preventive action but also facilitates maintenance planning. In the preceding section, we have noted that the basis of condition-based maintenance is the observation, measurement and analysis of the prognostic parameters and also the fact that the monitoring of the prognostic parameter(s) can, in some cases, be carried out while an equipment is running, whereas in some other cases, the equipment has to be shut down for the purpose of observation and measurement of the prognostic parameter(s). We have also noted that the monitoring methods generally used for plant and machinery are visual monitoring, performance monitoring, vibration monitoring, sound-level or noise monitoring and wear-debris monitoring. The characteristic features of these commonly used monitoring methods are given in Table 2.2. These monitoring techniques are now highly developed and sensitive, and they can be used to monitor complex expensive machinery, either continuously or periodically. The use of these techniques can lead to the detection of failure initiation thus, allowing sufficient time to plan and execute necessary preventive action.

Nakajima, in his introductory book on TPM [17], notes that until the 1970s, PM activity in Japan consisted mainly of periodic preventive maintenance, which he calls time-based maintenance, featuring periodic servicing and overhaul. He adds that in the 1980s, there was a greater use of predictive, or condition-based, maintenance and during the 1980s, periodic preventive maintenance was rapidly being replaced by predictive maintenance. In India, however, in many process plants, condition monitoring is not being practised [20], although the maintenance professionals are gradually becoming aware of the benefits to be derived from the implementation of condition-based maintenance.

Table 2.2. Monitoring Methods in Common Use for Detection and Identification of Equipment Problems

Monitoring Method	*Detection of existence of problem by measurement of*	*Determination of the nature of the problem by analysis of*		
Visual monitoring	Overall appearance	Colour	Shape	Texture
Performance monitoring	Rate of output	Uniformity of rate	Quality level	Uniformity of quality
Vibration/noise monitoring	Overall vibration/ noise level	Frequency content	Signal wave-from	Signal statistics
Wear-debris monitoring	Amount of debris	Size-distribution of debris	Shape of debris	Chemical composition of debris

Condition monitoring helps in overcoming the problem of excessive maintenance on the one hand and inadequate maintenance on the other. It also results in greater safety of plant and equipment, increased plant and equipment availability, reduced maintenance costs and in general more efficient plant operation and better employee morale and job satisfaction. There are certain other benefits which may result from the implementation of condition-based maintenance. These are as follows:

(i) Possibility of detection of weak components of equipment at the commissioning stage.

(ii) Improved product quality.

(iii) More effective negotiations with plant manufacturers and/or repair contractors.

(iv) Opportunity for better specifications of future plants.

(v) In some cases, the machine can be run at increased load and/or speed, if necessary, through the application of on-line monitoring.

The implementation of condition-based maintenance for critical process plant equipment can be adequately justified by its advantages of greater safety and increased equipment availability. In process plants, sometimes instant shutdown is not permissible and in case of such equipment, the evaluation of time-dependent deterioration enables the equipment to be stopped safely, thus making available valuable leadtime during which necessary planning can be done. Further, on-line monitoring of critical equipment also enables timely alarm, which, in turn, ensures that the machine condition is adequate where instant shutdown is both necessary and permissible. Moreover, increased equipment availability results in greater output and higher productivity and this is achieved by a combination of more running time, or uptime (because of higher MTBF[7]) and less maintenance time, or downtime (as a result of lower MTTR). The increase in MTBF is achieved through a reduction in the number of unforeseen plant stoppages, proper utilisation of production windows[8] available for maintenace work and the optimisation of time between planned overhauls. The reduction of MTTR is obtained through the avoidance of various consequential damages from unexpected failures, planning of maintenance work, including spare parts in advance, reduction of inspection/diagnosis time after shutdowns and the need to strip serviceable equipment for inspection during annual overhauls.

All condition monitoring is not of the on-line variety. In some cases, an equipment needs to be shut down for an observation and measurement of the prognostic parameter(s). Moreover, equipment inspection also requires stoppage, or shutdown, of the equipment. The decision of a shutdown, whether it is for condition monitoring, periodic inspection, component replacement, or minor repair or adjustment, is a very difficult one since it entails loss of production and revenue. This is particularly true in continuous process plants where the shutdown of an equipment may call for the shutdown of a line, or the entire plant. At the same time, non-performance of these essential maintenance tasks may result in catastrophic failures, which, in turn, may cause longer shutdowns and greater losses of revenue. Opportunistic maintenance is a term which is applied to maintenance work which is carried out during an equipment or plant shutdown, but which is not directed at the primary cause of failure or shutdown. In other words, an equipment can be stopped for either maintenance or non-maintenance reasons and whenever such stoppages take place, there exist opportunities for carrying out preventive maintenance of the shutdown variety, which cannot be performed while the equipment is running. In a study carried out in a medium-sized machine building plant, it was found that on certain machine-tools, such as gear hobbers, copying lathes and even vertical boring machines and plano-millers, the stoppages due to production reasons had been large and that the maintenance downtime which occured in subsequent periods (quarters, in this case) could have been significantly reduced if the opportunities of carrying out necessary preventive maintenance tasks during these shutdowns had been properly utilized[1]. In the manufacturing industry, such significantly large production windows can and do sometimes occur as illustrated by this case study. However, in continuous process plants, the production windows available are much smaller since they are primarily caused by the non-availability of raw materials/raw stock, and in such cases, opportunities for preventive maintenance are available on the failure of an equipment of the system. In a system consisting of many equipment, the failure of one of its constituent equipment may present an opportunity for carrying out preventive maintenance work on other equipment of the system. Similarly, the failure of a multi-component equipment may present an opportunity for carrying out preventive maintenance on other components along with the corrective maintenance work on the failed component. The efficacy of opportunistic maintenance was illustrated in a case study carried out on a 210 MW thermal power unit [21]. However, the use of opportunistic maintenance, which, in a thermal power unit, consists mainly of preventive maintenance work on load-bearing equipment, calls for computerised maintenance planning and control methods and procedures/ algorithms [21].

Till now, in this section, we have discussed two effective methods of preventive maintenance of equipment, particularly for equipment which are used in continuous process plants, namely condition-based maintenance and opportunistic maintenance. We have also noted that in continuous process plants, preventive maintenance activities requiring a shutdown of the equipment, can, in the majority of cases, only be performed during opportunities and an effective use of opportunistic maintenance can improve plant availability and also increase the useful life of plant and equipment. In this context, it is important to note that scheduling of preventive maintenance inspections and also other preventive maintenance activities, such as periodic replacements of wearing parts, programmed replacements of bearings and other such items and even some 'fixed-interval' minor repairs and adjustments can only be economically established on the basis of the analysis of past failure and maintenance records [15]. This is also true in case of equipment wherein periodic on-line monitoring of a prognostic parameter (such as vibration for rolling-element bearings) is employed since analysis of past data provides an inference of the time-dependent deterioration and therefore, spacing of the inspection interval; even setting of the admissibility criteria, or acceptance limits, should be based on the analysis of the condition monitoring data [3]. These preventive maintenance activities can retain an equipment in a satisfactory condition, but effective maintenance must also be directed towards reliability growth since the intent of a reliability programme is also to extend satisfactory performance of an equipment into the time domain to the maximum degree possible, which, in simple words, implies that the times between successive failures of an equipment should tend to become larger and larger [2].

Designing-Out-Of-Maintenance Activities - Maintenance Prevention (MP) and Maintainability Improvement (MI)

Modernisation and the pressing need for higher productivity have brought with it sophisticated equipment and machines. Such sophisticated machines tend to have a high probability of failure. These failures cause disruption in production and also result in an increase in the direct costs of maintenance. This direct cost of maintenance does not include the cost of lost production due to breakdowns etc. and it has been shown that in the manufacturing industry, the loss due to breakdowns is almost as much as the direct costs of maintenance. Moreover, certain studies have shown that 30 per cent of all maintenance expenditures is wasted. Therefore, considerable savings can be effected, and simultaneously higher revenue can be earned by improving the availability of manufacturing plant and equipment. Availability, in its turn, is a function of both reliability and maintainability.

We may conclude, therefore, that the increasing complexity and sophistication of modern equipment has brought with it the requirements of greater reliability and improved maintainability. Reliability of an equipment is defined as the probability that it performs its purpose adequately over the period of time intended, under the specified operating conditions or environment. The definition of reliability embraces four elements namely, probability, satisfactory performance, time or life, and operating conditions. The mean time to failure (MTTF) for a replacement part, or the mean time between failures (MTBF) for a repairable system, such as an equipment used for production, and therefore, the total operation time, or uptime, in any given time period, such as a week, a month, or a year, is a function of the reliability of the equipment. Maintainability, on the other hand, denotes the ease with which maintenance can be conducted, when required, since even in the most critical equipment, reliability cannot be absolute and failures do occur. Maintainability is defined as the probability that the equipment or machine will be restored to specified conditions within a given period of time when the maintenance action is performed in accordance with the prescribed procedures and resources [14]. Thus, from the point of view of maintainability, the objective is to design and develop equipment which can be maintained in the least time, at the least cost and with the minimum expenditure of resources, without affecting its performance. Thus, the maintenance practices to be adopted and the actual repair time, the level of spares inventory and the cost of lost production will depend on the maintainability of the equipment, and the mean time to repair (MTTR), and therefore, the total downtime of the equipment, is a function of its maintainability. Availability, which is defined as the probability that the system is operating satisfactorily at any point in time under stated conditions, is a ratio of the uptime to the total time, which, in turn, is the sum of uptime and downtime. Thus, availability is a function of both reliability and maintainability, and is a more practical measure of equipment performance as well as the effectiveness of maintenance practices and procedures adopted, since it includes both reliability and maintainability.

When we talk of designing-out-of-maintenance, we are discussing activities which are directed at reducing the need for maintenance of the equipment, and the greater the availability of the equipment, the lower the need for its maintenance. Thus, designing-out-of-maintenance activities are directed at improving the availability of plant and machinery. From our earlier discussion, we have seen that such activities can either be directed at improving the reliability of the equipment as denoted by an increasing MTBF, and/or improving its maintainability which, in turn, is denoted by a decreasing MTTR. These activities, or efforts, are essentially of two types:

(i) Reliability and maintainability improvement efforts carried out at the stage of design, manufacture and installation (and also commissioning) of the equipment, and

(ii) Reliability and maintainability improvement efforts carried out by the user of the equipment during its useful life.

This is illustrated in Fig. 2.4 wherein the equipment availability improvement efforts have been initially classified under two heads, as noted above.

The Japanese use the term maintenance prevention (MP), for the first type of activity. This activity is directed at facilitating maintenance-free design in new equipment [18]. Nakajima further clarifies that MP activities are carried out during the design to commissioning stage of the life of the equipment and 'the goal of the MP activities is to reduce maintenance costs and deterioration losses in new equipment by considering past maintenance data and latest technology when designing for higher reliability, maintainability, operability, safety and other requirements' [18]. The equipment designer can use a number of techniques to enhance the reliability of the equipment. Some of the important methods, which are used during the design stage, are as follows:

(i) Use of effective and creative design;

(ii) System simplification using a smaller number of components and taking into account maintainability considerations, such as accessibility of components, test points, adjustment points and connectors, modular design etc.;

(iii) Improving the reliability of individual components (parts improvement method);

(iv) Use of over-rated components; and

(v) Use of structural redundancy and here the designer can either use unit redundancy, component redundancy, redundancy for the weakest/weaker link(s), or a combination of these methods keeping in mind the costs.

For an effective design, the designer must be able to identify important failure modes and failure situations, and attempt to eliminate these failure modes and failure situations [11]. If he cannot eliminate some of them, then he must take actions to mitigate the consequences of the important failure modes and failure situations. For the purpose of identifying failure modes and failure situations and assessing their effect on system reliability, the designer can use reliability block diagrams/system logic diagrams and failure modes and effects analysis (FMEA),

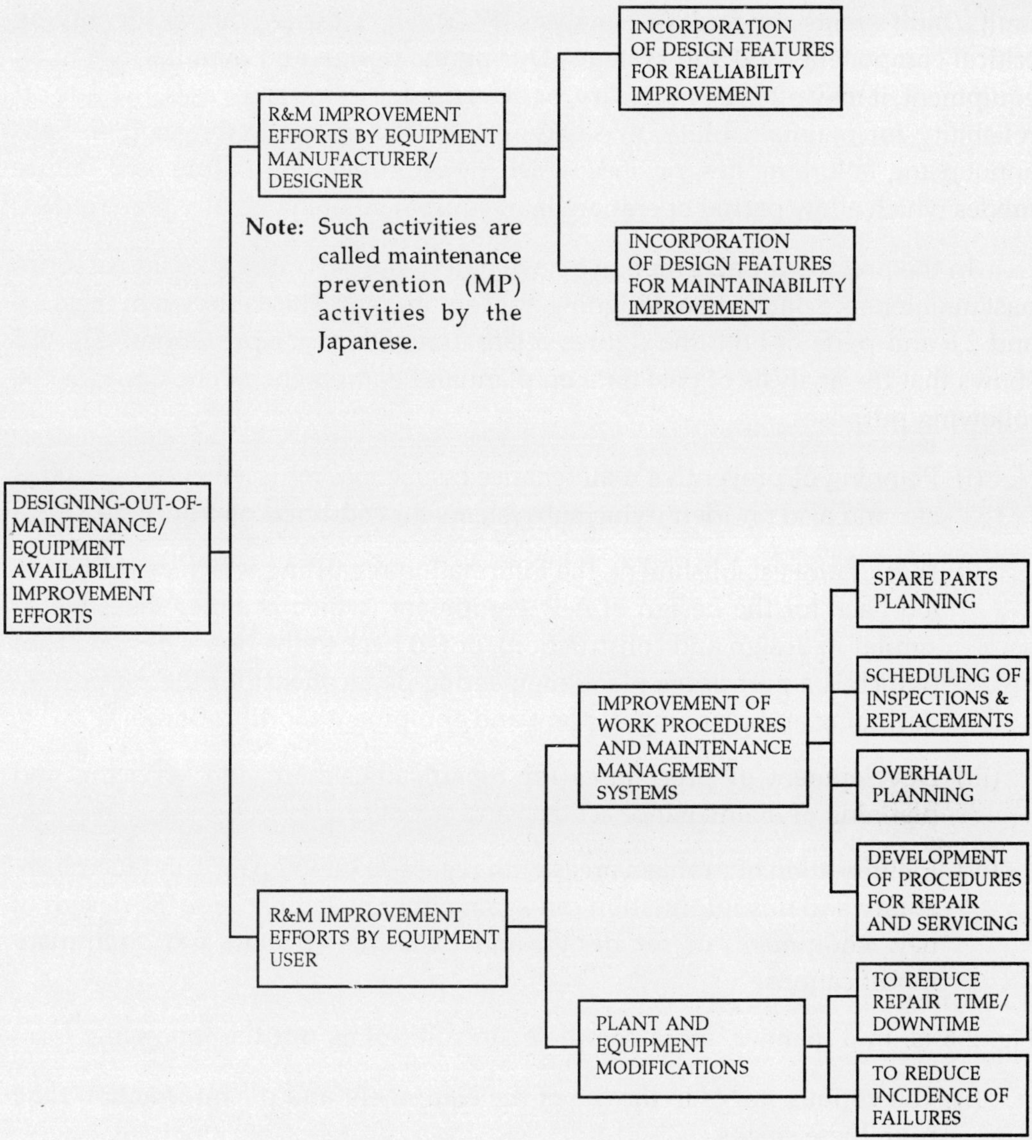

Fig. 2.4. Designing-Out-Of-Maintenance Efforts/Activities

or the failure modes, effects and critically analysis (FMECA). The designer must be able to distinguish between a failure mode and a failure mechanism. Failure mode is the observable behaviour of an item when it fails, as for example, the failure of an electric motor due to bearing seizure, whereas failure mechanism is the cause of the observable failure mode [11]. Fault trees can also be constructed for undesirable faults/fault events and fault tree analysis (FTA) can be carried out for identifying critical components and sub-systems. During the design and manufacture of an equipment, it may often be necessary, or even desirable, in some cases, to trade off reliability for maintainability, or safety, or one failure mode for another. Self-announcing failure modes, or ones which signal impending failure, and failure modes which allow partial operation of an equipment are generally preferred.

In the preceding paragraph, we have noted that MP must take into account past maintenance data when designing new equipment. This is shown in Figs. 2.5 and 2.6 and parts of both the figures relate to maintenance prevention. Fig. 2.5 shows that the analysis of past data on plant and equipment can be used for the following purposes:

(i) Planning of preventive maintenance inspection, replacements, overhauls etc. and also for identifying subsystems for condition monitoring;

(ii) Weak point establishment, the information regarding which can either be fed back for the design of new equipment (which is either the same or similar in design and construction), or fed back to the user's design office (which is a part of his plant engineering department) for the purpose of designing and planning of plant and equipment modifications;

(iii) Development of procedures for repair, adjustment and servicing and planning of maintenance actions; and

(iv) Identification of problem areas with regard to maintenance and maintainability and this information can again either be fed back for the design of new equipment, or for design and planning of plant and equipment modifications.

Fig. 2.6 is, in a manner, more complete since it points out the following:

(i) The various stages in the life of the equipment and the information flow from these stages,

(ii) Use of information/data from commissioning and early life period of the equipment for design of new equipment and also for design of plant and equipment modifications by the user of the equipment; and

(iii) Use of maintenance data obtained after incorporation of plant and equipment modification again either for the design of new equipment or for planning of other improvements/modifications.

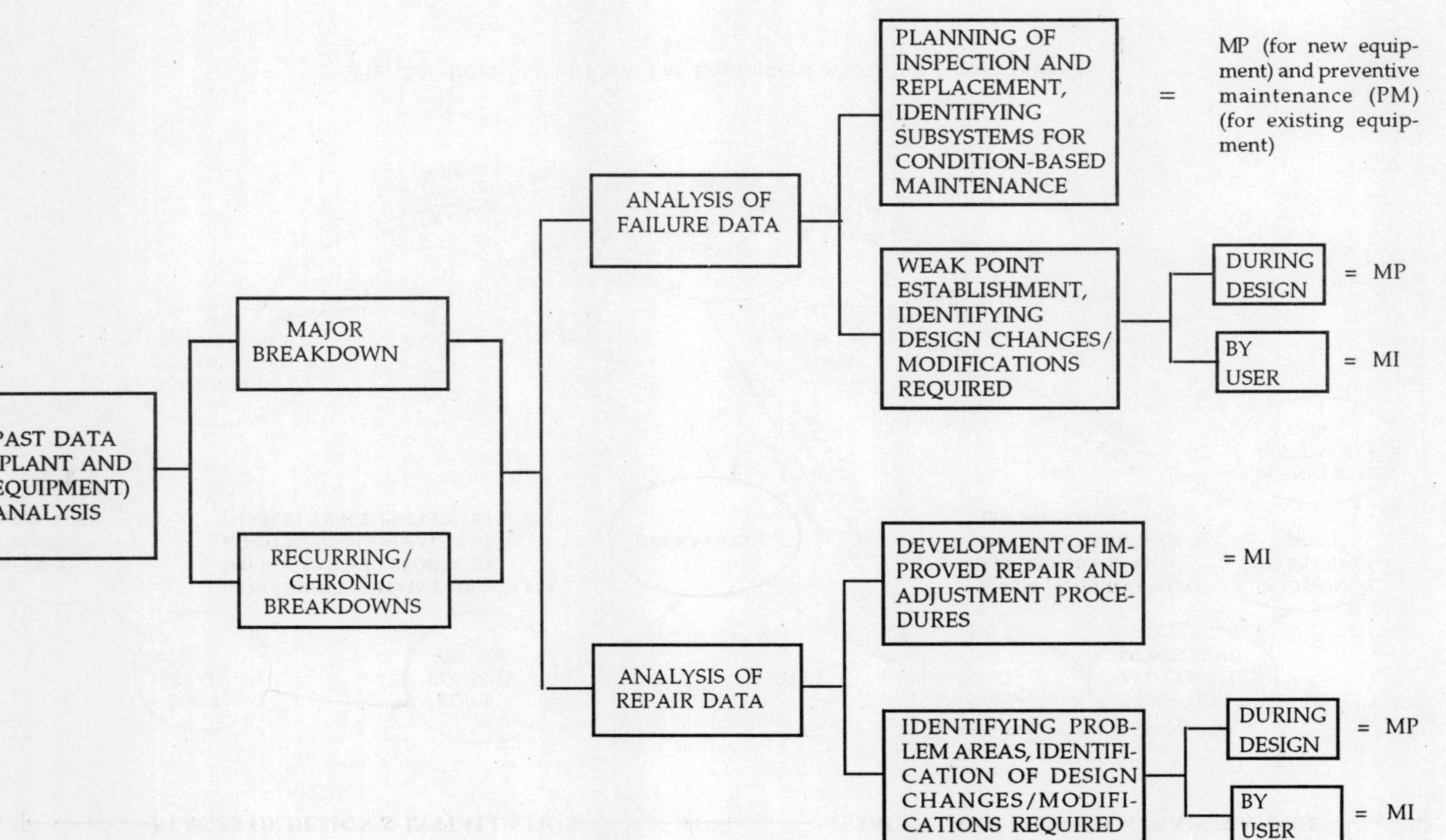

Fig. 2.5. Analysis of Past Data/Maintenance History

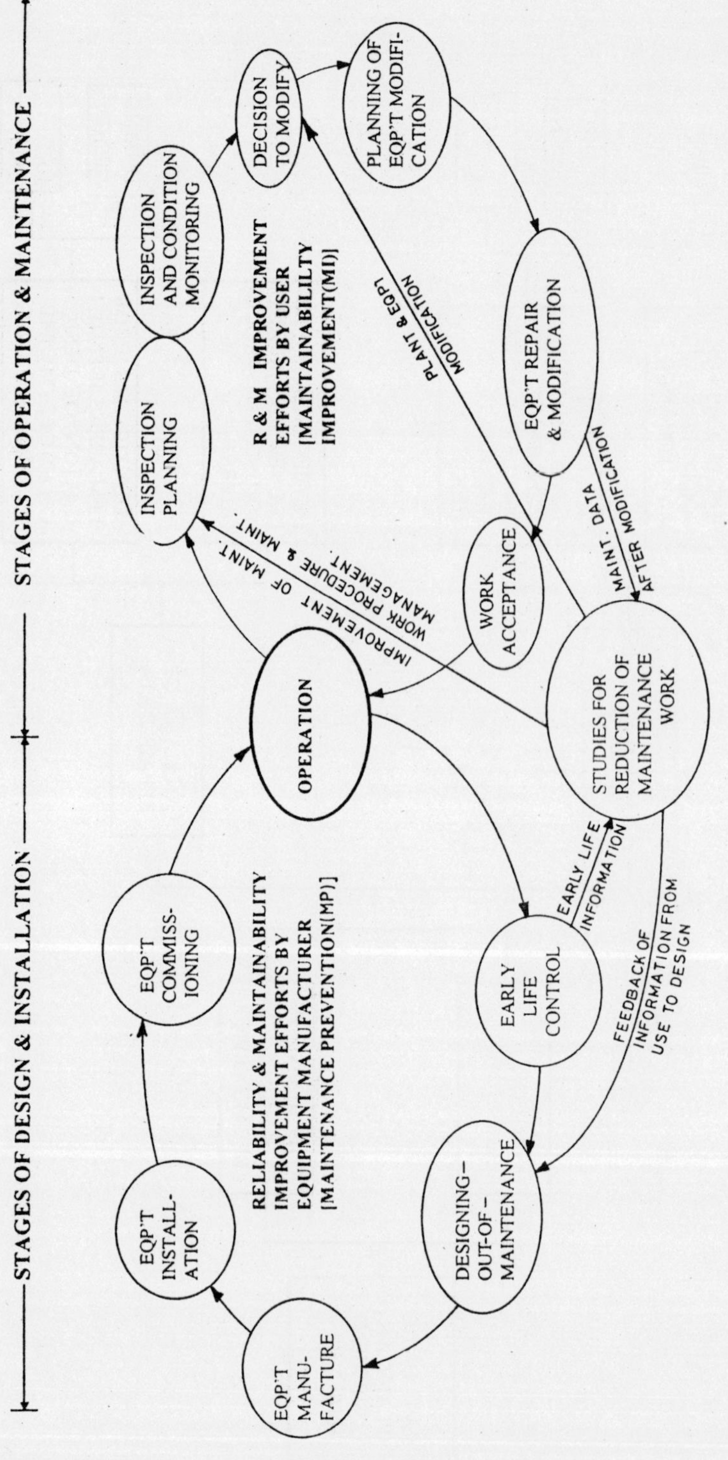

Fig. 2.6. Information Flow For Equipment Availabilty Improvement

Both Figs. 2.5 and 2.6 point out that the past operational and use data and problems encountered must be fed back to the equipment designer for MP. But is the designer of an equipment also the user of the equipment? The important point to remember is that the user of the equipment is generally not the equipment designer and manufacturer. In most cases, the equipment manufacturer and the equipment user are two different companies-different organisations, and the designer, who is also the original equipment manufacturer, is hardly ever the user of the equipment. For effective MP, and to ensure that the reliability and maintainability requirements are adequately met in the new equipment design, both equipment manufacturer and the equipment user must cooperate [11]. Such interaction between the equipment manufacturer and user is not always forthcoming. The lack of interaction between the manufacturer and user is also a weakness of the cyclic model of functional maintenance enunciated by Wiegel and also Evans' circular model of the main functions of terotechnology. Wiegel had recognized the need for such interaction [26]. We shall return to this point and discuss it further in the subsequent chapter but the lack of this interaction also brings up the need for reliability and maintainability improvement activities by the equipment user as shown in Figs.2.4 and 2.6.

This brings us to what the Japanese call maintainability improvement (MI). As already explained earlier, maintainability is used to mean the ease of maintenance and therefore, MI refers to activities that can reduce the time needed for the maintenance of plant and equipment [23]. The reduction of maintenance could also be due to a reduction of the incidence of failures, and accordingly, MI, theoretically, should also include activities which are directed at reliability improvement. This has accordingly been shown in Fig. 2.4, where plant and equipment modification activities have been shown to include those which are directed at the reduction of the incidence of failures in addition to those which are meant to reduce the time required for the maintenance action. However, in actual practice, most of the reliability and maintainability improvement efforts which are carried out by the user are directed at the improvement of maintainability. Thus, the term used by the Japanese is quite appropriate, although some of the plant and equipment modification efforts may also result in higher MTBFs. MI thus includes both:

(i) Development of improved repair and maintenance procedures, and maintenance management systems; and

(ii) Plant and equipment modifications, as shown in Figs. 2.4, 2.5 and 2.6.

The main objectives of MI activities are:

(i) The identification of the important causes of poor maintenance and excessive downtime; and

(ii) The elimination, if possible, of these causes without introducing new ones.

In cases where it is not possible to eliminate the causes, the objective is to mitigate the effect of these causes by minimising the downtime for each type of failure. As shown in Figs. 2.5 and 2.6, past data of recurring, or chronic, as well as high-cost, or major breakdowns is analyzed with the objective of reducing the MTTR. A reduction in MTTR can be achieved either by the use of improved work procedures and maintenance management systems, or through plant and equipment modifications. The analysis of MTTR may call for breaking the repair time down into its elements, such as travel, logistic and preparation time, time required for diagnosis, dismantling and repair time, and time required for reassembly, adjustment and try-out. MI activities are directed at the reduction of MTTR, and mean time for scheduled maintenance. In one of the earliest published applications of terotechnology, Rappini [22] reported very significant improvements obtained through modifications to plant and machinery at an integrated iron and steel-works in Italy. These modifications were based on the feedback of information and experiences of the maintenance engineers and the inferences drawn therefrom to the design department of the steel-works. Rappini reported savings of £40,000 in the annual cost of spares and 1900 hours of maintenance time as a result of modifications and alterations made on the hot rolling mills alone and estimated a saving of £300,000 annually in the maintenace costs and a reduction of one per cent in production loss due to emergency stoppages in the case of alterations contemplated for the 150 tonne basic oxygen furnace. The report clearly shows that the alterations and modifications to plant and equipment had significantly reduced both the maintenance time and maintenance expenditure, and thus were part of a major project of designing-out-of-maintenance carried out in the steelworks. At the same time, these were essentially activities directed at maintainability improvement (MI).

Thus, designing-out-of-maintenance consists of all activities aimed at equipment availability improvement and includes both MP and MI, as shown in Figs. 2.4 and 2.6. In actual practice, however, much of the designing-out-of-maintenance work is carried out by the equipment user in the form of maintainability improvement. This condition will change because increasing competition will bring with it greater interaction between equipment manufacturers and equipment users. This is very welcome since designing-out-of-maintenance effort is more effective if it is carried out at the design stage. Ikeda has described a few of the salient features of the MP design system at the Fuji Photo Film Company [13]. The planned maintenance system, which includes periodic preventive maintenance, gave way to the MP design system as a result of a study which showed that (i) a poorly designed equipment exhibited low availability and total life, (ii) post-failure repair times were longer in the case of equipment where maintainability had not been given due consideration during its design, and (iii) with increasing automation, product quality had become increasingly dependent on the condition of the equipment. The MP design system had the objective of ensuring that reliability, maintainability and safety aspects were given due consideration during the stages of equipment selection, development of equipment specifications, installation and running trials. While all the information was concentrated in the plant design section, the maintenance engineers were involved during the design of equipment so that reliability, maintainability, standardisation of components and assemblies were optimised and the availability of spare parts ensured at the same time. The MP design section also took active part in the commissioning of the equipment to make sure that the early failure period was minimised and the equipment started producing at the rated capacity at the earliest. Since this is a report of the work done in a Japanese company, one might get the impression that MP design activity had not either been suggested or carried out elsewhere. Finniston, in a paper published in 1973 [12], had reported the work done by the British Steel Corporation. Based on this, Finniston has recommended the following measures:

(i) Special attention to maintainability considerations, including the standardisation of capital replaceable items such as valves, pumps, motors and bearings;

(ii) Pre-testing of certain critical items before installation, particularly since in the case of an integrated steelworks, components, machines and equipment cannot be prototype tested;

(iii) Pre-definition of the installation practice and methods and procedures to be followed with proper planning of the installation work (by the manufacturer and user together);

(iv) Setting up of a team by the user which would be responsible for the installation and commissioning and which would work from the stage of design with the manufacturers of various machines and equipment and be responsible for formulating the acceptance trials; and

(v) Proper planning of the operating trials and proper evaluation of the final equipment designs from the point of view of maintainability and formulation of specific maintenance actions and systems required.

Productive Maintenance = PM + MP + MI ?

Now we come to the basic question — what is the difference between the two PM's—preventive maintenance and productive maintenance? We know now that preventive maintenance is not just routine, or periodic preventive maintenance, that is, it is not just cleaning, lubrication and periodic inspections. We know that prevention of failures also calls for replacements, servicing and overhaul of equipment, and predictive maintenance, wherein the health, or condition, of a component/machine/equipment is monitored and maintenance action is taken based on the analysis of the condition monitoring data. We also know that in continuous process industries, such as thermal power plants, fertilizer plants etc., preventive maintenance activities can only be carried out during opportunities, and, thus, in continuous process industries, preventive maintenance takes the form of opportunistic maintenance. We have also seen that designing-out-of-maintenance includes both MP and MI. But is productive maintenance, preventive maintenance (including periodic and predictive maintenance) together with designing-out-of-maintenance, or in other words, productive maintenance = PM + MP + MI?

No, it is not just PM + MP + MI. Productive maintenance is more than the sum of preventive maintenance and designing-out-of-maintenance. As clearly stated by Takahashi and Osada [23], `PM activities mean not only preventive maintenance, but also a widerPM that focusses on the lifetime economic feasibility' of equipment, tools and accessories used in production. They explain this by adding that `the requirements of this kind of PM are creating equipment with a greater possible overall efficiency.' Preventive maintenance and designing-out-of-maintenance activities are aimed at the elimination/minimisation of loss due to equipment breakdowns, that is, they are used to attain the objective of zero breakdowns. Loss of production caused by equipment and machine breakdowns is not the only kind of loss which affects the productivity of equipment and machines. Productivity is affected by other kinds of losses as well, and these other losses are as follows:

1. Setup and adjustment losses;
2. Losses due to idling and minor stoppages;
3. Loss due to reduced speed or operation at less than full load;

4. Loss due to defects in process and production of defective products; and
5. Loss due to reduced yield from startup of the machine to the point of stable production.

These five together with the loss due to downtime caused by equipment breakdowns are called 'six big losses.' These six big losses cause a reduction in the overall equipment effectiveness and the aim of productive maintenance is improvement of overall equipment effectiveness. The aim of productive maintenance has been clearly indicated in the definition of TPM which we had discussed in Chapter 1.

Nakajima, in his introductory book on TPM [17], states that the word "total" in "total productive maintenance" has three meanings, which describe the principal features of TPM. These three meanings are as follows:

1. Total effectiveness and this indicates TPM's pursuit of economic efficiency or profitability.
2. Total maintenance system which, in turn, includes maintenance prevention (MP), maintainability improvement (MI), and preventive maintenance.
3. Total participation by employees which is obtained through autonomous maintenance by production operators through small group activities.

The first two meanings, namely total effectiveness and total maintenance system, are the aims of productive maintenance and the third meaning pertains to making productive maintenance total through the use of autonomous maintenance by operators. Therefore,

Productive maintenance > PM+MP+MI, and
Productive maintenance = Total maintenance system +
elimination of five remaining big losses.

References

1. Arankalle, M.N., Development of Maintenance MIS in a Medium Scale Machine Building Plant, Unpublished M.Tech Thesis, Indian Institute of Technology, Kharagpur, December 1987.
2. Ascher, H. and Feingold, H., *Repairable System Reliability*, Marcel Dekker, Inc., New York, 1987, pp (iii), 1 and 2.
3. Bhadury, B., Sinha, B.K. and Basu, S.K., 'Analysis of Bearing Vibrations of a Paper Machine', *Mechanical Engineering Bulletin*, Vol. 16, No. 2, 1985, pp. 68-83.

4. Bhadury, B., and Basu, S.K., 'Modelling Total Life Cycle Cost', *Proceedings of the Institution of Mechanical Engineers* (London), Vol 200, No. A1, 1986, pp. 31-40.

5. Blanchard, B.S., 'Introduction,' in *TPM Development Program: Implementing Total Productive Maintenance* (S. Nakajima, ed.), Productivity Press, Cambridge, Massachusetts, U.S.A., 1989, pp. XXI-XXIV.

6. Blanchard, B.S. and Lowery, E.E., *Maintainability*, McGraw-Hill, New York, 1989, p 20.

7. Blegen, H.M. and Nylehn, B., 'Organising the Maintenance Funcion—An Analytical Approach', *The International Journal of Production Research*, Vol. 7, No. 1, 1968, pp. 23-32.

8. Carter, A.D.S., 'Achieving Quality and Reliability', James Clayton Lecture, *Proceedings of the Institution of Mechanical Engineers* (London), Vol. 188, No. 13, 1974, pp. 201-213.

9. Collacott, R.A., *Mechanical Fault Diagnosis and Condition Monitoring*, Chapman and Hall, London, 1977.

10. De La Mere, R.F. and Ball, K.J., 'Early Life Availability of Chemical Process Plant,' *Reliability Engineering*, No. 2, 1981, pp. 289-302.

11. Evans, R.A., 'Reliability, Accessibility and Maintainability,' in *Quality Management Handbook* (L. Walsh, R. Wurster and R.L. Kimber, eds.). Marcel Dekker, New York, 1986, pp. 197-249.

12. Finninston, H.M., 'Terotechnology and Management at BSC,' *Journal of the Iron and Steel Institute*, July 1973, pp. 481-485.

13. Ikeda, A., 'A Reliability and Maintainability Design System and Its Development,' *Terotechnica*, Vol. 1, No. 1, May 1979, pp. 17-24.

14. Jardine, A.K.S., *Maintenance, Replacement and Reliability*, Pitman Publishing, London, 1973, p 23.

15. Lee, W., 'Organisation and Management of a Preventive Maintenance Program', in *Proceedings—International Conference on Optimum Resources Utilisation Through Tribo Terotechnology and Maintenance Management (Tribo-Maint. '81)*, New Delhi, Nov. 30-Dec. 6, 1981, Sarita Prakashan, New Delhi, 1983, pp. 1193-1216.

16. McBrady, K.W. and Kier, J.W., 'The Value of Preventive Maintenance', in *Modern Maintenance Management*(E.J. Miller and J.W. Blood, eds.), D.B. Taraporevala, Mumbai, 1971, pp. 122-138.

17. Nakajima, S., *Introduction to TPM*, Productivity Press, Cambridge, Massachusetts, U.S.A., 1988, pp. 8 and 11.

18. Nakajima, S. (Editor), *TPM Development Program: Implementing Total Productive Maintenance*, Productivity Press, Cambridge, Massachusetts, U.S.A., 1989, pp 26 and 287.

19. Parkes, D., 'Maintenance: Can It Be an Exact Science?,' in *Operational Research in Maintenance* (A.K.S. Jardine, ed.), Manchester University Press, 1970, pp. 1-7.

20. Parkes, D., 'Terotechnology, Resource Utilisation and Productivity,' in Proceedings—*International Conference on Optimum Resources Utilisation Through Tribo Terotechnology and Maintenance Management (Tribo-Maint. '81)*, New Delhi, Nov. 30-Dec. 6, 1981, Sarita Prakashan, New Delhi, 1983, pp 41-50.

21. Rao, A.N. and Bhadury, B., 'Maintenance Planning for Thermal Power Plants: A Discussion,' Paper # 93 WM 141-2 EC of *IEEE Transaction on Power Systems.*

22. Rappini, G.E., 'Some Aspects of Terotechnology at Italsider,' *Journal of the Iron and Steel Institute*, June 1973, pp. 389-405.

23. Takahashi, Y. and Osada, T., *TPM: Total Productive Maintenance*, Asian Productivity Organization, Tokyo, Japan, 1990, pp 21 and 201.

24. Watson, C., 'Is Preventive Maintenance Worthwhile?', in *Operational Research in Maintenance* (A.K.S., Jardine, ed.), Manchester University Press, 1970, pp. 142-173.

25. White, E.N., 'Challenges to Maintenance Engineers Grow,' *CME*, October 1986, pp. 20-22.

26. Wiegel, W., 'Functional Maintenance: A Systems Approach,' *Metals Technology*, January 1974, pp. 6-12.

27. Woodley, B.J., 'Condition Monitoring', *Tribology International*, Vol. 11, No. 1, February 1978, pp. 29.

Endnotes

1. Although maintenance, by itself, may not add value to the product, timely and adequate maintenance does add value to the physical assets. We shall discuss this concept of value-added maintenance later in this chapter.

2. In the manufacturing industry (which, in India, is known as the engineering industry), by and large, maintenance is not considered that important and it takes second place not only to production but also to production planning and control, materials management and quality control functions. However, with the advent of automation and CNC machines and machining centres, maintenance has become an important function in the manufacturing industry as well.

3. We have already noted that timely and effective maintenance actions result in proper care and upkeep which, in turn, prolong the useful life of the equipment. Further, longer the useful life of the equipment, the greater is its life cycle profitability. We shall discuss this in greater detail in the next chapter.

4. In B.S. 3811: 1984 standard, terms and definitions used in maintenance are presented in a form which enables maintenance managers to communicate with engineers

working in disciplines such as reliability, quality control, cost control and computer applications.

5. The reader will recollect that in Chapter 1, we had noted that the Japanese plant engineers, scientists and academicians still tend to think of preventive maintenance to include only routine jobs, or periodic preventive maintenance jobs, and periodic inspections.

6. This is the design office of the continuous process plant, which in Wiegel's case was an integrated iron and steel-works. In India, in continuous process plants - iron and steel-works, fertilizer plants etc. - there are maintenance planning bureaus/maintenance planning offices, or planning departments, and engineers in these bureaus/departments analyze the data fed back to identify areas of plant and equipment modifications and designing-out-of-maintenance.

7. MTBF — mean time between failures, and
   MTTR — mean time to repair.

8. Periods of time during which plant is shut down due to production reasons, that is, for non-maintenance reasons.

Terotechnology, TQM and TPM

In this chapter, we will try to establish the links between TPM, terotechnology and Total Quality Management (TQM). Many readers may surmise that TPM is a derivative of terotechnology, since both preach the care of physical assets and promote life-cycle management of the manufacturing plant and equipment. Similar views may be held about TPM and TQM in as much as TPM possibly took the idea of maximisation of equipment effectiveness for the life of the equipment from terotechnology and involvement of all employees in all departments and employee participation from TQM. Whether TPM originated from terotechnology, or TQM, or both, is probably not very important. Whatever be the origin of TPM[1], it is more important to understand the similarities and differences between TPM and terotechnology, and TPM and TQM. This knowledge will help in an understanding of the 'enablers' of TPM — the prerequisites — things which enable the implementation of TPM. For this reason, in this chapter, instead of trying to establish the historical sequences and origins of concepts and practices of TPM, we will try to carry out a comparison first between TPM and terotechnology and then another between TPM and TQM. We will conclude our discussion with an enumeration and brief discussion of the enablers of TPM.

In the first two chapters, we have already discussed the history, objectives/goals and constituents, or elements, of TPM. We have, however, not discussed terotechnology and TQM, in any detail. For a proper comparison of terotechnology and TQM with TPM, it is necessary to first discuss terotechnology and TQM. We will, accordingly, discuss the why, what and how of terotechnology and TQM, one after the other in the following two sections, before we take up the comparisons. Books have been written on terotechnology and TQM, and discussions in this chapter, cannot, and do not, profess to be total, or complete, in any sense. Instead, the discussions will be limited to the basics/fundamentals and such elements which will make possible adequate understanding of terotechnology and TQM to permit detailed comparisons of their salient points with those of TPM.

Terotechnology

Terotechnology professes an urgent need to care for, or to take care of, the physical assets which an organisation possesses and has the objective of pursuit of economic life cycle costs. The pressing need for the application of this concept emanated from the fact that modernisation and the urgent need for higher productivity have brought with it sophisticated equipment and machines. Such sophisticated units or plants, or in general, systems, in many cases incorporate newer, and therefore not adequately proven technologies and designs and also consist in most cases of a larger number of assemblies/subassemblies/components, and therefore, tend to have high probabilities of failure. These failures cause disruptions in production resulting from a loss of availability of the system and also result in an increase in the direct cost of maintenance. The cost of maintaining modern industrial systems is very high and as we have noted earlier, this direct cost of maintenance does not include the cost of lost production due to unavailability of the system, which, in turn, is as much as, if not more than, the direct cost of maintenance. Thus, the need is the fulfilment of two seemingly contrary objectives, namely, the maximisation of availability and the minimisation of the life cycle costs of maintenance. These are also the objectives of terotechnology.

Before we go on to a detailed discussion of the concept, we will briefly, through an example, illustrate the importance of equipment reliability in terotechnology and the need for minimisation of the total life cycle costs of the equipment. Let us examine a situation in which a manufacturing organisation wants to buy a machine/equipment, and has three alternative machines for consideration. These we shall call products A, B and C. The three elements of life cycle cost of an equipment/machine are the cost of acquisition or the first cost, the cost of maintenance of the equipment over its life cycle (and these two together make up the cost of ownership), and the cost of use or the operating cost of the equipment. The cost of acquisition, or the first cost of the equipment, increases with increasing reliability. The cost of maintenance, on the other hand, is obviously high when the equipment reliability is low and tends towards zero as the reliability approaches unity. The cost of use, or the operating cost, can be assumed to be independent of reliability. The sum of these three basic elements of cost is the total life cycle cost, which is obtained as a convex curve as the reliability goes from zero to unity as is shown in Fig. 3.1. Let us for a moment also consider the cost of lost production, or the loss of revenue due to unreliability of the equipment, which is clearly also a function of equipment reliability, decreasing as reliability increases. If the loss of revenue is also taken into account, we have another total life cycle cost curve as shown in the figure. We, thus, see that equipment reliability affects the cost of ownership, that is, two of the three basic life cycle cost elements and thus, affects the total life cycle cost of the system and it also affects the cost of lost production, or the loss of revenue. Moreover, we have plotted two curves of total life cycle costs, one including the loss of revenue and another excluding it, to illustrate further the importance of reliability and to show that the value of reliability at which an optimum life cycle cost is obtained is higher when the loss of revenue is taken into account. In this example, we find that from the point of view of the user, product C is the best choice since it gives the lowest total life cycle cost including the cost of lost production, followed by product B. Product A, though cheaper (that is, one with much lower first cost), would result in much higher total life cycle cost, with or without the loss of revenue due to equipment unreliability.

WHAT IS TEROTECHNOLOGY?

Terotechnology emerged as a concept — which stresses the need to care for the assets which a manufacturing plant possesses. The term terotechnology has been derived from the Greek word *terein* which literally means 'to take care of.' Terotechnology has been defined 'as a combination of management, financial, engineering and other practices applied to physical assets in pursuit of economic life cycle costs.' Further, it is also stated that the practice of terotechnology

> "is concerned with the specification and design for reliability and maintainability of plant, machinery, equipment, building and structure with their installation, commissioning, maintenance, modification and replacement, and with feedback of information, performance and costs [15]."

Obviously the physical assets to which this new concept can most effectively be applied are those which have a useful or productive life of many financial years, the bulk of such assets being plant and machinery. Also the application of this concept would obviously seem to be all the more important in the capital-intensive

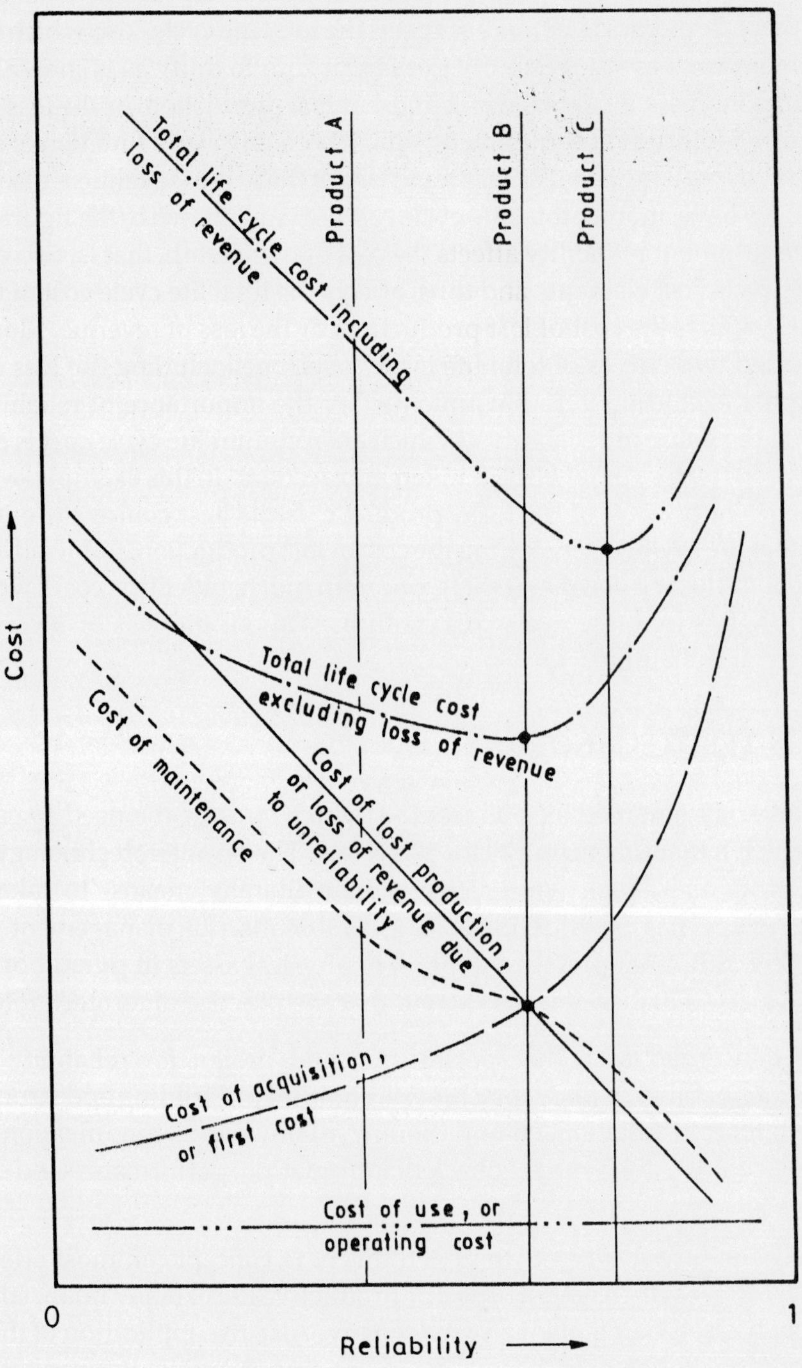

Fig. 3.1. Effect of Equipment Reliability on Life Cycle Cost and Its Constituents

continuous process industries, wherein with increasing sophistication and automation, both the cost of replacement and the total cost of maintenance over the equipment life cycle, including the cost of lost production, have become much more than ever before. Thus, for such physical assets, terotechnology stresses the objective of pursuit of economic life cycle costs through the building in of reliability and maintainability during the stages of development of equipment specification and design, effective maintenance, which may include repair, component replacement, equipment overhaul and modification during the life cycle, and feedback of information, performance and costs. The concept has been explained very succintly by Darnall in the following words [6]:

> "In future, terotechnology will be an essential element of good husbandry, of quality and of the ability to understand that an artefact commits resources both in its making and in its subsequent use .... The outcome of such an approach may result in a product which has a high initial cost and a long reliable life, or which is cheap with a short life and anticipated replacement or breakdown .... Terotechnology has a simple objective — that of minimising the whole life cost of ownership[2] — but its practice can be complex involving interdependencies and relationships of a diversity of resources — people, money, material, ideas and techniques."

MAIN FUNCTIONS OF TEROTECHNOLOGY

In Chapter Two, we had noted that the Committee for Terotechnology was formed in 1970 by the Government of the United Kingdom and that this Committee took two years to come up with the definition of terotechnology (the one we have discussed in the preceding paragraphs). This Committee also developed a description of the activities involved, which emphasized that the practice of terotechnology demanded an involvement of multi-disciplinary personnel and also work at the multi-agency level with the objective of minimising the on-going cost of maintenance of plant and machinery.

Discussion of terotechnology is incomplete without a mention of Wiegel's 'functional maintenance' [29] which stressed the need to identify critical equipment centres and weakspots and through planned maintenance reduce the cost of maintenance, thereby also increasing the plant and equipment availability. Wiegel's cyclic model of functional maintenance, shown in Fig. 3.2, for the first time defined a built-in system of feedback from the maintenance department to the design office

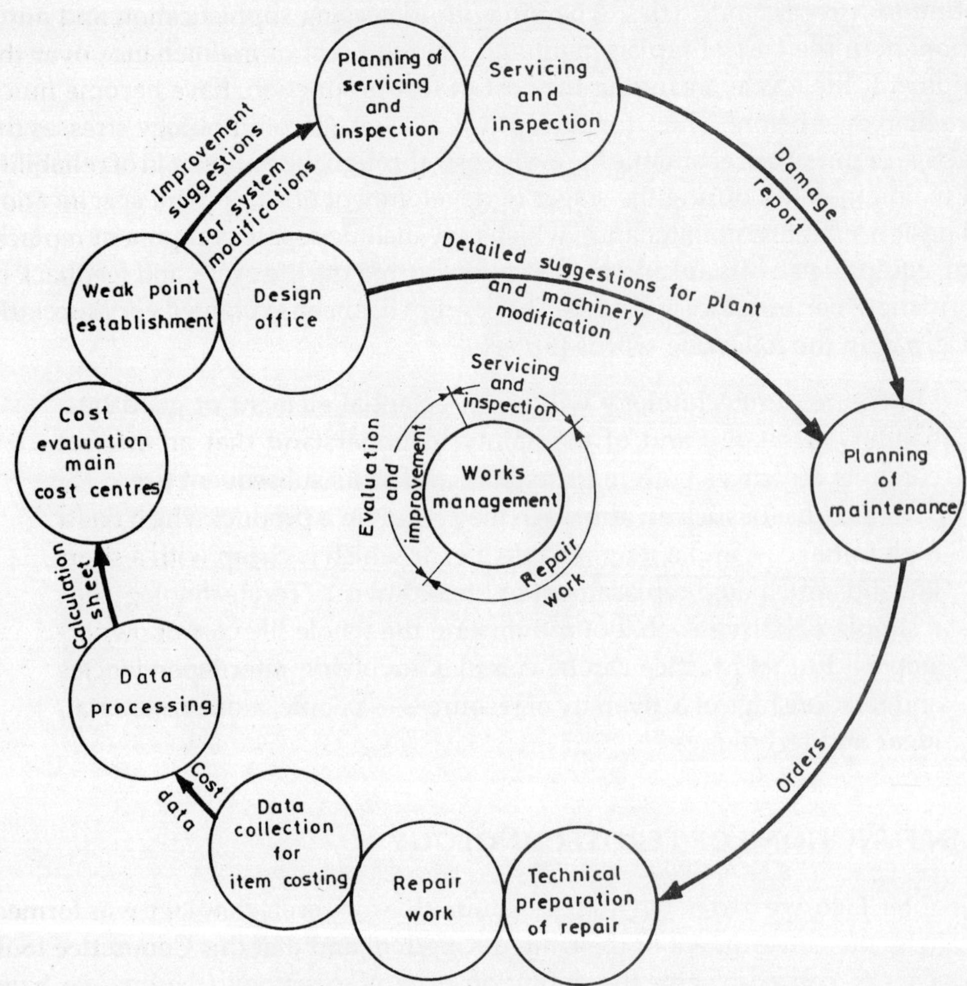

Fig. 3.2. Cyclic Model of Functional Maintenance

through the costing department, whereas the design office, after evaluation and identification of the weak points, fed forward to the maintenance department suggestions for modifications to plant and machinery. Keeping the system flexible and recognizing the principle of management by exception, Wiegel's model had an inherent capability of constant improvement. Evans [9], in his 'circular model' of the main functions of terotechnology, propounded in 1974 and shown in Fig. 3.3, has enlarged the systems concept enunciated by Wiegel and has stresed, in addition to the feedback loop defined earlier, the need for feedback of information gathered during the stages of installation and commissioning and also during use from the production department to the designer. The model also includes the feed-forward

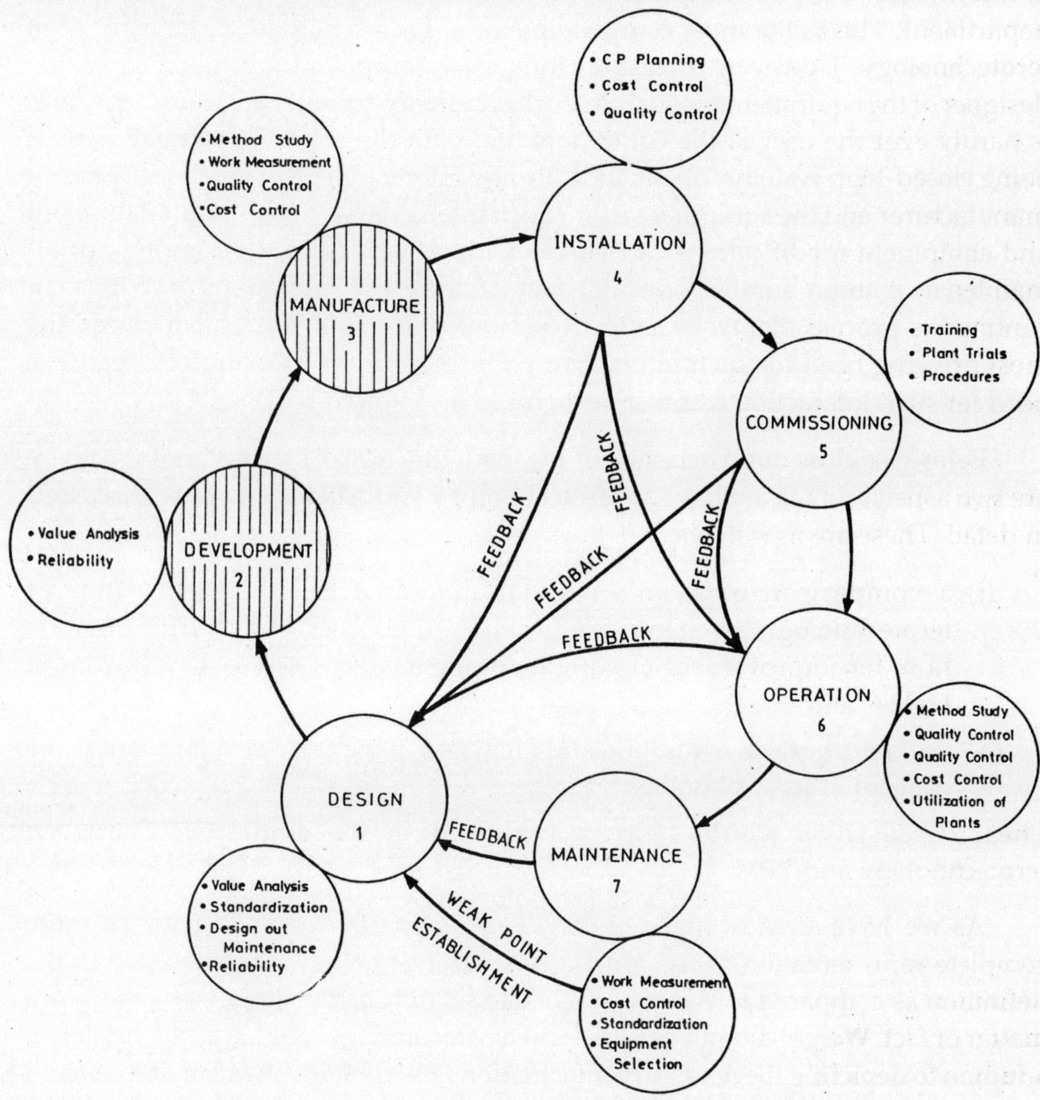

Fig. 3.3. Terotechnology - Circular Model of Main Functions

Note: Terotechnology looks at equipment life cycle from the point of view of the user and thus although strictly speaking, detailed design and drafting, product development and manufacture are essential parts of plant/equipment life cycle, from the view of terotechnology, the expenses incurred on these activities are just parts of the purchase price of the equipment, paid by the user. For this reason, development and manufacture are shown hatched in this figure.

of information from the installation and commissioning stages to the production department. This is the most complete pictorial representation of the concept of terotechnology. However, in case of industrial equipment and machinery, the designer of the equipment is usually also the original equipment manufacturer and is hardly ever the user of the equipment and both the models described earlier, being closed-loop systems, do not indicate any interaction between the equipment manufacturer and the equipment user.[3] Such interaction is most essential for plant and equipment modifications carried out with the objective of designing-out-of-maintenance and a number of senior maintenance and operations executives of continuous process plants, in their discussions with the author, have voiced the most pressing need for such interaction with the equipment manufacturers. The need for such interaction was also recognized and voiced by Wiegel [29].

Before we close our discussion of the main functions of terotechnology, there are two aspects which are basic to terotechnology and which need to be discussed in detail. These are as follows:

(i) a comparison of Evan's circular model of the main functions of terotechnology, given in Fig. 3.3, with the model depicting the information flow for improvement of equipment availability used in TPM, given in Fig.2.6; and

(ii) the contributions of Rappini and Finniston in the early development of the concept of terotechnology.

These discussions would help in highlighting the similarities between terotechnology and TPM.

As we have already noted earlier, Evan's circular model is a much more complete representation of the functions of terotechnology as enunciated in the definition as compared to Wiegel's cyclic model of functional maintenance.[4] As a matter of fact, Wiegel did not use the term terotechnology and his cyclic model, in addition to depicting the necessary information flow for improvement of plant and equipment availability, starting with the damage, or breakdown, report and going right upto the establishment of weak points (cost centres/equipment requiring special attention), stresses the need for:

(i) planning in maintenance and technical preparation of repair activity;

(ii) weak point establishment and developing improved preventive maintenance systems including modifications in preventive maintenance schedules (schedules for preventive inspections, servicing and overhauls); and

(iii) feedback from the user, or production, departments to the design office, which, in turn, passes on detailed suggestions for plant and equipment modifications to the maintenance department.

Wiegel proposed that the cost of maintenance actions should be evaluated based on actual failure and repair data and these costs should be used for establishment of weaknesses. The work on these weak points should include work in both areas, that is, preventive maintenance and maintainability improvement. Evan's model is more complete not only because it includes all the stages of the life cycle of the equipment, namely design, development, manufacture, installation, commissioning, operation and maintenance, and also lists the important activities/functions for these seven stages (in circles by the side of each stage), but also because it brings out the need for feedback from installation and commissioning in addition to the feedback from operation and maintenance stages of the life cycle. Readers should also note that against design, the activities shown include standardisation, reliability considerations and designing-out-of-maintenance. Thus, the circular model lays more stress on maintenance prevention.[5]

Now let us get down to the task of comparing the models proposed for terotechnology and TPM and the information flows given in Figs. 3.3 (and Fig. 3.2) and Fig. 2.6. Both the models lay stress on the need for planning of maintenance work (both preventive and corrective maintenance) and for preventive maintenance actions. Both the models also stress that planning of preventive maintenance inspections should be based on suggestions for improvement of preventive maintenance system and work procedures and these, in turn, are derived from the analysis of past maintenance data. However, the TPM model suggests that special studies directed at reduction of maintenance work should also be carried out and the suggestions for improvement of preventive maintenance procedures should also take the information obtained from these studies into account.

Similarly, both the models stress the need for feedback of data and information, and the feedback and feedforward loops in two models are also very similar. Both the models stress the importance of feedback of information and data from use/operation and maintenance to design for identification of areas calling for designing-out-of-maintenance efforts. However, because the TPM model uses twin circles, instead of one, to depict the information flow — with one depicting the design and installation stage and the other dedicated to the operation and maintenance stage of the life cycle of the equipment — it can clearly differentiate the maintenance prevention (MP) from the maintainability improvement (MI) efforts. This is clearly an improvement over the cyclic and circular models of terotechnology since this permits detailing and clarification of activities and feedback information required for the MP and MI efforts. However, this should not, in any manner, be taken to imply that terotechnology does not recognize the need for both MP and MI. The need for MP is clearly and explicitly indicated in the definition and that for MI is implied through the stress on feedback of information, data and costs. The emphasis on both MP and MI will become more obvious during the discussion of the contributions of Rappini and Finniston.

Rappini's application of terotechnology [20] stressed the need for quicker response by the maintenance engineers to production problems and to the feedback of the experiences gained and inferences drawn by them to the design department. As reported by Rappini, these inferences were based on a thorough analysis of failure trends, history of requirements of spares and inspection reports etc. and the information fed back was used to make improvements and modifications to plant and machinery to reduce the direct costs of maintenance, both man-hours and cost of spares, as well as the costs of lost production. Both Wiegel and Rappini achieved considerable savings in the costs of maintenance and a corresponding reduction in the loss of production due to breakdowns by analysis of past failure data and by creating an organisational structure for proper planning of maintenance activities and timely feedback of inferences drawn from the analysis of recurring failures. Finniston, in his paper, highlighted the work done by the British Steel Corporation in the four important areas of activities of terotechnology, as viewed by the user of an equipment, which are installation, commissioning, maintenance of plant and equipment, and feedforward to production and feedback to design [12]. Finniston advocated that in the design of the equipment, special attention should be paid to maintainability considerations, including the standardisation of capital replaceable items such as valves, pumps, motors and bearings. He also suggested that certain critical components should be pretested before installation and stressed the fact that not enough attention was being paid to the activities of installation and commissioning of complex process plants, such as equipment used in a large steelworks. Finniston accordingly recommended the (a) setting up of a team by the user, which would be responsible for installation and commissioning, and which could then work with the manufacturers of various machines and equipment and be responsible for formulating the acceptance trials, (b) pre-definition of the installation practices, methods and procedures to be followed with proper planning of the installation work by the manufacturer and the user of the equipment together, and (c) proper planning of the operating trials, and proper evaluation of the manufacturer's final designs from the point of view of maintainability and also specific maintenance actions and procedures required, particularly in the case of innovations and new design features. These measures would not only reduce the total project cost, but also assist in avoiding expensive failures later.

The earliest applications of terotechnology were in the steel industry, in as much as Wiegel, Rappini and Finniston were involved in the management of the maintenance function of integrated iron and steel-works in Germany, Italy and the UK respectively. This is not surprising since the steel industry is one of the most capital-intensive industries and the concept which espouses the care of physical assets would draw the maximum attention in such plants. The reader should also note the diversity of approach of these three pioneers of terotechnology[6]. Whereas Wiegel concentrated on detailed planning of maintenance activities, Rappini's basic thrust was directed to modifications of plant and equipment, and lastly, Finniston argued the necessity of detailed planning of the installation and commissioning jobs. As a matter of fact, Finniston, for the first time, highlighted the importance of the installation and commissioning jobs and brought out the fact that if these jobs are not executed properly then this could adversely affect the direct cost of maintenance of the equipment over its life cycle as well as the useful life of the equipment (the length of life cycle). He also stressed the need for planning of these jobs. Finniston's recommendations have been incorporated in Evan's circular model, wherein not only are network (critical path or CP) planning of installation work and development of procedures for commissioning trials highlighted as necessary activities, but also the feedforward of information from these stages of equipment life cycle to operation and feedback from these stages to design are included. Finally, before we move on, we should return to the discussion of MP and MI and review the work of Rappini and Finniston to see whether both MP and MI are included in the concept and practice of terotechnology. Taking Rappini's contribution, we note that Rappini concentrated his attention on maintainability improvement. He also stressed the need for the analysis of past maintenance data, feedback of inferences drawn and creation of responsive and effective maintenance organisation and maintenance system and procedures. Finniston, on the other hand, advocated maintenance prevention and in this regard, he stressed certain specific aspects such as maintainability considerations and ease of maintenance, standardisation of capital replaceable items of plant and equipment and pre-testing of critical components and items before installation.

ELEMENTS OF EQUIPMENT LIFE CYCLE COST AND TRADE-OFF IMPLIED IN TEROTECHNOLOGY

The defined objective of terotechnology is the pursuit of economic life cycle cost, but it looks at life cycle costs from the point of view of the user. According to him, the life cycle of an equipment begins with the identification of its need by him after which he draws up the necessary and relevant plant/equipment specifications and thereafter the user acquires the plant/equipment only after an evaluation of alternatives and equipment justification. The equipment life cycle, thus, extends right through its acquisition, use and maintenance upto its final retirement or disposal. This is illustrated in Fig. 3.4. The user makes investments for the acquisition of an equipment on (i) drawing up of the necessary specifications, (ii) invest-

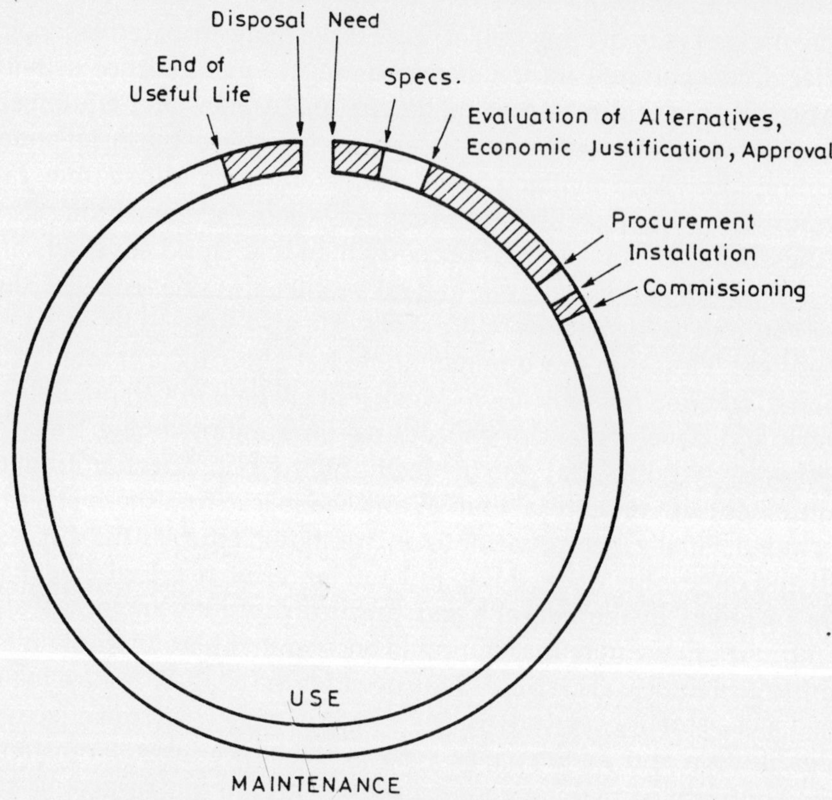

Fig. 3.4. Equipment Life Cycle From the User's Viewpoint

ment appraisal, (iii) capital cost, or the actual purchase price, (iv) installation, and (v) commissioning. The return on this investment starts when the equipment or machine comes into use for the manufacture of saleable product(s) and continues until the plant is disposed off at the end of its useful life. However, during the period of its use, the manufacturing organisation has to bear the costs incurred in its maintenance, in the form of repairs, replacement of components, modification and periodic overhauls.

For the purpose of asset management, therefore, the life cycle cost of an equipment or plant can be sub-divided into the following three main constituents:

1. *Cost of Ownership* - includes the cost of acquisition, as explained earlier, the cost of maintenance, including repair, replacement, modification and overhaul, during the life cycle of the equipment, and the cost of monitoring the condition and performance of the equipment.
2. *Cost of Use* - includes the costs of materials, energy, including fuel, and manpower used to produce goods or services.
3. *Cost of Administration* - includes data acquisition, recording, analysis and documentation with regard to the asset.

To simplify decisions on optimisation of life cycle performance as well as organisation and costing methods, it is recommended that appropriate fractions of the costs of administration be included in the costs of use and ownership, namely, the data collection, analysis and documentation with regard to production, productivity etc. in the cost of use, and those for condition monitoring and inspection of equipment under the cost of ownership. Thus, the two main elements of life cycle cost are, therefore, the cost of ownership and the cost of use. Moreover, the cost of ownership can be sub-divided into the first cost, or the acquisition cost of the equipment, and the cost of maintenance, which must also include the cost of monitoring the condition of the machine.

The most important stage in the life of an asset, whether it be a single machine, an equipment, or an entire plant, is the stage of investment appraisal. It is at this stage that the management has to consider the trade-off between the cost of ownership and the cost of use. But the point to remember here is that the cost of ownership has two constituents — the cost of acquisition and the cost of maintaining the equipment over its life cycle, and not just the cost of acquisition or, for that matter, just the capital cost or the price paid by the company to procure the equipment. A company considers the acquisition of an asset either (i) as a replacement, or (ii) for the purpose of cost reduction, or (iii) as a part of a budgeted expansion/modernisation/diversification programme. At the stage of investment appraisal, due consideration must be given to the following aspects:

(a) the expected return on investment from the use of the asset,

(b) market and marketability of the product(s) to be produced by the asset, particularly in a changing economic environment taking cognizance of the external forces, market trends, both domestic and export, new technology and obsolescence and governmental controls,

(c) the expected life of the asset,

(d) the required availability and whether the asset is required to be used continuously or intermittently,

(e) the reliability of the various alternatives,

(f) ease of maintenance and maintainability of the various alternatives,

(g) the cost and availability of spares,

(h) the training of operational and maintenance personnel required, and

(i) the means — instrumentation and systems — provided by the manufacturers and/or required to be used to monitor the condition of the equipment and to predict the health and the remaining useful life.

All companies generally make a detailed economic evaluation before the acquisition of any production equipment or plant and the methods used are return on investment calculations (now-a-days most companies are using the present worth method taking into account the interest rate, that is, they are using discounting), or the replacement cost method between two equipment capable of producing the same output (discounting should be used in this case as well). However, in such detailed economic justifications, the total installed cost of the equipment and the estimated pay-back period are, in a majority of cases, the only considerations for deciding on one equipment over another. This shows that in the majority of cases, the trade-off considered is between the total installed cost, which is the total acquisition cost less the cost incurred for development of specifications, investment appraisal and in some cases even installation and commissioning, and the cost of use, whereas the trade-off required to be done is between the cost of ownership, as defined earlier, and the cost of use. Herein the point to remember is that in case of industrial plant and equipment, the total acquisition cost is only a small fraction of its cost of ownership, that is, the total cost of maintenance over the life cycle of the equipment, in most cases, far exceeds the first cost or the acquisition cost. Therefore, such an economic evaluation may result in the procurement of an equipment with lower acquisition cost but one that will result in higher incidence of failure and/or poorer maintainability features resulting in lower availability and higher costs of maintenance over its life cycle. To highlight this, Blanchard [3] uses a simile wherein he likens the total life cycle cost to an iceberg with the first cost or the acquisition cost only being visible above the surface. This brings us to the second trade-off, that between the cost of acquisition and the total estimated cost of maintenance and to the assertion that the total estimated cost of maintenance over the equipment life cycle must be given due consideration during the stage of investment appraisal.

In the preceding paragraph, we have shown the need to estimate the total equipment life cycle maintenance cost and to consider its trade-off with the total cost of acquisition during the stage of investment appraisal. However, it must also be realized that the maintenance cost over the equipment life cycle is essentially a time-dependent function since reliability is an exponentially decaying function of time. Thus we may view the objective of attainment of economic life cycle from a slightly different angle. This can be explained by first developing a mathematical formulation of the total life cycle cost of plant/equipment.

Let **C** be the total cost of acquisition,

U be the cost of operation or use of the equipment per unit of time,

(**Note:** usually for job costing, the cost of operation or use per piece or per unit of time is worked out, or estimated).

T be the life time or useful life of the equipment in time units, and

$f(t)$ be the time-dependent maintenance cost:

then the cost of operation or use over the life time of the equipment = U.T., the maintenance cost over the life time of the equipment = $\int_{\phi}^{T} f(t)\,dt$, and

C_T, the total life cycle cost of the equipment = $C + \int_{\phi}^{T} f(t)\,dt + U.T.$

To obtain the objective of optimisation of total life cycle cost, there is a trade-off between the cost of ownership and the cost of operation, U.T., and this decision is made at the stage of investment appraisal. However, once this decision is taken, the cost of acquisition becomes a constant and the cost of use, from the point of view of optimisation, also becomes a constant having been decided upon over the life cycle based on estimates. Therefore, once the equipment is procured, installed and commissioned, the objective of terotechnology can only be attained by the minimisation of the total cost of maintenance over the life cycle of the equipment. Thus, the practical embodiment of terotechnology in operating plants is the achievement of maximum availability at minimum cost of maintenance over its useful operating life.

IMPORTANT NOTES ON LIFE CYCLE COSTING

It has already been explained in the preceding sections that the estimate of life cycle cost is of primary interest at the stage of investment appraisal and that such investment may be considered for the replacement of an existing plant or equipment, or for the acquisition of new plant or equipment as part of an expansion/ diversification/modernisation scheme. The application of life cycle costing to a plant replacement situation in a chemical industry has been described by Riddell [22]. He has examined an existing plant and has considered two alternative strategies. The two strategies considered are as follows:

Strategy I : allow the existing plant to continue with little or no capital expenditure until such time that falling standards in safety/performance necessitate its replacement, and

Strategy II : allow the existing plant to continue with no further capital expenditure and demolish the plant after a life time of about 15 years replacing it with an asset built with the technology of the time.

This study has shown that the total life cycle costs of such assets are 4.5 times of the initial capital costs, that is, the costs of acquisition. It has also been shown that the cost of acquisition or fixed capital, operator salary and wages, cost of services incurred for the use of the plant (including cost of energy) and the cost of maintenance are similar in value and lie in the range of 22-31 per cent. From the study, it has been found that rebuilding the plant after 15 years would result in a saving of £ 3 million as compared to the strategy of continuing to run the plant for about 30 years. Most importantly, based on this study, it was recommended to the works management that the major cost constituents of the total life cycle costs of the physical assets of the works should be monitored with a view to developing an optimum policy for the management of physical assets. However, a manufacturing organisation possesses a very large number of physical assets in the form of buildings, structures, plant, equipment and machines and the collection of data on the elements of life cycle costs for all the assets will turn out to be a stupendous task. Moreover, it is neither necessary nor worthwhile to monitor the life cycle performance of all the assets that an organisation owns. Accordingly, it is recommended that the asset register (in India, the statutory auditors, in keeping with national acts, demand that fixed asset registers and details of fixed assets be maintained scrupulously) may be redesigned to record and control life cycle cost elements of critical plant, equipment and machines, that is, only such critical equipment with long planned lives for which there is a need to monitor the life cycle cost [2]. A suggested format for the asset register is given in Fig. 3.5.

Riddell's study not only brought out the fact that life cycle costs can be estimated at both the plant level and the individual equipment (item of the plant) level and that life cycle costing is a powerful tool for effective asset management,

ASSET NO
(as per Fixed Asset Register Serial/Code)

GENERAL INFORMATION						
Asset Nomenclature	Date Acquired	Date Commissioned	Planned or Budgeted life	Description of Imp. Accessories/Spl. Tooling	Dept./Cost Centre (where installed)	Product Lines (for which used)
Technical Details/Description		Purchase Price (Total) = Break-up: Main Equipt. = Accessories =				

FOR PURPOSES OF TAX RETURNS AND STATUTORY ANNUAL REPORTS													
Asset Class (per IT Act)	Depreciation Allowed (per IT Act)	Depreciation Charged in Annual Returns											
		Year 1 ( )	Year 2 ( )	Year 3 ( )	Year 4 ( )	....	Year ( )	Year ( )	Year ( )	Year ( )	Year ( )	Year ( )	

YEAR	LIFE-CYCLE COSTS																	
	COST OF USE							COST OF MAINTENANCE										
	Planned Cost	Actual cost	PERFORMANCE				Planned Total Cost	Actual Total Cost	Cost of M/Power		Cost of Spares		Cost of Lost Time		PM Performance			
			Prod. hrs		Non-Prod. hrs				Plan	Actual	Plan	Actual	Hrs. lost	Cost	Bk. down		Plan maint.	
			Plan	Actual	Plan	Actual									Hrs	%	Hrs	%
Year 1 ( )																		
Year 2 ( )																		
Year 3 ( )																		
.																		
.																		
.																		
Year ( )																		

Salvage Value	Estimated Sale Price =	Actual Sale Price =	Date of Sale	Date of closure of card	Card Closed Signed________ Dept.______

Fig. 3.5 Suggested Format for Asset Register

but also showed that collecting and maintaining cost and performance data from existing plant and equipment over several years is necessary for developing reliable estimates of life cycle costs which can then be used as useful inputs during the stage of investment appraisal of new plants and equipment. Thus, once an asset is purchased, installed and commissioned, it is necessary to set up procedures for the recording and monitoring of life cycle costs and life cycle performance. The concept of life cycle costing and asset management, in the context of terotechnology, is new and considering the fact that the normal accounting system is geared to producing statements for management control over a twelve month period and finally the annual accounts, it is difficult to introduce a system for control of costs attributable to any given asset which has a useful life of many financial years. Also, in normal accounting practice, the direct costs of materials, labour, tooling etc. are identified for different product lines for job costing and a specified number of overhead account heads are used for expenses, the labour being costed by the use of man-hour or machine-hour rates which again have subjective allocations of indirects or burden. Thus, sometimes sight is lost of expenses directly attributable to an asset since some of them go under different overhead expense accounts. As against this, for the purposes of calculating the life cycle cost, all costs attributable to a given equipment or asset need to be identified as far as practicable. Hewgill identifies the major strength of life cycle costing as that of treating all costs as cash paid out (or received) at a particular time in the life time of the asset and therefore, the life cycle cost forecast reads like a cash flow statement [14], which, in turn, is more readily understood by engineers. For life cycle costing, the main problem, however, is that of separation of cost elements associated with the physical asset from the cost elements associated with the products being produced by these assets. In this regard, Riddell [22] has suggested some guidelines which may be found useful by practitioners. Another point to remember is that for life cycle costing, the forms and reporting procedures like work orders, job cards, route sheets, stores issue notes, idle hour reports, scrap or rejection reports etc. will have to be reworked so that the data can be identified by an asset in addition to the normal job and overhead account heads and the use of asset codes will make the form simple.

ESSENCE OF TEROTECHNOLOGY

We may conclude our discussion of terotechnology by briefly recapitulating the why, what, where, when and how of terotechnology for the purposes of enlisting the important points, which, in turn, will be necessary for its comparison with TPM. The essence of terotechnology can be captured in the following points:

1. Terotechnology is essentially a concept and its enunciation also stressed this quite clearly. Terotechnology was enunciated to bring home to organisations the need (for them) to take care of (their) physical assets.
2. The objective of terotechnology is the minimisation of the life cycle costs of assets and the bulk of such assets are plant and equipment.
3. The achievement of this objective of minimisation of life cycle cost of a plant or equipment calls for the following:
   (i) maximisation of plant, or equipment, availability,
   (ii) minimisation of the cost of maintenance over its useful life, and
   (iii) prolonging its useful life.

Note: A close observation of Fig. 3.4 brings home quite clearly that the time required for early life activities, namely development of equipment specifications, evaluation of alternatives, procurement of the equipment, its installation and commissioning, should be as small as possible and its useful life as long as possible for ensuring an adequate return on investment. Moreover, maximisation of equipment availability and minimisation of cost of its maintenance are complimentary and the latter cannot be achieved without the former, and, as we have already noted, after the acquisition of the equipment by the user, minimisation of life cycle costs can be achieved only through the minimisation of the cost of its maintenance over the life cycle.

4. The most important contributions of Wiegel and his 'functional maintenance' are the following:
   (a) for the first time, he pointed out to the maintenance practitioners and manufacturing organisations that maintenance activities can and should be planned, and
   (b) he also enunciated a closed-loop system of maintenance of plant and equipment, stressing the need for feedback of maintenance data, information and costs, and showed that such feedback was essential for achieving the twin objectives of maximisation of equipment availability (with minimisation of the costs of maintenance) and extension of its useful life.

In the paper he presented at the terotechnology conference held in Delhi in 1981, Parkes [19] stated that inadequate planning of maintenance and adherance to traditional maintenance systems result in totally inadequate plant engineering practices, which, in turn, result in frequent breakdowns of continuous process plants in critical sectors like power generation and fertilizers etc. He adds that in developing nations, in most of the plants, the availability of plant and equipment is very low, condition monitoring is not practised and maintenance planning is totally inadequate. Maintenance records are not properly maintained and equipment history cards are generally not used as aids to maintenance planning. Such a situation is not at all desirable and in such cases, the attainment of the objectives of terotechnology will call for the following:

(a) A thorough analysis of past failures and detailed planning of maintenance activities.

(b) An organisational structure which ensures that such analyses and planning are carried out and inferences drawn and the policies resultant therefrom are fed back to design and also fed forward to the production/operation departments. Thus, terotechnology stresses that in addition to the traditional tasks of repair and routine preventive maintenance, the following activities have to be carried out for the attainment of three sub-objectives given under 3(i), (ii) and (iii) earlier:

   (i) detailed planning of all maintenance activities, that is, detailed planning of both corrective maintenance and preventive maintenance jobs (please see Fig. 2.3),

   (ii) feedback of maintenance data, information and costs, and a thorough analysis of such data not only to identify weak spots (plant and equipment which are prone to recurrent failures) and areas/plants/equipment/mechanisms requiring modifications, but also as a necessary input for adequate planning of maintenance tasks,

   (iii) development of detailed suggestions for modifications of plant and machinery, and such modifications are called maintainability improvements (MI) under TPM, and

   (iv) reliability and maintainability considerations and considerations of ease of maintenance in the design of new plant and equipment, and we have seen that such activities are called maintenance prevention (MP) efforts under TPM.

5. Terotechnology was developed in the continuous process industry and the earliest known applications were also carried out in the process industry.

Total Quality Management

Quality is synonymous with fitness for use. All human societies, right from the dawn of civilization have made use of natural and artificial materials and forces to provide for its members products, which include both goods and services. An essential requirement of these products is that they must meet the needs of those members of society who will actually use them. Another way of stating this is that the product must satisfy the needs of its customers, or users, and the internationally accepted definition of quality, as given in ISO 8402[7], is as follows:

> "the totality of features and characteristics of a product or service that bear on its ability to satisfy stated or implied needs."

Thus, quality of a particular product is the extent to which it satisfies the expectations of its customers(s). The manufacturer/supplier of the product must, therefore, determine the needs and expectations of its customers and convert these customer expectations and requirements into engineering specifications. These specifications then become the basis for the design and manufacture of the product and the product made to the design conforms to the specifications. The measure of quality then becomes the degree of conformance to these specifications.

Now, when we talk of controlling someone or something, we mean that we carry out checks and corrections, as and when required, and we exercise restraint and direction to assure that the results/outputs obtained are as required. We may, therefore, define quality control as a system of verification and maintenance of a desired level of quality in product, or a process, and this may include activities as diverse as inspection, calibration of equipment, gauges and instruments, foolproofing/mistake-proofing of processes, process controls, process and product optimisation and efforts directed at quality improvements. Quality control has come a long way. At the turn of the century, quality control consisted essentially of component inspection and product inspection and testing. Such was the state of affairs for a very long time and quality control was synonymous with inspection and the head of the quality control function was called the Inspection Manager. At best, quality control was taken as a necessary evil since the job was one of sorting — sorting out the acceptable from the nonconforming, or vice versa. Nowadays, companies consider product quality to be a competitive weapon and more and more companies are turning toward total quality management. We will briefly recount this passage from inspection to total quality control (TQC) and total quality management (TQM) before going on to a detailed discussion of TQM.

FROM INSPECTION TO TQC AND TQM

Quality as a necessary function has been with mankind from a very long time. Even the primitive people who were gatherers and users of natural materials faced quality problems, such as identification of edible plants and fruits and differentiating them from the poisonous ones. However, herein we are discussing quality and quality control in the context of manufacturing and as far as this is concerned, quality emerged as an important function around the first decade of the twentieth century with the emergence of improved technologies, complicated products and corporations engaged in the manufacture of a number of different products in large volumes. Although the concept of division of labour came with the Industrial Revolution, bringing with it a production system wherein a worker no longer made the entire product and only made a part thereof, quality problems were not experienced initially since the products manufactured during the early period were comparatively simple. With the introduction of complicated products, it became necessary to inspect components and products after their manufacture.

Thereafter in the early 1920s, W.A. Shewhart developed a statistical chart for the control of product variables. Later in the same decade, H.F. Dodge and H.G. Romig suggested and developed the use of acceptance sampling as a substitute for 100 percent inspection. Shewhart's control charts and the Dodge and Romig tables of acceptance sampling heralded the beginning of statistical quality control (SQC). As a matter of fact, the emergence of Shewhart's process control charts ($\overline{X}$ and R charts) was a major milestone in the development of quality control, being a radical departure from the past. Process control was added to the list of quality tasks, or activities, required to be carried out during production and attention shifted from the product (inspection concentrates on the product) to the process used to produce the product. With the advent and increased use of SQC by industry, quality control was recognized as a scientific discipline and it was included in the list of courses (subjects) taught in universities and colleges. With it came recognition by industry, and the person who headed the quality control function was designated as the Quality Control Manager (the designation was upgraded from that of Inspection Manager). This was the state of affairs from the mid/late 1930s till the 1960s.

Till the early 1960s, therefore, the quality function had moved from inspection to quality control with the stress shifting from the product to the processes used to manufacture the product. The subsequent move from quality control to quality assurance and thereafter, to TQC and TQM is much more interesting. The 1960s saw the advent of quality circles (and as a matter of fact, the first quality circle was formed in Japan in the year 1960). This much is known and widely recognized, but a lot more happened after the 1960s. These years saw a number of events and also produced a number of new thoughts and insights on quality. Among these, the following had the greatest impact on the evolution of the quality movement:

(i) Juran's quality trilogy,

(ii) Enunciation of the spiral of progress in quality and Fiegenbaum's definition of TQC,

(iii) Development of quality circles and widespread recognition of the importance of participation, and

(iv) Company-wide quality control — implementation of the concept of TQC in Ford Motor Company in 1986.

A brief and sequential discussion of these concepts and insights will help us trace the movement from quality control to quality assurance and thence to TQC.

Juran's quality trilogy, for the first time, defined the three constituents of the quality function and also stressed the fact that these three constituents are both essential and inseparable. The first constituent is quality planning. Quality planning not only involves determining the quality policy and the quality levels of different products, and linking product and process design to achieve the desired quality characteristics, but also includes the essentials which enable the achievement of the desired product quality, such as design reviews, planning of inspections and tests, planning of process controls, vendor evaluation and selection, training of operators and inspectors and field performance evaluation. Moreover, quality planning precedes quality control and without adequate planning, one cannot exercise effective control. The second constituent of the trilogy is quality control and this consists of conducting inspections and tests, control of vendor performance, and determining actions to correct discrepancies and implementing them. Thus, this part of the trilogy also provides the information needed for quality improvements. The third constituent of the triology is the ultimate objective of quality function — of the entire quality effort. All the planning and subsequent control are totally useless unless they lead to improvements in product and process quality. Juran's trilogy, therefore, pointed out to the professionals the three essentials of quality and with this realization came a new definition of quality control, namely

> "the use of techniques and activities to achieve, sustain and improve the quality of a product."

Juran's trilogy also brought out the overriding importance of planning for quality. With it came the reaiization of the need for the development of work instructions, procedures and systems. Thus, the need for and importance of a well-thought out and documented quality system emerged from the quality trilogy and with it came quality assurance. The stress was on the quality system since the system provides the assurance that product and process quality are as they should be.

The attainment of product and process quality, thus, requires the performance of a wide variety of activities. Such activities range from the study of customers' quality needs, transforming these needs into engineering specifications and development of product designs to satisfy these needs, to design reviews, development of process controls, conduct of inspections and tests, and field performance and complaint analysis, right upto corrective actions, which, in turn, may include revision of engineering specifications and product and process designs. In a tiny enterprise producing a single product, all these tasks are carried out by only one or at best a few persons. In a modern corporation, engaged in the manufacture and marketing of a diverse range of products, however, specialized departments are created to carry out specific functions, such as product design, manufacturing planning, materials management/purchasing, production, inspection, test, and service. Moreover, when it comes to launching either a new or a changed product, these functions usually follow a given sequence. This sequence is depicted by the spiral of progress in quality shown in Fig. 3.6. The point to remember is that each of these departments carry out some of the essential activities, or quality tasks, and each, therefore, contributes its share to the attainment of product quality and also its sustenance and improvement. The spiral of progress in quality, therefore, brings out quite clearly that the achievement, sustenance and improvement of product quality requires the active involvement of various departments/groups in an organisation. The objective cannot be achieved by just the production and the quality assurance departments, and it requires a total effort — the involvement of persons from every function in the organisation. Fiegenbaum's definition of TQC is a combination of the essence of the quality trilogy with this need for total involvement. Fiegenbaum defines TQC as:

> "an effective system of intergrating the quality development, quality maintenance, and quality improvement efforts of the various groups in an organisation so as to enable engineering, production, marketing, and service at the most economical levels which allow for full customer satisfaction[11]."

With the coming of TQC, the stress shifted to people.

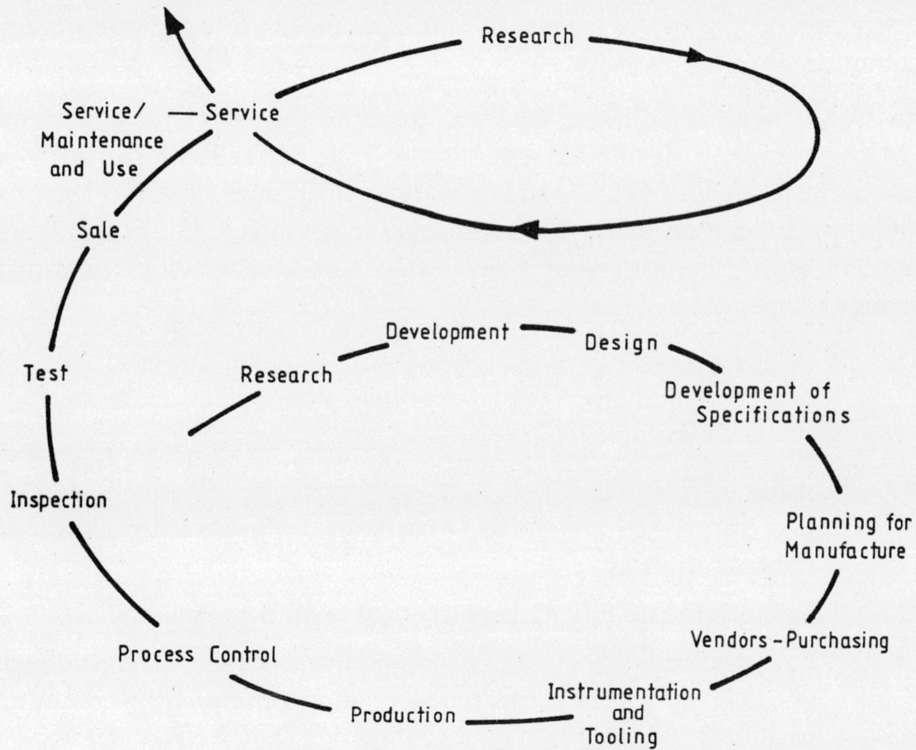

Fig. 3.6. Spiral of Progress in Quality

The individual operator in a manufacturing plant is the key to the production of quality components and products, since it is he who is primarily responsible for ensuring conformance to specifications. Moreover, it is also the individual operator who understands the manufacturing process well enough to make useful suggestions for the improvement of products and processes. In recent years, it has also been realized that the operators and inspectors can make useful contributions to the quality planning effort. The involvement of operators and supervisors in the preparation of work instructions and procedures has been found to be very useful. Thus, the operators, the inspectors, and for that matter, the entire tradeforce can make useful contributions to quality development, quality maintenance and quality improvement efforts. The best method of ensuring involvement is participation. This was the philosophy and motive behind the development of quality circles in Japan. With the success of these circles, came the recognition of the importance of employee participation in the efforts directed towards quality and productivity growth. The 'total' in TQC and TQM not only implies involvement of all departments/groups in the organisation but also the involvement of all employes, at all levels, in the organisation. Such involvement requires a motivated and committed workforce and proper use of employee participation can bring about motivation and commitment in the workforce.

In 1986, Lawrence Sullivan, who was then the Quality Control Manager of Ford Motor Company, developed a version of TQC. He called it company-wide quality control (CWQC). CWQC is an application of TQC as defined by Fiegenbaum and this application is probably the closest one can get to TQC. Sullivan suggested that implementation be carried out in seven stages, and the activities identified for the different stages are as follows:

Stage 1: includes inspecting and auditing of components and finished goods, and solving quality problems as they arise.

Stage 2: concentrates on quality assurance during production, in particular using statistical methods to identify quality problems (use of SQC), and improved machines/processes to reduce the number of nonconformities.

Stage 3: expands the quality assurance effort to all departments.

Stage 4: focusses on educating and training all employees, including managers, to create a greater awareness of and (consequently) commitment to quality.

Stages 5&6: concentrates on review of product and process designs and reduction of process variability through continual improvements. Product and process designs should be gone into and they should be linked to effectively improve quality and lower internal (production) costs.

Stage 7: reviews customers' needs and requirements and ensures that they are adequately translated into operational documents, such as specifications, drawings, process sheets, and process control charts.

CWQC brought into focus the importance of education and training and also the fact that education and training are necessary for all employees, right from top management down to the inspectors, machine operators and assembly workers, and including office personnel, sales and service people and even the dealers of the company's products. Education and training provide the fundamental basis of positive quality motivation for all company employees, and with the use of effective leadership and top management commitment, these motivated employees can subsequently be transformed into individuals committed to quality.

With CWQC, the quality movement had come all the way from inspection, through quality control and quality assurance, to total quality control, and with each of these developments, the stress and also the management attitude towards product and process quality changed. The evolution of the quality movement is shown in Fig.3.7. The point to remember here is that each of these developments enriched the quality discipline; with new insights, new activities were added and everything that was done earlier was not necessarily discarded. For example, with the coming of SQC, process control did not totally replace inspection and inspection of products and components was not stopped. What actually happened was that the stress shifted to processes and companies realized that processes had to be controlled to ensure minimisation (if not avoidance) of nonconforming products. Inspection was still carried out, wherever necessary, but with the advent of SQC, 100 per cent inspection was replaced, in many cases, by sampling inspection. Quality assurance and TQC further enriched the discipline; as a matter of fact, they brought in radical changes in the prevailing precepts and attitudes. The quality function is not viewed as a necessary evil any longer; instead it is considered as an important strategic weapon. TQM has been derived from TQC. It was soon realized that the objectives of TQC cannot be achieved without effective leadership and top management commitment. With this realization came TQM; and TQM is TQC plus leadership and top management commitment.

WHAT IS TQM?

Whereas terotechnology is a concept, TQM is a philosophy — a philosophy which integrates the quality development (quality planning), quality maintenance (quality control) and quality improvement efforts of all employees and various groups, or departments, in an organisation to enable manufacture and service at the most economical levels with the objective of full customer satisfaction.[8] The key words of this definition, or the beacons of this philosophy, are quality improvement, total involvement, least cost/economy in utilisation of resources, and customer satisfaction. Also total involvement can only be achieved with the help of effective leadership and top management commitment. Moreover, since TQM is a philosophy, 'it is not something that an organisation does but the way in which an organisation does everything' [4]. The point to remember here is that TQM is a management philosophy — a philosophy directed at value-added management, using total involvement to achieve this goal through continuous improvement of products, processes, procedures and systems.

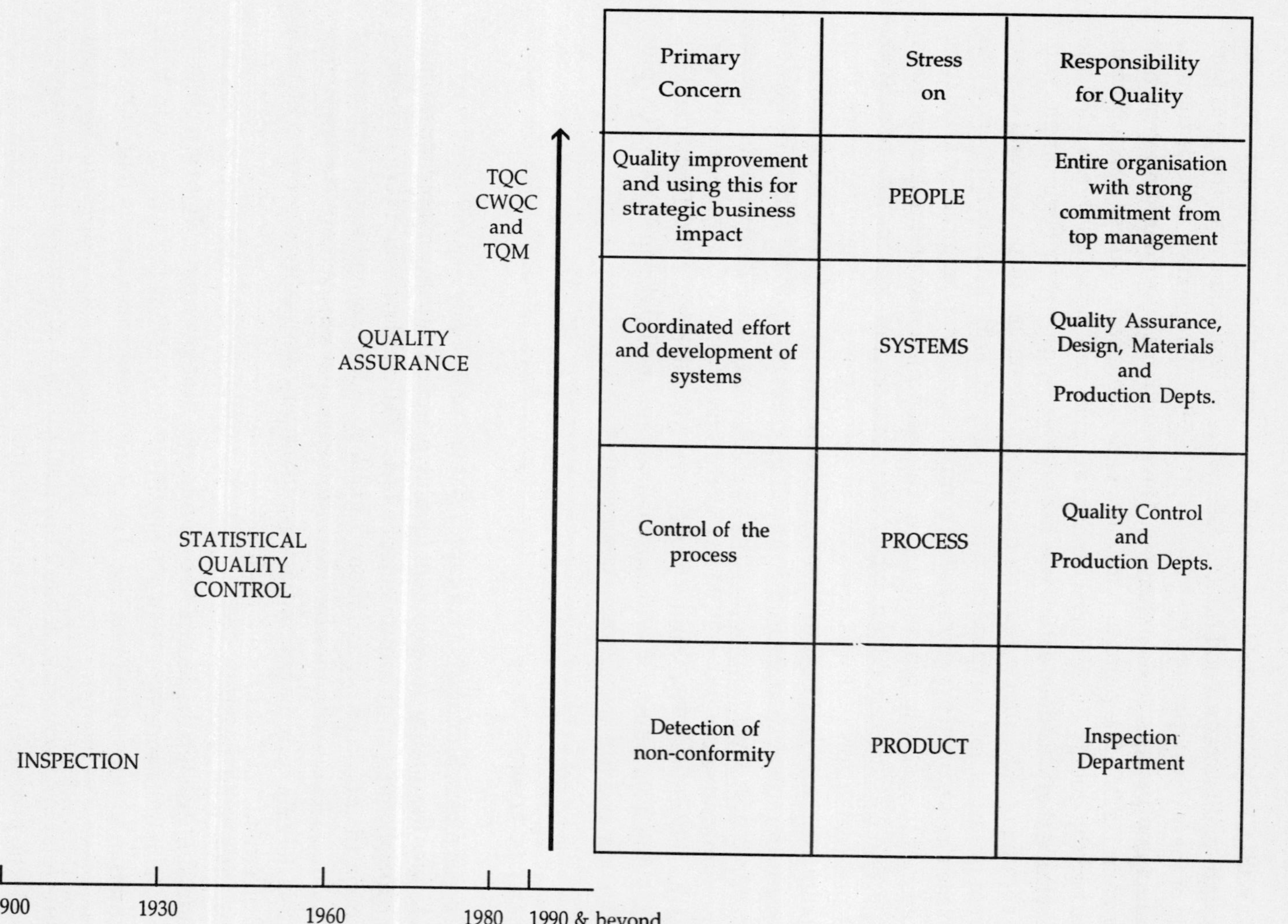

Fig. 3.7. Evolution of the Quality Movement

Quality Progress (a journal of the American Society for Quality Control) conducted a survey and asked its readers to submit papers on TQM applications — papers which either defend or attack TQM — since the need for the survey arose from a feeling in certain people which tended to suggest that TQM was just another fad and would ultimately fail. The results of this survey were published in the July 1995 issue (the call for papers was published in the October 1994 issue). The replies received included case studies and in depth analysis of TQM applications, which clearly pointed out that TQM is a strategic weapon — 'a firm foundation upon which a company can build its business' [1]. Many of the replies also included a definition of TQM and some of these definitions are given below:

— 'A business philosophy that seeks to improve the results, including financial performance, of an organisation's management system; guarantee its long-term survival through a consistent focus on improving customer satisfaction' [7].

— 'A management philosophy that builds a customer-driven, learning organisation dedicated to total customer satisfaction through continuous improvement in the effectiveness and efficiency of the organisation and its processes' [5].

— 'A strategic architecture requiring evaluation and refinement of continuous improvement practices in all areas of a business' [23].

— 'The processes, methods, and systems that organisations use to delight customers and, at the same time, help reduce costs, increase revenue, and empower employees' [8].

— 'An ongoing journey of continuous, measurable improvement championed by responsible individuals at all levels of the organisation' [16].

— 'The continuous improvement of all activities. It is a methodology as well as a way of life' [21].

— 'Is all employees working together in a systematic way to make improvements for customers' [10].

— 'Is customer focus, teamwork, improvement, mission driven' [17].

The readers will readily note that these definitions are all along the lines of the one given in the preceding paragraph and these definitions point out to us that:

— TQM is a philosophy;

— It is customer driven;

— It stresses continuous improvement in all activities and in all areas of business;

— Involvement of individuals at all levels of the organisation; and

— It is aimed at value addition (reduction of costs and increase in revenues).

Various authors at various times have taken T in TQM to mean:

— total customer satisfaction,

— total quality control, and

— total involvement.

However, it is generally recognized that the T in TQM stands for total involvement, and customer satisfaction, being a measure of product quality, comes under the Q in TQM. Thus, for a better understanding of the philosophy, we may redefine TQM as follows:

Total — involvement of everyone in the organisation, at all levels and in every function.

Quality — have to understand and satisfy customers' needs — both internal and external customers.

Management — the leadership and commitment which have to be provided to achieve all these.

Thus, T in TQM is concerned with people — their motivation and participation in continuous improvement,[9] Q with product and process quality and customer satisfaction, and M with managing people — coordinating and directing their efforts towards the common goal(s)/objective(s) and creating an environment which encourages innovation and change. This can be abbreviated as follows:

T	+	Q	+	M	=	TQM
↧		↧		↧		
People Process		Quality Process		Management Process		

COMPONENTS OF TQM

Product and process quality are derivatives of/resultant from the quality contributions of many different individuals with many different technical, production/manufacturing and managerial skills. These individuals have to willingly and enthusiastically participate in the quality effort to ensure development of specifications, drawings, procedures, processes and methods for a high level of product quality, maintenance of this level of quality, followed by a well-coordinated and effective quality improvement effort. This comes from a positive commitment to quality. Achieving widespread commitment to quality involves a broad range of activities. It is based on the following:

(i) sound quality policy,

(ii) customer orientation and efforts directed at full customer satisfaction,

(iii) careful quality planning and development of a quality system, and

(iv) enlightened management of quality and productivity.

Development of clear specifications, design for manufacture and assembly, process design and design of process controls, careful screening and control of vendors and suppliers, and routine feedback and evaluation of quality data, among many others, contribute to the achievement of the objectives of TQM. Sound technological methods are thus basic to quality control and improvement. However, effective human relations are also basic to this effort and TQM programmes must emphasize the assurance of quality motivation and development of the right kind of attitudes. Everyone must believe in the company, its management and in the importance of good quality. For this is needed an enlightened management—a management with a commitment to quality and which realizes the importance of education and training, and of employee participation. Nowadays it has become fashionable to speak of employees as the most important asset of a company, but how many managers really and truly accept that the individual employee knows his work better than his superior and are prepared to create an environment wherein the employee will work willingly and enthusiastically towards quality improvement of products and processes. Moreover, quality commitment for top management must be more than a matter of lip service. The most earth-shaking pronouncements and slogans in support of quality fade into nothingness for the operators and inspectors when an order is received to ship products of substandard quality to meet a delivery commitment. It is important to remember that the quality attitudes of personnel are influenced by the actions and deeds of their superiors that occur in connection with their jobs and these have a much more significant effect than do the slogans, pep-talks, education and training. Therefore, it is worthwhile to remember that a superficial commitment on the part of management does more harm and must be avoided at all costs. What is required instead is effective leadership with a strong belief in the importance of quality.

Therefore, the two basic components of TQM are the following:

1. quality sciences and technologies, and
2. human relations techniques.

These two components have to come together for the achievement of TQM as shown in Fig. 3.8. The figure also lists separately the various activities, or constituents, of these two basic components. The necessary constituents of quality technologies, for example, include the following:

(i) Quality function deployment (QFD).

(ii) Quality planning and development of a quality system as per ISO 9000, or the Malcolm Baldridge National Quality Awards (MBNQA) criteria.

(iii) Process controls — statistical process control (SPC) for the manufacturing industry and SPC with engineering process control (EPC) for the continuous process industry.

(iv) Management of quality of suppliers and vendors.

- Translating customer requirements into engineering specifications and design of appropriate manufacturing process control system - QFD.
- Planning for quality and development of quality management system - ISO 9000/ MBNQA.
- Process control -SPC and SPC with engineering process control for continuous process industries.
- Supplier quality management.

- Creation of vision, statement of mission and development of quality policy.
- Creating awareness about importance of quality and communication of quality policy.
- Education and training.
- Development of fora for participative management and support for employee involvement and participation
- Effective leadership and top management commitment.

Fig. 3.8. Basic Components of TQM

Similarly, the constituents of the human relations techniques are the following:

(i) Creation of a vision, statement of mission and development of quality policy.

(ii) Communication of quality policy to all employees (or better still, to all stakeholders) and creation of awareness about the importance of quality.

(iii) Education and training of all employees.

(iv) Creation of an environment which promotes employee involvement and participation.

(v) Effective leadership and top management support to the TQM programme.

Having discussed the definition of TQM and its various components, we are now ready to discuss the way in which the various components must come together to achieve the objectives of TQM. The TQM philosophy must have a foundation; a foundation on which the rest of the edifice will be built. What are the constitutents of the foundation of TQM? Similarly, the edifice must have a roof to provide the required protection, support and direction. Further, one must necessarily have columns to hold up the roof. What constitutes the roof, and which are these pillars? Let us call this edifice the house of TQM. It is important to consider and discuss the construction of this house, since the basic structuring of a TQM programme in any manufacturing organisation must be based on this construction. The house of TQM, thus, provides the structure of the TQM programme. This structure is shown in Fig. 3.9. The foundation is provided by the following components:

1. Creation of a vision, statement of the mission, and development of quality policy.
2. A well-conceived and documented quality management system.
3. Awareness, education and training for all employees.

The five pillars of the structure are as follows:

4. Customer orientation and customer focus in all functions and activities.
5. Emphasis on process design and use of process controls.
6. Employee participation and use of participative approaches in the management of quality and productivity.
7. Continuous improvement.
8. Supplier quality management.

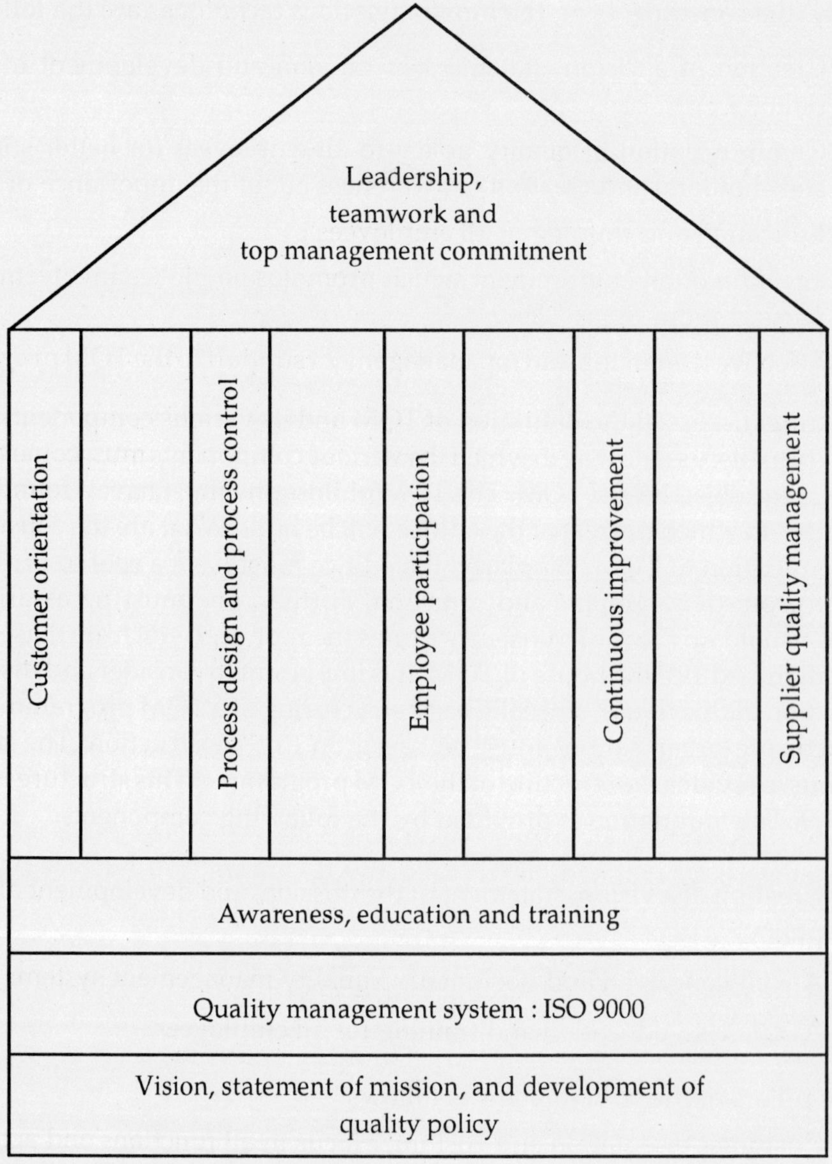

Fig. 3.9. House of TQM - Structure of a TQM Programme

Finally, the roof of the house consists of the following components:

9. Teamwork.
10. Leadership and top management support.

This structuring of the components of TQM also emphasizes certain very important points. It also answers a number of questions and clears some misconceptions. Some of these are as follows:

(i) Many companies profess that they have implemented TQM and their justification is an ISO 9001 or ISO 9002 certificate. Getting the ISO 9001/ 9002 certification is not the same as implementing TQM. It is a very useful step — an important stepping-stone to TQM. Quality planning and a good quality management system is one of the main foundations of TQM; but it is a means to the end and not an end in itself.

(ii) Employee involvement and continuous improvement are the two most universally recognized trade marks of TQM, and they are, accordingly, considered as two of the five pillars of TQM. However, they cannot be achieved without:

— an awareness of the importance of quality,

— knowledge of the corporate quality policies, and also the continuous improvement, or the plan-do-check-act (PDCA), cycle, and

— education and training

for all employees of the organisation. Education and training (including an awareness programme) must consist of both formal classroom instruction and on-the-job training in continuous improvement and problem-solving and trouble-shooting (the seven basic quality tools) and also in brainstorming, fundamental statistics and advanced statistical methods. All employees must know the seven tools, and only a few need to know the more advanced techniques. Thus, awareness, education and training provide an important foundation on which continuous improvement and employee motivation, involvement and participation can be built.

(iii) Likewise, customer satisfaction is also a trade mark of TQM, but customer focus is not just good intentions. It requires a lot of hard work from getting a clear understanding of customer needs and requirements right through product design, manufacturing planning and process controls upto after-sales service. QFD provides a practical framework for some of these activities but QFD, in turn, must go hand-in-hand with a good distribution channel, adequate inventories of spare parts, prompt and efficient service, and provision of training and maintenance support to the customers.

(iv) TQM cannot be achieved without leadership, teamwork and top management support. Also these three cannot, in essence, be separated since top management commitment to quality is a catalyst for both teamwork (some call it cross-functional management) and effective leadership. At the same time, TQM is not just leadership, teamwork and top management support as many behavioural scientists seem to profess. These are components of TQM and they work only when the foundation exists and the pillars are also there (they are being practised).

We have talked of the need for an enlightened management. TQM needs an environment and this environment promotes a culture which encourages learning, innovation, participation and empowerment; a culture which promotes quality improvement in all functions and all activities through collective effort. Such a culture can only be created by an enlightened management, which is:

— a management which recognizes the importance of quality,

— a management which is prepared to let go and shed autocratic and bureaucratic behaviour,

— a management based on trust and shared values.

This culture may be termed as total quality culture. Saraph and Sebastian have defined this culture as "the total of the collective and shared learning of quality-related values as an organisation develops its capacity to survive in its external environment and to manage its own internal affairs" [24]. The development of total quality culture requires a vision and a clear statement of quality mission and policies, education and training for all, and an organisational structure which promotes a sense of belonging to the organisation and enables self-direction and change. Total quality culture is an enabler of TQM since such a culture is necessary for continuous improvement, motivation, participation and teamwork. Some of the identifying characteristics of total quality culture are as follows:

(i) total employee involvement,

(ii) continuous improvement in all spheres of activities,

(iii) process-oriented management,[10]

(iv) top management commitment to product quality, and

(v) intolerance of waste in any from, such as scrap, rework, lost production capacity and inventory.

ESSENCE OF TQM

In keeping with our format, we should conclude our discussion of TQM by briefly going over the important points, which we could use later for comparison with TPM. The following points attempt to present the essence of TQM:

1. TQM is a philosophy. It has been derived from TQC, which, in turn, evolved as a natural outgrowth of the quality movement. TQC is an effective system of integrating the quality planning, quality control and quality improvement efforts of various groups/departments/functions of the organisation. The objective of TQC is continuous quality improvement for full customer satisfaction at minimum cost. This is also the objective of TQM.
2. TQM is more of a management philosophy since what is more important is the manner in which TQM is implemented, or the way in which the various activities are carried out by the organisation.
3. TQM stresses total involvement — involvement of all employees at all levels — for attaining the objectives of continuous quality improvement and full customer satisfaction.
4. The two basic components of TQM are quality technologies and human relations techniques. The quality technologies or tools, which are essential, are QFD, quality planing and development of a quality system, statistical process control (or SPC with EPC) and supplier quality control.
5. Although the quality technologies are essential components of TQM, it is the human relations techniques which are the enablers of TQM. TQM needs a motivated workforce, willing and enthusiastic participation, and teamwork. For these it uses proper communications and awareness training, education and training for all employees, effective leadership and creation of a conducive environment.
6. Continuous quality improvement is attained through the use of a participative management approach. Moreover, TQM stresses the willing and enthusiastic participation of employees. Accordingly, TQM promotion is carried out through the use of a particular type of small group autonomous activity known as quality circles (or QC circles, by the Japanese). In quality circles, participation is voluntary, and not mandatory.

7. The stress in TQM is on prevention of quality defects and nonconforming products and towards this end, TQM makes extensive use of education and training. The workforce is given training in the seven basic tools, which are essentially techniques for problem-solving and troubleshooting.
8. Finally, since the bulk of quality control and quality assurance techniques were developed for the manufacturing industry, that is, organisations engaged in the manufacture of discrete products, TQM has also found greater application in the manufacturing industry.

Terotechnology and TPM

Let us first take up for comparison the application and objective(s). Both terotechnology and TPM are applied to physical assets, the bulk of such assets being plant, machinery and equipment. However, terotechnology does not limit itself to plant, machinery and equipment, and includes in its ambit, buildings and structures as well.[11] TPM, on the other hand, considers only equipment and that too equipment used for manufacturing/production, since, in addition to breakdown losses, it talks of setup, yield/low capacity operation and quality losses. Next we come to the objectives. We have already noted that both terotechnology and TPM promote life-cycle management of plant and equipment. We have also surmised that TPM possibly took the idea of maximisation of equipment effectiveness for the life of the equipment from terotechnology and its objective of economic life-cycle costs. This is true but that is where the similarity of objectives ends. A brief exposition of the differences between the objectives and emphases of terotechnology and TPM are as follows:

1. Minimisation of life-cycle cost vs. maximisation of life-cycle effectiveness.

   Both terotechnology and TPM stress the urgent need to take care of plant and equipment and prolong their useful life; that is, one of the goals in both the cases is the maximisation of the useful life of the equipment. However, whereas the aim of terotechnology is the minimisation of the life-cycle cost, that is, the sum of the costs of ownership and use over the life cycle of the equipment, TPM strives to minimise the loss of effective productive capacity of the equipment. One stresses the need to reduce costs and the other to increase the net productive capacity available for value addition to the product(s). Equipment effectiveness is a measure of the value added[12] to the product, being produced/manufactured, through the use of the equipment, and value addition is significantly reduced by the six major equipment-related losses.

2. Preventive maintenance vs. productive maintenance.
3. Application of management, financial, engineering and other practices vs. use of total involvement and a motivated workforce.

We will need to discuss points 2 and 3 in greater details in the following paragraphs.

Whereas both terotechnology and TPM attempt to extend the useful life of production equipment through proper care and maintenance, terotechnology stresses the maximisation of equipment availability and minimisation of the cost of maintaining it over its life cycle. As opposed to this, TPM stresses the maximisation of overall equipment effectiveness, and this measure of overall equipment effectiveness is the product of availability, performance rate and quality rate, as defined in Chapter Two. Thus, TPM tries to maximise overall equipment effectiveness through the minimisation of the loss of effective productive capacity of the equipment, or the maximisation of the value-added operating time, as shown in Fig. 4.1. TPM recognizes that breakdown loss is just one of the major losses and the minimisation of the loss of value-added operating time also calls for attention to the other five major equipment-related losses, namely, setup and adjustment, idling and minor stoppages, speed/reduced capacity utilisation, quality and start and restart losses. In some instances, the loss due to one (or more) of the other causes, such as stoppages, setup or quality, is greater than the loss due to breakdowns.

We now come to the most important difference between terotechnology and TPM. Terotechnology talks of using management, financial and engineering tools and practices for the achievement of its objective of economy of life-cycle cost of plant and equipment. It does not in any way recognize, or even mention in passing the importance of involving all employees of the organisation in this important task. Wiegel's cyclic model and Evan's circular model only bring out the need to involve the production/operation department for feedback of information and data with regard to equipment failures and deficiencies and the design department for suggesting modifications to plant and equipment. The establishment of weak points and suggestions for modifications of maintenance procedures and systems remain the responsibilities of the maintenance department. Terotechnology, thus, seems to believe in the (organisational) structural straitjacket and the 'I operate, you fix' tradition. It also does not explicitly recognize the need to motivate the grassroots, namely, the equipment operators and the maintenance tradesmen, and of using them:

(i) to ensure the proper care and upkeep of the equipment; and

(ii) for suggesting improvements in the operating and maintenance procedures and practices and also in the design of plant and equipment.

TPM, being a Japanese innovation, recognizes this and places great importance on it. It not only recognizes the importance of motivation and employee participation, but also ensures a motivated workforce and total involvement through:

(i) autonomous maintenance, training of equipment operators and maintenance skills training (these will be discussed in detail in Chapter 5); and

(ii) TPM promotion and use of small group activity to ensure the participation of all employees, including the grassroots. (this will be discussed in detail in Chapter 6).

Nakajima, in his book entitled *'TPM Development Program,'* talks of another difference between terotechnology and TPM. He says:

— "terotechnology involves the equipment supplier, engineering firms and the equipment user. TPM, on the other hand, is practised only by the equipment user" [18].

This difference in the domains[13] of terotechnology and TPM is illustrated in Fig. 3.10. Although conceptually the objective of economic life-cycle cost of plant and equipment can only be achieved by active cooperation between, and joint efforts of, the equipment designer, equipment manufacturer[14] and the equipment user, since the designer and manufacturer of the equipment is hardly ever the user of the equipment, in real life, the practice of terotechnology is usually the responsibility of the equipment user. We have discussed this earlier in this chapter under main functions of terotechnology and we have also noted that 'terotechnology looks at equipment life cycle from the point of view of the user' (please see Figs. 3.3 and 3.4). Therefore, although the concept of terotechnology must necessarily involve the original equipment manufacturer (who is also usually the designer) and the equipment user, it is usually practised by the equipment user. In this regard, therefore, in real life, there is no difference between terotechnology and TPM. One of the basic differences between the practice of terotechnology and TPM, however, is autonomous maintenance. One of the characteristic features of TPM is autonomous maintenance, which holds the equipment operators responsible for daily maintenance tasks and certain routine maintenance activities, and this differentiates it from terotechnology.

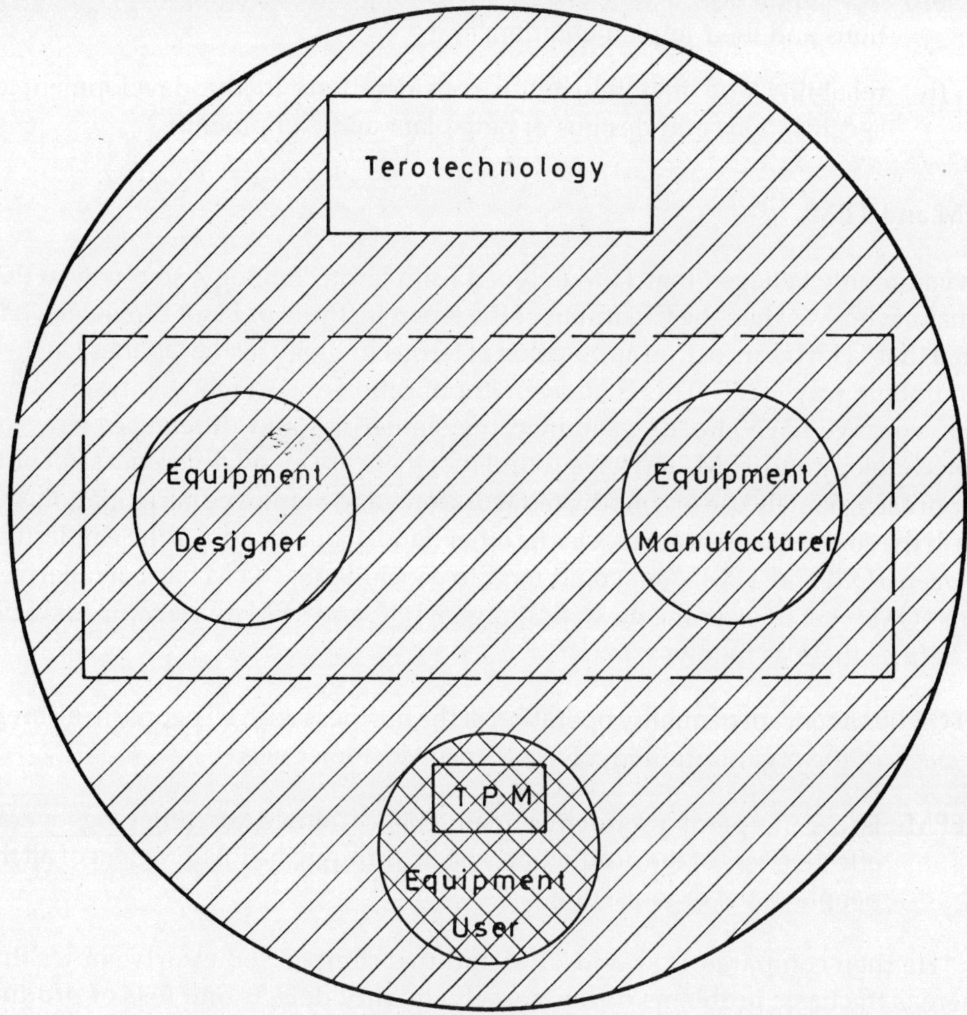

Fig. 3.10. A Comparison of Domains— Terotechnology and TPM

Note: The dotted line implies that in most cases, equipment design and manufacture are carried out by the same organisation.

In all other respects, terotechnology and TPM are similar. The similarities include the following:

(i) analysis of past failures (and in TPM, these include all losses and not just breakdown losses) and planning of maintenance activities;

(ii) a plant-oriented organisational structure, which permits feedback of data, analysis, planning, and feed forward of information and policies;

(iii) development of detailed suggestions for plant and equipment modifications and their implementation; and

(iv) reliability and maintainability considerations in the development of specifications and designs of new plant and equipment.

TQM and TPM

It is commonly believed that TPM evolved from terotechnology, so much so that Tamaki, who was then the Chairman of the Japan Institute of Plant Engineers, had stated that "TPM is, in fact, an application of terotechnology by the Japanese in their own unique way" [27]. This is an oversimplification and in many ways, it is not quite true. We have already examined the similarities and differences between terotechnology and TPM, and have found that there are many differences not only in approach, namely use of a motivated workforce and employee participation, but also in the contents and practice. On the other hand, if one examines the similarities between TQM and TPM, one would tend to conclude that TPM has been derived from TQM.[15] Let us examine the definitions of TQC and TPM given by Suzaki [25]. He defines them as follows:

TQC: is a concept of quality operation of the business with all people in all areas of the organisation involved to meet customer needs.

TPM: is a concept of productive maintenance aimed at achieving overall effectiveness of the production system through the involvement of all the people in the organisation.

He then compares TQC and TPM and this comparison clearly shows that whereas the basic problems differ, namely, quality defects and loss of productive capacity, and obviously the technologies (tools/techniques) also differ, both use education and training, employee involvement and a mindset, or attitude, which is intolerant of defects and waste. This is a mindset which does not accept that "it is natural for machines to breakdown: produce defects and suffer minor stoppages" [26]. We do not wholly agree with the definitions given above, in as much as we feel that whereas TQC, or TQM, is a philosophy, TPM is a practice and not a concept or a philosophy. However, we feel that the similarity in approach overshadows everything else, so much so that one feels that TPM is a part of TQC/TQM, or in other words, TPM is a subset of TQM. This is particularly true when it comes to the operation of continuous process industries, and in such industries, the implementation of TPM is one of the stages of implementation of TQM. We will discuss this in detail in the last chapter when we take up real-life case applications of TPM.

In TPM, the development of the right attitude, which is characterized by a sense of ownership of the equipment, the pride of craftsmanship and a realization of shared responsibility with equipment operators and maintenance tradesmen is no less important than the actual tasks of maintenance. Moreover, just as in TQM, TPM cannot succeed without (i) top management commitment to the care and upkeep of production plant and equipment, and (ii) participation of all who are in any way concerned with this task. Thus, the driving force, or the philosophy, behind TPM is to improve the quality of people by building the right attitudes so that they would want to not only maintain the equipment but also to improve them. This way the employees will strive for the improvement and growth of the company [26]. Thus, we find that the human relations techniques which are used in TQM are also essential for the success of TPM.

Other than the fact that the ultimate goals differ, namely, in TQM, it is the elimination of defectives, whereas in TPM, it is the elimination of the loss of productive capacity, the most fundamental difference between TQM and TPM is the participative approach used, that is, the difference between quality circles and PM groups.[16] TQM uses quality circles, whereas, the small groups in TPMare called PM groups. Both these approaches are used to facilitate the

(i) participation of the grassroots (shop-floor workers/equipment operators, maintenance tradesmen, quality control inspectors etc.), and

(ii) involvement of all employees in the TQM/TPM efforts, or in other words, promotion of TQM/TPM — related activities in all functions and departments and at all levels.

However, there are some basic differences between quality circles and PM groups and these are essentially related to the structure, goals/problem selection, mode of participation, and operation. These differences are given in Table 3.1. The reader will note that quality circles are informal organisations independent of the existing organisational structure whereas PM groups, on the other hand, are formal organisations created by the management for TPM promotion within the existing organisational structure. The differences in the structure, problem/theme selection and conduct of activities arise from the difference in the basic objectives and for this reason, the beginnings and basic objectives of the two approaches have been noted right at the top of the table.

Table 3.1: Basic Differences Between Quality Circles and PM Groups

	Quality Circles	*PM Groups*
Beginnings and basic objectives	As study groups to teach quality control techniques to production supervisors (and hence the name), and these, in turn, evolved into problem solving groups for workers/operators	As groups formed for participation of workers to enable them to take up and solve problems of concern to the organisation and to work toward organisational goals.
Structure of the groups	— Formed by workers themselves — Independent of the existing organisational structure — Leaders usually selected by circle members.	— Formed within the existing organisational structure — Leadership usually assumed by supervisors.
Mode of participation	Voluntary	Mandatory
Goals/themes selected, or selection of problems	Themes of discussion and problems to be tackled are selected by circle members. These themes may have no direct bearing/connection with the improvements goals of the organisation.	PM groups must choose themes and goals which are consistent with the goals of the organisation. Thus, problems are usually those which are of concern to the management.
Operation/conduct of activities.	— Usually conducted outside working hours — No overtime paid for attending meetings.	— Generally conducted during working hours — If conducted outside working hours, then overtime is usually paid.

CONCLUDING REMARKS

TPM has taken the essence from both terotechnology and TQM — the concept of life cycle effectiveness from terotechnology's objective of minimisation of life-cycle cost and the need for participation, employee involvement and organisational commitment and leadership from TQM. However, TPM is neither a concept nor a philosophy. It is a practice which can, therefore, be actually implemented in a phased and structured manner. The implementation of TPM will reduce losses and this will, in turn, result in an increase in production and improvement in productivity. The fact that TPM was developed in the manufacturing industry (unlike terotechnology which was developed in the continuous process industry) should not, in any way, inhibit its implementation in the continuous process industry. In the last chapter we will discuss a real-life illustrative example and also a case study of implementation of TPM. Both these applications are from the continuous process industry. As a matter of fact, in the author's opinion, just like terotechnology, the implementation of TPM will have a much greater impact in the continuous process industry (as compared to the manufacturing industry).

The practice of TPM consists of a number of activities, which include the following:

(i) Autonomous maintenance tasks are performed by the equipment operators. Through autonomous maintenance, the production operators are, in a way, given ownership of their equipment. This not only makes them feel responsible for the care and upkeep of their equipment, but also brings in them, a pride of craftsmanship and a feeling of belonging to the larger group — the organisation. This promotes involvement, commitment to the equipment and the task, and a desire to contribute towards improvements to the equipment and the process.

(ii) Training of operators in the proper operation and upkeep of the production equipment. Moreover, this training includes training in equipment inspection, which, in turn, stresses the need for an orderly shopfloor. Orderly shopfloor implies a clean, tidy and orderly workplace. These initiatives not only bring about an improvement in equipment availability, but also inculcate employee involvement and commitment and in this way also contributes to continuous improvement efforts.

(iii) Training of maintenance technicians to improve their skills. Together with greater confidence and job satisfaction, this brings a sense of belonging in the maintenance technicians. This, in turn, brings a desire to participate in the continuous improvement efforts.

Education and training of the workforce forms a very important part of TPM practice. In this regard, TPM is very similar to TQM. We have noted above that employee involvement and participation of the grassroots in the improvement goals of the organisation follow as natural outcomes of autonomous maintenance and education and training of the employees. We will discuss autonomous maintenance and education and training of equipment operators and maintenance tradesmen in Chapter 5.

In productive maintenance, the overall equipment effectiveness is obtained by multiplying equipment availability, its performance rate and the quality rate. The initiatives taken in TPM towards reduction of defects in the form of scrap, rejects and rework compliment the TQM efforts of the organisation. The practice of TPM, therefore, is an essential requirement in the implementation of the TQM philosophy. This is particularly true in case of the continuous process industries, wherein TPM can provide a foundation on which the improvement in results and increase in value-addition resulting from reduction in production costs and increase in revenues can be structured. TPM, thus, becomes a necessary step in the quest for TQM, and therefore, in a way, TPM is a subset of TQM. This will be discussed further in the last chapter of this book when we take up the real-life implementation of TPM.

References

1. Bemowski, K., "TQM: Flimsy Footing or Firm Foundation," *Quality Progress*, Vol. 28, No. 7, July 1995, pp. 27-28.

2. Bhadury, B., *Some Applications of System Analysis in Terotechnology*, Unpublished *Ph. D. Thesis*, University of Burdwan (India), July, 1985.

3. Blanchard, B.S., "Life Cycle Costing — A Review," *Terotechnica*, Vol. 1, No. 1, May 1979, pp. 9-15.

4. Butz, H.E. Jr., "Strategic Planning: The Missing Link in TQM," *Quality Progress*, Vol. 28, No. 5., May 1995, pp. 105-108.

5. Corrigan, J.P., "The Art of TQM," *Quality Progress*, Vol. 28, No. 7, July 1995, pp. 61-64.

6. Darnell, H., "Guest Editorial," *Terotechnica* Vol. 1, No. 1, May 1979.

7. Dobbins, R.D., "A Failure of Methods, Not Philosophy," *Quality Progress*, Vol. 28, No. 7, July 1995, pp. 31-32.

8. Early, J.F. and Godfrey, A.B., "But It Takes Too Long," *Quality Progress*, Vol. 28, No. 7, July 1995, pp. 51-55.

9. Evans, D.W., "Terotechnology — How It Can Work?," in I. Mech. E. (London) Conference, University of Durham (September 4-5, 1974) *Mech. Engg. Pubs.*, London, 1975, pp. 73-80.

10. Feinberg, S., "Overcoming the Real Issues of Implementation," *Quality Progress*, Vol. 28, No. 7, July 1995, pp. 79-81.

11. Feigenbaum, A.V., *Total Quality Control*, McGraw-Hill Book Company, New York, International Student Edition, 1986 (McGraw-Hill 1961, 1983), p. 12.

12. Finniston, H.M., "Terotechnology and Management at BSC", *Journal of the Iron and Steel Institute*, July 1973, pp. 481-485.

13. Heath, J.A., "A Few Good Ideas for a Good Idea Program," *Quality Progress*, Vol. 27, No. 1, July 1994, pp. 35-38.

14. Hewgill, J.C.R., "Towards Economic Life Cycle Costs," in *Terotechnology Handbook*, Her Majesty's Stationery Office, London, pp. 12-19

15. Hewgill, J.C. and Parkes, D., "Terotechnology—Philosophy and Concept," *Terotechnica*, Vol. 1, No. 1, May 1979, pp. 3-8.

16. Landes, L., "Leading the Duck at Mission Control," *Quality Progress*, Vol. 28, No. 7, July 1995, pp. 43-48.

17. Moe, J.L., "What Does Employee Involvement Mean?," *Quality Progress*, Vol. 28, No. 7, July 1995, pp. 67-71.

18. Nakajima, S. (Editor), *TPM Development Program: Implementing Total Productive Maintenance*, Productivity Press, Cambridge, Massachusetts, U.S.A., 1989, p. 12, 349.

19. Parkes, D., "Terotechnology, Resource Utilization and Productivity," in *Proceedings—International Conference on Optimum Resource Utilization Through Tribo-terotechnology and Maintenance Management* (Tribo-Maint. 1981), New Delhi, Nov. 30-Dec 6, 1981 (Publisher — Sarita Prakashan, New Delhi, 1983), pp. 41-50.

20. Rappini, G.E., "Some Aspects of Terotechnology at Italsider," *Journal of the Iron and Steel Institute*, June 1973, pp. 389-405.

21. Rau, H., "15 Years and Still Growing," *Quality Progress*, Vol. 28, No. 7, July 1995, pp. 57-59.

22. Riddell, H.S., "Life Cycle Costing in the Chemical Industry: Two Case Studies," *Terotechnica*, Vol. 2, No. 1, January 1981, pp. 9-21.

23. Roosevelt, B., "Quality and Business Practices: Essential Ingredients for Success," *Quality Progress*, Vol. 28, No. 7, July 1995, pp.35-40.

24. Saraph, J.V. and Sebastian, R.J., "Developing a Quality Culture," *Quality Progress*, Vol. 26, No. 9, September 1993, pp. 73-78.

25. Suzaki, K., *The New Manufacturing Challenge: Techniques for Continuous Improvement*, The Free Press (A division of Macmillan, Inc.) New York, 1987, pp. 6 and 8-24.

26. Suzuki, T., *New Directions for TPM*, Productivity Press, Cambridge, Massachusetts, U.S.A.,1992, pp. IX-XIV, 7-12, 17-20.

27. Tamaki, A., "Total Productive Maintenance and Its Impact on Japanese Industry," *Terotechnica*, Vol. 2, No. 1, January 1981, pp. 3-4 (Guest Editorial on Total Productive Maintenance).

28. Webster's Third New International Dictionary, Vol. I, Encyclopaedia Britannica, Chicago/London, 1966, p. 670.

29. Wiegel, W., "Functional Maintenance: A Systems Approach," *Metals Technology*, January 1974, pp. 6-12.

Endnotes

1. Probably it did not directly originate from either, since all three were developed at around the same time. However, TPM may have benefitted from the work done in the West on terotechnology and from work done on quality control, quality circles and small group activity in Japan. But this is only natural. As a matter of fact, TPM, being more of a practice than a concept, has taken freely from other disciplines and technologies.

2. The fact that minimising the whole life cost of ownership, which, in turn, can be attained by the minimisation of the time dependent cost of maintenance over the life cycle, would result in 'economic life cycle cost' will be explained later in the sub-section on the constituents of the equipment life cycle cost.

3. The design office shown in Wiegel's cyclic model is the design office of the steel-works which can recommend comparatively minor/restricted equipment modifications to reduce the incidence of recurrent failures etc. These, however, can also be effective as has been brought out by Rappini [20].

4. Readers should note that Wiegel used the term functional maintenance. The use of this term implies that maintenance is functional only if it includes all the activities needed for improvement of plant and equipment availability.

5. As opposed to this, Wiegel's model proposed maintainability improvements primarily because, as noted earlier, the design office in the cyclic model is the design office of the user organisation.

6. This is rather interesting particularly because the three applications were conducted at around the same time and with the same overall objective.

7. ISO 8402 contains the quality management and quality assurance vocabulary and is a part of the ISO 9000 standard.

8. ISO 8402 does not define TQM but says that quality management is that aspect of overall management function which determines and implements the quality policy and includes strategic planning, allocation of resources and other systematic activities such as quality planning, operations and evaluations. It also says that attainment of the desired quality requires the commitment and participation of all members of the organization.

9. Willing and active participation in continuous improvement is synonymous with employee empowerment. 'Empowerment means giving power to someone. In TQM culture, empowerment is providing adequate training in continuous process improvement tools and enough time to apply them' [13].

10. A process-oriented management is quality-conscious and is organised around the core processes that meet customer requirements.

11. This is a minor difference. Also, this is basically due to the fact that terotechnology was enunciated by managers and engineers of continuous process industries whereas the roots of TPM lay in the manufacturing industry. In the continuous process industry, buildings and structures constitute a significant portion of the investment and for ensuring the economy of life-cycle cost of the plant/project, one has to consider the costs of installation, maintenance, modification and replacement of buildings and structures, as well.

12. Added value is the difference between the sales revenue and the total cost of resources utilised to produce the product.

13. Domain, as per Webster's Third New International Dictionary, is a field of control, or more appropriately, a circumscribed realm of concern [28].

14. In most cases and particularly for production equipment and machines, design and manufacture are carried out by the same firm, or in other words, equipment designer and equipment manufacturer are not two different entities or organisations. This is the reason for the dotted line in the figure.

15. In Japan, TQM is referred to as company-wide quality control. Also this belief is further bolstered by the fact that both TQM and TPM were developed by the Japanese.

16. As we have noted earlier, quality circles are referred to as QC circles by the Japanese. Also the PM groups, which are called TPM groups in Japan, are based on the American zero defects model and have evolved from the ZD groups. The ZD groups, in turn, resulted from the combination of the concept of zero defects with quality circles [18].

Eliminating Six Big Losses

In Chapter One, we had noted that the first of the three motives for the advocation and subsequent adoption of TPM, as identified by Takahashi [20], was adoption of the life cycle approach for improving the overall performance of production equipment. As discussed in Chapter Three, terotechnology also stresses and promotes adoption of the life cycle approach for the management of physical assets. It is the stress on overall performance which differentiates TPM from terotechnology and productive maintenance from preventive maintenance. We have noted and briefly discussed these differences in Chapters two and Three, but we are restating them in this chapter to stress the fact that efforts at improving the overall performance of plant and machinery must not only be directed at losses due to ineffective maintenance, but also towards the other losses which limit the effectiveness of production equipment. After all, the formal definition of TPM, as noted in Chapter One, clearly states that the aim of TPM, is the maximisation of equipment effectiveness and as a further clarification, it is also noted that this implies efforts directed at the improvement of the overall effectiveness of production equipment. Wireman, in his book on TPM, explains the first two clauses of the formal definition of TPM, namely maximising equipment effectiveness and establishment of a total system of PM covering the whole life of equipment, for ensuring equipment capacity and implementing a programme of maintenance for the entire life of the equipment [23]. He goes on to state that ensuring equipment capacity implies efforts directed at ensuring that the equipment performs to its specifications — operates at its design speed, produces at the design rate which results in quality products at these speeds and rates. This implies efforts aimed at the maximisation of equipment utilisation (and not just the maximisation of equipment availability), and there are six significant causes of reduction of equipment utilisation. These are as follows:

1. Losses due to ineffective maintenance, and these, in TPM terminology, are called breakdown losses.
2. Setup and adjustment losses.
3. Losses due to idling and minor stoppages of equipment.
4. Loss due to operation at reduced speed, or at less than full (design) load—this Wireman calls reduced capacity loss [23].
5. Loss due to poor product quality - due to defects in process and production of defective items.
6. Loss due to reduced yield from the startup of the equipment to the point of stable production - and this Wireman calls 'startup/restart loss' [23].

These are the six major equipment losses and the stress it places on the elimination of these major losses is one of the three identifying characteristics of TPM, as noted and discussed in Chapter One. In this chapter, we will discuss each one of the losses, and the steps which can be taken to eliminate them, separately one after the other.

The reduction of equipment utilisation has three constituents, which have to do with the availability of the equipment, the rate at which the equipment is performing, and the product quality performance of the production equipment (this, in TPM literature, is called the 'quality rate,' in keeping with the performance rate). Thus, the overall equipment effectiveness has three constituents, namely, availability, performance rate, and quality rate and the overall equipment effectiveness

$$= \text{availability} \times \text{performance rate} \times \text{quality rate.}$$

Note: *These three constituents are also measures of equipment effectiveness.*

These three constituents, the six big losses and the method of calculating these three constituents from the shop, or equipment performance, data are given in Fig. 4.1. The terms used in the figure are explained as follows:

(i) Loading time is the available time on the equipment for production/productive work. This is the total time available minus the necessary time for planned or essential activities, such as time lost due to meetings,

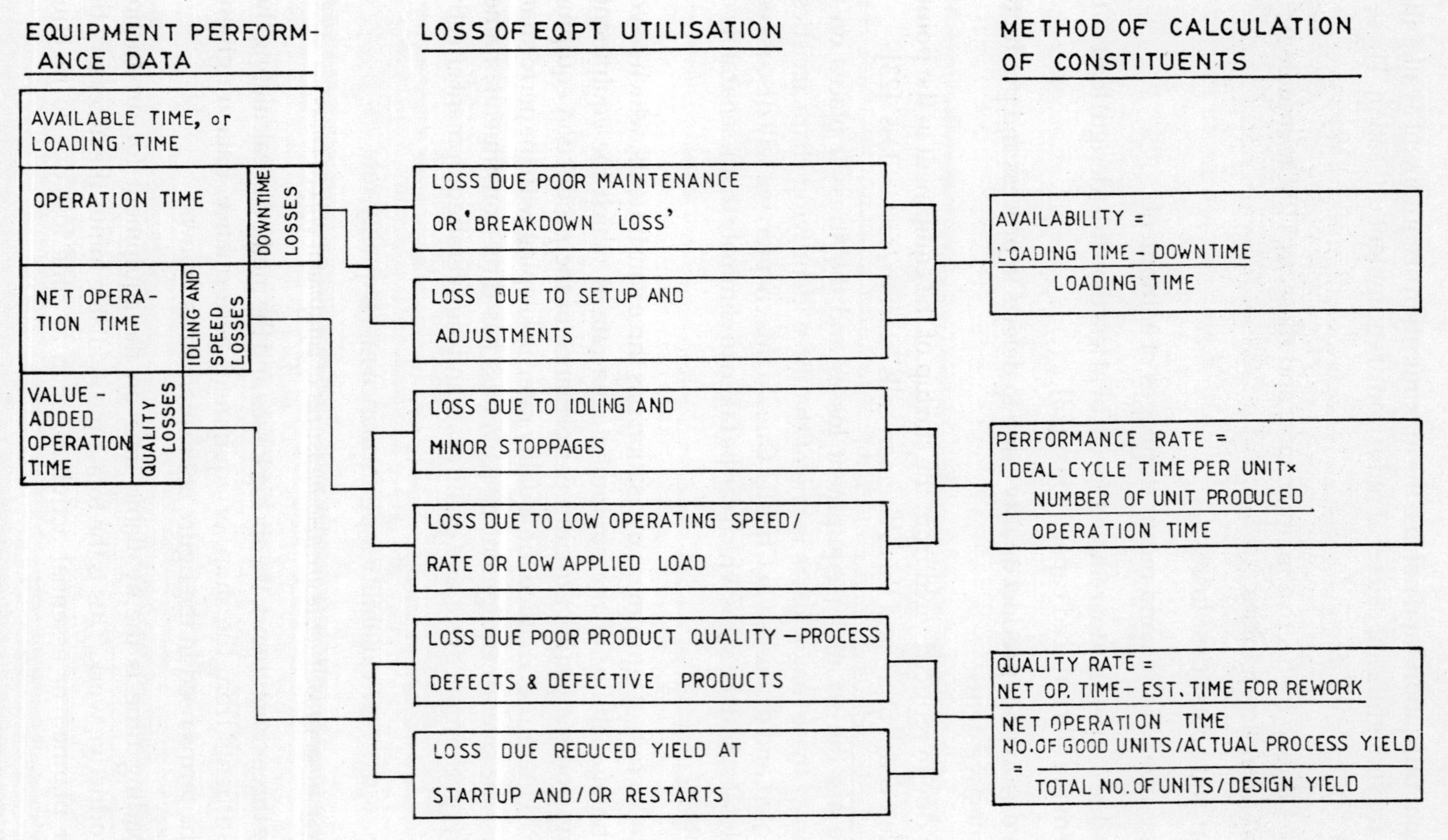

Fig. 4.1. Calculating Availability, Performance Rate and Quality Rate

scheduled tea/coffee breaks or precautionary rest periods, and also breaks in production schedules or planned production stoppages for planned/preventive maintenance work, and, on rare occasions, scheduled production stoppages for non-maintenance reasons.

(ii) Operation time is loading time minus the downtime, or the time the machine is down for reasons other than given under (i). Such downtime includes time lost due to equipment breakdowns, setup of equipment, tools, dies and accessories, and adjustments to the equipment. These adjustments are generally carried out by operators, and take less than 10 minutes.

(iii) Net operation time is the time the equipment or the machine is operated at its design speed, or at the design rate of production, or at the design load. The time lost due to idling and minor stoppages of the machine, and operating it at a reduced speed or at a reduced rate of production are subtracted from the operation time to get the net operation time. The term 'design load' has also been included to take account of process plant equipment which are either derated and/or operated at low loads for various reasons. An example of this would be a 210 MW thermal power unit being operated at 150 MW because two out of six pulverizers are down. In thermal power plant terminology, such outages are called partial outages.

(iv) Value-added operation time is the net operating time during which actual value addition is carried out. This is obtained by subtracting the total estimated time for rework of defective/nonconforming products from the net operation time. Thus, the time required to make up for the quality losses is subtracted from the net operation time to get the value-added operation time.

In Chapter One, we had noted that the objectives of TPM are zero breakdowns and zero defects. As a matter of fact, the aim of TPM is much more. In addition to the minimisation of losses due to inadequate maintenance of equipment and poor product quality, the minimisation of losses due to setup and adjustments, idling and minor stoppages, operation at lower speeds and/or lower rates of production, and lower yield at startup and/or restart of equipment are also included. The minimisation of the total loss, which is the sum total of the six big losses, will ensure the maximisation of productive, or value-added, utilisation of the equipment. Many practitioners seem sceptical about Japanese techniques, such as TPM, TQM and JIT. The main reason for this sceptism is the feeling that objectives, such as zero breakdowns, zero defects and zero inventory, are utopian and can never be achieved. Zero breakdowns do not necessarily mean that the loss due to breakdowns should actually be reduced to zero, since it would be extremely difficult, if not impossible, to do that. However, attempts can be made to get as close as possible to zero and this is what is actually meant by zero breakdowns. The term zero should, in all fairness, be read as 'tending to zero.' In the context of the six big losses, it must be realised that, as opposed to the other four losses, setup and startup losses cannot be reduced to zero.[1] For these two losses, the objective is to minimise them, and for the other four losses, the aim is to eliminate them. Having discussed the six big losses and identified the three measures of equipment effectiveness, we can now discuss the steps and methods of eliminating/minimising them.

Eliminating Breakdown Losses

Unlike terotechnology, which is essentially a concept, TPM is a practical model. In this section, we propose to discuss the implementation of the objective of zero breakdowns. However, before we can do that, we will need to understand the different types of breakdowns and also the difference between chronic and sporadic losses, and also take a relook at the types of maintenance and maintenance systems. Accordingly, this section will be divided into the following four subsections:

1. Types of breakdowns.
2. Chronic and sporadic losses.
3. Types of maintenance and maintenance systems revisited.
4. Implementation of zero breakdowns — four phases and five activities.

TYPES OF BREAKDOWNS

For most people, breakdown signifies some kind of a malfunction, or failure, which results in the total stoppage of a machine. Such failures in which the equipment stops completely result in the total loss of equipment or machine capacity. Failure is the termination of the ability of an item to perform its required function, and when it is applied to an equipment or a machine, required function, implies performance as per its design specifications. Therefore, we see that failures need not always be catastrophic bringing the machine to a grinding halt; a failure can also take the form of deterioration or wear of its component part. Whereas catastrophic failures are easily recognised and immediately dealt with, deterioration of the equipment which results in a reduction of its function, or capacity, is not so easily recognised. Moreover, even if recognised, such conditions are overlooked. To attain the objective of eliminating breakdown losses, it is imperative to recognise that there are two types of breakdowns, and these are as follows:

(i) Function loss, or capacity loss breakdowns.

(ii) Function reduction, or capacity reduction breakdowns.

Both types of breakdowns result in losses of equipment capacity. A function loss breakdown results in the total loss of capacity and a function reduction breakdown results in a partial loss of capacity. Now, the first objective of TPM is maximising equipment capacity and the maximisation of equipment capacity demands that adequate and timely actions be taken to deal with both these types of breakdowns. Function loss breakdowns are dealt with on a war footing as emergency repairs. As opposed to this, function reduction breakdowns receive a much lower priority. Moreover, since in case of function reduction breakdowns, the equipment can still be run, in many cases, for short-term considerations, the equipment is allowed to run at a reduced capacity. What is worse, in many cases, over a period of time, operation at a reduced capacity — at a lower operating speed, with lower applied load, at a lower productivity level or production rate — is taken to be normal. The operator is asked to continue operation of the equipment at a reduced capacity.

Function reduction breakdowns must also receive the necessary attention. As opposed to short-term gains, long-term profitability should be the primary concern of the organisation. This is all the more important because capacity reduction breakdown represents the largest cost to most manufacturing organisations[16],[23]. Wireman[23] gives the examples of an equipment which produces a defective product whenever it operates at a speed higher than 80 per cent of its design speed. When this happens, the organisation takes the easy route and asks the operator(s) of the equipment not to run the equipment at speeds higher than 80 per cent of its design speed. Over a period of time, this becomes the standard practice. This way the orgnisation loses 20 per cent of the equipment capacity but the organisation chooses to follow this route since correction of the problem would have taken time and effort (and during this time, production would have suffered). In the short-term, this alternative may seem attractive but in the long-term, it would be very expensive (and unnecessarily so) since the organisation would have to invest in an additional machine just to meet the demand on its production capacity. The procurement of an additional machine could have been avoided had the necessary time and effort been taken to correct the problem when it was first noticed. Operation at reduced manufacturing speed resulting in longer cycle times is the most common example of the loss due to function reduction breakdown. Shirose and Goto [16] give other examples of function reduction losses. They state that long setup and adjustment times, frequent idling and minor stoppages, and production of a larger number of defectives during startup and during processing may be results of function reduction breakdowns. Thus, this kind of breakdown could also result in other kinds of losses.

In most cases, function loss breakdown of the equipment is caused by the failure of some component of the equipment. Preventive maintenance and condition monitoring inspections are designed to detect normal deterioration and wear of critical components of the equipment. Thus, maintenance practices are directed at the prevention of such failures. Function loss breakdowns can also be due to infant mortality, or running in failures and poor operating and maintenance practices. Therefore, in case the preventive and predictive maintenance programmes are effective and implemented properly, the incidence of function loss breakdowns can be minimised. As opposed to this, function reduction breakdowns are generally caused by the neglect of a chronic equipment problem [23]. Thus, whereas function loss breakdowns are sporadic in nature, function reduction breakdowns are chronic minor breakdowns. Such minor and chronic problems require timely and innovative solutions. When a function reduction problem is detected, it should be analysed and solved since 'it is more economical to solve the problem than it is to reduce the operating standards' [23].

CHRONIC AND SPORADIC LOSSES

What we will discuss in this subsection relates to all the six major losses. We are discussing it under breakdown losses because this is the first of the six losses and an item which relates to all six must find a place with the first one. It is also due to the fact that the effect of chronic losses is most acutely felt in the case of equipment breakdowns and product quality problems. The dictionary [7] meaning of chronic is 'lasting a long time or deep seated and long continued'and chronic usually relates to a disease. Sporadic, on the other hand, is 'scattered, occuring here and there and now and then.' Thus, chronic is used to refer to an undesirable condition, or phenomenon, which is either deep seated and continues over a long time, or occurs repeatedly over a long period of time. As opposed to this, a sudden or an unexpected occurrence which occurs rarely is referred to as sporadic. The difference between chronic and sporadic losses is illustrated in Fig. 4.2.

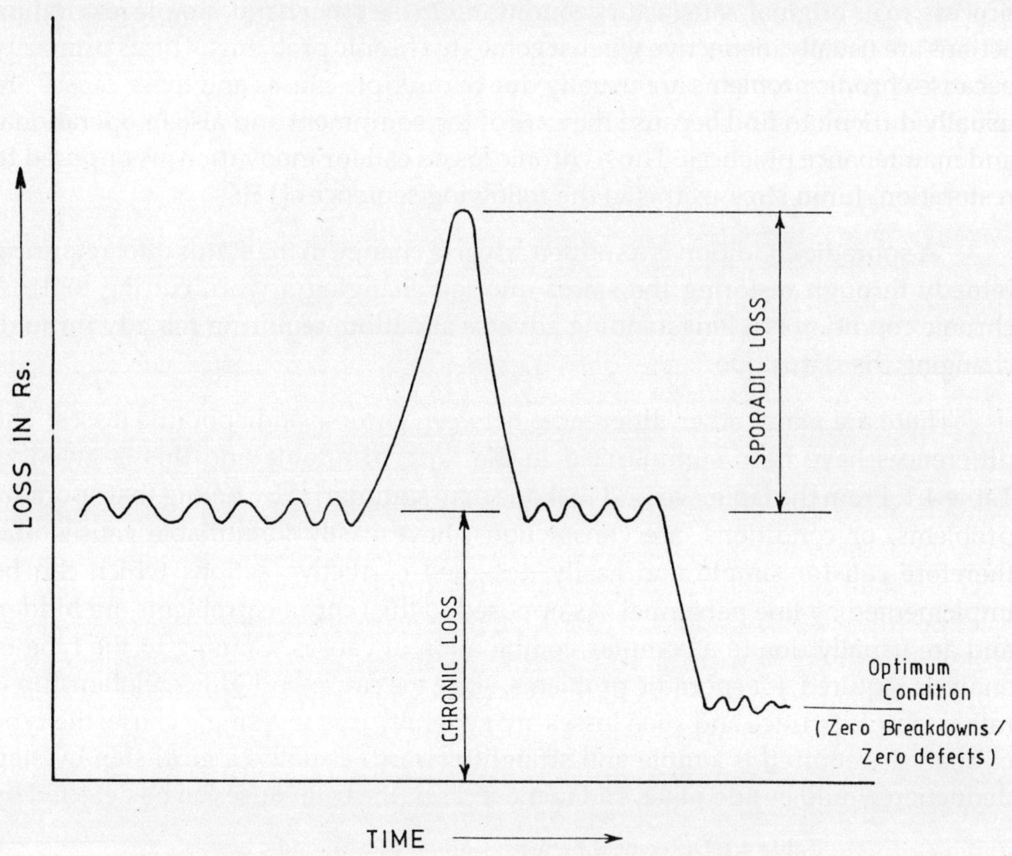

Fig. 4.2. Difference Between Chronic and Sporadic Losses

Chronic breakdowns, or chronic defects, occur repeatedly over a long period of time and keep on occurring till something radical or different, is done to get rid of the cause, or causes, of such breakdowns, or defects. Chronic losses are caused by conditions, which, over a period of time, get to be perceived as normal, and such losses only become obvious, or come to be recognised, when they are compared with optimum conditions. The figure illustrates a case wherein after the chronic loss had been recognised, necessary efforts had been made to bring the level of loss down to the desired optimum level. Sporadic breakdowns, or sporadic defects, on the other hand, are sudden and unexpected occurrences and these occur only occasionally. The cause for a sporadic problem can be easily found out. Sporadic breakdowns, or sporadic defects, are usually due to a single cause (recall control charts and the existence of an 'assignable cause') and thus can be removed by restoration — a repair or corrective action which restores the equipment, or the process, to its original, satisfactory condition. On the other hand, simple restoration actions are usually ineffective when it comes to chronic problems. This is primarily because chronic problems are usually due to multiple causes and these causes are usually difficult to find because they are of the equipment and also of operational and maintenance practices. Thus, chronic losses call for innovation, as opposed to restoration. Juran stresses this in the following sentences [11]:

"A sporadic condition is a sudden adverse change in the status quo, requiring remedy through restoring the status quo (eg changing a worn cutting tool). A chronic condition is a longstanding adverse situation, requiring remedy through changing the status quo."

There are many other differences between chronic and sporadic losses. The differences have been summarized in the form of a table and this is given as Table 4.1. From the table, we find that one may summarize by noting that sporadic problems, or conditions, are conspicuous, have easily identifiable causes and therefore call for simple and easily designed corrective actions which can be implemented by line personnel. As opposed to this, chronic problems are hidden and are usually due to a complex combination of causes. Coming to the type of analysis required, for sporadic problems, since the cause-and-effect relationship is rather simple to trace and such losses are generally due to a single cause, the type of analysis required is simple and straightforward. Usually, logical step-by-step deduction would be adequate, and in most cases, the true cause can be detected by

Table 4.1. Differences Between Chronic and Sporadic Losses

	Characteristics of	
Aspect	*Sporadic Problems*	*Chronic Problems*
Visibility	Conspicuous - conditions created considerably different from routine operating conditions	Hidden - tend to be overlooked since losses hard to measure
Frequency of occurrence	Low - only occasionally	High - occur frequently
Method of detection	No special method necessary since visibility is high	Can only be detected by comparing the actual condition with the theoretical (design) standard/specification, or optimum condition/level
Economic impact/ loss	A single problem very costly but cumulative effect and cost minor	A single occurrence has small impact, or loss, but cumulative effect, or loss, considerable
Resulting impact on supervision and management	Substantial - sudden nature of problem attracts immediate attention and action	Small and due to repetitive/continuing nature of problem accepted as unavoidable/inevitable

Aspect	*Sporadic Problems*	*Chronic Problems*
Causation	Cause-and-effect relationship simple to trace. Generally due to a single cause	A single cause is rare; usually multiple causes or worse still, a complex combination of causes
Type of solution required	'Restore the *status quo*'	'Change the *status quo*'
Type of analysis required	Usually simple—'ask why five times'	Intricate and complex—cause-and-effect analysis, correlation analysis and design of experiments and analysis of variance
Corrective action to be taken by	Usually the line personnel in production, or design, can attend to it.	Will need specialists in process engineering, maintenance, and/or quality assurance

'asking why five times,' in keeping with the teachings of Taiichi Ohno of Toyota [17]. As opposed to this, the type of analysis required for chronic problems is usually intricate and complex. It also calls for detailed knowledge of the system/process and the equipment. This, together with the need for the application of sophisticated techniques, such as correlation analysis, design of experiments and analysis of variance etc., calls for the involvement of specialists in identifying, planning and implementation of corrective action(s).

The characteristics of different types of equipment losses are given in Table 4.2. A closer look at the table would show the reader that five out of the six big losses have been included in the table and the only loss which has not been

Table 4.2. Characteristics of Equipment Losses

Sl. No.	*Type of loss*	*Conspicuous, or clearly evident*	*Hidden*
1.	Breakdown loss		
	(a) sporadic breakdowns	✓	
	(b) chronic breakdowns		✓
2.	Setup and adjustment loss	✓	✓
3.	Idling and minor stoppage loss		✓
4.	Speed loss		✓
5.	Qualty loss		
	(a) sporadic defects	✓	
	(b) chronic defects		✓

explicitly included is the startup loss[2]. We have noted earlier that the difference between sporadic and chronic losses is clearly felt (or seen) in cases of equipment breakdowns and product quality inadequacies. However, the table shows us that, in addition to chronic breakdowns and chronic defects, idling and minor stoppage and speed losses are also hidden. Moreover, there are some setup and adjustment losses which are hidden (whereas the others are quite obvious). As a matter of fact, idling and minor stoppages and reduced speed operations are also overlooked and considered normal exactly in the same way as chronic breakdowns and chronic defects. Two examples of chronic losses have been cited by Shirose [15]. He gives the example of a punch press which has been operating at 200 strokes per minute although it has been designed to run at 250 strokes per minute. In this case, the speed loss of 50 strokes per minute will remain hidden till such time that the operating (or actual) speed is compared with the design speed, or design capacity of the press. The second example is one of setup loss. Shirose cites the case in which setup currently takes one hour. He states that if the setup time can be brought down to 30 minutes by improvement in the technical and operating procedures and methods, then only will the hidden loss of 30 minutes become evident. The above discussion clearly brings out the importance of chronic problems/conditions. We must, therefore, briefly examine how such chronic losses occur, why these losses are neglected and also some of the actions which can be taken to reduce, and if possible, eliminate these chronic losses.

In case of minor stoppage, speed loss and setup and adjustment loss, a chronic loss is often both unanticipated and unnoticed. Thus, in case of these kinds of losses, it is important to recognise the existence of a loss. One must remember that if the loss is not recognised, then, over a period of time, it will be accepted as a part of normal operation. To ensure that such chronic losses are recognized, the following rules must be strictly adhered to:

1. do not neglet any unusual or undesirable condition or occurrence; and
2. wherever possible, compare the actual performance or data, with the design (specified) or optimum value. When the loss is duly recognised, the condition must be thoroughly investigated before planning and implementing any remedial action. It is best to remember that:
   (i) chronic losses are due to multiple causes and in most instances, due to a complex combination of a number of causes, and
   (ii) a hastily or improperly planned action may result in either a symptomatic treatment — a stopgap measure, or an inappropriate or unsuccessful

remedial action, or an incomplete remedial action — one that is not carried out thoroughly or properly.

In cases where the remedial action is either inappropriate or incomplete, then the chronic loss will be neglected. Sometimes the remedial action is prevented because of pressures of production and delivery requirements. In such cases, temporary and stopgap measures are taken and the problem, or the condition persists. This is also tantamount to neglect. Sometimes remedial action is not taken even after the condition has been observed because the extent of the problem, or the economic impact of the condition, is not recognised. When the magnitude of the loss is not clearly understood, in most cases, the tendency is to under-estimate the effect. Sometimes even when the impact is correctly understood, it is assumed that the remedial action would turn out to be too expensive and/or the operational practices would minimise the impact of the problem. The various reasons for neglect of chronic losses in industrial organisations are shown graphically in Fig. 4.3.

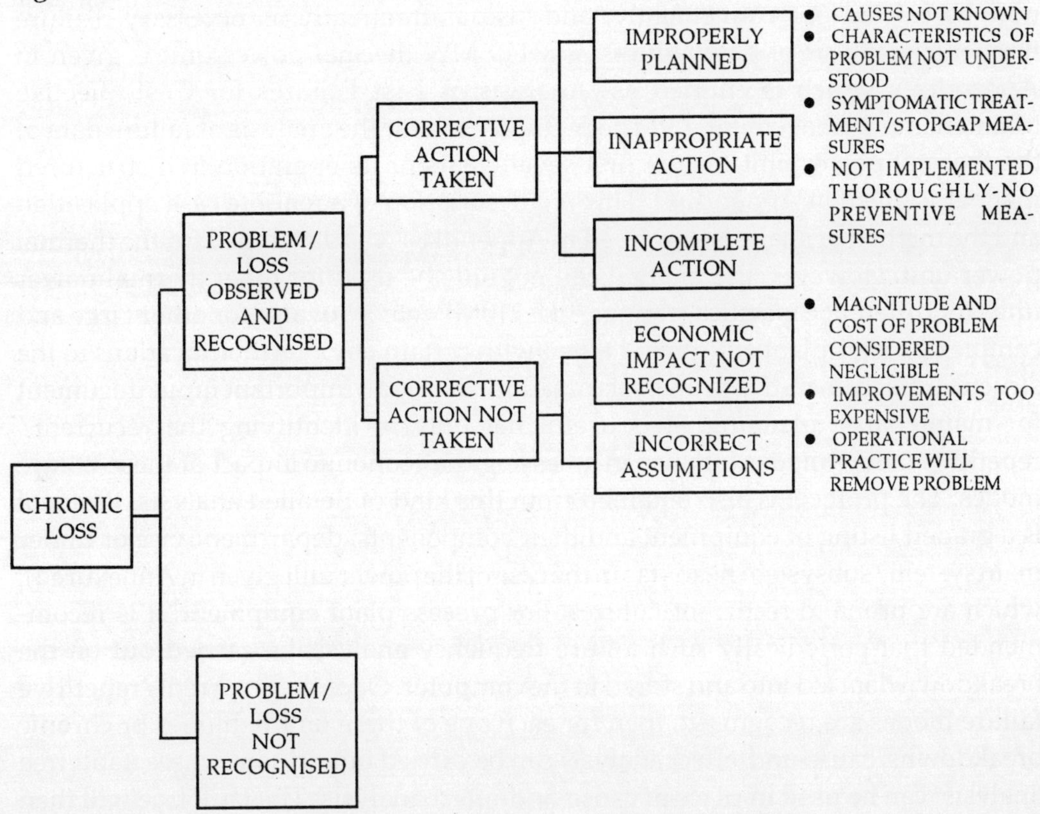

Fig. 4.3. Reasons for Neglect of Chronic Losses

From Fig. 4.3, it is clear that the first step towards reduction, and subsequent elimination, of chronic losses is identification, or recognition, of the problem. In this context, the reader should recall the discussion of maintenance prevention (MP) and maintainability improvement (MI) in Chapter Two. We had noted therein that designing-out-of-maintenace requires, as a first step, the identification of important failure modes and failure situations and this is accomplished through the analysis of past operational and use data as had been shown in Figs. 2.4 and 2.5. In Fig. 2.5, it was shown that the analysis of past data is carried out to identify major breakdowns and also recurring/repetitive, or chronic breakdowns. Chronic losses can be recognised only through such an analysis of past data.[3] This is particularly true in large process plants. This is the first step in the reduction, and subsequent elimination of chronic losses.

In case of capital equipment used in processs plants, without detailed analysis of past failure data, it becomes very difficult to identify the recurrent/repetitive failure modes. With the availability of computers, such analysis of past data can now be carried out conveniently, and also as frequently as necessary. Failure frequency analysis of past failures of a 110 MW thermal power unit is given in Appendix-I, which is entitled as 'Analysis of Past Failures for Cost-Effective Maintenance Management' [2]. The method used for the analysis of failure data of the thermal power unit for the first seven years of its operation in a structured manner is given in Appendix-I. This is a description of a real-life case application and the method of analysis described in Appendix-I was developed for the thermal power unit. However, the method can not only be used for other thermal power units (of different capacities/ratings, like 210MW etc.), but also for other large and complex process plant equipment albeit with certain obvious modifications to the structure. Such an in-depth analysis of failure data is an important input document for maintenance planning. It is useful not only in identifying the recurrent/ repetitive failure modes but also in assessing the economic impact of these failure modes. The protocol is also obtained from this kind of detailed analysis. Protocol is a graded listing of equipment and their components, departmentwise or under main system/subsystem heads (as in the case of the power unit given in Annexure I), which are prone to recurrent failures. For process plant equipment, it is recommended that periodically such failure frequency analysis be carried out on the breakdown data fed into and stored in the computer. Once the recurrent/repetitive failure modes are recognised, then for each one of these failure modes or chronic breakdowns, cause-and-effect analysis can be carried out. In some cases, fault tree analysis[4] can be used in place of cause-and-effect analysis. The fault tree will then have the chronic breakdown as the TOP EVENT, and accordingly, a fault tree will have to be developed for each of these chronic breakdowns. Shirose recommends the use of P-M analysis in place of cause-and-effect analysis [15]. He states that for the identification of causes related to chronic equipment problems, cause-and-effect analysis is not as effective as P-M analysis. P in P-M stands for phenomenon or problem and M stands for mechanism/machinery, manpower and materials.[5] The procedure of P-M analysis consists of the following seven sequential steps:

(i) Problem definition and clarification.

(ii) Physical analysis of the problem.

(iii) Enumeration of all relevent conditions which are needed to produce the problem.

(iv) Evaluation of each of the conditions identified under step (iii) in relation to factors, such as equipment — machinery, tools and accessories, materials and operational methods and practices.

(v) Enumeration of all factors which influence the conditions.

(vi) Investigation of all items listed under step (v) to identify the causes.

(vii) Formulation of corrective action for each of the factors.

TYPES OF MAINTENANCE AND MAINTENANCE SYSTEMS REVISITED

Once the causes of the chronic losses are identified, then corrective actions can be planned and implemented to reduce, and subsequently eliminate, these chronic losses. In Chapter Two, under designing-out-of-maintenance — MP and MI, we have discussed actions directed at improving reliability and maintainability of equipment. One of the methods of reducing chronic breakdown losses is by improving the reliability and maintainability of the production equipment.[6] In Chapter Two, we have also noted that availability is a function of both reliability and maintainability and is thus, a more practical measure of performance of the production equipment. Equipment availability manifests itself either as intrinsic availability or as operational availability. Intrinsic or inherent availability of an equipment is a function of its quality of design[7] and depends on the reliability and maintainability features incorporated into it during its design. Thus, 'the first line on an engineering drawing expressly begins to define the work needed by the maintenance engineer and the downtime and loss to the user, not to speak of the cost of manufacture, quality assurance, sales promotion, etc.' [8]. The operational availability of the equipment, on the other hand, is also dependent on its quality of manufacture. Moreover, deficiencies in assembly of the equipment or assembly defects, installation errors, maloperation, and poor maintenance of the equipment also result in the loss of operational availability. Thus, we may conclude that whereas intrinsic availability is dependent on the reliability and maintainability features incorporated in the design of the equipment, the operational availability also depends on the following:

(i) quality of manufacture — the care that is taken by the equipment manufacturer during the machining and fabrication of the components/parts which together make up equipment,

(ii) care taken during assembly operations — for the subassemblies and the final assembly of the equipment — by the equipment manufacturer,

(iii) installation practice and care taken during the installation of the equipment — most often, the installation is carried out by the equipment manufacturer at the equipment user's premises,

(iv) operational methods and practices — by the operators (who belong to the user organisation), and

(v) maintenance practices and the care taken during maintenance of the equipment by the equipment user.

Work by the pioneers of terotechnology has stressed the importance of reliability and maintainability features incorporated in the equipment design, the quality of manufacture and assembly and also the installation and commissioning methods and practices. These are essential preconditions for ensuring that the equipment functions as per the design/design specifications. In Chapter Two, in our discussion of designing-out-of maintenance, we had discussed the work of Finniston, in which he had stated that not enough attention was being paid to the activities of installation and commissioning. Accordingly, he had stressed that, in addition to reliability and maintainability features during design of an equipment, special attention should be paid to detailed planning and proper execution of installation and commissioning jobs. However, the loss of availability due to inadequate quality of design, quality of manufacture and assembly, and improper installation and commissioning practices and methods is much less than the loss of availability resulting from improper/inadequate and inconsistent practices and methods adopted during the operation and for the maintenance of the equipment [15]. Correct, adequate and consistent methods and practices used during operation and for maintenance of the equipment are necessary to maintain an optimum equipment condition so that it may be used fully as per its design specifications. TPM stresses the importance of these functions and activities and states that functions and activities which are necessary to maintain the optimum equipment conditions are as important as the essential conditions for optimum functioning of the equipment, that is, correct and adequate operation and maintenance of the equipment is as important as the factors of equipment design, manufacture, assembly, installation and commissioning, These two together give the user of the equipment the ability to use the equipment fully, as desired by him and as designed.

The activities necessary for the optimum operation and maintenance of the equipment are given in Fig. 4.4. In the figure, starting from the principles of productive maintenance and terotechnology enunciated in Chapters Two and Three, and following the logic described in the preceding paragraph, we have deduced the five activities necessary for achieving zero breakdowns. These five activities are maintaining basic equipment conditions, maintaining operating standards, restoring equipment to optimum functioning, improving design weaknesses and improving operating and maintenance skills. We will discuss these five activities together with the four phases of implementation of zero breakdowns later in this section, but for the moment let us get back to Fig. 4.4. Four of the five activities have been explicitly shown in the figure. However, the fifth activity, namely improving operating and maintenance skills, has been broken up in two parts. These two parts are preventing repair/restoration errors and preventing maloperation of the equipment. The two parts, have, in turn, been included in the two arms of the figure. The reason for doing this needs a closer inspection of the figure. One arm of the figures includes activities such as restoration, improvement of design weaknesses, and prevention of restoration errors, whereas the other arm includes activities like the maintenance of basic equipment conditions, maintenance of operating standards, and prevention of maloperation of equipment. The former are activities which are part of the maintenance function and need to be carried out by the maintenance personnel, whereas the latter are activities which can and should be carried out by the operators of the equipment.

Restoration is repair and is necessary because, over time, deterioration takes place. The thing to remember is that when small changes are repeatedly neglected, then they can also develop into major breakdowns. Restoration is an activity of returning the equipment and/or its constituent component(s) to its/their original and proper, or design, condition. Restoration, thus, attempts to return the production equipment to its original, design, state and this is done by taking action to detect deterioration and also corrective measures to eliminate its source. In TPM,

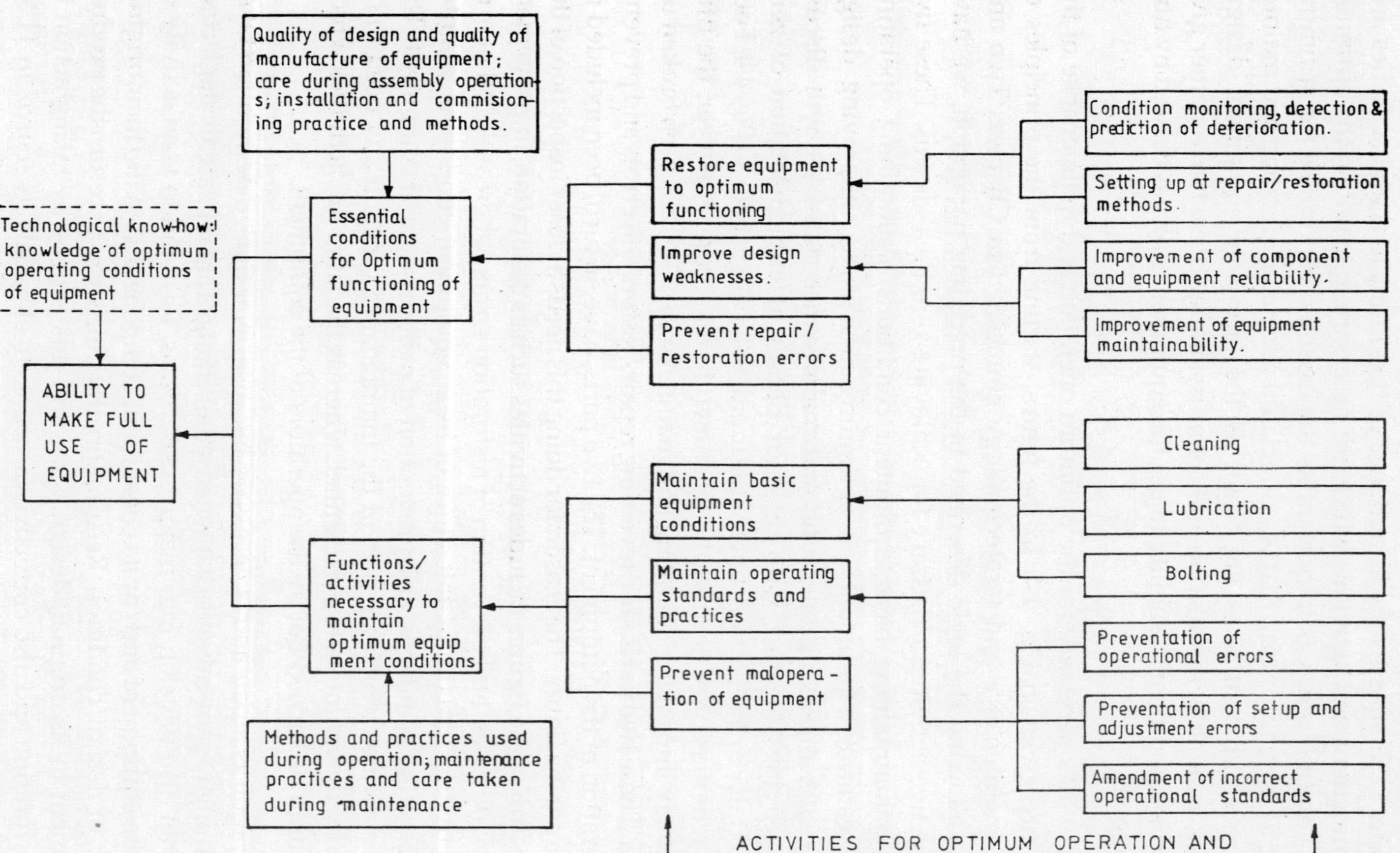

Fig. 4.4. Optimum Operation and Maintenance of Equipment

we define two kinds of deterioration and these are natural deterioration and accelerated deterioration. Natural deterioration is the normal wear-out that occurs inspite of proper use and maintenance. This kind of deterioration is duly recognised by the designer and accounted for by him. On the other hand, accelerated deterioration is caused by human beings and occurs over a much shorter period of time. Most often, it results from the following factors:

(i) neglect of vital functions required for maintaining optimum equipment conditions, such as cleaning and essential lubrication, and

(ii) neglect of natural deterioration.

Accelerated deterioration can, and must, be prevented in order to derive the full use of equipment by maximising equipment availability.

Cleaning also reveals deterioration which when neglected, tends to increase over time and spreads to other parts. Sometimes a single loose bolt in a flange coupling of a pipe joint can cause a major accident (and resultant breakdown), and a loose bolt in a plummer block of a large end bearing can cause a major accident. Moreover, a loose bolt can increase shaking, which, in turn, loosens other bolts and causes equipment breakdown. Thus, proper bolting, that is, ensuring that there are no broken or loose connecting parts, such as nuts, bolts and washers, can also prevent breakdowns. Cleaning, lubrication and bolting are, therefore, activities which are essential to maintain basic equipment conditions, as shown in Fig. 4.4. In Chapter Two, we have noted that periodic preventive maintenance, which includes activities like daily and weekly oiling and greasing, changing of oil, changing of filter and cleaning of the equipment and accessories etc., is a necessary part of the maintenance of the equipment and also that such activities have to be carried out right from the beginning to the final retirement, or disposal, of the equipment, at pre-determined intervals. Periodic preventive maintenance can, in turn, be broken up in two parts. These two clearly identifiable and separate parts are as follows:

(i) activities such as cleaning, lubrication, bolting, and such periodic inspections of an equipment which can be carried out by the operators, and

(ii) inspections which require equipment shutdown and/or maintenance and diagnostic skills, periodic replacements of wearing parts, programmed replacements of capital items, such as bearings, and periodic overhauls.

Whereas researchers and practioners in the areas of preventive maintenance and terotechnology had always recognised the importance of periodic preventive maintenance, they had not recognised the importance of this break-up. This is necessary to bring into focus the simpler, but essential tasks which fall under the first category and also to ensure that these tasks get done and chronic losses are not neglected. TPM recognises that these activites are often neglected since operators do not carry them out and maintenance personnel are hard-pressed for time and opportunity to perform them. TPM stresses the importance of these activities and also recognises that the operators of the equipment are in the best position to carry out the activities. Under TPM, the operators are required to carry out these activities of cleaning, lubrication, bolting and daily and weekly/monthly inspections which can be classified under a third type of maintenance, and can be termed as autonomous maintenance. Thus, under TPM, we have three types of maintenance, namely, corrective maintenance, autonomous maintenance, and preventive maintenance. This is shown in Fig.4.5 and the sub-classifications of these three types of maintenance are also shown in Fig. 4.5. If the reader compares Fig. 4.5 with Fig. 2.3 and our earlier discussion of types of maintenance in Chapter Two, he will notice that the only difference is breaking up of periodic preventive maintenance and creation of a third type of maintenance — autonomous maintenance. We will discuss autonomous maintenance in greater detail in the next chapter, but we conclude our discussion of types of maintenance by noting that this classification is most appropriate since it is most logical, as evident from Figs. 2.1, 2.2, 2.3 and 4.5 and our discussions in Chapter Two and in the preceding paragraphs.

As shown in Fig. 4.5, the three maintenance regimes are corrective maintenance, autonomous maintenance, and preventive maintenance. Corrective maintenance includes both breakdown maintenance and maintenance activity directed at reliability and maintainability improvement of the equipment, and preventive maintenance includes both periodic activities which need to be carried out by maintenance personnel (as indicated in the preceding paragraph) and predictive maintenance. Predictive maintenance is also known as condition-based maintenance and consists of activities of equipment diagnosis and condition monitoring. We have already discussed corrective maintenance and condition-based maintenance in detail in Chapter Two and we will discuss autonomous maintenance in the next chapter.

Production equipment are becoming larger and more complex. Greater complexity has arisen from the fact that production processes being adopted involve severe operating conditions and in many cases, such equipment employ single stream series design with minimal redundancies [6]. On one hand, larger equipment use greater number of components, and on the other, safety margins in design have been reduced substantially thus, increasing the strain on the components. The

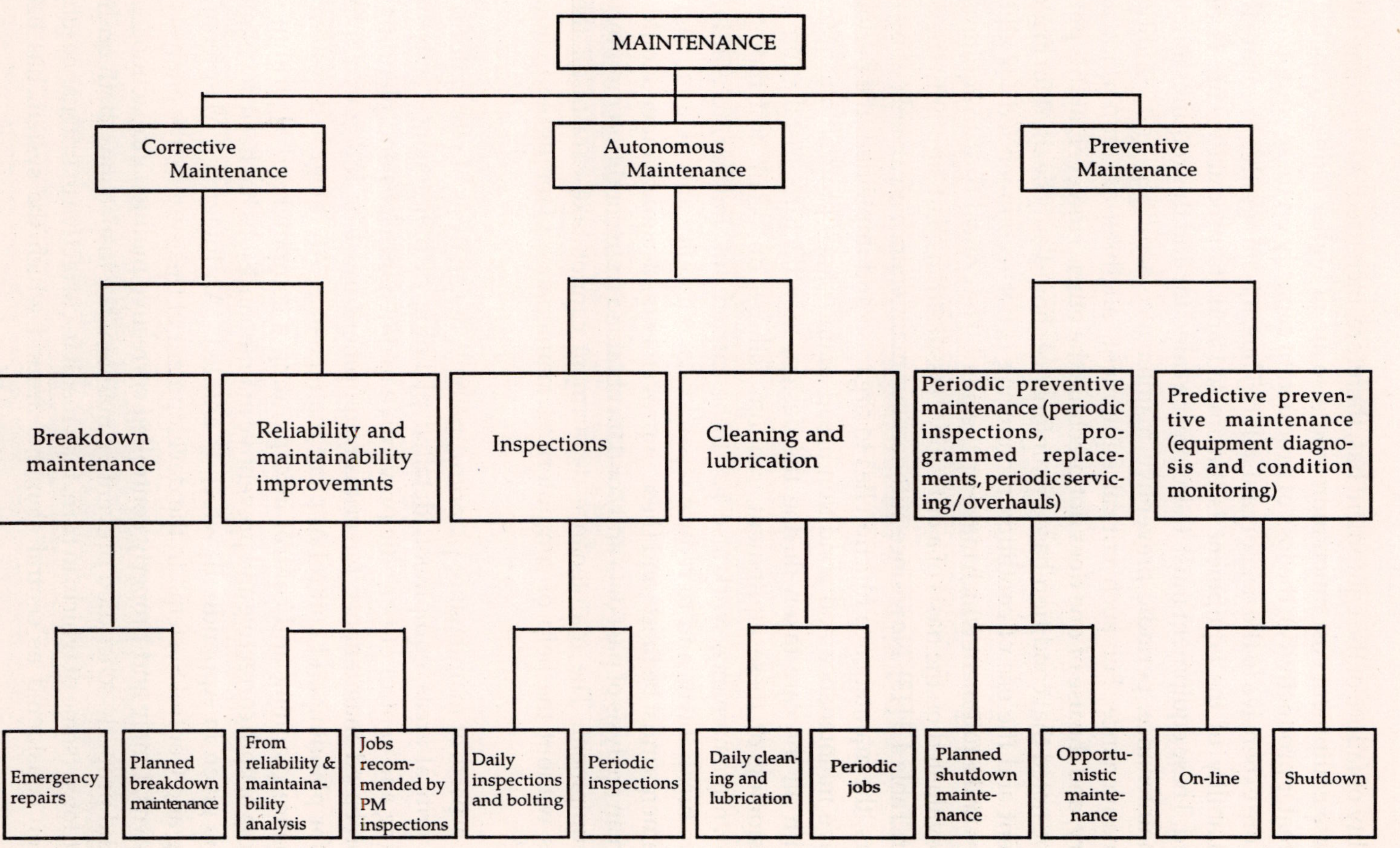

Fig. 4.5. Types of Maintenance — **Classification Under TPM**

probability of failure of the equipment has, therefore, increased. At the same time, since these equipment cost much more and also are of higher ratings (capable of much greater productivity), the loss of production capacity on these equipment is much more expensive to the user organisation. Thus, it is imperative to ensure that the availability of the equipment is maximised and its productive life is also increased. These equipment must, therefore, be cared for and this requires autonomous maintenance, periodic preventive maintenance activities, and condition-based maintenance. For such critical equipment, all three are important and necessary, and the use of one does not preclude the other. However, at this point, it must be noted that condition-based maintenance should only be used for critical equipment and the use of condition monitoring is not recommended for all the machines and equipment which make up the plant. The criticality of an equipment may be evaluated on the basis of a criticality classification chart similar to the one shown in Table 4.3 [18]. Now since autonomous maintenance is carried out by the operators, the maintenance function has to organise and implement the periodic preventive maintenance and condition-based maintenance programmes. Moreover, with all the care taken during the design, manufacture, installation and commissioning of these equipment, random failures do occur and therefore, breakdown maintenance work also has to be carried out. Further, to eliminate repetitive breakdowns and to reduce repair costs, reliability and maintainability improvements must be made and these improvements/design changes should be based on an analysis of past data and/or data obtained from condition monitoring of the equipment. The maintenance department cannot take care of all these activities without the help of computerised maintenance planning and control systems.

All aspects of maintenance planning, namely, the analysis of past failures to identify critical areas/equipment, detailed planning of maintenance activities, scheduling and control of periodic preventive maintenance jobs and planning of condition-based maintenance for critical equipment must be integrated into a system for planning and control of plant maintenance. An integrated system of maintenance planning and control incorporating a computerised algorithm for scheduling of both corrective and preventive maintenance jobs has been developed [3] and is given in Appendix II, which is entitled 'An Integrated Maintenance Planning and Control System.' In the development of this system, the analysis of breakdowns, timely and properly controlled corrective maintenance actions and timely and properly scheduled preventive maintenance inspections, both on-line and shutdown (some of which, in turn, may result in corrective maintenance jobs), have been considered as central elements around which the system has been

Table 4.3: An Illustrative Equipment Criticality Classification System

Effect of breakdown on	*Equipment Classification (A highest and C lowest)*		
	A	*B*	*C*
Safety - effect on the workplace, including human beings	Will result in a serious accident which will cause seven or more days of lost production	Will result in an accident which will stop production; or operation of equipment regulated by law	No risk of an accident and no production stoppage
Environment	Effects will extend outside the factory and will cause seven or more days of lost production	Effects will extend outside the factory; or operation of equipment regulated by law	No risk of environmental damage; pollution caused can be taken care of inside the factory
Product quality	Will directly affect product quality	Downstream processes will be seriously affected.	Negligible effect on downstream processes.
Production quantity/rate	Production will be stopped for seven days or more	Will seriously affect work in other sections.	No effect on other sections
Maintenance	Breakdown frequency/ maintenance cost very high	Breakdown frequency twice or more per year and repair cost Rs. 300,000 or more	Breakdown frequency less than twice per year and repair cost less than Rs. 300,000.

constructed. The job card, or job order, has been retained as both the instruction sheet and control instrument for all the corrective maintenance activities and periodic preventive maintenance jobs. The procedure has been kept simple with the minimum number of inputs and only such outputs, or reports, are produced which are really necessary for the purposes of maintenance planning and control. The system proposed in Appendix II may have to be altered by way of reconstruction of some of the forms and type of reports to suit the size of the company and the specific factors affecting maintenance, but the framework of the system will be applicable universally.

IMPLEMENTATION OF ZERO BREAKDOWNS—FOUR PHASES AND FIVE ACTIVITIES

Having discussed the differences between the two types of breakdowns, chronic and sporadic losses, and types of maintenance and maintenance regimes in the context of TPM, we are now in a position to discuss the method of implementation of the programme of zero breakdowns. Before we go to the five activities which are necessary for achieving zero breakdowns and the four phases of implementation of the programme, let us return briefly to our discussion of chronic and sporadic losses. This time around we will be more specific and only discuss the causes of chronic breakdowns. Sporadic breakdowns are sudden problems and are generally easy to restore. As opposed to this, chronic breakdowns are generally difficult to eliminate. Neglected function reduction conditions which are treated as minor generally lead to chronic breakdowns. Chronic breakdowns cause accelerated deterioration of the equipment and its constituent components, and also result in one or more of the five other major equipment losses, such as increased setup and adjustment, frequent idling and minor stoppages, reduced speed or reduced capacity, quality and yield losses, and also energy and manpower losses. The determination of the causes of a chronic breakdown is the first step towards its elimination and this requires a detailed cause-and-effect analysis. All the possible causes must be considered and this, in turn, is only possible if the analysis is carried out in a structured manner. Structured analysis enables the total enumeration of all possible causes of a chronic breakdown by listing out the possible causes under different heads, or major causes, which, in this case, are as follows:

1. Equipment design problems.
2. Daily, or periodic, maintenance problems (or, in TPM terminology, autonomous maintenance problems).
3. Preventive maintenance problems.
4. Equipment improvement problems.
5. Problems with maintenance technologies and skills.

A cause-and-effect diagram which shows the possible causes of chronic breakdowns is given as Fig. 4.6. A closer observation of Fig. 4.6 will indicate to the reader the fact that chronic breakdowns are the result of weaknesses in the equipment management system. These weaknesses include inherent design weaknesses, absence of any attempt at reliability and maintainability improvement of the equipment, conditions wherein only emergency/stopgap repairs are possible and inadequate daily maintenance leading to accelerated deterioration of the equipment.

Zero breakdown implies the minimisation of all breakdowns — function loss and function reduction breakdowns, and controllable and uncontrollable breakdowns. Controllable breakdowns must be eliminated and the frequency and severity of uncontrollable breakdowns[8] must be minimised. Action must be taken to minimise the incidence of chronic breakdowns, and this requires work in the

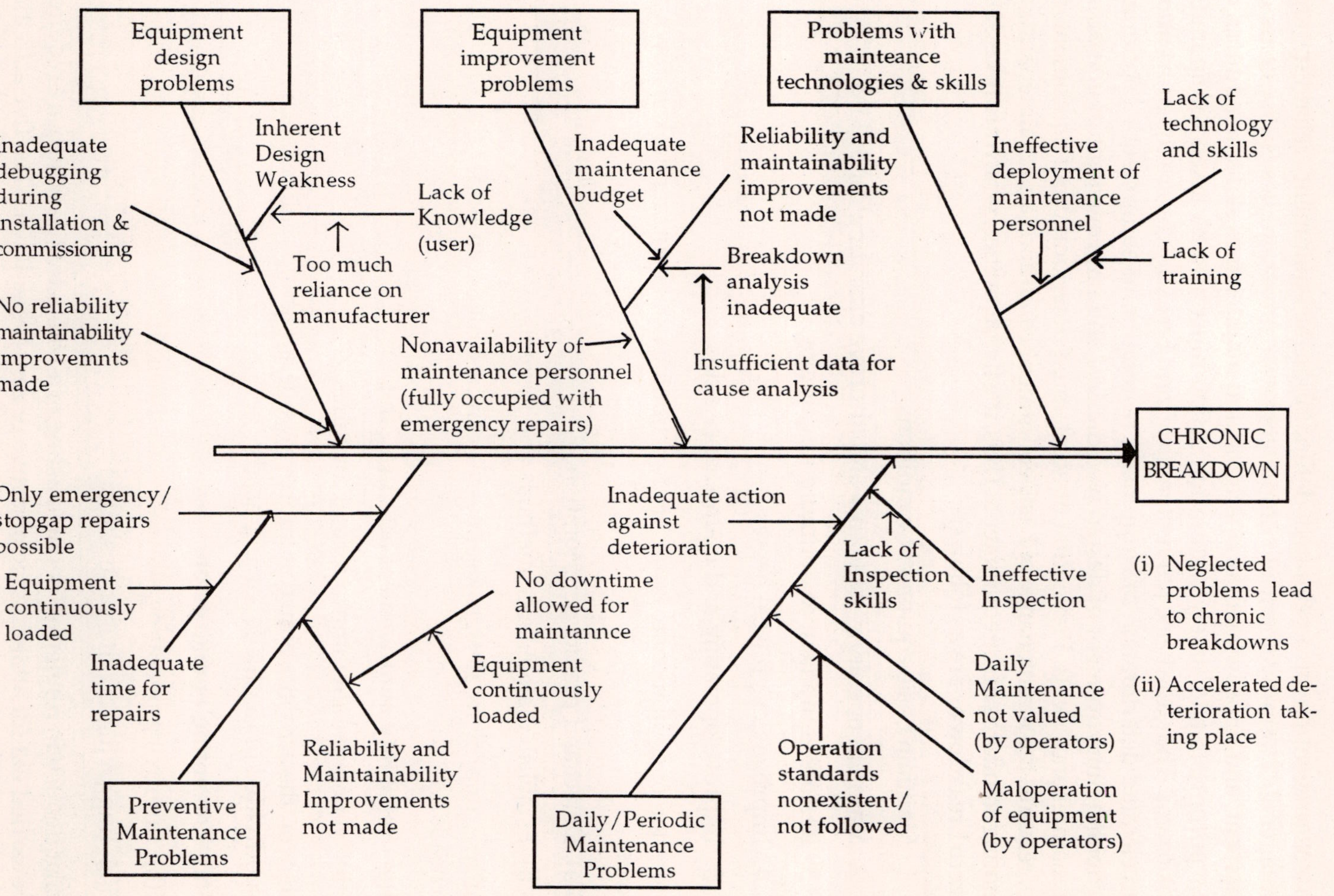

Fig. 4.6. Causes of Chronic Breakdowns

areas of prevention of accelerated deterioration of equipment, reliability and maintainability improvement of components and subassemblies/subsystems of equipment, and improvement of operating and maintenance skills. In addition to this, appropriate and timely restoration action must also be taken for sporadic breakdowns. Thus, the basic requirements of zero breakdowns are the prevention of accelerated deterioration of equipment, restoration of equipment to optimum functioning, improvement of design weaknesses, and improvement of operating and maintenance skills. Prevention of accelerated deterioration of equipment, in turn, requires the maintenance of basic equipment conditions and maintenance of operating standards of the equipment. Thus, the five activities, which are necessary for zero breakdowns are as follows:

1. Maintain basic equipment conditions.
2. Maintain operating standards and improve operating conditions.
3. Restore equipment to optimum functioning.
4. Improve design weaknesses.
5. Improve operating and maintenance skills.

Restoration of equipment to optimum functioning can be further broken down as follows:

3(a) Detect and predict deterioration.

3(b) Establish maintenance methods and systems.

Similarly, improving design weaknesses can be broken up under the following two heads:

4(a) Reliability improvement activities, and

4(b) Maintainability improvement activities.

Moreover, the activities aimed at improving operating and maintenance skills can be subdivided under the following heads:

5(a) Preventing human errors.

5(b) Improving operating skills.

5(c) Improving maintenance skills.

Similar deduction results in a detailed listing of all the activities which are required to be carried out for attaining the objective of zero breakdowns. The five activities for zero breakdowns are shown in Fig. 4.7. The detailing of these basic activities—further breakdown to obtain a detailed list of activities required—is also given in Fig. 4.7.

The list of the activities given in Fig. 4.7 need the attention of both operation and maintenance departments. Some of these activities have to be carried out by the operators and the remaining have to be done by maintenance personnel. All the activities shown under maintenance of basic equipment conditions have to be taken care of by the operating personnel. Similarly, all the activities under improvement of design weaknesses have to be carried out by the maintenance department. The remaining three basic activities, namely, maintenance of operating conditions, restoration of equipment and improvement of operating and maintenance skills, require the combined attention of both the operation and maintenance departments. For example, in case of restoration of equipment, whereas activity 3(b) — establishment of maintenance methods and systems — is the responsibility of the maintenance department, activity 3(a) — detection and prediction of deterioration — needs the attention of both operators and the maintenance personnel. Daily, and also some periodic equipment inspections are the responsibility of the operators and the remaining activities under 3(a) need the attention of the maintenance personnel. Similarly, coming to activity 5, whereas 5(b) and 5(c) pertain to the operation and maintenance departments respectively, activity 5(a) has to be shared by them. This need for joint responsibility is one of the basic characteristics of TPM. We have noted this in Chapter One but we must stress this again. If TPM is to succeed, then the 'I operate, you fix' attitude of old has to be replaced by the principle of joint ownership of equipment/machines.

All these activities cannot be implemented overnight and for that matter, nor can they be carried out in one sweep. We must remember that in most cases, the manufacturing organisation (contemplating the implementation of TPM) is in a state of reactive maintenance. This state is characterised by the following attributes:

(i) only emergency and stopgap repairs are undertaken by the maintenance department;

(ii) problems are attended only when they are brought to the notice of the maintenance department;

(iii) training in maintenance skills is viewed as an unnecessary expense;

(iv) the maintenance department tries to keep some records but the quality of data is poor and an organised maintenance system does not exist; and

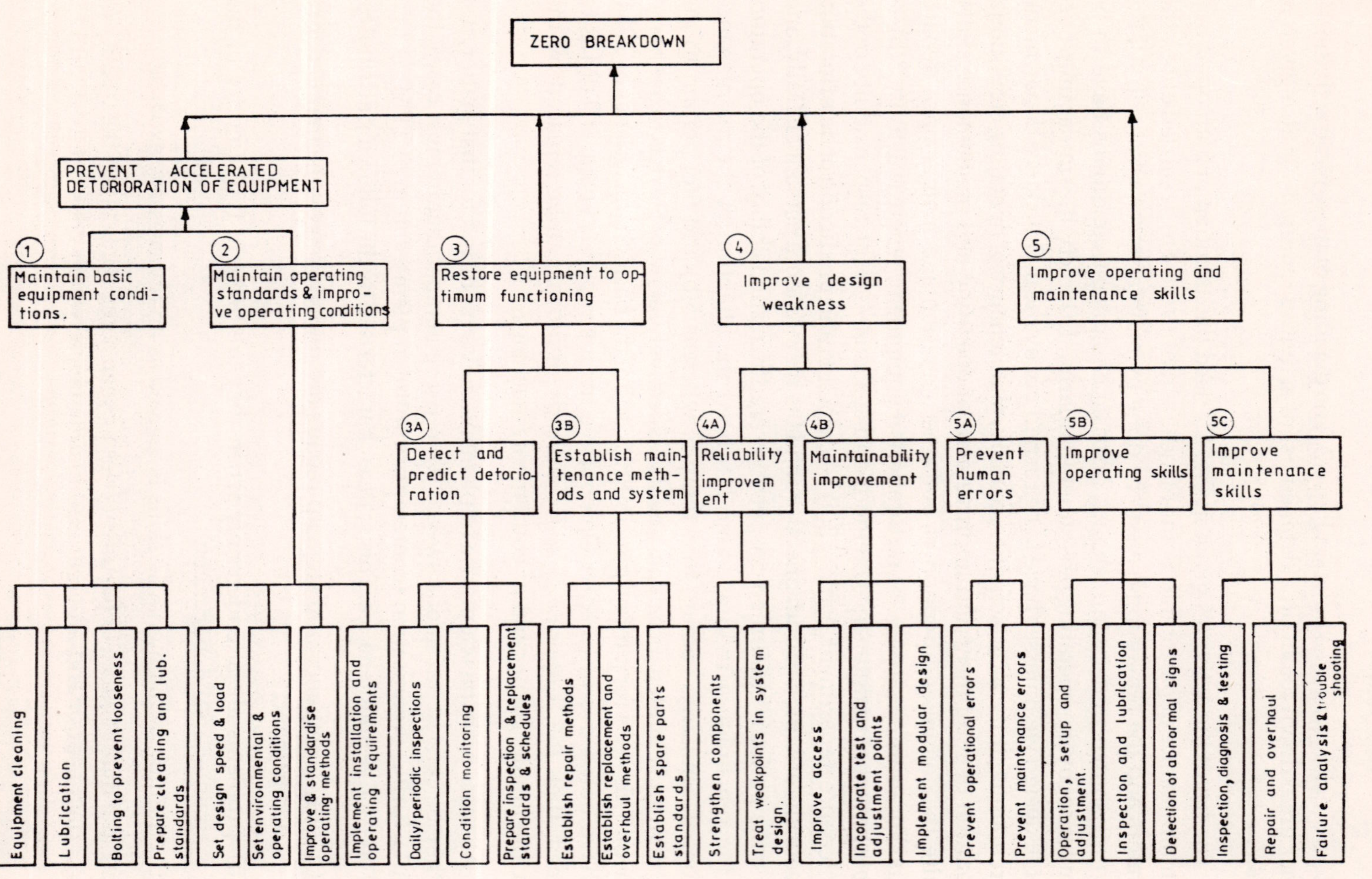

Fig. 4.7. Five Activities for Zero Breakdown

(v) top management attitude towards the maintenance function can be best summed up by the following remark:

> "We don't know why the equipment breaks down - that is what we pay maintenance for" (to see that it does not) [23]

There are many companies in this state and in many cases implementation of zero breakdowns has to be done in this kind of environment. Going from reactive maintenance to productive maintenance requires phased implementation; specifically the implementation of zero breakdowns has to be done in four phases. These four phases are given and explained in Table 4.4.

Phased implementation, and the use of the four phases, becomes necessary because of the following basic reasons:

(i) Accelerated deterioration of the equipment has to be effectively arrested and the equipment has to be taken to a state of natural deterioration. Moreover, thereafter, the basic equipment conditions and the basic operating standards of the equipment have to be maintained as otherwise the equipment will again revert to a state of accelerated deterioration. This requires adequate preparation and involvement of both operating and maintenance personnel.

(ii) The effective application of periodic replacements, servicing and periodic overhauls requires longer and stabler life spans of components and equipment. If this is not the case, then periodic preventive maintenance would turn out to be ineffective and also expensive. In one of the earliest published applications of preventive maintenance in a sinter plant of an integrated iron and steel-works, the effectiveness of preventive maintenance was questioned [22]. This was primarily because the equipment had not been restored to a reasonable state of functioning and equipment failures were uncontrolled and too frequent.

(iii) Similarly, the application of condition-based maintenance needs as a prerequisite the proper application of periodic preventive maintenance. Unless the equipment and the components have reasonably long life, the operation of the equipment cannot be studied/observed over a period which is long enough to determine the prognostic parameters and setting up of the acceptance levels of the parameters. This needs an observation of deterioration/wear over a long period of time.

Thus, we see that TPM is a method of achieving the aim of maintenance-oriented plant management not via an easy route of capital investment but via a positive investment in human resources in order to fully utilise existing equipment through improved equipment availability and through

Table 4.4. Four Phases of Implementation of Zero Breakdowns

Pre-TPM Implementation Phase	*Implementation of Zero Breakdowns*			
	Phase I	*Phase II*	*Phase III*	*Phase IV*
Reactive Maintenance	*Prepare for Periodic Preventive Maintenance*	*Periodic Preventive Maintenance and Designing-Out of Maintenance Activities*		*Predictive, or Condition-Based, Maintenance*
State of affairs:	*Activities:*	*Activities:*	*Activities:*	*Activities:*
* Only emergency repairs undertaken * Skills training viewed as unnecessary * No organised maintenance information system * Some records kept and quality of data poor. *Activities to be undertaken* * Consider activities in phases I to IV and develop appropriate maintenance organisation * Assess ability and skills of maintenance personnel and determine gaps * Setup a spare parts management system * Setup a maintenance planning and control system (computerisation of the manual work order system similar to one given in Appendix II)	* Through Pareto analysis of past equipment performance data, identify critical equipment. * Restore these critical equipment to a reasonable state of functioning by removing visible and pressing problems through repair/replacement of components. * Analyse operation of critical equipment and for them - set up operating standards, and - set up cleaning and lubrication standards.	* Extend work done in phase I to other equipment (not so critical) * Take up reliability and maintainability improvement of critical equipment by improving design weaknesses * Improve operating skills * Improve maintenance skills * Prevent operating errors. * Prevent maintenance errors.	* Set up periodic preventive maintenance standards namely, - inspection standards: daily and periodic - replacement standards - servicing/overhaul intervals and methods * Study the operation of critical equipment, and for them determine - prognostic parameters to be monitored - condition monitoring method to be used - acceptance level/acceptability criterion.	* Start condition-based maintenance of critical equipment * Carry out failure analysis to determine failure frequencies and dominant (repetitive) failure modes * Carry out technical analysis for components - Fatigue - Rupture/Shear, etc. * Carry out corrective maintenance work based on above analysis for maximising availability and extending life.

labour-saving (improved maintainability resulting in smaller repair times) as a result of plant and equipment modifications.

Minimising Setup and Adjustment Losses

In the manufacturing industry,[9] for most process designers and planners, setup time reduction has become a very important issue. With smaller batch sizes, it is now imperative to reduce the setup time. However, when the process designer or shop engineer talks of setup time, he is talking about the total non-operation time (time during which the machine, or equipment, is shut down) between the completion of one component, or product, and the start of production of another component, or product, on the same equipment, or machine. This generally includes both setup and adjustment times. If this time is reduced, then obviously the batch, or lot, size which is economical to run reduces and this reduction in the economic batch size gives the industrial organisation the needed flexibility. Increase in flexibility makes life much easier for both the production planning and sales departments allowing them to be more responsive to customers' requirements. This increases competitiveness and may make the difference between winning or losing a customer order, or a contract. Thus, reduction of setup and adjustment time not only increases equipment availability by reducing downtime, but also increases flexibility of the manufacturing process.

Setup is recognised as a necessary part of all processes. This is more evident in the manufacturing industry wherein there is the setup of machine tools, involving exchanges of jigs and fixtures, changing of tools, setting of speeds and feeds, making trials production runs(s), inspecting parts and adjustment of machines, tools etc., or setting up of presses, which involves exchange of dies, making trial runs, checking of trial part and making necessary adjustments. However, setup is also an essential part of the process in batch production operations carried out in continuous process industries, such as chemicals and pharmaceuticals. Herein setup may include washing, purging, disinfecting and charging with fresh materials, in addition to setting the temperature, pressure, time etc., making trial production runs, checking quality of the product, or yield of the process and making the necessary adjustments. Setup time, as understood in the industry, thus includes both setup and adjustment times. The time that is spent after the setting up of the machine, or the equipment, in getting it to produce a quality product is the adjustment time. If the setup is perfect in the first place, then this additional time will not be required. Thus, whereas setup loss cannot be totally eliminated, the loss of time for adjustment can be eliminated. Therefore, in this section, we will discuss measures to minimise setup loss and eliminate adjustments. We will divide this section into the following three subsections:

1. Improving setups.
2. Eliminating adjustments
3. A structured programme for improving setup and adjustments.

IMPROVING SETUPS

The setup loss is the loss of operating time, or the downtime, due to a setup. Thus, this is the time during which the machine, or the equipment, is shut down. But there are a number of things which can be done when the machine is running, that is, there are a number of setup activities which can be carried out when the equipment is in operation. Such activities are called external setup activities. Therefore, the most important thing in improving setups is recognising the difference between external and internal setup activities. The difference between external and internal setup activites is given below:

External setup activities are those which can be carried out while the machine, or the equipment, is in operation and for which the machine does not need to be shut down. As opposed to this, internal setup activities can only be performed when the machine, or the equipment, is shut down, or stopped.

Once we recognise this difference, then we can study setup operations with a view to separating external and internal setup activities. Thereafter, we can convert as many of the internal setup activities to external setups as possible. Once this is done, then one can take steps to shorten the internal setup time. Conversion of internal setup activities to external setup is possible since, in most industrial processes, many external setup tasks are hidden in the internal setup time. There are a number of internal setup tasks (carried out after the machine is stopped) which can be done earlier while the machine is in operation processing an earlier job.[10] Dies and jigs can be prepared and kept ready, and cutting tools and spanners/ wrenches can be kept ready close to the machine. Thus there are five fundamental steps required for improving setups and these are as follows:

1. Study the setup operation, as it is currently being performed, and break up the operation into its 'elements,' or activities. (Some of these activities would be external, whereas the remaining would be internal).

2. Carry out a thorough method study of the setup operation (address each activity and ask three basic questions — what?, why? and how?), and
   a) eliminate unnecessary activities (or 'foreign elements' as the industrial engineers call them) and identify activities which are essential for the process,
   b) combine activities, wherever possible, and
   c) simplify and improve the setup operation.
3. After the eliminate-combine-simplify step, check the activities of the simplified operation and separate the external and internal setup activities.
4. Convert as many of the internal setup activities to external setups as possible.
5. Shorten the internal setup time.

The fourth step of conversion of internal setup activities to external setup requires considerable thought and ingenuity. However, the following list of suggestions can serve as useful guidelines:

(i) For a number of internal setup activities, there is a need for preparation and arrangement, such as collection of hand-tools, torque wrenches, slip gauges and templates. These can be separated and the task of collection and keeping them properly arranged close to the equipment can be carried out externally.

(ii) Fixtures, dies, jigs, and even gauges, can be pressembled and kept ready.

(iii) Cutting tools can be preset so that the task of centreing and adjusting on the machine can be eliminated.

(iv) Standardisation of fixture parts and use of these standard parts can eliminate the need for using shims and spacers during internal setup.

At the end of this step of externalisation, wherever possible, the final list of external setup activities is available with the planner. Then the planner must determine the preparations to be made, or the method of carrying out the external setup. This method must be documented as a written step-by-step procedure and this document must be used during the actual setup. This ensures that the external setup tasks of preparation, presetting, preassembly etc. are carried out properly and all the tools and accessories are in proper condition and position before the internal setup starts. If this does not take place, then these tasks will have to be carried out during the internal setup. Formalisation and standardisation is as necessary for external setup as it is for internal setup.

The fifth step of shortening the internal setup time is the most important step, because it is, after all, the basic objective of the whole exercise. The smaller the time required for internal setup, the faster the equipment can start producing the new/next component, or product. The most important thing in reduction of internal setup time is the standardisation and documentation of the work procedures. This ensures the avoidance of unexpected problems and delays. There are some measures which can effectively reduce the internal setup time and these are as follows:

(i) Simplifying clamping mechanisms — use of standard clamps, reducing the number of bolts and nuts, standardisation of bolts and nuts used, and use of more efficient and quick-acting clamping devices (both quick-clamping and quick-release), such as hydraulic, cam-operated, and pneumatic clamps.

(ii) Use of parallel activities, by identifying activities which can be performed simultaneously by two or more persons.

(iii) Use of division of labour and optimising the number of persons in the crew (people should not come in each others way).

At this stage of our discussion, we must bring out the importance of discipline and training in improvement of setup and adjustment. Discipline in the workplace is derived from two of the 5 Ss used in Japanese industrial organisations—*seiri*, which stands for orderliness, or organisation, and *seiton*, which stands for tidiness. Orderliness is important in setup jobs and has to do with removing unnecessary items/things, proper arrangement of items and allocation of space for placing, storing and stacking, and development of standards for organisation of the workplace. Tidiness comes from strict adherence to these standards. Orderliness and tidiness are necessary to ensure that one does not have to:

* search for anything,
* unnecessarily move anything, and
* use anything that is not specified in the procedures.

These three simple rules are derived from *seiri* and *seiton* and they must be kept in mind. Training ensures proper adherence to improved methods and standards. Training should be such that strict adherence to the procedures becomes second nature for the operators and setup crews.

ELIMINATING ADJUSTMENTS

After a setup is completed, in most cases, some adjustments have to be made to ensure that the product meets the quality requirements (or the component meets the drawing specifications). The ultimate goal is the elimination of all adjustments, and it must be stressed that this goal is attainable since, as noted earlier, if all factors are set to specifications during the external and internal setups then this can be achieved. However, when the setup operations are first analysed, it is found that whereas there are some adjustments which are avoidable and can be eliminated, there are some unavoidable adjustments, which cannot be eliminated, unless the mechanism, or the equipment, is redesigned and modified. Accordingly, initially the aim is the elimination of all avoidable adjustments and minimisation of the time lost on account of essential unavoidable adjustments. For this, all the adjustments which are currently being made should be taken up one at a time and an indepth analysis of the purpose, cause(s), the actual methods used, and the final effectiveness (of the adjustment) should be carried out.

Adjustments are usually made to accurately position a job, or a stop, centre a cutting tool, and set the depth of cut, the feed, or set the timer, or some other parameter on the production equipment. Therefore, the purpose of adjustments falls under three main heads, namely, positioning, centreing and setting, and the setting can be done on a dial, with the help of a handwheel, or with the help of slip gauges, or marking block, or with the help of set screws. The primary causes of adjustments are as follows:

1. Accumulation of errors—this requires use of shims and this cause accounts for a large percentage of the total adjustment time.
2. Improper work methods, or procedures, which are not clear to the operators, or setup crews.
3. Lack of standards, datum planes, reference surfaces, or marks.
4. Lack of a measuring method or devices.
5. Insufficient rigidity of the equipment, or an accessory, or a fixture.
6. Inherent inadequacy of the mechanism, or the equipment which calls for intervention by the operator.

Whereas some of these causes can be removed comparatively easily, some others may be difficult to remove and may call for major equipment redesign and modifications. The latter gives rise to unavoidable adjustments. The remedies for the avoidable and unavoidable adjustments are given in Table 4.5. The unavoidable adjustments cannot be eliminated, but the remedies given in the table will streamline the procedure and make it more convenient for the operators, or setup crews, to perform the adjustment. This will help minimise the loss of time needed for the adjustment. The importance of standardisation of the procedures, documenting it, training the operators and having them practise it cannot be overemphasized. Moreover, the fact that all adjustments must ultimately be eliminated must not be lost sight of. All inadequacies must be addressed and necessary modifications must be made to the mechanism or the equipment. Towards this end, the setting of annual improvement targets can be helpful.

Table 4.5. Causes and Remedies of Adjustments in Setup Operations

Causes of Adjustments	*Prognosis/ decision*	*Remedies*
Accumulation of errors	Avoidable/eliminate	Increase precision
Improper work methods	—	Standardise
Lack of standards, datum planes, reference surfaces/marks	—	Select
Insufficient rigidity of the fixture/work-holding device	—	Strengthen/Improve clamping
Insufficient rigidity of the equipment	Unavoidable/minimise	Establish adjustment procedure
Lack of measuring methods	—	Set fixed value/Use constant value settings
Inherent inadequacy of mechanism/equipment	—	Train and improve skills.

A STRUCTURED PROGRAMME FOR IMPROVING SETUP AND ADJUSTMENTS

Adjustments cannot be separated from setups and any attempt at improvement must be directed at both setup and adjustments. Improvement of setup and adjustment operations requires a systematic programme which must look at both setup and adjustment in the context of the important factors of the manufacturing process, such as the characteristics of the machines and accessories, tools, jigs and fixtures, etc., and the proposed method, or the 'process plan,' and also the desired, or the targetted improvement. The programme consists of the following six basic steps:

Step 1. Analysis of the manufacturing process:

— equipment/machine;

— accessories and ancillary equipment;

— jigs, fixtures, dies and gauges;

— process details/details of the method, such as the sequence, estimated times, quality specifications and cautions and checks; and

— setup operation details, including earlier work done to reduce setup and adjustment time and points calling for improvement.

Step 2. Setting the desired, or targetted improvement - this must take into account the equipment restrictions, or the inherent inadequacies of the equipment and the method, if any.

Step 3. Analysis of the preparatory work:

— tools, measuring instruments, gauges and templates;

— materials handling/transport devices; and

— workplace/workstation layout.

Step 4. Improving setup.

Step 5. Analysis of adjustments to eliminate avoidable and minimise unavoidable adjustments.

Step 6. Finalising reengineered methods and its implementation:

— reinvestigate external and internal setups and ascertain optimal conditions;

— establish improved setup and adjustment procedure;

— document and formalise the procedure; and

— train operators/setup crews.

The programme for improvement of setup and adjustment must aim at very significant reductions. Large reductions call for bold and seemingly radical measures, which may include redesign and modification of equipment and automation of setup/parts of the setup operations. In Japanese industry, the practice of modifying general purpose machine tools and presses to bring about large reductions in setup time is very common. Presses are modified so that the old dies can be quickly slid out of the press while new dies are pushed in from the other side; such modifications are commonplace.

The achievement of a large reduction may call for additional expenditure of a considerable amount and such an outlay may not always be possible. In such cases, to start with, targets could be set at modest levels and improvements which result in fairly significant reductions without major additional expenditure could be identified. Herein it is important to remember that one of the areas where major improvements can be made at low cost is the simplification of the adjustment process, which may consist of creating good reference surfaces, employing simple measurements methods, use of go-no-go gauges, and using simple standardised adjustments. Moreover, delays, or hold ups of setup operations, are sometimes caused by the nonavailability of a material handling device, such as a crane or a forklift. Diecarts and specially designed pushcarts for fixtures reduce the need for forklifts and cranes.

Reducing Losses Due to Idling and Minor Stoppages

In this section, we will discuss the losses caused by idling and minor stoppages of production equipment. Idling of equipment occurs when the flow of material, or workpieces, stops with the result that processing stops, but the equipment continues to run. Idling of an engine in a car implies that the engine is running but the car is not moving. In case of minor stoppages, the equipment stops automatically after an instrument mounted on the equipment detects a problem. The problem can be an obstruction, an imminent collision, overloading of the equipment, or its malfunction. Instruments and sensors are provided to prevent damage to the equipment and production of defective/nonconforming products/components. Idling is different from a minor stoppage in as much as during idling, the equipment continues to run without producing, while during a minor stoppage, the equipment is stopped as a result of a temporary problem. However, in both these cases, the production is stopped till the operator intervenes and removes the cause of stoppage of production. Therefore, idling is also a form of minor stoppage of production. But why do we call these minor stoppages? Takahashi and Osada call them brief stoppages and this term seems more appropriate than minor stoppages since time is what differentiates these stoppages from longer stoppages of production. They define a brief stoppage as one in which the duration of the stoppage is between one second and five minutes, and one which does not require intervention by the maintenance personnel [21]. However, the fact that the duration is less than five minutes does not mean that the loss due to such brief stoppages is negligible. On the other hand, such stoppages account for a significant loss of production. This is particularly true in organisations which use a large number of automated production systems. The larger the amount of automation, larger is the loss due to idling and minor stoppages, and in modern factories with a large number of automatic equipment, these losses and associated defects prevent the equipment from being used to their full capacity. Takahashi and Osada describe the results of a study conducted by them in a plant with a number of presses and welding machines. They found that there were as many as 9,000 cases per day of brief stoppages of less than five minutes [21]. They also found that longer duration stoppages were comparatively very few, namely, only 25 cases per day of abrupt breakdowns of five minutes or more, and just three cases per day of long-term breakdowns of one hour or more. This study clearly shows that the loss due to brief stoppages is very significant and also that such stoppages account for greater losses of production than do the stoppages of longer duration. This is more so in an assembly line environment and in factories using transfer lines and automated production systems [16].

Brief stoppages occur for a number of reasons. Takahashi and Osada list a number of possible reasons, including some which are non-work related, such as excessive conversation among workers, unnecessarily pushing a switch button twice, bending to pick up a fallen part and manual removal of scrap beyond what is really necessary [21]. Such causes can be eliminated but work related problems cannot be totally eliminated, and these work related causes of brief stoppages may include manual dislodging of a workpiece/material stuck in a material conveying duct/chute, changeover of part bins, occasional product quality checks, stoppage caused by overloading of equipment, and a stoppage caused when a robot assembler fails to pick up a part correctly and mis-assembly starts. However, loss due to brief stoppages can be minimised and it is important to remember that the improvement in equipment utilisation is directly proportional to the reduction in the loss due to brief stoppages.[11] Moreover, brief stoppages not only affect plant productivity, "but also contribute to a subconscious mistrust of mechanised equipment on the part of the operators" [21].

The following characteristics of brief stoppages make it difficult to adopt a structured programme aimed at their reduction:

1. Since, in these stoppages, work is restored easily and comparatively quickly, the problems are neglected, the losses remain unnoticed and little effort is made to get to the bottom of the problems and remove the causes.
2. The conditions of occurrence of these stoppages vary widely. Moreover, their location also changes constantly. Both these reasons make them liable to be ignored.
3. It is difficult to quantify the loss due to these brief stoppages.

Because of these reasons, these stoppages are not given sufficient importance and the losses remain unnoticed. Further the operators and maintenance personnel treat these problems superficially adopting stopgap measures, and the actual physical conditions are not studied with the result that the action taken is always inadequate. As is obvious from the results of Takahashi and Osada's study, brief stoppages affect the performance rate, or the productivity, of the equipment. Accordingly, all such stoppages must be taken seriously and every occurrence must be analysed and action must be taken to prevent recurrences. The following strategies can be used for the reduction of the incidence of brief stoppages:

1. **Remove minor defects in material transporting and transfer devices and mechanisms** — most of the brief stoppages are caused by material getting stuck in ducts and chutes, etc. Therefore, to prevent such incidents, defects must be found in all devices and mechanisms used for transport and transfer of material/blanks/workpieces, and these defects must be corrected.
2. **Maintain basic equipment conditions** — ensuring that the basic equipment conditions are maintained can, in turn, ensure the prevention of occurrence of minor stoppages. The basic tasks of cleaning, lubrication and bolting are very important. The management must, therefore, see that the operators understand the importance of these tasks and that the cleaning, lubrication and bolting standards for all production equipment are strictly adhered to.
3. **Review operations, determine optimum equipment conditions and maintain operating standards and procedures** — many stoppages are caused by incorrect and inadequate setup and adjustment operations. Periodic review of equipment operations and ensuring that the operators are trained adequately to maintain the operating standards and procedures can go a long way in reducing minor stoppages. Moreover, the installation of the equipment must be reviewed in the context of the manufacturing process and the processing conditions. Based on this, the optimum conditions, such as pressure, temperature, amplitude and frequency of vibration, rate of material supply/rate of feed of stock, etc. must be determined and steps must be taken to maintain these conditions during processing.
4. **Make equipment modifications and eliminate design weaknesses**— under serial (1), we have considered only minor defects in material transport and transfer devices. In addition to three strategies mentioned under serials (1), (2) and (3), significant reduction in the incidence of brief stoppages also requires an in-depth analysis of the mechanism used for material transfer, positioning

and gripping, etc. This analysis is a technical analysis and it must consider the actual physical conditions. Such an analysis should lead to improvements and equipment modifications. Moreover, design weaknesses in these areas and also in monitoring and detection systems must be identified and eliminated (including safety devices and interlocks).

Eliminating Speed or Capacity Loss

There are innumerable examples particularly in the continuous process industry, where equipment are operated at much less than the full, or designed load, or capacity. An example of this is the following:

> An 82.5 MW thermal power unit has been derated to 71 MW and for years, its maximum capacity has been considered as 71 MW, whereas it was designed to produce 82.5 MW of electricity.

When an equipment is operated at lower capacity, the process plant incurs a loss and capacity loss can be expressed as the difference between the maximum theoretical capacity of the plant, with existing raw materials and processes, and its actual operating capacity [18].[12] In the manufacturing industry engaged in machining, fabrication and assembly, such losses of capacity also take place. For the manufacturing industry, consider the following example:

A machine tool is being operated at a rate at which it takes four minutes to machine a component, whereas theoretically, if the machine is operated as it is designed to be, it should take only three minutes.

The capacity loss is one minute per component or 40 components per shift of 480 minutes. Capacity loss, in TPM terminology, is also known as speed loss to denote that the equipment is being operated at a lower speed, or at a lower rate, of production. Therefore, speed, or capacity loss can be defined as the lost production caused by the difference between the designed rate of production, or capacity, of the equipment and its actual operating rate of production, or capacity. Thus speed, or capacity losses are caused by reduced operating rate of production. Speed, or capacity losses also affect the performance rate, or productivity, of the equipment.

These losses are incurred because the equipment cannot be operated at its designed, or theoretical rate, or capacity. It could be because at a higher rate of production, or at a higher load, either quality defects or minor stoppages frequently occur. Accordingly the management decides to operate the equipment at a lower rate of production, or at lower load. The quality defects, or minor stoppages, at higher production rates, or loads, could be due to inherent design weaknesses, or they could be due to changes in the product line, changes in the product shapes (greater complexity of shapes), or changes in input raw material, or feedstock (its quality, physical properties etc.). Some equipment are not operated at the designed, or specified rate, or load, because in the past quality, or mechanical problems had been experienced and these problems were never solved. Sometimes when production rates, or loads, are increased, quality, or mechanical problems appear (and they usually appear suddenly at a certain load, or rate). These problems are, however, not experienced at lower loads, or production rates. Under these conditions, instead of taking the time to investigate these problems and making serious attempts to resolve them, it is decided to follow the easier path of running the equipment at lower load, or production rate. Over a period of time, the lower production rate is taken as the standard rate, or load, for the equipment.

In some cases, due to inherent design weaknesses in the equipment, or mechanism, at the installation and commissioning stage itself, the decision is taken to run it at a lower load, or production rate. At this stage, instead of accepting this lower rate, or load, the user organisation should insist that the equipment be run at higher loads, or rates, to expose the hidden defects. The equipment manufacturer must be required to demonstrate that the equipment is capable of being operated at the designed, or specified rate, or load, and the commissioning trials should be carried out for a reasonably long period of time. Increasing the load, or production rate, is a simple and effective way of exposing hidden defects. Insufficient debugging at the installation and commissioning stage is the cause of most of the speed, or capacity losses.[13]

In addition to insufficient debugging and undetected and unresolved design defects, inadequate daily maintenance and improper operating practices and standards are the other common causes of speed, or capacity losses. The maintenance of basic equipment conditions and maintenance of operating standards and improvement of operating procedures are necessary to prevent speed, or capacity losses as well. A detailed cause-and-effect analysis is necessary for identification of the causes. In this case, the use of P-M analysis may also be necessary. We had very briefly discussed P-M analysis earlier in this chapter under chronic losses. More information on P-M analysis is available in Chapter Two of the book entitled TPM Development Program edited by Nakajima [15]. Once the causes are identified, steps have to be taken to correct the problem. This requires a thorough investigation of the mechanisms and subsystems, which has necessarily to be an engineering analysis. Such an analysis should lead to redesign and modification of the mechanism(s)/subsystems.

Reducing Product Quality Losses

Many maintenance practitioners are probably surprised by the fact that TPM has two professed objectives, namely zero breakdowns and zero defects. Whereas it is true that plant and equipment breakdowns are the primary concern of maintenance, but what probably intrigues them is the inclusion of zero defects with zero breakdowns. They probably fail to understand the connection between defects and maintenance. This is because of the fact that in most industrial organisations, maintenance and quality are two separate departments — two functions so far removed from each other that those who work in these departments probably do not see any relationship between their functions at all. The fact that product quality is dependent on the manufacturing process used, and the state or health of the manufacturing process is, in turn, dependent on the condition, or state of repair and maintenance, of the production equipment and machines probably escapes many people. There are many factors which affect product quality and of them, the five most important factors in the manufacturing and production environment are material, men, machines, mechanisation (or automation) and methods (the 5 Ms for product quality). The last three factors are the basic ingredients of the manufacturing/production process. Therefore, product quality is dependant on the production process and production equipment and machines. Quality is not achieved by inspection, or by screening out defective products; it can be achieved by ensuring that no defects are created by production processes [18]. TPM draws attention to the maintenance-related quality problems and including zero defects with zero breakdowns is TPM's way of stressing the importance of product quality in the modern business environment (recall our discussion in Chapter One wherein we have stressed the importance of elimination of wastes).

In this section, we will discuss the losses due to poor product quality—the losses which are caused by defects in the manufacturing/production process and production of defective items. Defects in process and production of defective items result in scrap and rework.[14] In this section, we will discuss activities directed at the elimination of losses due to scrap and rework of components and products, and losses due to reduced yield at the startup and restart of equipment will not be included. Startup/restart losses will be taken up separately in the following section.

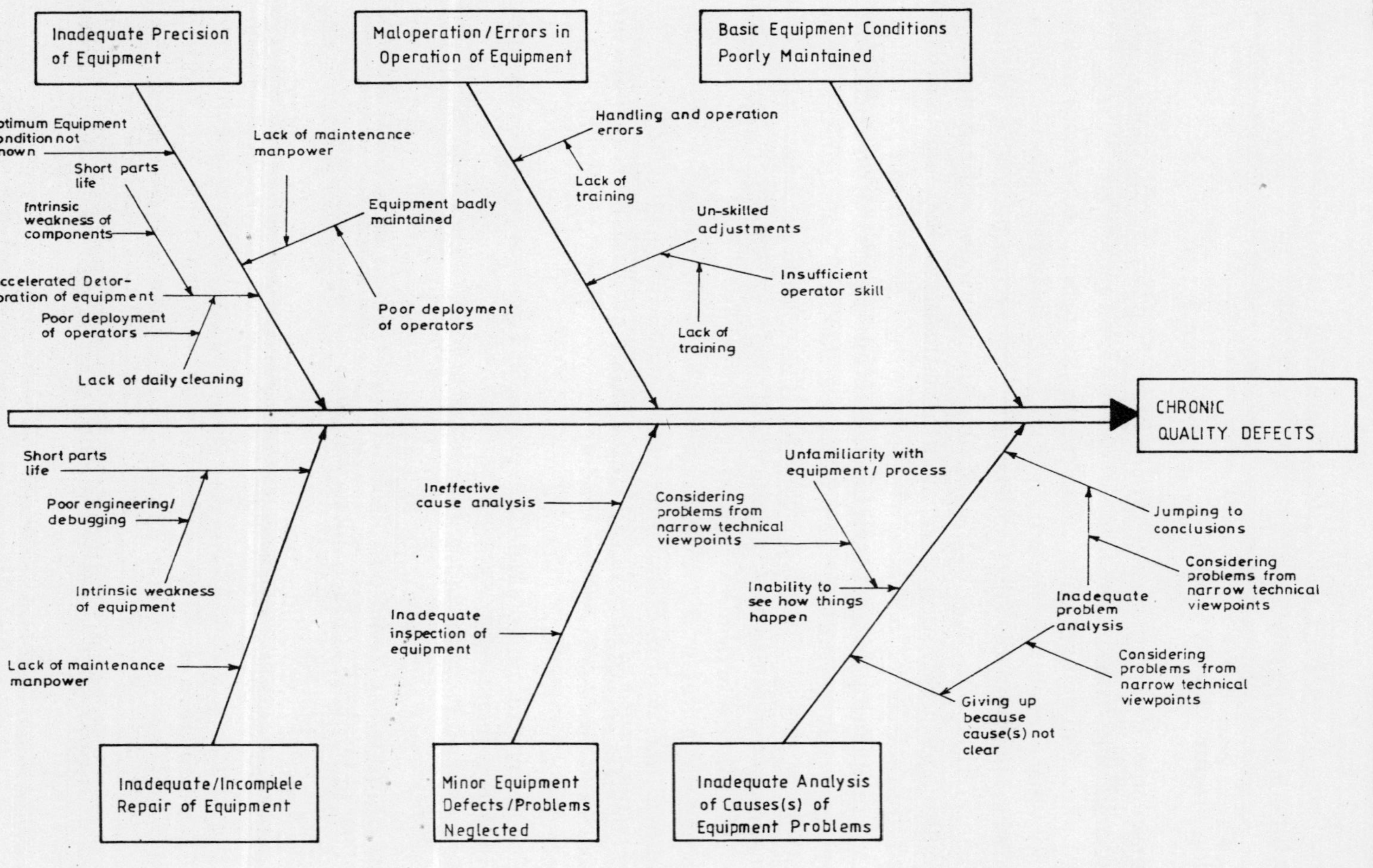

Fig. 4.8. Typical Causes For Chronic Qualty Defects.

Maintenance-related quality losses can be subdivided into two broad classes, namely, chronic and sporadic losses as shown earlier in Table 4.2. We have discussed the characteristics of chronic and sporadic losses, and we have noted that chronic defects are caused by equipment operating with some kinds of deterioration, or malfunction, which, over a period of time, are taken as normal operating conditions. Further, we have also noted and discussed the fact that in many cases, the problem or loss is not recognised, and even in cases, where the problem or loss is duly observed and recognised, sometimes the corrective action is not taken. Moreover, as shown in Fig. 4.3 and discussed earlier in this chapter, the corrective action taken is sometimes inappropriate and/or improperly planned, and at some other times, it is incomplete. Stopgap measures are taken, the corrective action is not implemented thoroughly, and no preventive measures are instituted. We have also noted that the reason for this state of affairs is the fact that chronic defects are usually the result of a number of causes and intricate and complex analysis is required to determine the causes of chronic defects. The typical causes of chronic defects are shown in Fig. 4.8. Fig. 4.8 is given in the form of a cause-and-effect diagram for clarity of illustration and to facilitate understanding. The different possible causes and their relationships can be better shown and explained with the help of a cause-and-effect diagram as opposed to a flow chart or a block diagram. In addition to cause-and-effect analysis, the identification of causes may call for P-M analysis as well. Herein we will repeat our earlier assertion that causes-and-effect analysis , if carried out properly, can be as systematic as P-M analysis, but we add that for identification of the causes of chronic maintenance-related quality losses, P-M analysis[15] may be more useful in the understanding and analysis of the physical phenomenon.

Chronic defects can not be totally eliminated, but systematic identification of chronic defects and thereafter, for each one of the identified chronic defects, a systematic analysis to identify the underlying cause(s) can help in a significant reduction of chronic quality loss. In this regard, we reiterate Juran's advice in stating that the aim must always be a defect-free product. The aim of zero defects implies the need for never-ending quality improvement, and chronic quality defects call for quality improvement efforts since the chronic level of quality continues till some specific quality improvement action is taken to change it [12]. This is shown in Fig. 4.2, wherein quality improvement efforts have been shown to be successful in bringing down the quality loss from the regular level of chronic loss (say eight per cent) to the optimum level, which is the level of loss at the optimum conditions, as achieved. However, continuous improvement efforts can ensure that this level is lowered further. Thus, we conclude that in case of chronic quality defects, the objective is to reduce the losses due to chronic quality defects, or in other words, to reduce the incidence/occurrence of chronic defects. A further reference to Fig. 4.2 will also bring out clearly the important distinction between chronic and sporadic quality problems. The 'spike' or sudden peaking shown in the figure is a sporadic rise from the historic level of chronic quality loss. This sporadic loss is due to some sudden change in the process — an assignable cause for the sporadic quality defect. The incidence of such assignable causes can be prevented. The prevention of sporadic quality defects calls for a thorough and detailed engineering of the process. For each critical quality characteristic, detailed process design must be carried out and for the process, or the machine, optimum operating conditions must be determined. Thereafter, with the basic machine conditions adequately maintained, a process capability study should be carried out with the process, or the machine, running according to the optimum operating conditions. Process capability study is a part of process design and serves as a verification of the adequacy of the process chosen for the quality characterisic. If the process capability is found to be adequate, then necessary process controls are instituted for the monitoring of the process. Thus, like the process capability study, process control is also an integral part of the detailed process design, being an in-built control mechanism to ensure that the process is running as per design. Thereafter, the process can be monitored by the use of periodic/infrequent quality audits and process controls may be discontinued.

Table 4.6 presents in a sequential manner the steps required for (i) reduction of chronic quality defects, and (ii) prevention of sporadic quality defects. The fundamental point to remember here is that attainment of zero defects implies the reduction of product quality losses to a level, which is very close to zero, and this calls for both fire fighting and improvement activities. Fire fighting efforts are necessary when during process control, the process is found to have deviated, as for example, a point is found outside the control limits indicating the occurrence of a sporadic defect. Prevention of sporadic defects calls for proper design of the process,[16] adequate process control and an ability to restore the process to a state of control as quickly as possible by removing the assignable cause whenever a shift/deviation, or increased dispersion, of the process is detected. As opposed to this, reduction of chronic defects calls for quality improvement efforts and quality improvement must aim for zero defects. Moreover, the goal of zero defects demands a mindset wherein nothing short of perfection is acceptable [11]. All chronic defects must be found out and removed one by one. Also when undertaking quality improvement work, it is best to remember Juran's advice. Juran says that

Table 4.6. Reducing Product Quality Losses

Reduce Chronic Defects	*Prevent Sporadic Defects*
Step 1 By Pareto analysis of historical data on quality losses, — identify chronic defects, and — list them in the descending order based on their criticality, that is, as per their contribution to losses.	**Step 1** From product specifications and component drawings, — identify the quality characteristics to be maintained, and — list them in the descending order based on their criticality, that is, as per their effect on the primary product function(s).
Step 2 For each of the chronic defects, take up quality improvement programmes, one at a time.	**Step 2** For each product and each identified quality characteristic, take up process design and process control activity, one at a time.
For Each One	**For Each One**
Step 3 Identify the phenomenon. Phenomenon implies not only the mode of occurrence of the problem/defect, but also the equipment/machine and the mechanism which is either responsible or affected.	**Step 3** Design the process, that is, — study the effect of nonconformance on the functional characteristics of the component, or the product, — select the equipment/machine, accessories, jigs, fixtures, tools and gauges, — determine the process/method: the processing steps/operations, and — determine the cautions and intermediate quality checks required.
Step 4 By cause-and-effect analysis or P-M analysis, identify 'causal factors.' These are all factors which may conceivably produce the perceived phenomenon, including those which are logically proved to produce the phenomenon.	**Step 4** Determine the optimum operating conditions of the machine/process.
Step 5 For these 'causal factors,' or variables, determine the normal conditions, or settings. (these are optimum, or specified conditions or settings.)	**Step 5** Determine basic machine conditions which must be maintained.
Step 6 Take steps/corrective action to bring the variable(s) or causes to the normal/desired condition/setting.	**Step 6** Run process with optimum operating conditions and basic machine conditions, and carry out a process capability study.
Step 7 Monitor results and follow up to 'stabilise causal factors,' that is, make sure that the factors or causes stay at the normal condition or setting.	**Step 7** If process capability adequate: — run process maintaining optimum operating conditions and basic machine conditions, and — institute process controls. If not, return to step 3.
Carry Out Steps 3-7, For All Chronic Defects	**Step 8** Monitor performance and carry out quality audit(s).
**Elimination of chronic quality defects calls for never ending improvement.*	**Carry Out Steps 3-8 For All Critical Quality Characteristics of All Products.**
Zero Defects Must be the Ultimate Goal	

there are two journeys required to be undertaken for quality improvement, namely the diagnostic journey from the symptom to the cause followed by the remedial journey from the cause to the remedy [12]. The tools which can be used for the former are cause-and-effect analysis and P-M analysis. Thereafter, once the causes are determined, technical knowledge and work experience are used to determine the remedy. Without knowing the real causes the remedy cannot be determined. Product quality is a function of the state of the process and in many cases, the process is affected by the condition of the machine/production equipment - the state of its repair and maintenance and the operating conditions and procedures. Accordingly, maintenance-related quality losses account for a large percentage of all product quality losses and reducing quality losses demands the correction of both chronic and sporadic equipment/machine problems [23].

Eliminating Startup/Restart Losses

In TPM literature, the sixth major loss has been identified as the reduced yield loss and it has been defined as the loss incurred during the early stages of production because of reduced yield from machine startup to stable production {13][14]. We have also noted earlier in this chapter that Wireman has chosen to designate this loss as the startup/restart loss and Wireman defines it as the loss incurred each time a process must be shut down and restarted.[17] He explains this by adding that this loss might be due to the production of an unacceptable product till the equipment reaches a certain operating parameter such as temperature, or speed [23]. This explanation also categorizes the startup/restart loss as a defect, or quality loss. The above discussion explains why, in TPM literature, startup/restart losses are not considered separately and instead are generally clubbed with product quality loss, that is, with the losses due to quality defects in process and rework [15]. The author could also have followed the oft-trodden conventional path, and taken the startup/restart loss as part of product quality losses instead of discussing it separately as a loss which is quite distinct in character from the losses which occur after the initial failure, or running-in failure, region of the life cycle. Before we can actually discuss the sixth major loss, it is necessary to briefly discuss equipment life cycle and the 'bathtub curve.'

After years of research examining the failure data of many types of components and machines, several modes of failure have come to light. This is best illustrated by the well-known 'bathtub curve,' which is shown in Fig. 4.9. The curve is a plot of the hazard rate, h(t),[18] against time, and time, in this case, denotes the life cycle of the equipment. The bath-tub curve has been found to be most applicable in describing the failure modes over the life cycle of equipment, which are, in turn, made up of different sub-systems, sub-assemblies and assemblies. The life cycle of an equipment, can be sub-divided into three distinct periods, or regions. These three regions are as follows:

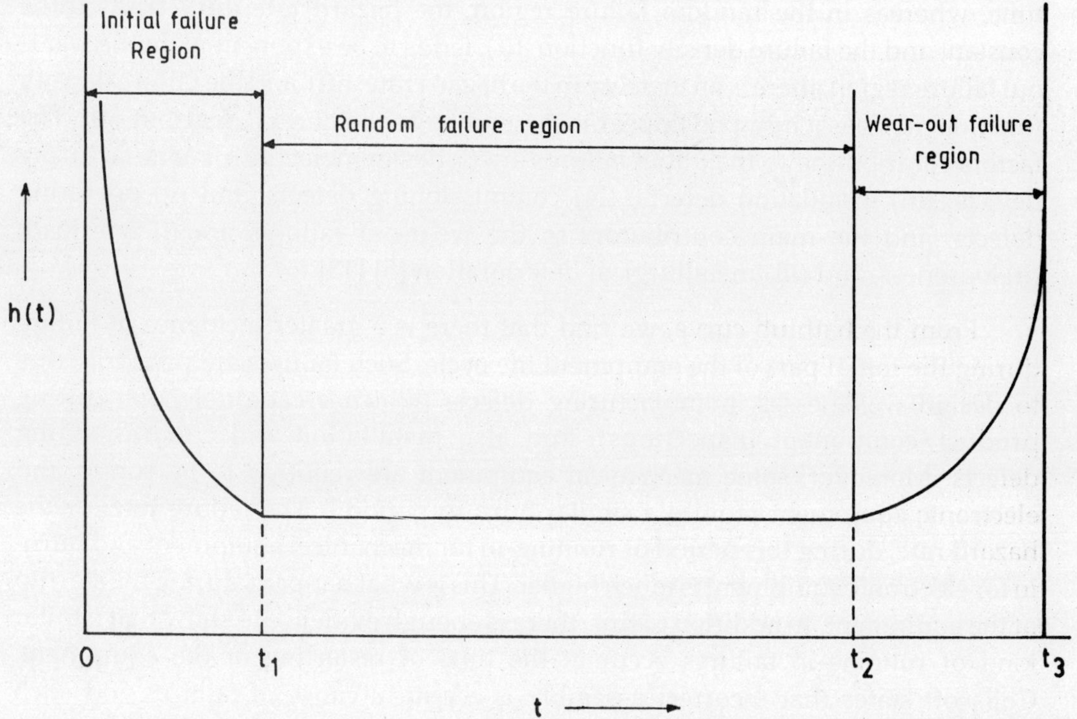

Fig. 4.9 Bath-tub Curve

(i) Early failure, or initial failure, or running-in failure, or burn-in region - when a batch of new items just produced, or assembled, is placed in operation, the initial failure rate is generally somewhat higher than that encountered a short time later. This is mainly due to the initial failures of components owing to weaknesses and manufacturing defects.

(ii) Incidental, or random, failure region — this is the middle region in which fewer failures take place. In general, failures seem to occur when the environmental or operational stresses exceed the design strength of the components.

(iii) Wear-out failure region — as the component or the equipment reaches old age, there are signs of deterioration and many failures occur.

In Fig. 4.9, period 0 to t_1 is the initial failure region, period t_1 to t_2 is the random failure region, and the period t_2 to t_3 depicts the wear-out failure region. In the initial failure region, both h(t), hazard rate, and f(t), failure density function, decrease with time, whereas in the random failure region, the hazard rate, h(t), tends to be constant and the failure density function, f(t), tends to be exponential. In the wear-out failure region, there is an increase in the hazard rate, h(t), and the failure density function, f(t), has a humped appearance (tending to the normal distribution). The factors contributing to the initial failures are (i) design defects, (ii) manufacturing defects, (iii) installation defects, (iv) commissioning defects, and (v) operating defects, and the main contributors to the wear-out failures are (i) overload, (ii) looseness, and (iii) metallurgical deterioration [5] [13].

From the bathtub curve, we find that there is a greater incidence of failure during the initial part of the equipment life cycle. Such failures are primarily due to design weaknesses, manufacturing defects (which escape detection during product/component inspections), and also installation and commissioning defects. Moreover, some mechanical equipment are required to be run-in and electronic equipment require a similar burn-in period.[19] The failure rate, or the hazard rate, during this period of running-in for mechanical equipment and burn-in for electronic equipment is much higher. This is what happens during the startup of the equipment. In addition to this, there is enough evidence to show that similar kind of running-in failures occur at the time of restarting of the equipment. Collacott states that incorrect assembly is a critical cause of failures and such incorrect assembly may occur during servicing. Accordingly, he reports evidence of an increased number of running-in failures caused by periodic overhauls [5]. This has been corroborated by Bhadury and Basu, who report that in a study conducted on a 110 MW thermal power unit, it was noticed that there was a period of running-in when the unit was restarted after a capital maintenance shutdown[20] (shutdown for overhauling of the entire unit) [1]. We may conclude, therefore, that during startup and restart, there is a loss incurred due to equipment breakdowns, and the breakdown loss during the startup and restart is greater than what it is after a while (after the equipment has been run-in or burnt-in). In addition to this, there are quality losses during startup and on restart of the equipment this quality loss can be either due to reduced yield or due to production of defective components/ products. In addition to this, in the process industry, there is a loss of productive capacity during startup — a loss of time from the startup of the equipment to attainment of stable production [18]. This loss of time may be because all products, or components, produced during the startup period have to be scrapped and/or due to adjustments and minor changes of setting required and minor stoppages experienced till the equipment attains stable operation. Therefore, during startup and restart of production equipment and systems, the following losses are incurred:

(i) product quality loss - reduced yield and production of defectives,

(ii) breakdown loss - running-in, burn-in due to design weaknesses, manufacturing defects, and/or installation and commissioning defects,

(iii) adjustments, and

(iv) minor stoppagges.

Please note that adjustments and minor stoppages are also caused by intrinsic weaknesses in system design (and some of it is also due to lack of training on the part of production operators).

It can still be argued that these four components of the startup and restart losses can be considered separately clubbed with the respective losses, namely, breakdown loss incurred during startup and restart with breakdown losses, time lost on account of adjustments with setup and adjustment losses, loss of capacity due to brief stoppages during startup and restart with idling and minor stoppage losses and loss due to reduced yield and nonconforming products during startup and restart together with product quality losses. Why do we need to consider these together (and not separately) under startup and restart losses, particularly because they are different kinds of losses? This is being advocated because of the following reasons:

(i) although the amount of loss incurred during startup and restart varies depending on the type of production system/equipment, condition of the equipment, level of engineering of the process and technical skills of operators etc., in actual practice, startup and restart losses turn out to be surprisingly high [15];

(ii) these losses are not only latent but also considered as inevitable in most cases [15], and clubbing parts of this loss together with other losses will lead to further neglect and uncritical acceptance of these losses; and

(iii) although four components of the loss are different in character and some may argue that breakdown loss has nothing in common with product quality loss, for example, the remedy for the four components is the same.

The remedy is design, manufacture, installation and commissioning of production equipment and systems to ensure high reliability, maintainability, safety and usability. This activity, in TPM parlance, is known as maintenance prevention, or MP. Therefore, to attain an objective of reducing six major losses and thereby maximise equipment availability and effectiveness, it is essential that the startup and restart losses be recognised as a major loss by the user of the equipment and steps be taken to minimise this loss right at the time of development of equipment specifications, and design of the equipment and its manufacture. This is the MP design stage and the MP design team must develop equipment specifications to not only ensure that reliability, maintainability and safety features are incorporated but also usability features are given due consideration. The usability features may include quick setting devices, ease of adjustment, automatic/semiautomatic controls, fast warm up, that is, getting to optimum parameter (temperature, pressure etc.) levels quickly, preheating/ preparation of stock/material etc. The team must also ensure that these features are incorporated into the equipment design by the manufacturer and adequate quality control measures are also instituted to guard against manufacturing defects. The incorporation of reliability, maintainability, safety and usability features at the stage of design of capital equipment and adequate and appropriate quality control measures taken during its manufacture have a direct bearing on the breakdown, quality, adjustment and brief stoppage losses incurred during startup and restart of equipment. We have already discussed the importance of detailed planning and proper execution of the installation and commissioning activity and this plays a vital role in the minimisation of startup and restart losses.

To ensure that all this is done properly, it is necessary that the user organisation set up a project management team at the time of acquisition of new production equipment. This team must include both maintenance and operations personnel and it must be made clear to them that they will be responsible for operating and maintaining the equipment after it is installed and commissioned. This team must be held responsible for MP design of the new equipment. Harvey and Eastburn report the steps and care taken by such a project management team during the setting up of the Thrybergh Bar Mill Facility of the British Steel Corporation [9]. This project team should rightfully be called the MP design team and Ikeda discusses the objectives of the MP design system at the Fuji Photo Film Company [10]. The responsibilities of the MP design team must include the following:

(i) equipment selection,

(ii) development of equipment specifications,

(iii) incorporation of MP design features and usability features in the design of the equipment,

(iv) overseeing the design of the equipment, its sub-systems, and controls in the manufacturing organisations,

(v) inspection of critical components and sub-systems during the manufacture of the equipment,

(vi) development of plans and procedures forthe installation ofthe equipment, and

(vii) development of commissioning procedures and conduct of the commissioning trials.

During the commissioning trials, the startup and restart procedures must be developed, fine tuned and documented. The team must also take part (with the manufacturer's engineers) in the preparation of the operation and maintenance manuals for the equipment.

With the rapid growth of technology, production equipment, particularly those used in continuous process industries, are tending to get more sophisticated. The requirements of higher productivity, coupled with greater automation, is bringing with it innovations in equipment design. The user organisations do not have any experience with these innovations and the accordingly, even with all the care, thought and foresight, certain unexpected problems are being encountered with new equipment after installation. If these problems are noticed during commissioning trials, then corrective action can probably be taken. However, either due to lack of time during commissioning and urgency of the need to start production or the fact that certain problems were not observed at the time of commissioning of the new equipment, some problems persist. It must be remembered here that MP activities are essentially early equipment management activities and include activities of designing-out-of-maintenance during the design, manufacturing, installation and commissioning of production equipment. These problems must be duly analysed and the user organisation must plan an equipment improvement project and take up activities directed at improving design weaknesses as soon as possible. Thus, even in case where a new equipment acquisition project management team, or an MP design team, is duly constituted and care is taken during the acquisition of the new equipment to design-out-maintenance and to incorporate the necessary usability features, equipment improvement activities may be necessary.

Moreover, as noted earlier, operation errors are also a major cause of early equipment problems and startup and restart losses. Therefore, operator training becomes important and improvement of operation and maintenance skills can assist in reducing startup and restart losses. Thus, we may conclude that the reduction of startup and restart losses calls for the following activities:

1. Maintenance prevention and early equipment management (installation, commissioning and initial debugging activities).
2. Improvement of design weaknesses.
3. Improvement of operating and maintenance skills.
4. Maintenance of operating standards and improvement of operating conditions.
5. Maintenance of basic equipment conditions.

CONCLUDING REMARKS

We had noted in the first chapter that the objectives of TPM are zero breakdowns and zero defects, and defect-free production and maximisation of equipment availability are, in turn, necessary for zero inventory levels and the implementation of just-in-time production systems. We have also noted that productive maintenance (and TPM) is directed at the maximisation of equipment effectiveness and this objective is larger than the objective of maximisation of equipment availability. The maximisation of equipment effectiveness, in turn, requires the reduction of the six big losses discussed in this chapter. The attainment of the objectives of TPM and the success of TPM implementation, therefore, depends very largely on the work done (by the equipment user), or the steps taken, towards the reduction of the six big losses. In this chapter, we have discussed the six big losses, one after another, and identified the steps which are necessary to reduce these losses. A close study of the steps reveals an interesting fact, namely that except for setup and adjustment losses and sporadic quality losses, reduction of the remaining five big losses, by and large, require the same steps. These steps are as follows:

(i) Restoration of production equipment to optimum functioning, or operations, after a failure,

(ii) Maintenance of operating standards and improvement of operating procedures,

(iii) Maintenance of basic equipment conditions,

(iv) Improvement of operating and maintenance skills,

(v) Improvement of design weaknesses and equipment defects, and

(vi) Maintenance prevention and early equipment management activities, including adequate debugging at the installation and commissioning stages.

Moreover, steps (ii) and (iii) can only be carried out if the following two steps are carried out earlier:

(i) review of operations and determination of optimum operating conditions, and

(ii) review of operations and study of the process to determine the basic equipment conditions which must be maintained.

This is shown in Table 4.7 and it helps to summarize the steps required for the reduction of five big losses. To this list of eight steps, we must add the following four steps required for the reduction of setup and adjustment losses:

Table 4.7. Steps to Eliminate Five Big Losses

Step/Remedial Action	*Will assist in reducing/eliminating*				
	Breakdown losses	*Idling and minor stoppages losses*	*Speed/ capacity losses*	*Defect and rework losses*	*Startup and restart losses*
1. Restore production equipment to optimum functioning after a failure	✓	—	—	✓	—
2. Review operations and determine optimum operating conditions.	✓	✓	✓	✓	✓
3. Review operations/study process and determine basic equipment conditions which must be maintained.	✓	✓	✓	✓	✓
4. Maintain operating standards and improve operating procedures.	✓	✓	✓	✓	✓
5. Maintain basic equipment conditions.	✓	✓	✓	✓	✓
6. Improve operating and maintenance skills.	✓	✓	✓	✓	✓
7. Improve design weaknesses and equipment defects.	✓	✓*	✓	✓	✓
8. Maintenance prevention and early equipment management activities.	✓	—	✓	—	✓

* In this case, the activity is directed towards removing defects in material transporting and material transfer and positioning and gripping devices and mechanisms.

(i) Study of existing setup and conversion of as many internal setups to external setup as possible.

(ii) Detailed methods analysis (industrial engineering analysis) of the internal setup (remaining) and adjustment operations and development of improved setup and adjustment procedures.

(iii) Implementation of the reengineered setup and adjustment procedures.

(iv) Modification of existing production equipment to reduce setup and adjustment losses (wherever feasible and also economically justified, that is, where saving is greater than the cost of modification).

Finally, we must add the step necessary for the elimination of sporadic defect losses. This step is one of process design, conduct of process capability study, institution of process controls and quality audit for each critical quality characteristic of the products being produced. Thus, we may conclude by noting that there are six basic steps for the reduction of five big losses with two prerequisite steps, four steps for the reduction of setup and adjustment losses and process design, process capability study and process controls for the elimination of sporadic defects.

We have already discussed improvement of design weaknesses and equipment defects earlier in this chapter and also in Chapter Two under designing-out-of-maintenance. Similarly, maintenance prevention has also been discussed in Chapter Two and again in this chapter. Our discussion of the six big losses in this chapter has highlighted the importance of maintenance of basic equipment conditions, maintenance of operating standards and improvement of operating conditions, and improvement of operating and maintenance skills. Moreover, the improvement of maintenance skills has a positive effect on the activity of restoration of production equipment. We will discuss these issues in the next chapter under the heading of "autonomous maintenance and maintenance skills training."

References

1. Bhadury, B. and Basu, S.K., "A Study of Hazard Rates of Mechanical Systems," in Proceedings-National Conference on Effective Maintenance for High Productivity, Central Mechanical Engineering Research Instituted (C.M.E.R.I), Durgapur (W.B., India), April 12-14, 1985, pp. MMM 5.1-5.13.

2. Bhadury, B. and Basu, S.K., "Analysis of Past Failures for Cost-effective Maintenance Management: A Case Study," in Proceedings - National Conference of Reliability

Engineering, Indian Institute of Technology (I.I.T), Kharagpur (W.B., India). Dec. 12-13, 1985, pp. 28.1-28.30.

3. Bhadury, B. and Basu, S.K., "A Computerized Maintenance Planning and Control Algorithm," *IE(I) Journal-PR* (The Institution of Engineers (India) Journal-Production Engineering Volume), Vol. 68, July 1987, pp 1-8.

4. Carter, A. D.S., "Achieving Quality and Reliability," James Clayton Lecture, Proceedings of the Institution of Mechanical Engineers (London), Vol. 188, No. 13, 1974, pp 201-213.

5. Collacott, R.A., *Mechanical Fault Diagnosis and Condition Monitoring*, Chapman and Hall, London, 1977.

6. De La Mere, R.A. and Ball, K.J., "Early Life Availability of Chemical Precess Plants," *Reliability Engineering*, Vol. 2, 1981, pp 289-302.

7. Geddie, W. (Editor), *Chambers's Twentieth Century Dictionary*, W & R Chambers Ltd., London, 1964.

8. Hewgill, J.C. and Parkes, D., "Terotechnology - Philosophy and Concept," *Terotechnica*, Vol. 1, No. 1, May 1979, pp 3-8.

9. Harvey, G. and Eastburn, K., "Terotechnology: A Case-Study in the Application of the Concept," *Terotechnica*, Vol. 1, No. 1, May 1979, pp 25-38.

10. Ikeda, A., "A Reliability and Maintainability Design System and Its Development," *Terotechnica*, Vol. 1, No. 1, May 1979, pp 17-24.

11. Juran, J.M. and Gryna, F.M. Jr. *Quality Planning and Analysis: From Product Development Through Usage*, McGraw-Hill Book Company, New York, 1970, pp 9, 5-21.

12. Juran, J.M. (Editor-in-Chief) and Gryna F.M. Jr. (Associate Editor), Jwan's Quality Control Handbook, McGraw-Hill Book Company, New York, Fourth Edition, 1988, pp 5-21, 22-3 and 22-31.

13. Nakajima, S., *Introduction to TPM*, Productivity Press, Cambridge, Massachusetts, U.S.A., 1988, pp. 14, 37.

14. Nakajima, S., "*An Introduction to TPM*," Chapter 1 in *TPM Development Program: Implementing Total Productive Maintenance* (S. Nakajima, Editor), Productivity Press, Cambridge, Massachusetts, U.S.A., 1989, pp 1-26 (p10).

15. Shirose, K., "Equipment Effectiveness, Chronic Losses and Other TPM Improvement Concepts," Chapter 2 in *TPM Development Program: Implementing Total Productive Maintenance* (S. Nakajima, Editor), Productivity Press, Cambridge, Massachusetts, U.S.A., 1989, pp 27-84 (pp 30, 35, 42, 50, 71-74).

16. Shirose, K. and Goto, F., "Eliminating the Six Big Losses," Chapter 3 in *TPM Development Program: Implementing Total Productive Maintenance* (S. Nakajima, Editor), Productivity Press, Cambridge, Massachusetts, U.S.A., 1989, pp 85-164 (pp 87, 138 and 153).

17. Suzaki, K., *The New Manufacturing Challenge: Techniques for Continuous Improvement,* The Free Press (A division of Macmillan, Inc.), New York, 1987, pp 113-123.

18. Suzuki, T., *New Directions for TPM,* Productivity Press, Cambridge, Massachusetts, U.S.A., 1992, pp 55, 86-90 and 103.

19. Tajiri, M. and Gotoh, F., *TPM Implementation, A Japanese Approach*, McGraw-Hill Inc., New York, 1992, p. 5.

20. Takahashi, Y., "Maintenance-Oriented Management Via Total Participation - Total Productive Maintenance, A New Task for Plant Managers in Japan," *Terotechnica,* Vol. 2, 1981, pp 79-88.

21. Takahashi, Y. and Osada, T., *TPM: Total Productive Maintenance,* Asian Productivity Organisaiton, Tokyo, 1990, pp 67-69.

22. Watson, C., "Is Preventive Maintenance Worthwhile?," in *Operational Research in Maintenance* (A.K.S. Jardine, Editor), Manchester University Press, Manchester, England, 1970, pp 142-173.

23. Wireman, T., *Total Productive Maintenance: An American Approach*, Industrial Press Inc., New York, 1991, pp 4, 21, 22, 35 and 61.

Endnotes

1. There will always be some loss incurred due to necessary setup of equipment and tools and dies etc. which needs stopping of the machine. Similarly, in many machines, there will be some loss of yield at startup, and in some cases, also at restart.

2. Implicitly, the startup loss is also included since yield loss is also a form of quality loss.

3. In the preceding paragraphs, we have stated that chronic losses become obvious only when they are compared with optimum, or design, conditions/levels. Such comparison is necessary since it results in the loss being observed. However, true recognition comes only when the economic impact, or the loss of productive capacity, is recognised. This recognition is aided by the analysis of past data.

4. Fault tree analysis is a tool which was primarily developed for use during the system design stage (initial phase of design of new systems/equipment). It is a top down approach, in which a system fault is traced down through the system to identify the basic causes (which are called the BASIC EVENTS). However, this method of analysis can also be used effectively to trace the basic causes for some critical and chronic

system failure modes of existing systems. Thus, it can also be used for identifying causes of chronic failures of complex equipment during operation or use.

5. P-M analysis is very similar to cause-and-effect analysis. Shirose states that cause-and-effect analysis has certain inherent weaknesses when it comes to listing of all relevant factors, such as machinery, manpower, materials and methods, and also determination of corrective actions. He feels that P-M analysis is more systematic in its approach [15]. However, Shirose's stand can be disputed, and cause-and-effect analysis carried out systematically and properly can be equally effective.

6. Elimination of chronic breakdown losses would, however, require increasing the operational reliability of the equipment to a level where the incidence of failures is very largely minimised (if possible, brought down to zero). Here maintainability will not come into the picture and major work will be required in the area of MP.

7. As per the European Organisation for Quality Control (EOQC), the quality of manufactured product is a combination of its quality of design and quality of manufacture [4]. Quality of design is the value inherent in the design' a measure of the excellence of the design in relation to the customer's requirements,' whereas quality of manufacture 'is a measure of the fidelity with which the product, taken at the point of acceptance, conforms to the design.'

8. Some of these uncontrollable breakdowns may be catastrophic. Such seemingly uncontrollable breakdowns also give prior warning signals. Detection of these warning signals and taking appropriate action to prevent catastrophic failures are the aims of predictive maintenance.

9. In India, manufacturing industry is more commonly known as engineering industry. The manufacturing industry produces discrete engineered products, such as TVs, motor cycles and cars, as opposed to bulk production of chemicals, fertilizers etc. in the continuous process industry. The manufacturing industry is very diverse and includes ship building, aircraft, machine building, machine tool, consumer electronics and the automotive industry.

10. With the recognition of the need for flexibility in the manufacturing industry, a number of steps have been taken to reduce the setup time. Use of CNC machine tools - CNC machines and machining centres - and use of cellular manufacturing have been particularly useful in reducing setup times in machining operations. In presswork, die carts are being more frequently used with the same objective in mind.

11. Although idling and minor stoppages interrupt production functions, they are not regarded as breakdowns and the time lost is called a stoppage and not downtime (in this context, please also refer to Fig. 4.1 and the discussion at the beginning of this chapter). The reasons for this are (i) the duration of these stoppages is small, (ii) the problems are quickly noticed and normal operations can be restored by simple measures such as removing the jammed workpiece and striking the start button, and

(iii) therefore, a breakdown slip need not be written and maintenance personnel asked to attend to the problem, However, when operators cannot correct these minor stoppages within a specified time (say 10 minutes), then some organisations designate these stoppages 'as breakdowns to emphasize their importance, even though no damage has occurred to the equipment' [19].

12. This loss can be expressed as the loss of production, or generation, in this example. However, since for financial statements, losses have to be stated in monetary terms, in case of continuous process plant operations, it is better expressed as the loss of revenue in rupees per day, per month, or per year.

13. This is particularly true in the process industry in India. Most of the equipment are imported and this makes matters worse. Later, when the user organisation wants to carry out trials at higher loads, or speeds, and investigate the problems encountered, assistance of the equipment manufacturer is not forthcoming. Even detailed drawings of mechanisms and components, necessary for technical evaluation and analysis, are not supplied by the equipment manufacturer.

14. In many cases (and this is particularly true in the manufacturing industry), only scrap is included in the internal failure cost and rework and retest are not included [16]. This is notwithstanding the fact that, in the majority of cases, rework turns out to be more expensive to the company than scrap, even in the short-term.

15. The reader is requested to refer to the discussion of P-M analysis given earlier in this chapter under chronic and sporadic losses (included under elimination of breakdown losses). P-M analysis was specifically developed by Shirose for elimination of chronic losses [15], and the author feels that the first five steps may be particularly useful in the case of chronic quality defects.

16. Process design and process control are seen as activities which are used in the manufacturing industry. But what is not so clearly understood is that process design and process control are also equally important in the operation of continuous process industries. Suzuki explains the work of process design and process control in the process industry under 'quality maintenance' in his book on TPM [18]. The tool proposed by Suzuki has been specially developed for control of maintenance-related quality losses in the process industry.

17. Since each shutdown has necessarily to be followed by a restart, this may be taken by some to imply that even essential shutdowns for preventive maintenance and also capital maintenance, or equipment overhauls, should be avoided. Practitioners must guard themselves against such seemingly logical, but incorrect, deductions.

18. h(t), hazard rate is the measure of the instantaneous rate of failure, that is, the probability of failure between time t and t+dt, given that there were no failures upto time t.

Mathematically, $h(t) = f(t)/1\text{-}F(t) = f(t)/R(t)$

where $f(t)$ = failure density function,

$F(t)$ = failure distribution function = $\int_0^t f(t)\,dt$, and

$R(t)$ = reliability function.

19. For this reason, the initial failure, or early failure, region of the life cycle is also called the running-in failure region and burn-in region.
20. However, this period of running-in after the overhaul was much smaller than the running-in period experienced during the startup (initial failure period). The slope of the curve was also smaller.

Autonomous Maintenance and Maintenance Skills Training

The Japanese refer to autonomous maintenance as self-initiated maintenance [11]. This seems adequate since some of the maintenance tasks are carried out by equipment operators under TPM and autonomous maintenance includes only the routine tasks of cleaning, lubrication, bolting and periodic inspections of the equipment. (We have already noted in Chapters One and Two that under productive maintenance and TPM, these tasks are performed by the equipment operators). The term self-initiated maintenance also highlights the fundamental change of attitude, which is a prerequisite of TPM—moving away from the 'I operate, you fix' syndrome. However, this change of attitude implies cooperation and the recognition of the fact that operations and maintenance are inseparable when it comes to the job of looking after the maintenance of production equipment and machines. The fact that these two functions have to work together for the maximisation of equipment effectiveness has been brought out quite clearly in the preceding chapter. Wireman uses the term team-based maintenance and this term is probably more appropriate since it brings out the need for the operator and the maintenance technician to work as a team. It also highlights the fact that the operation function does not replace the maintenance function and the operators take away only a part of the work load from the maintenance technicians [12].[1] We will use the term autonomous maintenance in this book primarily because this is the term that is used in TPM literature nowadays and is also understood quite well by the practitioners.

Autonomous maintenance has become synonymous with productive maintenance and TPM, and whenever one hears of TPM, the picture that emerges in one's mind is that of maintenance being performed by equipment operators. This thinking is so strong that if the more knowledgeable practitioners and maintenance professionals in India are asked to define TPM, the most likely answer will turn out to be as follows:

> "a model wherein the routine preventive maintenance tasks are taken care of by the equipment operators leaving the maintenance department enough time to attend to other essential and pressing maintenance functions."

This feeling is quite justified and we have already noted in Chapter One that autonomous maintenance is one of the key ingredients of TPM. But, what exactly is autonomous maintenance? Autonomous maintenance is maintenance performed by production operators [5], and the maintenance tasks which are generally performed by them under TPM include the following:

1. Cleaning, lubrication and bolting.
2. Daily and periodic inspections.
3. Minor repairs/adjustments and servicing.

With these routine preventive maintenance tasks out of the way, the maintenance department has enough time to attend to the important tasks of predictive, or condition-based, and corrective maintenance, which includes both restoration and reliability and maintainability improvement activities. But is this the essence of autonomous maintenance? Autonomous maintenance is not just handing over a few maintenance tasks to the production operators. It is much more than that. It is a strategy of giving production operators ownership of their equipment and making them feel responsible for its care [9]. In this chapter, we will discuss autonomous maintenance, the responsibilities of the maintenance department under TPM and the training of maintenance technicians.

Before we do anything else, let us briefly look at the need for autonomous maintenance. Why do we need autonomous maintenance and can we really have TPM without autonomous maintenance? In Chapter One, while discussing the history of TPM, we had noted the origin of autonomous maintenance. It may be mentioned, as a brief recapitulation that autonomous maintenance was instituted by Nippondenso in Japan in the late 1960s when it was noticed that the maintenance crew was finding it difficult to maintain the large number of automated equipment. The maintenance department needed help and the management thought it fit to change the allotment of duties of the production operators. The production operators were made responsible for the routine maintenance of their equipment. This story may give the wrong sort of message to many in India. Some of us may question the need for implementation of autonomous maintenance and justify this by quoting the story of Nippondenso and by saying that autonomous maintenance would only be necessary when the level of automation in our industries increases to that of Japan, or the industrialised nations of the West. They may also add that "we don't have to do it just because the Japanese have done it" to rub this in.

Let us consider the actual state of affairs in our industrial organisations. The main reason for the poor availability of equipment, plants and production facilities is that the basic equipment conditions are not maintained. The periodic preventive maintenance tasks of cleaning, lubrication, tightening of bolts and fasteners, replacement of wearing parts, equipment inspections and servicing are not performed. The maintenance department, in most cases, does not get the time to attend to these tasks and is too busy taking care of equipment breakdowns. Because these essential tasks are not performed, the condition of the equipment worsens and this, in turn, gives rise to a larger number of breakdowns. This makes matter worse and the maintenance departments find it all the more difficult to carry out the preventive maintenance tasks and ensure that the basic equipment conditions are maintained. Add to this the fact that equipment operating conditions are, in most cases, poor, operating procedures are not strictly adhered to and the operating standards are not maintained by the production operators. This also has a negative effect on the condition of the production equipment and, therefore, on equipment breakdowns. Increasing number of breakdowns also results in inadequate restoration activity and use of patchup repairs. The relationship between the operations and maintenance departments is adversarial. The two departments do not get along well; let alone the question of working together as a team. One blames the other for the poor condition of production equipment. As a result of this, the production equipment suffers. Because of this, the availability of our equipment, plants and production facilities is poor and things are getting worse every day. Consider also that globalisation and opening up of our economy will bring with it competition and this, in turn, will call for use of sophisticated and automated equipment and plants. We, in India, have to get out of this vicious circle and autonomous maintenance and implementation of TPM will provide us the means of doing this.

We must remember that in this age of competition, we cannot afford the luxury of poor equipment availability any more. The price that a manufacturing organisation pays for the loss of one hour of production on an equipment, or machine, is already very high and with the advent of modernisation and use of sophisticated machinery, this price is going to be much greater in the future. Also with rising prices of equipment and machinery and financial constraints brought on by budgetary limitations, the replacement of production equipment and machines is becoming more difficult. Maximisation of equipment availability and extension of the useful life of production equipment have become essential and these objectives cannot be achieved with the 'I operate, you fix' attitude of the past. Autonomous maintenance can help us attain these objectives.

The thing to remember is that autonomous maintenance is carried out to prevent accelerated deterioration of equipment and also to slow down the process of natural deterioration. The very basis of autonomous maintenance is the prevention of deterioration and this has been neglected in our factories, production facilities and process plants for far too long. Autonomous maintenance will enable the maintenance of basic equipment conditions and with it also bring back in the production operators the pride of craftsmanship. The operators will learn to take care of their equipment and machines and use them properly. This will also ensure the use of improved operating procedures and maintenance of operating standards. The accelerated deterioration brought on by excessive loading, maloperation and operating errors will also be prevented, and the incidence of equipment breakdowns will be reduced. The maintenance department will find time for important tasks, such as, predictive maintenance, analysis of past failures, strengthening of weak points and reliability and maintainability improvement activities. Thus, autonomous maintenance will not only take away a part of the workload of the maintenance department, but also bring into the organisation sanity, cooperation and a sense of belonging. Thus, we may conclude that autonomous maintenance is necessary for our factories and process plants and it is also essential for reduction of the six big losses. Accordingly, we cannot have TPM without autonomous maintenance.

Prerequisites for Autonomous Maintenance

In the preceding paragraphs, we have discussed the prevailing conditions in Indian manufacturing organisations and shown that to reverse the trend and work towards higher equipment availability and effectiveness, it is necessary to implement autonomous maintenance. We have also shown that autonomous maintenance is essential for the elimination of the six big losses and accordingly, it is an essential ingredient of TPM. But this is easier said than done since autonomous maintenance requires a change of attitude in the employees. Under autonomous maintenance, the operators of production equipment are required to attend to routine preventive maintenance tasks in addition to their allotted jobs of operating the production equipment. This implies that the operators are not only required to cooperate with the maintenance department and help in the task of maintenance of production equipment, but also to take on added responsibilities. Taking on added responsibility also implies acquiring a new skill. Similarly, under autonomous maintenance, maintenance technicians are also required to change their attitude. Many eyebrows will be raised on reading this statement; but for a moment, consider the fact that the maintenance personnel, in most of our factories and process plants, have been busy carrying out routine tasks and patchup repairs, and have not taken on condition-based maintenance jobs which require the ability to analyse condition monitoring data and based on this, to decide the best course of action, and also analysis of past failure data and failure modes to identify equipment weaknesses and then plan reliability and maintainability improvement activities. These jobs require updating of skills, acquisition of new knowledge and, in many cases, even learning of new skills. In addition to this, the maintenance technicians will also have to learn to cooperate with the production operators and not treat them as enemies. Thus, a most basic change of attitude is required from the production operators and the maintenance technicians. Of course, in most cases, it may be a lot easier to get the maintenance technicians to accept this than the production operators because the required change is going to be much more profound for the production operators. Now let us see whether it is going to be easy to bring about this change and implement autonomous maintenance. Also let us briefly discuss the basic prerequisites for this change.

The implementation of autonomous maintenance calls for an attitude of understanding and cooperation on the part of the employees. This, in turn, is derived from the employees sense of belonging to the organisation and the trust employees have in the management of the organisation. In India, in most of the industrial organisations, the industrial relations situation is not entirely conducive for the implementation of TPM. At best there is a gap — an absence of two-way communication—between the management and the employees, and in the worst cases, there is mistrust between the two. There is a lack of trust between the employees and the management and to this, in many cases, is added a lurking suspicion of the intentions of the management in the minds of the employees. This lack of trust has to be removed and this can be done by a clear demonstration of management's faith in TPM and its dedication to improvement and growth. The management has to take the necessary actions to bring about certain changes in the operations of the company. These changes are the prerequisites for the implementation of autonomous maintenance.

The prerequisites for the implementation of autonomous maintenance include the following changes/activities:

(i) recognition of the need for planning in maintenance and implementation of planned maintenance,

(ii) installation of history cards on all critical equipment and machines,

(iii) use of preventive maintenance and proper scheduling and control of all periodic preventive maintenance tasks including cleaning, lubrication, periodic inspections, periodic replacements, overhauls and servicing,

(iv) use of predictive, or condition-based, maintenance for critical equipment (particularly on rotating machines, like pumps and turbines — use of vibration and noise monitoring, and on gearboxes — use of wear-debris monitoring/ferrography),

(v) use of a maintenance planning and control system based on a work order, or job order, system (it can either be a manual system or a computerised system depending on the size and complexity of operations but as the size of operations increases, steps should be taken to computerise the manual system),

(vi) systematic collection of failure data and collection of costs of both breakdown and preventive maintenance jobs and feeding these back to the maintenance department via the data processing/management services department,

(vii) analysis of maintenance costs to identify areas/systems requiring special attention in the form of strengthening of components and subsystems and reliability and maintainability improvement efforts,

(viii) analysis of failure data and analysis of failure modes to identify the reliability and maintainability improvements needed, and

(ix) restructuring of the maintenance organisation to give it the required importance and power and also to ensure prevention of failures and an attitude of proaction as opposed to reaction and fire-fighting. The new structure must be capable of ensuring that all the preventive and corrective maintenance actions, detailed above, are properly planned and executed (for this, in larger process plants and manufacturing facilities, it may be necessary to create a maintenance planning bureau/cell/department).

These changes will demonstrate to the employees that the management wants to bring about major changes in the way the plant is being operated. The dedication of the top management to the efforts will be brought home by the expenditure of resources required for some of these activities. Once these activities and systems are installed and progressing satisfactorily, then the management can go to the employees and seek their cooperation in the task of implementation of autonomous maintenance.

When the organisation is brought to a stage where preventive and predictive maintenance programmes are operating satisfactorily, the maintenance tasks are being properly planned and the incidence of catastrophic failures has come down, failure costs and failure data are being fed back and based on them, corrective actions are being planned and executed, and the maintenance department has been restructured and given its due place in the organisation, the employees will realise that the management wants to ensure proper maintenance of plant and equipment. The benefits of these actions should be explained to the employees. The fact that better maintenance will lead to higher equipment availability and effectiveness, and this, in turn, will lead to greater revenues and higher profits must be explained to the employees. It is suggested that the results be quantified as far as possible and the employees and the employee union be taken into confidence. If these actions are taken then the attitude of the employees will change to one of understanding and cooperation. The employees will then be in a mood to accept the changes which will be brought about by autonomous maintenance. The management must also make it abundantly clear to the employees and the employee union that (a) the objective of the autonomous maintenance programme is not to eliminate any (not even one) maintenance jobs, and (b) if the equipment operators clean, lubricate, inspect and periodically service their own equipment, they will contribute to increased equipment effectiveness. If the trust in the management has been brought back (by the prerequisites) and these points are made clear to the employees, then, it is felt that, the equipment operators and maintenance technicians will accept the implementation of autonomous maintenance.

These preparatory tasks, or prerequisites, have been discussed in some detail primarily because they assume a special kind of importance in the Indian setting. What can be done easily in Japan may require quite a bit of preparation and effort here in India because of our cultural differences. The difference in the two cultures is not the subject matter of this book,[2] and herein we will only add that effective communication can only be built on trust and therefore, without mutual trust between management and employees, one cannot implement a major change, such as autonomous maintenance.

Allocation of Equipment Maintenance Tasks

We have already noted that maximisation of availability and extension of useful life of production equipment have become essential. These twin objectives have to be pursued relentlessly by all manufacturing organisations if they want to survive and grow in this age of competition. In the preceding chapter, we have also noted that for this it is necessary to ensure the following:

1. Proper operation of production equipment, maintenance of operating standards and improvement of operating conditions and procedures. These are necessary to prevent deterioration of the equipment. Correct operation of the equipment includes making necessary and proper adjustments, not only during setup but also periodically during operation of the equipment.

2. Maintenance of basic equipment condition to prevent deterioration. This should include not only the daily/routine maintenance acivities of cleaning, lubrication, tightening of bolts and fasteners, daily checks of the equipment and its conditions of use, and minor servicing, but also periodic preventive maintenance and predictive maintenance activities, such as inspections, condition monitoring, servicing, replacement of parts and overhauls and capital repair.

3. Restoration of equipment to optimum functioning since even with all the efforts directed at the prevention of deterioration, deterioration of the equipment and its components does take place. This results in failures, or breakdowns, which, as we have noted, can be of two types, namely function reduction and function loss breakdowns. Restoration is not just breakdown maintenance and it must include besides repairs, early detection of deterioration and early discovery of abnormalities.[3] The work of restoration must also include activities directed at the improvement of the maintenance function, such as establishment and improvement of methods and procedures for periodic adjustment of equipment, periodic servicing, testing and repair.

4. Improvement of design weaknesses. This must include attempts to improve both reliability and maintainability. Reliability can be improved not only by strengthening of components and subsystems and provision of redundancy (wherever it can be justified economically), but also by reducing overloading of the equipment and overstressing of its components and subsystems. Similarly, maintainability improvement calls for equipment modifications (to reduce the mean time to repair (MTTR)), analysis of repair data and the

establishment and improvement of procedures of inspection and testing, condition monitoring, diagnosis, servicing and overhaul.

From this discussion, we surmise that the activities which are required can be classified as follows:

1. Maintenance of normal operating conditions and standards.
2. Maintenance of production equipment and the activities included herein can be subdivided under the following subheads:
   — Routine maintenance;
   — Periodic maintenance;
   — Predictive maintenance; and
   — Breakdown maintenance.
3. Improvement of maintenance procedures and practices.
4. Improvement of the design weaknesses of the equipment.

At the begining of this chapter, we had questioned the need for implementation of autonomous maintenance and through a discussion of the conditions existing in our industrial organisations, we had concluded that the twin objectives of maximisation of equipment availability and extension of life can only be achieved if the production and maintenance departments cooperate. The maintenance department, by itself, cannot carry out all the activities mentioned earlier and some of these activities can, and should, be carried out by the production operators. But how is the apportioning of the tasks done?

An allocation of the equipment maintenance tasks between the production/ operation department and the maintenance department is given in Table 5.1. The allocation of tasks given in the table clearly shows that there are a number of tasks which are to be carried out by the production operators. These are the autonomous maintenance activities. Broadly, the autonomous maintenance programme includes correct operation, adjustment and prevention of overloading, cleaning, lubrication and bolting, daily and certain periodic inspections, minor repairs and servicing, and detection of abnormal signs and deterioration. The activities included are directed primarily at the prevention of deterioration, including its detection. In addition to the detection and prevention activities, minor adjustments, servicing and repair are also included. The tasks allocated to the maintenance department include the essential activities of inspection, condition-based maintenance, servicing and overhaul, planning and improvement of maintenance procedures and practices, and designing-out-of-maintenance. These essential tasks

Table 5.1 Allocation of Equipment Maintenance Tasks

Main Heads	*Equipment Maintenance Functions*	*Activities*	*Allocation*	
			Operation	*Maintenance*
1. Maintenance of normal operation		1.1 Proper operation — maintenance of operating standards	✓	
		1.2 Proper adjustment during setup and during operation.	✓	
2. Equipment maintenance	2.1 Routine maintenance	2.1.1 Cleaning	✓	
		2.1.2 Lubrication	✓	
		2.1.3 Tightening/Bolting	✓	
		2.1.4 Daily Inspections	✓	
		2.1.5 Minor Servicing	✓	
	2.2 Periodic maintenance	2.2.1 Periodic Inspections*	✓	✓
		2.2.2 Periodic servicing and replacement of parts		✓
		2.2.3 Periodic overhauls		✓
	2.3 Predictive maintenance	2.3.1 Condition monitoring		✓
		2.3.2 Analysis of condition monitoring data, diagnosis of fault and trend analysis		✓
	2.4 Breakdown maintenance	2.4.1 Early detection of abnormality and prompt reporting	✓	
		2.4.2 Repair of breakdowns		✓
3. Documentation and improvement — maintenance procedures and practices.		3.1 Improve inspection and testing procedures		✓
		3.2 Improve servicing and adjustment procedures		✓
		3.3 Improve repair procedures		✓
4. Improvement of design weaknesses — designing out-of-maintenance	4.1 Reliability improvement	4.1.1 Strengthen components		✓
		4.1.2 Prevent overloading/overstressing	✓	
		4.1.3 Analysis of failure data and failure modes		✓
	4.2 Maintainability improvement	4.2.1 Analysis of repair data		✓
		4.2.2 Improve diagnostic methods and procedures		✓
		4.2.3 Equipment modifications.		✓

* Although it is a task allocated to the maintenance department, certain periodic inspections are carried out by operations.

need time and cannot be performed if the maintenance department also has to attend to the daily/routine tasks which are better looked after by the equipment operators.

Ensuring Proper Operation of Production Equipment

Autonomous maintenance consists of the maintenance tasks performed by the production operators.[4] The operators are required to perform these tasks in addition to their basic job of running, or operating, the production equipment. Thus in TPM, the production operators are required not only to operate the equipment and produce components/products but also to take care of their equipment. We have also seen that maintenance of operating standards and procedures, that is, ensuring correct operation and preventing maloperation and overloading of the equipment, is a necessary input for elimination of breakdown losses (Chapter Four) and for maximisation of equipment availability and extension of its useful life (Chapter Five). In this section, we will briefly discuss the means and methods for ensuring that the production equipment is operated properly, that is, the operating procedures are adhered to, operating conditions and standards are maintained, maloperation of the equipment is avoided, and overloading of the equipment and overstressing of its components/subsystems is prevented.

It must be emphasized that operation and maintenance are dependent on each other. Poor operation leads to equipment failures and shutdowns. Assuring proper operation is, therefore, an integral part of autonomous maintenance and instruction in correct operation is, thus, an integral part of autonomous maintenance training. The operators must be told to run their equipment properly and with care and the need for ensuring correct operation must be explained to them. But telling them is not enough. They must be instructed in the correct operation of the equipment and such instructions must also include the construction, mechanisms and functions of the equipment and also the details of the processes to be performed on the equipment. During these instructions, the procedures for starting and stopping of the equipment, the daily and periodic maintenance activities including cleaning, lubrication, bolting and inspection, the precautions to be taken during operation of the equipment and details of minor adjustments, repairs and servicing must be covered. Unfortunately, such instructions, by themselves, are again not adequate and failures and accidents do take place. To prevent inadvertent and careless mistakes, a checklist for machine/equipment operation must be prepared. Such checklists must include all important points which have to be ensured and precautions which have to be taken by the operator of the equipment during startup, setup, operation, shutdown — both routine and emergency, and periodic inspection and adjustment of the equipment. Normal operating conditions, such as pressure, temperature etc. and also disposition of valves and controls, should also be noted for all major systems of the equipment. In a process plant, checklists must be prepared for all critical equipment and displayed prominently near the machine/equipment. These checklists can also be used to advantage for instructing new operators/trainees.

Essentials for Maintenance of Basic Equipment Conditions

We have already noted that maintenance of basic equipment conditions is an essential input for the elimination of breakdown losses (Chapter Four) and also for maximisation of equipment availability and extension of its useful life (Chapter Five). To many, it seems that maintaining basic equipment conditions and thereby prevention of deterioration is what autonomous maintenance is all about. Many detractors of TPM feel that in TPM too much importance is given to cleaning, lubrication, bolting and daily inspections and although these are necessary tasks, occasional nonperformance of these tasks would not necessarily be disastrous. Also the author has come across papers in journals which seem to profess that the application of one kind of maintenance (obviously the more modern kind) obviates the need for the practice of the other; as an illustration, this, therefore, implies that with the advent of condition-based maintenance, routine and periodic preventive maintenance will not be necessary. The practitioner will immediately react to this realising the danger of such a practice; lack of lubrication will definitely result in a seizure and a catastrophic breakdown, loose bolts in flange couplings cause leakages and loose bolts cause fracture of dies and tools and production of defective products. Takahashi and Osada have presented the results of a study which showed that around 70 per cent of all equipment problems, which if unattended would cause stoppages and production of defective products, are caused by (i) dirt and accumulation of dust and debris, (23 per cent), (ii) lack of lubrication and oil leakage (22 per cent), and (iii) looseness, excessive vibration and wobbling parts (24 per cent) [11]. Suzaki, in his book on manufacturing, states that the maintenance of normal equipment conditions is an essential input for the prevention of machine breakdowns and adds that the factors which cause machine/equipment problems include the following [8]:

(i) Dirty floor
(ii) Scattered chips on machine and floor

(iii) Dirty machine
(iv) Dirty oiler
(v) Flooded oil pan
(vi) Oil leakage
(vii) Empty oiler
(viii) Excessive vibration
(ix) Difficulties in equipment inspection
(x) Unnecessary things lying around and lack of organisation.

The last factor of Suzaki's list points to the importance of orderliness and tidiness, *seiri* and *seiton* in Japanese, which we have discussed in Chapter Four under improvement of setup and adjustments. In this section, we will discuss the importance of cleaning and cleanliness, lubrication, prevention of looseness and bolting, and daily and periodic equipment inspections. We will also discuss the requirements which are essential for the performance of autonomous maintenance. These essentials are (i) standards and checklists, and (ii) training and imparting of inspection skills. The discussion in this section will be presented in four subsections under the following headings:

1. Cleaning, lubrication and bolting.
2. Daily and periodic inspections.
3. Use of standards and checklists.
4. Equipment inspection training and development of "knowledgeable" operators.

CLEANING, LUBRICATION AND BOLTING[5]

We have already noted in Chapter Four that cleaning and lubrication are the two vital functions for maintaining optimum equipment conditions. We have also noted that looseness gives rise to excessive vibration which may result in a failure and shutdown. Mechanical looseness is also one of the contributors of wear-out failures of components [3]. Thus cleaning, lubrication and bolting are the three basic functions of autonomous maintenance. These three activities ensure the prevention of deterioration and maintenance of the basic conditions of production equipment.

Cleaning is the removal of foreign matter, dirt, debris and garbage and 'beautification of the equipment' [11]. Cleaning is an essential part of housekeeping. It not only beautifies the machine and its surroundings, but also helps in creating a tidy and orderly workplace. The most important thing about cleaning is that it gives the person a feeling of ownership; the operator who cleans the equipment before he starts work cherishes his machine and wants to take care of it. This also brings with it the pride of craftsmanship and the desire to do a job well. Cleaning is also a preventive action, since it prevents (i) breakdowns caused by dust, debris, scum and sludge, (ii) quality defects caused by dirt and contamination, and (iii) brief stoppages caused by dirt, dust and debris in chutes and material handling devices. We have already noted in Chapter Four that cleaning reveals deterioration and hidden defects. Certain defects, cracks and fractures are only visible after the part or the surface has been cleaned. Thus, cleaning is also inspection; during the process of cleaning, the operator checks to see whether everything is as it should be.

Lubrication reduces friction, smoothens movements and prevents wear of components. Lubrication also provides cooling and prevents overheating of components. Inadequate lubrication may result in a catastrophic failure caused by seizure. Insufficient lubrication may also lead to (i) indirect losses caused by poor operating conditions in sliding and rotating parts and in pneumatic systems, and (ii) accelerated wear caused by excessive friction. Such indirect losses can sometimes turn out to be more significant than catastrophic failures. Goto [5] gives the example of a company which reduced its electricity consumption by five per cent just by instituting methods and controls for proper lubrication. The common reasons for inadequate lubrication of equipment in factories and process plants include the following:

(i) Too many lubricating points and the time required for lubrication is not available.

(ii) Many of the lubricating points are inaccessible and this increases the time required for lubrication. Also some of the more inaccessible points are not lubricated.

(iii) Inadequate training of those who are responsible for the lubrication of machines/equipment.

Loose, broken, or missing nuts, bolts and other fasteners can cause major losses. At one end, catastrophic failures resulting in long shutdowns can be caused by loose or broken bolts and nuts and at the other end, looseness may result in losses caused by leakage and vibration. Takahashi and Osada [11] present the result of a study on bolt tightening conducted on 500 machines in a plant. The total incidence of looseness was found to be eight per cent in mechanical installations and as much as 19.3 per cent in electrical installations, such as control panels. The study also found that on some machines, more than half the joints needed tightening. Goto [5] reports the results of an analysis of causes of breakdowns in which it was found that 60 per cent of the breakdowns could be traced to faulty bolting. In another study, Goto reports that 48 per cent of all bolts and nuts were found to be either loose, missing, or otherwise defective [5]. These studies stress the need for including bolting as an essential part of daily maintenance together with cleaning and lubrication. Bolting is necessary for the prevention of accelerated deterioration of equipment. Bolting is an act of checking for loose, broken, or missing bolts, nuts, washers and other fasteners and taking corrective action. In a large plant, bolting may take a considerable amount of time unless it is aided and facilitated by some simple measures. These can be subdivided in two categories, namely, preventive and mistake-proofing measures. The preventive measures include the following:

(i) Stopping the use of just one bolt for tightening.

(ii) Use of spring washers and avoiding their reuse.

(iii) Ensuring the use of bolts of adequate/correct length.

(iv) Use of check nuts, or lock nuts, wherever possible.

(v) Use of torque wrench to tighten important bolts.

The commonly used mistake-proofing measures include the following:

(i) Marking, or otherwise identifying clearly, important bolts.

(ii) Using match marks on nuts to ensure proper tightening.

The preventive measures will reduce the incidence of loose and missing bolts and nuts. Checklists can also be prepared for critical machines/equipment and these checklists can be used during training. We will discuss the training of operators later in this section. Moreover, mistake-proofing aids are essential for the effectiveness of autonomous maintenance and some of these aids will also be discussed later in this chapter.

DAILY AND PERIODIC INSPECTIONS

Cleaning, lubrication and bolting prevent deterioration of the equipment. Another important constituent of autonomous maintenance is inspection. Inspection is carried out for the purpose of detection of deterioration, or a defect, or a problem, which if unattended, may cause a breakdown. Inspection is also a means of measurement. Thus, inspection measures natural deterioration and detects signs of accelerated deterioration. In TPM, daily and routine inspections are carried out by equipment operators. Inspections can be very effective, if they are carried out properly. However, in practice, the effectiveness of equipment inspection is adversely affected due to a number of reasons. Although the reasons cited are many and diverse, they can be grouped under three primary causes, which are as follows:

(i) Lack of time available to carry out equipment inspections.

(ii) Lack of motivation and interest (in the task of equipment inspection).

(iii) Lack of ability and necessary skills.

The operators often complain that not enough time is available for equipment inspections. Takahashi and Osada [11] state that the investigation of these complaints reveals that either too many items need to be inspected in a given time, the inspection methods are too difficult and time consuming, or the points, or areas, which are to be inspected are hidden from sight. The time required to be spent on equipment inspection depends on the number of items and parameters which are to be inspected and the ease with which each of these inspections can be performed. Each and every item, or operating parameter, of the equipment need not be inspected daily, and there are a large number of items which can be inspected periodically, instead. The inspection interval for periodic inspection can be weekly, fortnightly, monthly, and for some items even once a quarter. Thus, the first thing is to determine the inspection interval (and this must be done purely on technical and process considerations) for all the items and parameters which should be included under autonomous maintenance. Then these items should be grouped under different categories and when this is done, it will be found that the number of items in each group is much smaller then what had been anticipated. Thereafter, the activity of inspection should be studied and simplified, wherever possible. Also wherever necessary and possible, minor modifications must be made to the equipment to make the inspection points more accessible.[6] The time required for daily inspections should be around 10 minutes and the periodic inspections should not take more then 15-20 minutes [5]. Anything more then this will result in incomplete and ineffective inspections (On days in which periodic inspections have also to be carried out, around 30 minutes will be required and in a production shop, keeping aside 30 minutes for equipment inspection is itself rather difficult). After the daily and periodic inspections are determined and these activities are examined, simplified and improved, checklists should be prepared for each production equipment/machine.[7] These checklists should not only be used for training of operators, but also for performing the daily and periodic inspection tasks [9].

Unless the operator knows why a given item, an area, or a subsystem needs to be inspected and also realises the harm or loss/nonperformance of the inspection will cause, he will not be motivated to carry out the task. The operators, therefore, must be made aware of the need to inspect the item or area, and they must also be instructed adequately to carry out the inspection properly. If this is not done, then the operator may either not carry out the inspection at all (using lack of time as a convenient excuse), or just go through the motions and not perform the task properly. The purpose of equipment inspection is not just to detect problems in a machine or equipment, but to be confident that the inspected areas—the items or areas "that I inspected" — can be absolutely guaranteed [11]. This type of attitude is crucial for ensuring effective equipment inspection and can be developed through training.

USE OF STANDARDS AND CHECKLISTS

A walk around a factory floor reveals many dirty or sludgy oil pans, lubricating oil and grease ripples convered with dirt and dust, and clogged pipes in centralised lubricating systems. If this kind of a situation exists, then lubrication is useless no matter how often or how regularly it is performed. Such situations are quite common and two main reasons for their existence are lack of training and non-availability of checklists. Even the properly trained operator needs a checklist as it is a convenient *aide-memoire*—a reminder of all that needs to be done. The Japanese are big proponents of checklists [12].[8] They suggest its use not only as a training aid (for operators in autonomous maintenance), but also for performance of daily tasks of cleaning, lubrication, bolting and equipment inspections. Their faith in checklists is based on the belief that people can and do forget things and checklists prevent the bad effects of such forgetfulness.

Checklists are invaluable tools. The preparation of checklists calls for knowledge of the equipment — the construction, functions(s), mechanisms, operation and maintenance manuals provided by the supplier and the supplier's recommendations, and the knowledge of the process(es) to be performed on the equipment. Checklists for cleaning, lubrication, bolting and autonomous inspection must be prepared by the maintenance department although they are to be used by the equipment operators. In the preparation of the checklists, the maintenance engineers and technicians must consult the equipment operators and shop engineers, and together they must determine the activities to be carried out, points to be lubricated and items to be inspected. Checklists must be simple, brief and to the point. They must be written so that they are clearly understood by the operators, who have to use them. As noted earlier, if the checklists are properly and thoughtfully prepared, they can be used as valuable training tools. They not only remind individuals about the tasks to be performed or items to be inspected, they can also help operators detect out-of-tolerance conditions during equipment inspections. During training, the operators must be made to practice the tasks a number of times (with the use of the checklists). Through such practice, the contents of the checklists, namely, the tasks and the sequence in which they are to be performed in case of cleaning, lubrication and bolting and the 'know-what' and 'know-how' (what to look for and the technique of carrying out the inspection) in case of equipment inspection, get completely memorised and the operators can then carry out the autonomous maintenance tasks without the help of the checklists. The checklists must be displayed prominently at or near the machines as reminders and also aids, if and when needed. Some checklists for cleaning, lubrication and bolting and also for equipment inspections — for pneumatic/steam, hydraulic and electrical installations and for drive systems — are given as illustrations in Chapter Four of Nakajima's TPM Development Program [5].

Standards help to maintain the optimum equipment conditions. As compared to a checklist, a standard is a more complete document. In cleaning and lubrication, for example, whereas the checklists only enumerate the tasks to be performed and checks to be made, standards also define the method and tools used, the periodicity or cycle (whether daily, weekly, or monthly) and the estimated time required to carry out these tasks and checks. In case of equipment inspections, the standards also define the acceptance criteria, such as temperature must be between 30^0-50^0C, or the vibration must be below 25 microns. In standards, sketches are also provided showing the lubrication points and inspection areas/items. Generally, one standard can be prepared for all autonomous maintenance tasks for an equipment or a machine. This will include standards for cleaning and prevention of contamination, lubrication and equipment inspection giving therein the location/lubrication points, criteria, methods, tool(s), interval or periodicity, time required and the category of installation for equipment inspection, namely hydraulic, pneumatic, electrical, drive system, gearbox etc. As noted earlier, explanatory sketches/figures must be provided in the standards, if required. Conversely, two standards can be prepared—one for cleaning and lubrication, and another (separate) for equipment inspections. Examples of autonomous maintenance standards are given in Chapter Four of Nakajima's TPM Development Program [5].

Checklists and standards are useful aids. However, they serve two different purposes and it must be obvious from the preceding discussion that a standard is a more important document than a checklist. Moreover, checklists for equipment inspection are generally prepared subsystem-wise, for example, checklists for drive systems, transmission systems/gearboxes, hydraulic, pneumatic and electrical installations. As opposed to this, standards must always be prepared equipment-wise. Autonomous maintenance standards must be available for all critical equipment in a plant. The task of preparation of autonomous maintenance standards should be undertaken as an essential part of ISO9001/9002 documentation work. This will give the required fillip to the autonomous maintenance effort and the TPM implementation programme. There are two points which must be kept in mind during the development of standards and checklists. They are as follows:

(i) Simplicity—the planners and maintenance engineers must always remember Harold Dodge's oft-quoted advice, namely, "if you want a method or system used, keep it simple" [4]. Simplicity also facilitates control [6] and one must remember that in this case, self-control is necessary.

(ii) Involvement of the user — herein, as a reminder, we have Fumio Goto's observation, namely, "the biggest obstacle to adherence occurs when those who set standards are not the same people who must follow them" [5]. This will also facilitate maintenance and maintainability improvement, since involvement of the operators will encourage use of methods which are readily adaptable to change.

EQUIPMENT INSPECTION TRAINING AND DEVELOPMENT OF "KNOWLEDGEABLE" OPERATORS

The task of inspection requires mastering the skills required to perform it correctly.[9] To enable them to perform this task correctly, the operators must be given adequate training in equipment inspection. The difficult part of inspection involves measuring the extent of deterioration. This requires the ability to not only detect an abnormality, but also gauge exactly how bad the situation is. This, in turn, requires the skill to diagnose the problem and based on this, to predict the future damage it may cause. Thus once, the 'know-what' and 'know-how' of inspection of a mechanism or a subsystem are taught, then as a part of inspection training, each operator should be required to carry out the diagnosis.

Inspection training must be complete since the operators must learn enough to be able to set their own standards not only for daily and periodic inspections, but also for cleaning, lubrication and bolting. Inspection training must, therefore, include instructions in other essential tasks of autonomous maintenance. During the equipment inspection training, the importance of cleanliness, tidiness and orderliness must be clearly and unambiguously explained to the operators. The old idea that minor defects, such as a little dirt, abrasions, scratches, play, looseness or distortion are inevitable and do not cause breakdowns must be driven out of the minds of the operators. Operators must be convinced of the need to thoroughly eliminate all minor defects without deliberating as to whether they contribute to losses [10]. They must understand that from a TPM standpoint, such minor defects are regarded as the probable causes of defects unless it is known that they are absolutely unrelated to breakdowns and losses. Another important consideration in the design of an inspection training programme is that of safety—of the equipment and of human life. Accidents are bound to occur if the operators are not trained properly [12].

For development of an inspection training programme, subsystems which are common to most equipment and machines, such as drive systems, transmission systems, hydraulic, pneumatic and electrical installations etc., are identified and classified into several inspection categories. Then inspection checklists, standards and training programmes are developed for each of these categories by the maintenance engineers, preferably in consultation with production managers/ departmental managers. Thereafter, in TPM, training in equipment inspection is initially imparted to the production supervisors and PM group leaders by the maintenance engineers and technicians. This is done for all the categories of equipment subsystems, one after another. The supervisors and PM group leaders, in turn, then train the operators in their group. This is expected to enhance the leadership skills of the production supervisors and PM group leaders.[10] This method of training (of the supervisors and PM group leaders initially and through them to the equipment operators) has been very successfully used by the Japanese. The english translation of the term used by the Japanese for this method of instruction is "roll-out education" [10].

Training in equipment inspection should impart enough knowledge and skills to the equipment/machine operator so that he can detect signs of abnormal/ unusual conditions and problems which may subsequently develop into break-downs. This means that the operator should be able to sense an unusual condition during the operation of his equipment much before occurrence of a breakdown, or production of defective components/products. In TPM literature, such an operator is called a "*knowledgeable operator*." Tajiri and Gotoh [10] have given an explanation of this term and their explanation is as follows:

"The term `knowledgeable operator' does not mean an operator who can fix an equipment as well as a maintenance technician. Rather it emphasises that an important aspect of an operator's skill is to detect signs of losses."

The ultimate aim of autonomous inspection training is the development of knowledgeable operators.

We now come to a very important prerequisite of effective inspection and this is an "orderly shopfloor." A knowledgeable operator can detect signs or indications of abnormality in a workplace which is tidy and orderly. We must again invoke two of the 5Ss — *seiri and seiton*. We will discuss the need for *seiri and seiton* in greater detail in the following section, but before we close our discussion of equipment inspection training, we must stress the need for an "orderly shopfloor" or in other words, a shopfloor where deviations from normal conditions can be detected at a glance by anyone [10].

Seven Steps for Implementation of Autonomous Maintenance

Having discussed the allocation of equipment maintenance tasks and also the prerequisites for autonomous maintenance and essentials for maintenance of basic equipment conditions, we are in a position now to discuss the steps which have to be taken for the implementation of autonomous maintenance (or the stages of implementation of autonomous maintenance). Fumio Goto has developed the seven steps for the implementation of autonomous maintenance based on the experiences of companies who have successfully implemented TPM [7]. The seven steps of autonomous maintenance are given in Table 5.2. These seven steps can, in turn, be classified under the following three groups of activities:

Group I - Steps 1, 2 and 3 - Cleaning, lubrication and bolting.

Group II - Steps 4 and 5 - Daily and periodic equipment inspection.

Group III - Steps 6 and 7 - Workplace organisation, housekeeping and autono- mous management.

The seven stages, or steps, of implementation of autonomous maintenance are as follows:

1. Initial cleaning, lubrication and bolting.
2. Eliminating sources of contamination and improving accessibility to facilitate cleaning and lubrication.
3. Developing checklists and standards for cleaning and lubrication.

Table 5.2. Seven Steps for Implementation of Autonomous Maintenance

Activity Group	*Step*	*Activities*	*Goals*
I. Cleaning, lubrication and bolting	1. Initial cleaning	i) Clean equipment to remove dirt and dust ii) Remove unnecessary materials and discarded machine parts from the workplace iii) Lubricate and tighten bolts and nuts	i) Prevent accelerated deterioration ii) Learn that cleaning is inspection iii) Discover and remove hidden defects.
	2. Eliminating sources of contamination	i) Eliminate sources of dust and dirt/causes of contamination ii) Improve accessibility of areas/points difficult to clean and lubricate iii) Reduce time required for cleaning and lubrication **Note:** (ii) and (iii) may call for some equipment modification (minor in nature)	i) Increase equipment reliability (operational reliability) ii) Improve maintainability of equipment
	3. Cleaning and lubrication standards	i) Conduct training in cleaning ii) Establish lubrication control system (checklists) iii) Develop standards for cleaning, lubrication and bolting	i) Maintain basic equipment conditions (through deterioration prevention)
II. Daily and periodic equipment inspections	4. General equipment inspection	i) Conduct training in inspection ii) Discover and correct minor equipment defects through inspection iii) Modify equipment to facilitate inspection	i) Detect deterioration through visual inspection ii) Facilitate inspection*
	5. Autonomous inspection	i) Develop inspection checklists ii) Standardise and document cleaning, lubrication and inspection standards for all critical equipment/machines	i) Maintain optimum equipment conditions ii) Develop 'knowledgeable,' operators.
III. Workplace organisation, housekeeping and autonomous management	6. Workplace organisation and housekeeping	Standardise methods and controls for: i) Workplace cleaning and lubrication ii) Manufacturing/production process (es)	i) Review and improve plant/facilities layout ii) Develop 'orderly shopfloor' for better visual control

Contd..

Activity Group	Step	Activities	Goals
		iii) Product quality	
		iv) Data collection	
		v) Spare parts, dies, jigs and tools	
	7. Full autonomous maintenance	i) Record data and analyse MTBF and MTTR	i) Maximising equipment availability
		ii) Design and implement reliability and maintainability improvements	ii) Lengthen equipment life.

* *Visual inspection can be facilitated by simple means like serial numbering, markers and thermal tapes and by the use of gauges and indicators. Use of visual controls will be discussed later in the chapter.*

4. Training in equipment inspection, facilitating inspection and initiation of daily and periodic inspection by equipment operators.
5. Developing inspection checklists and standards and standardising and documenting cleaning, lubrication and inspection standards for all critical equipment in the plant.
6. Workplace organisation and housekeeping — imbibing the principles of tidiness and orderliness, *seiri* and *seiton*, in all activities relating to production equipment and production processes.
7. Full implementation of autonomous maintenance and achievement of the objective of autonomous management of production equipment.

The detailed activities and goals of the different stages are also given in Table 5.2.

Implementation of autonomous maintenance has to be done in steps or stages, because a major change such as this cannot be implemented any other way. The activities and goals given in the table clearly illustrate the fact that successful implementation of autonomous maintenance has to be progressive and enough time has to be given for each stage so that the activities are properly imbibed and goals for that stage are achieved before going on to the next stage. For example, unless equipment cleaning, lubrication and bolting, and orderly disposition of the workplace are attained and the operators learn and clearly understand that cleaning is inspection and through cleaning, hidden defects are discovered and subsequently removed, it is no use going to Step Two and taking on the tasks of eliminating sources of contamination and improving accessibility for cleaning and lubrication. Going to Step Two prematurely will only result in failure since the activities of Step One have not been completed and accordingly, the equipment and the operators have not been adequately prepared for the activities of Step Two. This holds good for all the steps, and management and employees alike should realise that the implementation of autonomous maintenance takes time. Enough time should be given at each stage and the operators must take the time needed to perfect each activity of each step.

There are three crucial inputs for the successful implementation of autonomous maintenance. They are so vital that they may be termed as keys to successful autonomous maintenance. They are as follows:

(i) Education and training.

(ii) Management involvement and cooperation between departments.

(iii) Employee participation and use of small group activities.

We will briefly discuss each of these three to comprehend the salient infrastructural requirements for the successful implementation of autonomous maintenance.

EDUCATION AND TRAINING

We have already noted the importance of education and training of operators—in proper operation of the equipment and in equipment inspection. We have also noted that education and training in autonomous maintenance should be progressive. It must not only impart knowledge and skills, but also bring about awareness and a change of attitude. The operators must become *'knowledgeable operators'* working in an *'orderly shopfloor,'* and such operators strive for perfection and continually try to improve. This calls for a feeling of ownership (of the equipment) and a sense of belonging (to the organisation). Knowledge, skill and self-confidence can only be achieved through a considerable amount of practice during training. Thereafter, sufficient time must also be spent in perfecting each activity of each step, as noted earlier.

There is, however, another aspect of education which is overlooked and this pertains to education of the management. Even before initiating the first step of autonomous maintenance, it is necessary to explain the objectives and benefits of autonomous maintenance and TPM to everyone in the management, right from top management to the shop-floor supervisors not only from the production/operations departments but also from all related departments, such as design/engineering, purchase/materials, accounting and personnel. A seminar should be organised by the maintenance department and in this seminar, the details of autonomous maintenance, the seven steps of its implementation and the goals for each of these steps must be presented and explained. In this effort, external expertise, if required, may be called for.

MANAGEMENT INVOLVEMENT AND COOPERATION BETWEEN DEPARTMENTS

Such a major change cannot be brought about without the support and direct involvement of the top and senior management of the company who must believe in the need to implement TPM. Only then can they bring about an attitudinal change in the middle management and in shop-floor supervisors. The employees and management alike should realise that in TPM, autonomous maintenance is not a voluntary activity. There are some managers and supervisors who take maintenance by equipment operators to be a voluntary and an unregulated activity. This misunderstanding is very damaging not only for the implementation of autonomous maintenance, but also to the TPM implementation programme. All levels of management must understand that (i) autonomous maintenance activities are mandatory and necessary, (ii) they are vital for the maintenance of optimum equipment conditions and maximisation of equipment effectiveness, and for achieving the company's goals of production, profits and growth, and (iii) autonomous maintenance requires a highly motivated workforce — both equipment operators and maintenance technicians — working in a supportive work environment.

Many hidden defects are exposed and many equipment malfunctions become evident during the implementation of autonomous maintenance. Such equipment problems must be corrected promptly. To the operators, prompt restoration of defects is a display of management's faith (and involvement in the programme) and as such, this needs management's attention and support. The maintenance department may require help to cope with this additional load of corrective maintenance activity. The management should monitor the progress of implementation of autonomous maintenance and offer advice from time to time, and should also provide the necessary infrastructural facilities for its implementation.

Cooperation between departments is most essential for the implementation of autonomous maintenance. The production/operation departments require the active cooperation not only of the maintenance department, but also of all related departments, as noted earlier. The cooperation between the departments is also necessary for TPM promotion and we will discuss this in the next chapter.

EMPLOYEE PARTICIPATION AND USE OF SMALL GROUP ACTIVITIES

TPM promotion is done through the use of small groups. Implementation of autonomous maintenance and TPM cannot be carried out without the participation of the employees. Employee participation is the most essential ingredient for the implementation of autonomous maintenance and for TPM promotion. The goals of each step of autonomous maintenance, noted in Table 5.2, are achieved through small group activities on the shopfloor.

PM group leaders are generally supervisors. We have already discussed education and training of production supervisors in autonomous maintenance activities and also their subsequent involvement in the autonomous maintenance implementation programmes. We will discuss the role of production supervisors in greater detail in the next chapter under TPM promotion through small groups, but herein we must stress that the active involvement of production supervisors is most crucial for the successful implementation of autonomous maintenance.

We have already noted that autonomous maintenance activities are mandatory. The equipment operators will carry out the autonomous maintenance tasks timely and properly only if they are convinced of the importance of autonomous maintenance, in particular and TPM, in general. This conviction comes through the active participation of the equipment operators in the autonomous maintenance programme. The equipment operators, as members of PM groups, take part in the (i) determination of standards for the autonomous maintenance tasks, the need for which we have discussed earlier, and (ii) monitoring the progress of implementation of autonomous maintenance, in the PM group meetings. Once the equipment operators are convinced, the activities of the different steps given in Table 5.2 are learnt and imbibed willingly and enthusiastically. Equipment operators, as members of PM groups, must then set concrete goals for themselves and for their groups to ensure that the goals of each stage of implementation of autonomous maintenance are achieved.

Need for and Benefits of Equipment Simplification

With the passage of time and advances in technology, new equipment and plants are being developed for production of goods and services. These new plants and equipment are much more complicated. Moreover, in operating industries, production processes are also being modified. The modification of production processes calls for addition to and modification of existing plant and equipment. This also makes the plants more complicated. Complicated plants and equipment are not only more susceptible to failures but also are much more difficult to maintain. Maintenance of basic equipment conditions becomes difficult. In such situations, autonomous maintenance is greatly facilitated by simplification of plant and equipment.

The process industry probably provides the best example of the difficulties created by changes in production processes resulting in modification of plants, laying of new pipelines and installation of additional electrical wiring and control panels. Herein the difficulties experienced in maintenance are also most obvious. Process changes in chemical and other process industries are usually brought about by cost reduction efforts and accordingly, many changes of production processes are made in a hurry. Old pipelines and electrical wiring are left in place. Sometimes even the old equipment, standby units and bypass lines are also left undisturbed [9]. These changes result in innumerable difficulties, including difficulty of access for cleaning, lubrication and inspection. Therefore, simplification should receive greater attention in process industries. It is also suggested that in process industries, simplification should be taken up as a part of the autonomous maintenance programme.

Suzuki suggests a six-step procedure for plant and equipment simplification. These steps are as follows[9]:[11]

Step 1: Study process specifications and understand production processes and equipment functions.

Step 2: Investigate and determine the reason(s) for introduction of complication(s).

Step 3: Determine the possible methods of simplification.

Step 4: Choose the best method and formulate improvement plans.

Step 5: Implement plans.

Step 6: Follow-up results and determine actual benefits of simplification.

Suzuki also provides a guide to simplification [9]. This guide applies mainly to chemical industries and oil refineries and in this guide, Suzuki suggests that to determine the possible methods of simplification, the need for and utility of mixers, valves, piping and pipelines and measuring instruments should be questioned with the objective of eliminating them altogether, or elimination of unnecessary duplication. Similar guidelines can also be prepared for other process industries.

The benefits of simplification are many and some of them are as follows [9]:

(i) Elimination of unnecessary piping, wiring, valves and fittings creates space, provides access and also makes the workplace more pleasant.

(ii) Improvement of workplace facilitates work and reduces operating errors.

(iii) Plant and equipment simplifications also facilitate visual controls and visual controls, in turn, facilitate the maintenance of basic equipment conditions.

(iv) Simplifications promote industrial safety.

(v) Reduction of process units and simplification of piping improves efficiency and helps save energy. Suzuki gives an example of a paper mill wherein simplification activities resulted in the reduction of electrical consumption by as much as 2,600 KW and the number of operators by about 50.

Visual controls are very useful aids in equipment inspection and we will discuss these in greater detail in the following section.

Mistake Proofing and Use of Visual Controls

Takahashi and Osada {11}, in their book on TPM, bring to our notice the following important fact:

> "It is easy to say that each should accomplish the goals set. To do so is another matter. People do not intend to break promises, but are forgetful, find tasks cumbersome or awkward and overlook things. That is why foolproofing, equipment augmentation and training are necessary."

This is a very important observation and this is something that must be realised by all engineers and managers. Operators, owing to the nature of their jobs, develop a strong bond with their equipment and want sincerely to take care of their equipment. They also want to do a good job and be recognised by their colleagues and superiors. It is the responsibility of the engineers and managers to design and develop a workplace which enables the operators to do their allotted jobs well-in time, properly and without mistakes. We have already discussed the subject of training of operators. We have also discussed the need for and benefits of equipment simplification and equipment modifications to support and aid maintenance of operating standards and procedures, and of the basic equipment conditions. In this section we will discuss means to prevent inadvertent and careless mistakes. We will not call it foolproofing—*boka-yoke* in Japanese. We will not do so since we believe very strongly that these mistakes are not committed by fools. Nor are they intentional—nobody is intentionally negligent. At the same time, due to momentary lack of attention, or overconfidence and carelessness, sometimes mistakes are committed. These mistakes are rare but in factories and process plants, human errors can sometimes turn out to be very expensive. Moreover, sometimes such errors cause accidents. Therefore, it is essential that mistakes be prevented by mechanical devices, electrical interlocks, ingenious means, or simple shop-floor methods. We will call these devices and means mistake-proofing measures—*poka-yoke* in Japanese, and in this section, we will discuss visual controls and these mistake-proofing measures.

Visual controls are the simplest and the most obvious means of protection against human errors and lapses. Visual controls facilitate equipment inspection. The state or condition of the equipment is clearly visible to the operator and this simplifies inspection. Visual controls also ensure that equipment inspections are carried out properly and lapses, if any, are visible and can be corrected before the occurrence of an undesirable event. The most commonly used methods of visual control are as follows:

1. *Matchmarks on nuts and bolts*

With these, the need for tightening is clearly visible to the human eye. Matchmarks are generally painted on both the nut and the bolt, or the body of the machine, by hand. Their use is essential in all areas where looseness, play, or vibration can cause deterioration/wear, an accident, or poor product quality.

2. *Marking of operating ranges on dials and gauges*

With this, abnormal operating conditions, if any, are clearly visible. Usually the face of the dial, (on the glass cover), is marked in green (for the normal operating range). In process plants, all gauges, such as pressure and temperature gauges, and vibration meters, must be marked to ensure safe operation of plant.

3. Marking of pipes to indicate the type of fluid being transported and also the direction of its flow

This facilitates maintenance and improves maintainability of process piping. It is particularly necessary for piping containing dangerous chemicals and environmentally harmful fluids.

4. Marking of valves and stopcocks

With this, the flow of fluid through the pipe is clearly discernible. Usually, open and close markings are done, using standard symbols, either by tagging or by hand painting. This improves maintainability, operability and safety of equipment and plant. Such marking is particularly necessary for valves in which the open and close dispositions are not so obvious.

5. Marking of type of lubricant (colour coding) and lubrication inlet points

This is a useful aid for proper lubrication during autonomous maintenance. It prevents missed lubrication points during daily and periodic lubrication and also prevents the use of wrong lubricant.

6. Marking of oil levels in oilers and level indicators

This guarantees the supply of the correct amount of oil and prevents failures resulting from inadequate lubrication. Usually, the maximum and minimum levels are marked (by thin lines) with the use of paint.

7. Marking of the sequence of inspection on the body of the equipment

Usually numbers, written in blocks or circles, are used to indicate the sequence. This is a useful aid and prevents missed inspections. These seven measures are sometimes known as the seven essentials of visual control [9].

We have already discussed the use of checklists for cleaning, lubrication, bolting and inspection. Together with the visual controls mentioned above, they should enable a proper conduct of autonomous maintenance tasks. In factories and process plants, mistake-proofing devices are generally used for the following purposes:

(i) Prevention of maloperation/wrong operation and overloading of the equipment.

(ii) Prevention of production of defective components/products.

(iii) Prevention of accidents.

The type of devices which are generally used can be classified under the following three categories:

(i) Electrical interlocks, cut-outs and protective devices which cut off power and thus stop possible misuse, overloading and further movement thereby preventing an accident. These devices and protections are generally built into the machine and should, therefore, be included in the maintenance prevention (MP) design.

(ii) Indicators which signal the occurrence of a problem. Such indicators, in the simplest form, can be a lamp, a siren, or both a lamp/bank of lamps and a siren to attract the necessary attention.

(iii) Mechanical stops, devices and fixtures which, for example, can be used to cut off the feed, stop a wrong size of blank or workpiece from being loaded, or block further movement. As opposed to electrical interlocks and cut-outs, indicators and mechanical devices are usually designed and installed by the equipment users. A number of ingenious methods are also used. Most of such devices and methods are based on suggestions received from employees. Small groups, be they quality circles or PM circles/groups, can be very effectively used in the development of simple measures of mistake proofing.

TPM Requires a Strong Maintenance Department

We have discussed the allocation of maintenance tasks earlier in this chapter and have noted that whereas daily cleaning, lubrication and bolting, daily and certain periodic inspections and some minor repairs and servicing are performed by the equipment operators, the maintenance technicians and engineers are responsible for the following activities:

(i) Periodic inspections.

(ii) Periodic servicing and replacement of parts.

(iii) Periodic overhauls.

(iv) Condition-based maintenance activities.

(v) Repair of breakdowns.

(vi) Planning and improvement of maintenance procedures and practices.

(vii) Analysis of inspection and condition monitoring data.

(viii) Designing-out-of-maintenance—MP and MI—activities, and this includes both reliability and maintainability improvement projects.

In this new arrangement, namely under TPM, whereas on one hand, the routine and some periodic preventive maintenance activities have been taken away from the maintenance department leaving them enough time for the other essential tasks mentioned above (which they could not attend to under the earlier set up), on the other hand, the maintenance technicians and engineers have to acquire knowledge and skills in new areas. These new areas include use of condition monitoring techniques, analysis of failure data to identify weak points and discern trends, analysis of repair data, use of reliability assessment techniques such as FMEA (failure modes and effects analysis) and fault tree analysis and also design for higher reliability and maintainability. Moreover, with the operators looking after their machines and equipment, the basic conditions of production equipment improve and with this the equipment availability of the production facility increases. Under these circumstances, much higher levels of efficiency and effectiveness will be expected from the maintenance department. The maintenance department also has to provide training, advice and guidance to the equipment operators in the performance of autonomous maintenance tasks. Wireman [12] provides a good analogy of the new relationship between equipment operators and maintenance technicians. He likens it to the relationship between paramedics and doctors. Whereas paramedics can provide first aid, a doctor is required to handle the real problems.

The maintenance technicians and engineers have to be capable of taking care of the real problems and doing this quickly and skillfully. We must also remember that the maintenance personnel are supposed to be responsible for training the operators. If the maintenance personnel are not trained properly, then they will not be able to impart the necessary training to the operators.

We may conclude that the maintenance personnel must have adequate knowledge about the technologies — process technologies, production equipment, pneumatic, electronic and microprocessor control systems etc., and techniques. The maintenance technicians must also possess the skills required to repair, service and otherwise restore not only simple mechanical systems but also electrical and electronic systems and devices. Moreover, with the passage of time, greater automation is being incorporated in production equipment and the maintenance of these equipment calls for newer knowledge and skills. In this context, let us briefly examine the state of affairs prevailing in our industries.

The state of maintenance of production equipment in our industrial organisations is woefully inadequate and for this reason, our industrial productivity is much lower than that of the developed nations. One of the reasons for this state of affairs is the lack of knowledge and skills of our maintenance engineers and technicians. Most of our engineers and technicians are not conversant with the technologies used in modern production equipment. Moreover, condition monitoring techniques, such as vibration and noise monitoring and ferrography, are now available and these techniques can be effectively used for predictive maintenance of production equipment, particularly in the process plants. This demands the acquisition of new knowledge and skills. Of course this is more in the form of updation of knowledge. In most cases, therefore, in addition to the need for updation of knowledge and skills, there is a need to impart basic knowledge and skills, particularly in pneumatic and fluid power, and in solid state and microprocessor control systems.

Training of Maintenance Engineers and Technicians

In certain books on TPM,[12] the term maintenance skills training has been used to denote the training of equipment operators (in maintenance skills) [10]. This seems rather restrictive and also confusing. We have, through our discussion in the preceding paragraphs, realised that the training in maintenance skills is required not only for the production supervisors and equipment operators, but also for the maintenance engineers and technicians. Maintenance skills training, in the title of this chapter, therefore, includes both these kinds of training, namely, training in autonomous maintenance tasks for the production supervisors and operators and training in condition-based maintenance, reliability assessment methods and tools, design for higher reliability and maintainability and restoration techniques and methods for maintenance engineers and technicians. In this chapter, we have already discussed the training of equipment operators in some detail. In this section, we will discuss the training of maintenance engineers and technicians. We will do this in two parts, namely, the types of training programmes and the course outlines for a few typical programmes.

TRAINING OF MAINTENANCE ENGINEERS

Maintenance has been a neglected discipline for far too long. In many of our industrial organisations, the maintenance department does not get the importance and the support which it deserves. The maintenance department is taken for granted and its existence is virtually not even acknowledged till a breakdown occurs. When that happens, the management suddenly wakes up to the need for proper maintenance of plant and equipment, and a number of promises are made and assurances given to the maintenance department. However, the moment the equipment is restored, the promises and assurances are conveniently forgotten and maintenance again takes a back seat. This picture does not only pertain to India; it seems that this portrayal is universal in character. Wireman [12] suggests that "to improve maintenance, the first step would be to change the name of maintenance; otherwise it would never get any respect." The author does not feel that a change of name is necessary. It is suggested instead that maintenance engineers and technicians must assert themselves, and through their efforts, they must show to the management that the twin objectives of maximisation of equipment availability and extension of the useful life of production equipment are essential ingredients for production, productivity, profits and growth.[13] For this the maintenance department must produce results. This, in turn, requires acquisition of knowledge and skills which will enable maintenance engineers and technicians to carry out all necessary preventive and corrective maintenance tasks, allotted to them, effectively.

Maintenance engineers need to acquire knowledge and skills in two specific areas.

(i) Use of condition monitoring techniques, particularly vibration and noise monitoring (for rotating machines), thermography and ferrography.

(ii) Use of reliability assessment techniques (such as FMEA and fault tree analysis, which we have mentioned earlier), analysis of past data and design for higher reliability and maintainability.

The training in condition-based maintenance must include both use of condition monitoring equipment (instruments and meters), and interpretation of condition monitoring data. Such training can be provided by manufacturers of condition monitoring equipment. There is also the possibility of organising in-house training programmes for maintenance engineers, wherein sessions can be conducted by specialists drawn from equipment manufacturers and from colleges/technical institutes and universities. For smaller organisations, the second alternative is preferable. In larger organisations, however, a mix of both may be called for—training in the use of the instrument(s) and in-house training by external experts. Training in the use and upkeep of the instruments, meters and gauges can be provided by the suppliers at their premises to a selected number of engineers. These engineers can then train other maintenance engineers, as needed. This is something similar to roll-out education discussed earlier under training of operators. The training provided by the supplier(s) can be followed by in-house training programme(s), wherein the background theory, diagnosis and prognosis, trend analysis and other relevant aspects of interpretation can be covered in detail.

Training in reliability assessment techniques, and reliability and maintainability design needs a different perspective altogether. These topics form a part of post-graduate education in Reliability Engineering/Quality and Reliability Engineering. Accordingly, colleges, technical institutes and universities, are the best sources for acquisition of knowledge in this field. Herein, as well, there are two courses of action. Maintenance engineers can be sent to the institutes and universities as industry-sponsored students. They may either be allowed to complete their M.Tech/post-graduate degree requirements, or permitted to take certain selected courses (a course is an instruction of one four and a half month semester duration in a particular subject). The first option is better but the second option can be followed if the engineers cannot be spared for that long a period (one and a half years are required for an M.Tech degree). In this case also, there is the possibility of deputing engineers for shorter-duration training programmes and summer/winter schools. These training programmes are of one or two weeks duration. Such training programmes can be very useful and this happens only if the training programme is a focussed one dealing with relevant topics only. In larger organisations, such programmes can also be arranged in-house. Experts from technical institutes and universities can be requested to conduct in-house training of maintenance engineers in specific areas.

TYPES OF TRAINING PROGRAMMES FOR MAINTENANCE TECHNICIANS

The kind of training required and the design of specific training programmes depend on the level of knowledge and skills of the maintenance technicians who are available on the rolls of the company. The types of knowledge and skills required are functions of the plant and the equipment. By and large, in most of the larger plants, the tradesmen who are involved in maintenance work are the following:

(i) millwrights/millwright fitters,

(ii) pipe fitters

(iii) electricians,

(iv) fluid power technicians/hydraulic and pneumatic equipment/appliance fitters, and

(v) electronics technicians.

In some industries, a few diesel mechanics are also employed to look after the diesel generating sets. In addition to this, welders and sheet-metal workers are also used in maintenance work. Whereas, training in the trades of welding, sheet-metal work, pipe fitting, millwright fitting and electricity (electrical repairing and wiring) are available in many of our Industrial Training Institutes (ITIs), trained persons in fluid power and electronics (particularly those who can attend to board-level repairs) are more difficult to find. Under the circumstances, depending on the trade and the type of training required, an industrial organisation can choose one or more of the following alternatives:

(i) Recruiting trained personnel with a few years of relevant experience in similar plants/installations.

(ii) Setting up of own training institute/centre to impart training in some or all of the trades.

"When all the possible options have been considered, experience shows that in-house training is the best method for training craftworkers"[12]. This is Wireman's recommendation for a developed nation like the USA, but this is more relevant and appropriate for developing nations like India, wherein it is difficult to find trained tradesmen in a number of specialist trades,[14] as has been noted earlier. For in-house training, the company has to set up and maintain its own training centre. Although this implies a considerably large investment, the returns on this investment is both visible and quick, since in-house training in maintenance skills can bring about significant improvements in both equipment availability and equipment effectiveness. The most important attribute of the maintenance technician is his troubleshooting ability and this includes both failure prediction and fault diagnosis. Thus, the training centre must be used not only for imparting introductory and advanced level training in various trades but also for training in equipment inspection and fault diagnosis. Training in inspection and fault diagnosis is equipment specific and training centres located inside the works are the best suited for this purpose. Moreover, these training modules and courses can be conducted by experienced technicians and supervisors. Training centres can also be used for training of operators. Such in-house maintenance training facilities are essential for continuous process industries.

Training programmes are also conducted by suppliers and manufacturers of production equipment, control instruments and control systems. However, these are more in the form of a pilot's jet conversion training. They require prerequisite knowledge and skills in the trade and they impart equipment-specific knowledge—knowledge of the construction, functions, mechanisms and the operating characteristics of the equipment, or the system, and care and precautions to be taken in its operation and maintenance. Training in certain maintenance skills specific to the equipment/system is also imparted in these programmes. These programmes are generally of a short duration. Since such programmes are usually held at the supplier's, or the manufacturer's premises (or a venue chosen by him), the participants get an opportunity to practise certain critical maintenance tasks and procedures. Such training programmes are comparatively few in number. However, their number is increasing. These training programmes are very useful and industrial organisations must take advantage of such opportunities. It is suggested that the concerned maintenance foremen/supervisors be deputed to such programmes so that they may, on their return, train the maintenance technicians.

OUTLINES OF A FEW PROGRAMMES

The training of maintenance technicians, whether they be millwright fitters, pneumatic system mechanics, electricians or electronics instrument and control system technicians, must concentrate on imparting the necessary skills and training in the practical repair and service functions. Unnecessary theory, such as stress or torque calculations, need not be included. However, to be able to impart the basic skills, some amount of theoretical inputs are necessary. These include material on tolerances and fits, mechanical fasteners, screw threads and threadforms, mechanical drives, gears and gear train calculations, rolling element bearings and choice of bearings for different applications, elements of pneumatic systems, selection, care and maintenance of hoses, friction, lubrication and choice of lubricating oils and greases, simple electronic controls and circuits, and integrated circuits and their selection for different applications.[15] Thus, the training should be a mix of classroom instruction and practical training, and the practical training should be imparted partly in laboratories and partly on site—on the machines and equipment. The classroom instruction should be broken up into modules and each module must be followed by a practical demonstration and this, in turn, should be followed by a practice session. For example, the rolling element bearing module must be followed by a practical demonstration and practice in the mounting of bearings. Similarly, pneumatic system mechanics and electronics technicians must get practice in repair and servicing of systems and controls.

Repair and servicing activities are equipment-specific and are also difficult to evaluate. "Repair quality is neither easily explained nor understood" and the quality of repair can only be tested by a trial run [11]. The quality of maintenance work is a function of the skill and also the care taken by the technician. Quality of work can only be ensured if the correct sequence of steps is followed and each setup of the maintenance job is properly understood and adequately practised so that the technician can apply the acquired skill at any time and under the most trying conditions. For this, the training modules must be based on and structured around what the Japanese call "one-point lessons." "One-point lessons are a means of accumulating, transmitting and verifying first-hand know-how from the shop floors and they range from work activities for equipment quality, safety and operation, to those concerned with equipment function, structure, troubleshooting and remedial action" [11]. One-point lessons are designed and written to impart training on a single point, or activity, or an element of a maintenance job. They generally stress a single point, such as the care to be taken in the mounting of a bearing, or the sequence of steps to be adopted for a specific fault detection. For a given job, the one-point lesson is used to explain how things should be done and also why they should be done that way. Diagrams and visual aids must be used as much as possible in the design of these lessons. Retention of technical information transmitted through visual aids, such as sketches, diagrams and photographs, is always better, and this way, one-point lessons would not only explain but also assist in learning by memorisation and practice. As noted earlier, each lesson must be followed by a live demonstration, and this should, in turn, be followed by adequate practice and if possible, by a test conducted under actual operating conditions. One-point lessons should be compiled and documented and these documents should then be organised under different training modules, which, in turn, are constituents of a particular training programme. Through such practice, not only can technical skills be enhanced but a mind-set and culture, which are conducive to building and sustaining the desired skills and motives, can be created in the workplace. This can also help in the creation of a maintenance system (just like a quality system). One-point lessons are very effective training tools and they should be used even for seemingly trivial things. For a developing nation like India, such one-point lessons written by maintenance engineers and/or supervisors trained at the foreign collaborator's works can turn out to be effective instruments for transfer of maintenance technology.

Now we are ready to discuss the outlines of training programmes in the various trades which are used for the maintenance of plant and equipment. As we have noted earlier, in addition to maintenance-specific trades, there are some tradesmen, such as welders and sheet-metal workers, who are used in maintenance jobs. We will not discuss the training of such tradesmen, since for these trades, maintenance activities do not call for any specific skills. Instead in the succeeding paragraphs, we will discuss the training programmes for maintenance-specific tradesmen, namely millwright fitters, hydraulic and pneumatic system mechanics, electricians and electronics technicians. We reiterate that in-house training is always preferable, particularly for continuous process industries, and accordingly, the company should recruit ITI graduates in the relevant trades and subject them to basic training programmes in these trades conducted in its own training centre.

The topics to be included in the training programmes depend to some extent on the equipment, level of instrumentation and automation, and also the company policy with regard to type of repair and servicing work which are to be done departmentally. Since maintenance is an equipment-specific activity, training programmes differ to some extent depending on the type of equipment, their structure and the instrumentation and controls used. Moreover, the training programme should also take into account the type of work that is to be done departmentally. Are the electronics technicians required to carry out component-level or board-level repairs? Some companies choose to do the less complicated work in-house and send the instrument or the controller, to the manufacturer or to a specialist company for complex repairs, whereas some other companies employ specialists who can attend to such complicated repair jobs.

The following points must be kept in mind during the development of the outlines of the training programmes:

(i) Both theory and practice are important and theoretical knowledge is becoming more crucial with the growing sophistication and automation of production equipment (and a good theoretical background is particularly necessary for diagnosing a fault or a condition).

(ii) Theoretical inputs should be limited to the amount necessary to support practice.

(iii) Training should be directed at developing troubleshooting and corrective maintenance skills.

Let us, as an illustration, discuss the outline of the training programme for millwright mechanics. The trainee millwrights must all be ITI-trained fitters who have undergone basic training in chipping, filing, marking, drilling, reaming and tapping. These trainees should be put through an intensive training programme which should, among others, include topics such as (i) care and maintenance of

V-belts and chains, (ii) types of lubrication and selection of lubricating oils and greases for different applications, (iii) drives, gears and maintenance of gearboxes, (iv) mounting, care and maintenance of bearings, (v) maintenance of sprockets, clutches and brakes, (vi) maintenance of pneumatic tools, and (vii) care and maintenance of dial gauges, timers, spirit levels, straightedges and other tools and instruments used by operators and mechanics. The trainees should also be given exposure to condition monitoring and its application through live demonstrations showing the use of vibration and noise meters and of ferrography. The mechanics should also undergo training in the daily and periodic maintenance activities required for the production equipment. This should include training in cleaning, lubrication, bolting, periodic servicing and minor repairs. This will enable the use of maintenance supervisors and tradesmen for training of equipment operators in autonomous maintenance. This, in turn, will go a long way in fostering goodwill and cooperation between the production and maintenance departments. The development of training programmes for other trades should also be based on these guidelines and done in a similar manner.

References

1. Aso, M., "Maintenance Skill Training," Chapter 7 of Nakajima, S. (Editor), *TPM Development Program: Implementing Total Productive Maintenance*, Productivity Press, Cambridge, Massachusetts, U.S.A., 1989, pp 329-347.
2. Bhadury, B., "Work Culture: An Exposition in the Indian Context," *Vikalpa* (the Journal of the Indian Institute of Management, Ahmedabad), Vol. 16, No. 4, October-December, 1991, pp 33-42.
3. Collacott, R.A., *Mechanical Fault Diagnosis and Condition Monitoring*, Chapman and Hall, London, 1977.
4. Dodge, Harold F., "A Quotation" in *On Q: ASQC's Journal of Record*, Vol. X, No. 4, April 1995, p 5.
5. Goto, F., "Autonomous Maintenance," Chapter 4 of Nakajima, S. (Editor), *TPM Development Program: Implementing Total Productive Maintenance*, Productivity Press, Cambridge, Massachusetts, U.S.A., 1989, pp 165-217 [illustrative checklists for autonomous maintenance activities given in Tables 4-1 and 4-7 on pp 174, 185, 187, 192, 193-195 and autonomous maintenance standards given on pp 182, 183 and 197 and 198].
6. Knipe, J., "Maintenance Management," Chapter 6 of *Terotechnology Handbook*, Department of Industries, Her Majesty's Stationery Office (HMSO), London, 1978.
7. Nakajima, S., *Introduction to TPM*, Productivty Press, Cambridge, Massachusetts, U.S.A., 1988, p. 76.

8. Suzaki, K., *The New Manufacturing Challenge: Techniques for Continuous Improvement*, The Free Press (a division of Macmillan, Inc.), New York, 1987, pp 113-123.

9. Suzuki, T., *New Directions for TPM*, Productivity Press, Cambridge, Massachusetts, U.S.A., pp 18, 69, 76-84.

10. Tajiri, M. and Gotoh, F., *TPM Implementation: A Japanese Approach*, McGraw-Hill, Inc., New York, 1992, pp 9, 53, 56, 75, 76.

11. Takahashi, Y. and Osada, T., *TPM: Total Productive Maintenance*, Asian Productivity Organisation, Tokyo, 1990, pp 227-246 and 289, 291, 303, 304.

12. Wireman, T., *Total Productive Maintenance: An American Approach*, Industrial Press, Inc., New York, 1991, pp 83, 84, 89, 144, 147, 170 and 171.

Endnotes

1. As per Wireman, operators perform about twenty per cent of the work that is performed by the maintenance technicians prior to the implementation of TPM.

2. The reader may, if he is interested, refer to a paper on work culture by the author [2]. In this paper, the author has discussed the characteristics of the Indian social milieu which are impediments to the development of a healthy work culture. The fundamental differences between the Indian and the Japanese cultures, in the context of work ethics and work culture, have also been discussed in this paper.

3. This detection/discovery of deterioration, or abnormality, is quite different from condition monitoring. This is discerning of an abnormality by an experienced individual with the help of his senses. This comes from long association and can be done by a person who has been using the artefact. TPM not only recognises the importance of such early warning and prompt reporting of an abnormality, it also suggests that the equipment operator should be given this responsibility since he, as the user, knows his equipment best. This kind of thing is what differentiates TPM from what has been professed and practised in maintenance engineering and management earlier.

4. In this book, the term worker has not been used, and instead production operator and maintenance technician have been used. This has been done for the following two reasons:
   (i) the term worker is very confusing since everyone in the organisation, including engineers and managers, who are knowledge workers, is a worker, and
   (ii) the term worker has feudalistic undertones and the sooner we get rid of everything that is feudalistic the better.

5. In the Indian environment, tightening will probably be used instead of bolting. The term bolting has been used, since in the original TPM literature, bolting is the term used for the activity of tightening all bolts and nuts and ensuring that there are no broken or loose fasteners, such as bolts, nuts and washers.

6. This should also be done for the lubrication points and grease nipples. Lubrication points which are inaccessible and hidden from view are generally found to be dirty and unattended — covered with dirt and dust and sometimes, even clogged. In most cases, minor modifications to the equipment is all that is necessary.

7. Whereas it is true that critical equipment are generally given greater attention, equipment inspection being an essential part of autonomous maintenance must be carried out for all production equipment and machines. Accordingly, checklists should be prepared for all of them.

8. Checklists are called checksheets in Japanese books which have been translated into English.

9. In the process industry, for the performance of this task, the operators must also understand the processes they operate. This is required in addition to an understanding of the construction, function(s), mechanisms and characteristics of the equipment they operate.

10. In most cases, production supervisors are the PM group leaders. There may be exceptions but, in TPM, such exceptions are rare.

11. The reader should notice the basic similarity between this procedure and that given in Chapter Four for improving setup and adjustments.

12. Masamitsu Aso, however, does include training of maintenance personnel [1]. Also, when he discusses curriculum and objectives of training programmes, he uses the term to specifically denote the training of maintenance technicians. This is more appropriate since the training of operators should be termed as autonomous maintenance training to avoid confusion.

13. Consider the following facts:

    (i) product is produced only when the equipment is running and the production volume and the revenue earned from the sale of the product are dependant entirely on equipment availability (this is particularly so in process plants); (ii) the cost of maintenance, which includes maintenance manpower cost, cost of spares and the cost of lost production, is, in most cases, very high and this cost has to be brought down through efforts aimed at maximisation of equipment availability; and (iii) the increasing cost of replacement of plant and equipment demands the extension of their useful life and this can be achieved through reliability and maintainability improvement efforts.

14. Consider also that retaining skilled tradesmen is becoming difficult since they are leaving in larger numbers every year for better paying jobs in the Gulf countries.

15. The list includes topics for all the relevant trades, and accordingly, only a few of these topics will be required for a given trade. For example, millwright fitters and pneumatic system mechanics need not be taught electrical and electronics but at the same time, mechanics dealing with pneumatics must have basic knowledge of instrumentation and control systems.

Small Group Activity and TPM Promotion

In the very first chapter, we have noted that one of the identifying characteristics of TPM is employee participation through the use of small group activity. As a matter of fact, to many, TPM, like TQM, is synonymous with employee participation and small group activity. Nakajima echoes the same thought when he says that "TPM has become widely known throughout the Japanese industry as an abbreviation for PM with all employees participating through small group activities" [16]. In Chapter Three, we had also noted that TPM has evolved from the coming together of the concept of life cycle effectiveness, and employee participation and use of autonomous small groups having taken the former from terotechnology and the latter from TQM (or more correctly TQC/CWQC, as it is known in Japan). Tamaki, who was then the chairman of the Japan Institute of Plant Management, summed this up very well by writing that TPM "is the combination of autonomous small group activity with life cycle approach in the pursuit of economic effectiveness" [22].

T in TPM stands for total involvement, which signifies the involvement of all employees at all levels and in all functions of the organisation. For this, the traditional departmental boundaries have to be transcended and employees in the various departments of the organisation have to work together to resolve equipment related problems, minimise the six major equipment related losses and achieve higher levels of equipment effectiveness. Since TPM uses small group activity to obtain employee participation for resolving equipment related problems and to bring about improvements in equipment effectiveness, this calls for creation of an organisation for cross-functional management of the activities of the small groups. This requires a structure which ensures that the activities of the small groups in the various functions and at various levels are directed, coordinated and linked. This is necessary to ensure the harmony of the goals of the various groups with the company goals. In TPM, this is ensured by the concept of TPM promotion and the TPM promotional structure.

In this chapter, we will discuss participation, the role of small groups and small group autonomous activity in TPM, and TPM promotion. We will first investigate the need for participation and also discuss the various barriers, or obstacles, to employee participation in industrial organisations. Herein, we will look at participation from the Indian perspective and discuss some of the problems which are probably unique to our subcontinent. Thereafter we will conclude our discussion of employee participation through an examination of the enablers of participation, or in other words, the various ingredients which can bring about employee participation and make it a way of life in an industrial organisation. Having looked at participation, we will move over to small group autonomous activity in the context of TPM, briefly discuss the various methods, or approaches, of participation used in industrial organisations before taking up the investigation of participation in small groups. First the identifying characteristics of PM groups and circles will be discussed. Thereafter, certain guidelines which can bring about effective participation in small groups will be examined. These guidelines are also called the principles of participation. With the background of employee participation and a brief discussion of small group activity in TPM, the operation of PM groups and circles and the concept and structure of TPM promotion will be taken up for discussion. In this context, we will also examine the role of management in TPM promotion. Moreover, the development of small group activity in an organisation and evaluation of the progress of PM groups will be briefly discussed.

Participation

As per Webster's Third New International Dictionary [24]:

> to participate is to take part in something, and participation is, accordingly, an action or state of taking part with others in an activity, or association with others in a relationship.

Thus, we see that although participation affords the employees an opportunity of taking part in problem solving and also for making suggestions for improvement of their jobs and their workplaces, the more important aspect of participation is that it helps to build relationships — relationships between employees and also relationship between the employees and the management. Participation aids in building bridges of understanding — bridges between various groups and functions and also a bridge between the employees and the management. Juran, in his book on 'Leadership for Quality,' states that 'it has long been known that experience and creativity of the workforce were underemployed assets of the companies' [12]. Participation helps to tap this asset and use it to attain the goals of the company. Thus, with participation, the company gains in two ways, namely:

(i) problems get solved, losses are reduced and work methods, processes and procedures are improved, and

(ii) morale of the workforce improves significantly, a favourable work environment is created and employee involvement and teamwork are obtained.

This fact is now increasingly being recognised. However, employee participation has yet to get universal acceptance. The reasons for this state of affairs are many and we will examine some of these reasons in this section and take a detailed look at participation so that we can understand its various aspects and implications.

NEED FOR PARTICIPATION

When we mention participation in an industrial setting, we usually imply worker participation in management. This usually sends shivers up the spines of some people who feel that this would make them lose some of their powers and their prerogatives. To some others, it signifies activities — meetings — which seem to add up to a colossal waste of time. Worker participation in management has been misunderstood very often and for this reason, we will not use this term. We will instead use the term employee participation. Employee participation implies that the employees are afforded an opportunity of taking part in solving problems and making decisions about their work/jobs and workplaces. This is usually much more than mere consultation and most often, the employee is given an opportunity of making suggestions about his work and workplace and taking part with his fellow employees in problem solving and also planning and implementation of new and improved work methods, procedures and systems. Let us first try to find out why we need participation before we try to analyse reason for peoples' antagonism to employee participation and participative approaches such as small group autonomous activity.

Industrial organisations who recognise the role of the human asset in reduction of losses, increase in production and improvement of product quality and productivity, appreciate the power of a motivated and committed workforce and accordingly, devote a lot of time and a substantial amount of resources for developing a work environment in which employees will willingly and enthusiastically participate in problem-solving and improvement activities. Employee participation is a powerful tool — a tool which can be used to harness the intrinsic power of the workforce, motivate employees and create a conducive environment. There are many good reasons for companies to seriously consider employee participation and make it an essential part of their operations. Some of these reasons are as follows:

1. An employee who has been working at a job for years is in a better position to:

   (i) identify problems with his job and his workplace and suggest remedial actions for these problems, and

   (ii) make suggestions for improvement of his job, and his workplace.

   The equipment operator, for example, understands his job, his machine and the manufacturing process well enough to make constructive suggestions. These suggestions can lead to reduction in wastage and losses, higher production, improved quality and greater productivity. Also what is more important is that, in most cases, the operator knows his job, his machine and the manufacturing process better than his superiors. If the organisation closes its eyes to this fact, it stands to lose.

2. Most employees want to do a good job. They want to contribute. In this context, the following comments of Sumant Moolgaokar, who was then the Chairman of the Tata Electric and Locomotive Company (TELCO) [15], on the attitude of people at work are very relevant and illuminating:

   (i) There is in each man something special which he would find satisfying to use and show his worth to his organisation and his community.

   (ii) It has long been established that people enjoy exercising their innate and trained abilities and that this enjoyment increases as the abilities become more complex.

   Employee participation and participative fora provide an opportunity to the employees to exercise their innate and trained abilities by solving work-related problems and making suggestions for improvement of their jobs, workplaces and related functions. This way they can also show their worth to the organisation. All that the organisation has to do is to set up a system for employee participation.

3. Employee participation is an effective tool for motivating the grassroots. When employees see that their ideas are being solicited and some of them are even being implemented by the organisation, then they feel encouraged to take on bigger challenges and strive for higher goals. Belcher of the American Productivity Centre, Houston, in his book on productivity, says [1]:
   (i) When employees have the opportunity to influence decisions that affect their jobs, they feel more in control of their destinies and less like cogs in a giant machine.
   (ii) An active solicitation of employees' ideas and their involvement in problem-solving processes greatly enhances the ability of employees to make a contribution to the organisation and to derive a sense of accomplishment and value.

   A person in control of his destiny is confident of himself and his abilities. Moreover, when such a person realises that he can actually make a positive contribution for the betterment of the organisation and that this contribution is recognised, he derives great pleasure and satisfaction. Such a person has positive motivation and a motivated workforce is one of the objectives of TPM.

4. Employee participation is a means of empowering employees. Empowerment means that employees feel that they have the responsibility and authority to participate in decision making and problem-solving at their appropriate level. Empowered employees take pride in their work and 'when men take pride in their skill or craft and try to perfect it, they give scope to their creative impulses where one man's gain is not another's loss' [15]. Participation thus helps bring back the pride of craftsmanship in the equipment operators and maintenance tradesmen. Moreover, empowered employees have a greater sense of belonging to the organisation [1].

5. This sense of belonging to the organisation is further buttressed by the recognition they get through employee participation for their job-related skills, problem-solving abilities and suggestions for improvement. Recognition and regular and frequent feedback reinforces good performance and also encourages self-development [1]. As a matter of fact, recognition is one of the three pillars of motivation, the other two being challenge in the work to be performed (a challenging task/assignment/job) and empowerment. We find, therefore, that participation provides two of the three pillars of motivation and helps in building a motivated workforce.

6. The common methods of employee participation enable a small group of employees to met regularly to identify and resolve work-related problems. This also satisfies the affiliation motive since most people enjoy being part of a team and working with the their colleagues towards the achievement of shared, or common objectives [1]. Participation thus fosters teamwork and collaboration among the employees of the organisation.
7. Lastly, when the management of the organisation promotes and actively supports employee participation, it unwittingly ushers in trust — trust between employees and the management. The employees start believing in the management and the organisation and this, in turn, helps in bringing about collaboration between the management and the employee unions/ associations.

From the preceding discussion we may, therefore, conclude that employee participation not only makes available to the organisation the latent skills and abilities of the workforce for problem-solving and improvement activities but it also fosters goodwill, motivation, teamwork and collaborative efforts. Mizuno, in his book on Company-wide Quality Control, says that:

> "Workers who reluctantly do only what they are told (to do) within their allotted time cannot produce good quality products. Good quality products are produced only when everyone (in the organisation) is willing to put his all into his work" [14].

Only when a conducive environment is created, that is, when the organisation has succeeded in developing the requisite culture, would everyone willingly and enthusiastically work towards the achievement of the organisational goals of higher product quality, productivity and growth. Employee participation is a basic ingredient of this culture (please refer to our discussion of total quality culture in Chapter Three). Participation helps in developing a motivated workforce with the right kind of a mindset or attitude, and as we have noted in Chapter Three"with the use of effecive leadership and top management commitment, these motivated employees can be transformed into committed individuals." Moreover, as has been pointed out by Mizuno [14].

(i) with the advent of sophisticated equipment, it has become necessary for operators to consult and learn from one another, and employee participation provides a forum wherein employees can exchange ideas and stimulate each other to do better work, and

(ii) a group of persons working together to solve a problem or come up with an improved method, or procedure, is more likely to succeed than a single individual trying to do it all by himself, and the most commonly used participative approach uses small group activity.

Employee participation becomes essential in TPM to ensure the (i) shedding of the 'I operate, you fix' attitude, (ii) implementation of autonomous maintenance, and (iii) involvement of all employees. For this reason, small group activity nurtured and promoted by the development and effective operation of PM groups is an essential ingredient of TPM implementation. Employee participation in the form of small group activity thus becomes an enabler of TPM.

BARRIERS TO PARTICIPATION

Juran, in his book on 'Leadership for Quality,' says that "it has long been known that experience and creativity were underemployed assets of the companies. More recently, it has become evident that workforce participation can also add significantly to company's quality performance" [12]. We have also, through our discussion, shown that workforce participation is an essential ingredient of TPM. Although there is an increasing awareness of the importance of employee participation, it does not come about easily. In general, most of the top managements have no problem in accepting employee participation and participative approaches, such as quality circles and TPM groups. As a matter of fact, in the majority of cases, the appeal of employee participation is the highest at the top management level, since on the one hand, managers, at this level, can easily perceive the possible gains which can be derived from the effective use of a motivated workforce, and on the other, the top management does not view employee participation as a threat to its sovereignty. The opposition to employee participation comes from the employees themselves. The greatest hurdle to employee participation comes from the difficulties experienced in explaining the objectives of participation and the need for its implementation to the workforce and convincing them of the management's sincerity and honesty. In addition to this, obstacles are also created by the middle management and supervisors, employee unions and, in some cases, staff specialists. Thus, the following groups (and institutions) are the barriers to participation [12]:

1. Middle management and supervisors.
2. Staff specialists.

3. Workers, owing to a feeling of insecurity.
4. Unions.

The greatest opposition to employee participation and the use of participative approaches comes from managers, particularly those at the middle management levels, and supervisors. Managers are concerned about losing their prerogatives. They feel that with the coming of employee participation they will no longer make decisions and the decisions taken will be influenced by the opinions expressed by the workforce in participative fora. Supervisors, on the other hand, feel that this is top management's excuse for coddling employees and employee participation is tantamount to being 'soft' on employees, which will, in turn, eventually lead to disobedience and indiscipline in the ranks and file. Moreover, middle managers and supervisors question the need for participation, or in other words, they feel that the time spent by the employees in meetings and improvement projects would be better spent on production jobs. Belcher, in his book on productivity, points out that loss of prerogatives and coddling employees are the most common misconceptions about employee participation [1]. These misconceptions are derived from the traditional industrial setup wherein the managers, or 'bosses,' were supposed to make decisions and give orders, and the employees were expected to carry out the orders given to them by the managers and supervisors. The basis of these misconceptions has been explained by Gondhalekar in the following words [9]:

"Traditionally, the management was expected to play the role of `brain' and the employees were expected to play the role of `hands.' The term `millhand,' which was used to refer to a worker for a whole century after the industrial revolution, sprang from this philosophy of separating the `planners' from the `doers.' It appeared to be the logical and correct way to the industrialised western world, and management theory was developed around it... (The professional managers) would know best, and the employees only needed to obey and implement what they were told."

Juran points out that staff specialists also oppose the implementation of employee participation [12]. They seem to view this as a threat and this apprehension stems from the mistaken belief that because of their education and training and long years of professional experience, they are the only ones who are capable of working on planning, data analysis, suggesting product and process improvements and designing and implementing cost reduction projects. Accordingly, they feel that planning, analysis and improvement activities are their sole domain and no one else should be allowed to meddle in their jobs — particularly not the 'doers.'

Such strait-jacketing and traditional attitudes sometimes lead to unwarranted and undesirable display of arrogance by the managers, supervisors and staff specialists which, in turn, breeds resentment and cynicism in the workplace [5]. The following excerpt from an expose by Cohen-Rosenthal explains what the workforce has to put up with in many industrial organisations [5]:

> "Each and every day, workers confront workplaces and work situations that put them down, demean their capabilities and defy their common sense. They see bosses who order them to do things they know to be wrong and wasteful. They see superiors using their positions as weapons... They see profesionals who use their professional status to ignore their ideas."

Over a period of time, such strong and negative experiences result in a loss of faith of the workforce in their management. Resentment gives way to cynicism and cynicism to a lack of trust. The workers do not trust their management and this loss of trust is a major stumbling block in the implementation of employee participation.

Due to resentment, cynicism and lack of trust in the management, the workers have misgivings about employee participation. Particularly in India, the workers generally do not want to be drawn into any kind of participation. Firstly, they consider it to be an eyewash since they doubt the sincerity of the management. Secondly, some of them feel that employee participation would turn out to be a forum for passing on to them the entire blame for poor production, low productivity etc. [3]. To the majority of workers, these are, however, not very strong reasons and they only give rise to a feeling of indifference. The main reason for their opposition to employee participation is a feeling of insecurity — the fear of loss of jobs. Employee participation is a tool for improvement activities, whether they be in the areas of product quality, productivity, or equipment availability/ effectiveness. Such improvement activities, in turn, lead to reduction of losses, higher equipment effectiveness and more efficient production, a possible fall out of which would be a smaller workforce. Accordingly, the employees view participation as a threat and to many employees a call for participation is, in one sense, 'asking them to participate in helping to eliminate jobs — their own jobs, or those of colleagues' [12].

The unions capitalise on this feeling of insecurity and, in their interaction with the workforce, they stress the possible reduction in the size of the workforce and the loss of jobs. The unions oppose any kind of employee participation since 'unions are wary of shifting employee loyalty from the union' to the management [12]. In a way, employee participation is a threat to the survival of unions since participation would necessarily bring the management and the workforce much closer and in such an ideal environment, the unions would have a much smaller, if any, role to play. The union officials, therefore, impress upon the employees the need to consider any proposal from the management very carefully since the management speaks with a "forked tongue." They also impress upon the workers the futility of taking part in improvement projects since, according to union officials, the profits from these projects will go to the management and the workers will not get adequate, or just, rewards.

CREATION OF A SUPPORTIVE ENVIRONMENT

Employee participation cannot be imposed from above. The employees — the middle-level managers, the first-line supervisors and the workers — have to feel the need for it and at the same time, the scheme of participative management has to have the active support of the management [3]. For this, the management must create an environment which supports and encourages participation — an environment which seeks, nurtures, rewards and celebrates the contribution of each employee. The basic elements of such an environment are:

(i) safe, open and supportive workplaces and work situations,

(ii) trust and a sense of belonging to the organisation, and

(iii) management commitment.

Active participation implies innovative thinking and creativity from all levels of employees. An environment that supports and encourages innovation and creativity is characterised by the following attributes:

1. *Resources* — For an employee to perform well and derive satisfaction from his job, he needs the wherewithal — whether it is a machine in good working order, or tools, fixtures and drawings, materials, necessary information, or adequate instructions. Non-availability of the required resources is a major source of demotivation and even the most competent and otherwise committed employees are often dissatisfied due to reasons like poor communications, poor design, bad materials, shortages, delays and inadequate tooling [2]. Moreover, employees need the time, facilities and funding to take up problems and solve them in new and innovative ways.

2. *Challenge* — The content, responsibilities and challenges of the job are important to most employees. An interesting and challenging job brings the best out

of most individuals. Moreover, groups of individuals and teams also do their best work when faced with a stiff challenge arising from the nature of the problem.

3. *Safety and Job Security* — Employees who have to worry about personal safety in the workplace and/or their job security cannot do good work and can, therefore, not also be expected to come up with creative ideas and innovative solutions to problems.
4. *Openness and Freedom* — The work environment should call for employee participation in decision making and seek their ideas and solutions to the problems facing them. Work becomes more challenging and interesting for employees as their knowledge and skills improve and as they are increasingly able to influence decisions affecting their jobs [7]. For such an environment, the prime requisites are openness and freedom enabling two-way communication between departments, and also freedom from needless constraints. An open environment, in turn, has two characteristic attributes — ranks and levels are not stressed and there is cooperation and collaboration between departments and divisions. Moreover, in this context, one must also recognise and take into account the following:
   a) People are less willing to accept pressure and close supervision than was the case a decade or two ago.
   b) The trend in our schools and our homes is also towards giving the individual greater freedom. There are fewer direct, unexplained orders in schools and homes and young people are participating increasingly in decisions which affect them.
   c) There is a substantial increase in the educational level of the workforce. As people acquire more education, their expectations with regard to the job and its content, responsibilities, challenges and freedom increase.
5. *Encouragement and Recognition* — A supportive environment encourages and supports new ideas. For this, the organisation and its management must show enthusiasm and support for innovative ideas and creative solutions to problems. Support for innovation calls for reduction of destructive criticism (by managers and supervisors) and unwarranted and excessive fear of evaluation (by professionals) in the minds of the employees. Moreover, good work and innovative ideas should be recognised and rewarded. The reward system should be reviewed to include acknowledgement of a job well done, constructive feedback to enable improvements and attractive rewards for perfor-

mance in quality, productivity and equipment effectiveness improvement ideas.

These attributes help to create safe and open workplaces and work situations which encourage and support employee participation. As such, some of these, such as safe, clean and well-ventilated workplaces, employment security, encouragement, recognition and rewards, help in creating a work environment which is conducive to employee participation and a conducive work environment is one of the enablers of employee participation, as shown in Fig. 6.1. We will discuss the enablers later in this section, but now we must turn to something without which employee participation becomes a farce. Employee participation also calls for a sense of belonging to the organisation, which, in turn, requires trust — faith and belief in the organisation and its management. An employee, whether he is an equipment operator, a maintenance technician, an office staff employed in the purchasing department, a supervisor, or even a middle-level manager, will only take part in any activity over and above his routine and assigned jobs and actively participate in improvement activities if he trusts the management and believes in what it is trying to do. Otherwise he will only do his assigned tasks — things he has been told to do - within the prescribed hours of work.

The top management of the company, therefore, has a very important role to play in developing the employees trust and bringing about a sense of belonging to the organisation in them. The management can create the right kind of 'climate' — one in which the individual employee not only does his job to the best of his capability but also willingly and enthusiastically makes his contribution to the betterment and growth of the organisation. The following are the basic prerequisites for the development of such a climate of trust:

1. The middle management must be convinced of the need and relevance of employee participation and also be assured that it will not, in any way, affect their powers of taking decisions. Moreover, the middle management must also be convinced that the scheme of participation will not affect production, productivity and other performance indices. Ideally the need, relevance, mode of participation, structure of committees and other details should come from the middle management [3]. It is important also to remember that if the middle management truly backs employee participation, then it would take necessary steps to convince the first-line supervisors about it. The top management must, therefore, obtain the backing of the middle management.
2. Most of the participative schemes have failed because management has not been able to convince the supervisors that employee participation will not

only benefit the company but also will not, in any manner, dilute the authority vested in them [3]. The first-line supervisors must also be convinced that discipline will not, in any way, be compromised. The first-line supervisors are management's link with the grass-roots and the management must, therefore, get their active support.

3. Last but not the least is the need for the management to recognise the feeling of insecurity that employee participation creates in the minds of the employees and face up to their aprehensions [12]. The management must convince the grass-roots — equipment operators, maintenance technicians, quality control inspectors and buyers in the purchasing department — that employee participation will not affect their livelihood, in any way. It must assure the employees that the company not only understands their apprehensions, but also has a plan to deal constructively with job displacements and reductions brought about by the successful implementation of improvement projects. The management must come out openly and discuss this plan with the employees and obtain their support. Such a plan must show new jobs and new vacancies created by growth, diversification, and use of improved technologies, and also reassignments, and programmes for retraining the displaced employees.

We have seen that an environment which supports and encourages participation is created by the top management of the organisation. However, the top management cannot create a supportive environment by itself; it needs the help and active support of the senior managers of the company. Also the top and senior management of an organisation will take the trouble and make the necessary efforts if they truly believe in employee participation. This belief has to be much more than tacit support; management support of employee participation has to be much more than a matter of lip service. In some instances, it is seen that whereas the top management of the company believes in the need for employee participation and advises the general managers of the constituent units, or divisions, to implement it, the unit management is ambivalent about the need and relevance of employee participation. This lack of support from the senior managers of the company leads to the failure of the scheme of employee participation [20].

Goetsch and Davis point out that management commitment is the most critical element in the implementation of employee participation [8]. They also clarify that complete management commitment is characterised by, and is the sum of, the following three attributes:

1. Direct involvement of the top and senior management.
2. Commitment of time.
3. Commitment of the necessary resources by them.

The top and senior management of the company must go beyond just professing their support to employee participation — they, as a group and also as individuals, must be actively involved. The management, as a group and as individuals, must also practise what it preaches. The most earth-shaking pronouncements made by the management in support of, say, product quality fade into nothingness for equipment operators when an order comes down to the factory to ship products of sub-standard quality to meet a delivery commitment. Such behaviour of the management does a lot of harm — it has a negative effect on the scheme. For the top and senior management, employee participation should be a matter of faith.

The workforce requires clearly stated goals and objectives and it is the management's responsibility to define these objectives. The management must also bring about compatibility between the stated objectives and the practices of the organisation and help the workforce to align itself to these objectives. These objectives give direction and meaning to their work. They also bring about cooperation and collaboration between departments and functions. Let us go back a little and examine the source of objectives and see how the management can ensure compatibility between the objectives on the one hand and the practices of the organisation and behaviours of the employees on the other. Objectives are derived from strategies and strategic goals are needed for the definition of objectives. This much is known and recognised but what is not appreciated is that strategic goals are derived from the vision and mission statements.[1] Vision and mission statements play an important role in the development of strategy by providing a framework to generate and then screen strategic options. What is more important is the fact that these statements are also the fountainhead of the right kind of values, which, in turn, give rise to practices and behaviours which support and sustain co-operation, collaboration and participation [23]. Vision and mission statements are, therefore, not only the starting points of all improvement projects, but also vehicles for alignment of the strategic and cultural paths of the organisation and for creating consistency between the objectives and practices and behaviours. The most important task of the top management is the creation of the vision and definition of the mission statements. This task must be done in consultation with the senior managers of the company and the vision must be created by consensus.

The creation of vision and definition of mission statements by the top management of the company displays to the employees the direct involvement of the management in the participative management process. Once the vision and mission statements are defined, the senior management must establish the objectives in the areas of, say, production, productivity, quality, equipment availability and equipment effectiveness, cost reduction and energy conservation. At the senior management level, these objectives are usually stated in a broad sense. Therefore, the senior management must also assist in the deployment of these objectives to the lower levels of management [12]. At the lower, namely departmental/divisional, levels, the specific projects, which must be carried out to meet these objectives, and the resources required for these projects are identified. The senior management personnel must take an active role in the scheme of employee participation. Senior managers must be members of the steering committee and the steering committee must meet periodically to take stock of the scheme and review progress of the activities of the PM groups and advise them with regard to the projects to be undertaken by them. Senior and middle level managers must serve on project teams responsible for the implementation of improvement ideas. Moreover, the middle level managers must serve as facilitators to the PM groups and provide them the necessary guidance and technical assistance. We have already stressed the importance of obtaining the backing of middle management. Herein we must point out that this backing should be in the form of involvement, nay commitment. The middle management must be actively involved in the scheme and the middle level managers must be prepared to spend the necessary time serving in various capacities. Finally, all levels of management must undergo the training needed to understand the concepts, objectives and mechanism of employee participation [12]. This is essential and for this the top and senior management and the middle level managers have to commit the necessary time.

The management must be prepared to commit the necessary resources. For employee participation, the most important input required is training — training of all employees, and the management must be prepared to commit the resources required for training. The time, effort and resources spent on training have a direct effect on the success of the scheme of employee participation. For a successful scheme, the training needs are extensive. Training is required for the top and senior management personnel so that they may develop people by using their education, experience and creativity to improve company operations. This, after all, is the objective of participation — it must make the employees more competent. The members of the steering committee and middle managers must undergo more extensive training. The first-line supervisor must undergo minimally the same training programme as is offered to the workforce [12]. They should have a detailed knowledge of the basic concepts of participation and also of the tools and techniques which are useful in the identification, analysis and solution of work-related problems. They must also have a clear idea about the functioning of the PM groups. Finally in this context, the management must recognise that training to the workforce and the first-line supervisors has to be conducted during working hours and the employees have to be released from their duties and assigned tasks for the period of training. The necessary resources must be made available for the conduct of meetings. In this regard as well, it is important to remember that the meetings of the PM groups are also usually held during the working hours. Resources required for the improvement projects must also be made available. Lastly, there are three important points which must be made and these are as follows:

a) The scheme of annual performance appraisal must be reviewed and revised. Performance in PM group meetings and on improvement projects must be given adequate weightage. If this not done, then the scheme of performance appraisal will become a stumbling block — a disincentive.

b) The scheme of recognition and reward for enthusiastic participation and improvement ideas should also be reviewed from time to time to ensure its continued attractiveness to the employees.

c) The management must face up squarely to the apprehension of the work-force [12]. As noted earlier, the management must be prepared to commit the resources required for retraining of employees who will be affected.

It is essential to have a tradeforce that is both diligent and committed and this can be achieved by careful thought to the needs of the individual employee and creating a supportive work environment—an environment that is conducive to the satisfaction of those needs [13]. A supportive environment can help usher in sincerity and competence in the workforce — a combination that will take the company forward. The management has a very important role to play in the task of creating a supportive work environment. They can create a compelling vision and communicate this to the employees so that the employees align with it and it becomes a shared vision. They can define the missions and provide the necessary resources to the employees, help to develop employees and empower them to tap and harness their energies and abilities.

ENABLERS OF EMPLOYEE PARTICIPATION

The creation of a supportive environment helps in developing a motivated workforce. Although, employee participation cannot be successfully implemented without a motivated workforce, it also requires two other basic ingredients, and these are:

— initiation of schemes of employee participation and availability of participative approaches, and

— training of members and leaders of the quality circles/PM groups in various aspects and facets of employee participation.

As a mater of fact, the factors which enable or bring about employee participation can be subdivided under three broad heads, which are as follows:

I. Creation of a motivated workforce.

II. Availability of participative approaches.

III. Training of members and leaders of small autonomous groups.

We shall discuss these three, one at a time, to be able to identify all the enablers shown in Fig. 6.1.

The first set of enablers of employee participation can be classed under the first ingredient identified by us, namely, creation of a motivated workforce. As shown in Fig. 6.1, this set includes the following:

1. Challenging and meaningful work.
2. Clear goals/objectives.
3. Education and job-related training to develop ability and skills.
4. Availability of necessary resources to carry out the assigned tasks/jobs.
5. A conducive work environment.

We have already noted that to most employees the content, responsibilities and challenges of the job are important and an interesting and challenging job brings out the best effort from most individuals. When an employee comes to work, he is there not only to earn a livelihood but also to do the assigned jobs and tasks well and to the best of his capability. But he will only do his best if he derives job satisfaction from the work assigned to him. The job should be interesting and also mildly difficult — something that needs the exercise of both mental capabilities and physical skills. However, an interesting and challenging job does not remain interesting and challenging if the goal/objective is not clearly defined. A person must know what he is required to do and achieve, and for this, the goal(s), or objective(s), of the jobs and assignments must be clearly stated and understood by him. We have already noted that these goals and objectives are derived from the

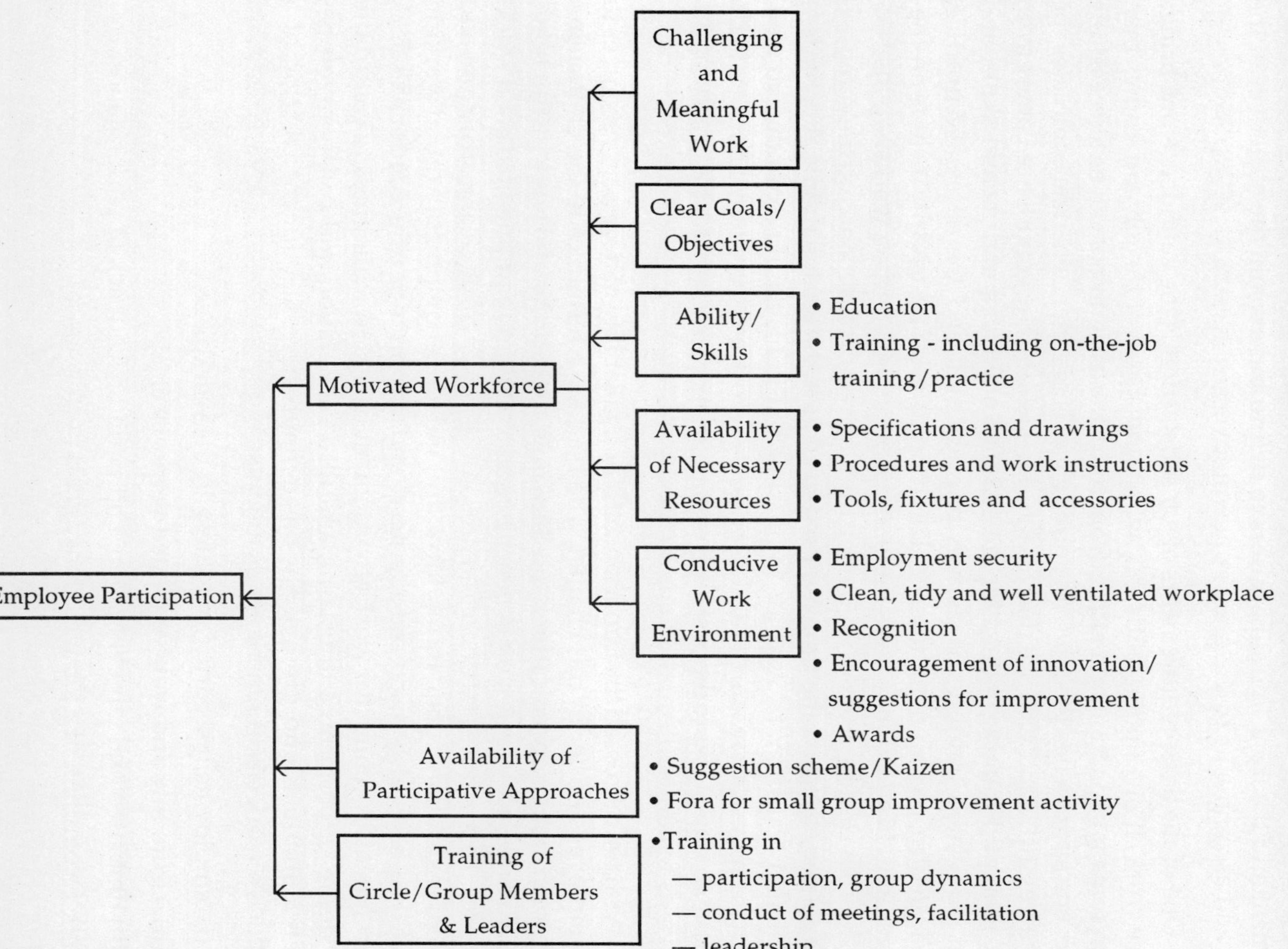

Fig. 6.1. Enablers of Employee Participation

missions/mission statements and thus it is the responsibility of the middle management and the front-line supervisors to define and explain the objectives of the jobs and assignments to the grass-root employees.

One of the basic requirements of job satisfaction is the confidence one brings to the work. If one understands the `what' and `how' of the job and knows that, given some imagination and effort (from him), the assignment can be successfully done, one approaches the job with confidence. Thereafter, when he completes the job successfully and well, he derives job satisfaction. The confidence comes from education and training. Education gives him knowledge and mental skills, and from job-related training, he derives physical skill and the necessary practice, which, in turn, gives him confidence. This training must necessarily include on-the-job training, in addition to class room and laboratory/training workshop instruction. Moreover, the period of on-the-job training required depends on the complexity of the job/task and the time required to acquire the essential skill. A confident and skilled craftsman takes pride in his skill and in his ability to do the job well. Given the necessary resources and a conducive work environment, he wants to do the assignments/tasks to the best of his capability and work hard for the organisation. He wants to contribute and belong to the organisation.

We have discussed the importance of the availability of necessary resources to the employees earlier in this chapter. The necessary resources to the craftsmen/tradesmen include specifications and drawings, procedures and work instructions, tools, fixtures, accessories, work benches, and machines/equipment in good working order. To the office staff, necessary resources may include clear instructions and procedures, stationery and forms, furniture, and office equipment in good working order. We have also discussed the need and importance of a conducive work environment. A conducive work environment ushers in willingness to contribute and desire to perform, enthusiasm, and also cooperation and collaboration between individuals and groups. The basic inputs necessary for the creation of a conducive work environment are as follows:

(i) employment security and safety in the workplace,

(ii) clean, tidy and well-ventilated workplace,

(iii) unbiased and fair evaluation, and periodic feedback of performance,

(iv) recognition of a job well done/good performance,

(v) encouragement of innovation/suggestions for improvement, and

(vi) awards for excellence — performance of a very high level and/or for good implementable ideas/suggestions for improvement in productivity, quality, and equipment availability and effectiveness.

We have noted earlier that a motivated employee wants to contribute to the betterment of the organisation. We have also noted that one of the essential inputs of a conducive work environment is encouragement of suggestions and ideas from the employees. Thus, the availability of a scheme of participation, or a forum where the employee can make his contribution, or his proposal/suggestion for improvement, is a basic requirement and accordingly, the second ingredient of employee participation is the availability of an approach/scheme for employee participation. The availability of a scheme, or an approach, is also an enabler of employee participation. A motivated workforce which can and wants to contribute cannot do so without the availability of a scheme, such as employee suggestion scheme or Kaizen [9], or an approach of employee participation, such as small group autonomous activity in the form of quality circles and/or PM groups.

The third ingredient of employee participation is the training of employees, who will participate, in the concept and mechanics of participation. It is also an enabler of employee participation. A scheme, or approach of employee participation, such as Kaizen, or PM groups, cannot succeed without the provision of adequate training of the employees in the various aspects and facets of participation. The members and leaders of quality circles and/or PM groups must undergo training in participation. Herein it must be pointed out the this training is quite different in its content and structure from the job/work-related training discussed earlier. It also must be remembered that this training does not and cannot replace job-related training but it can complement it and make the employee more useful to the organisation. The training of circle/group members in participation must include training on the need and concept of employee participation, in group dynamics and the tools and techniques used for identification, analysis and solution of work-related problems such as brainstorming, Pareto analysis, checksheets and histograms, scatter diagrams, binomial plots and correlation-regression analysis, cause-and-effect diagrams and control charts. The training of circle/group leaders must be more extensive and their training should also include training in facilitation and conduct of meetings and in leadership.

Small Group Autonomous Activity

Belcher, in his book on productivity, says that [1]:

> "Organisations often pay scant attention to the potential contributions of the workforce at large, relying instead on management personnel to achieve higher levels of productivity. Since involvement of the workforce is minimal, the results are predictable: apathy, mistrust and resistance...

(under the circumstances) management must drag an unresponsive and ponderous organisation to higher levels of performance against its will."

This state of affairs is characteristic of many large industrial organisations in India — particularly those wherein effective attempts at involving the grass-root employees have not yet been made. We have discussed the need and usefulness of employee participation and have noted that "efforts at the development of an environment in which the employees can and will contribute to performance improvement are typically characterised by employee involvement strategies" [1]. There are many methods, or strategies, of involving the grass-root employees starting from information sharing, and including small group autonomous activity through the effective use of small groups in the form of quality circles and/or PM groups, right upto the use of empowered groups. Quality circles are small groups of employees from the same work area (of the same bureau/cell/section/shop/department), or doing similar type of work, who voluntarily meet regularly for about an hour every week to identify, analyse and resolve work-related problems not only to improve quality, productivity and the total performance of an organisation, but also to enrich the quality of worklife of the employees [6]. We have noted earlier that the driving force, or philosophy, of TPM is to improve the quality of people by building in them the right kind of attitudes and developing a sense of ownership of the equipment and belonging to the organisation, and also that this is attained through the use of participation of the grassroots and through TPM promotion. In this regard, it has great similarity with TQM. We have also noted that TPM also uses small group activity for employee involvement and participation and in TPM, these small groups are called PM groups (in Japan, they are called TPM groups). Thus, we find that PM groups are created with the same objective of employee participation, and through the use of small group activity, PM groups enable employees not only to take up and solve equipment-related problems of concern to an organisation but also to derive a sense of ownership and job satisfaction.

The techniques, or strategies, commonly used for employee involvement and participation can be classified under three heads, as follows [1]:

I. Employee involvement techniques:

   1. Information sharing schemes.
   2. Suggestion schemes/systems.

II. Problem-solving techniques:

3. Task forces.
4. Small group autonomous activity.

III. Higher-order participative technique requiring organisation restructuring:

5. Use of empowered groups/teams.

The techniques which are aimed just at involving the employees, as opposed to using them for problem solving or decision making are lower order strategies which are comparatively simple and can be implemented without a major commitment of management time and resources. Under the information sharing scheme, the management shares with the employees on a regular basis, information about the nature and challenges of the business, plans and performance of the organisation, and the rationale behind organisational changes and decisions which affect employees and their jobs. A suggestion system, on the other hand, is a more organised approach of employee participation and is aimed at obtaining and evaluating ideas and suggestions for improvement from the employees.

As we go up the ladder, we come to schemes, or techniques, which involve the employees in problem-solving. In these techniques, employee participation is greater than in the lower-order techniques. The strategies included in the middle-order set of techniques are the creation and use of task forces, and employee participation through the use of small group autonomous activity. As a problem-solving technique, the use of task forces is the least demanding in terms of management time and resources. A task force is an ad hoc group of managers and employees brought together to solve a particular problem. The members of the task force are chosen by the management and the problem is also defined by the management. Moreover, the group is normally disbanded after the completion of the task at hand, that is, after the solution to the problem has been developed and presented to the management. In contrast, the use of small group activity requires management commitment in the form of time and resources in developing a motivated workforce and in sustaining employee motivation through provision of necessary time and resources for training, conduct of meetings and implementation of improvement ideas, encouragement of new and innovative ideas/suggestions and recognition of outstanding circles and groups and awards. Small group activity depends on the enthusiastic work of examining, analysing and solving problems done by small groups of employees usually from a common work area/shop/ department, or area of plant, or company activity. Unlike task forces, these small groups are permanent problem-solving teams consisting generally of 8 to 12 employees, who are members of a particular circle or group. This group meets periodically — usually for one hour every week — to take up, analyse and solve work-related problems of concern to the group and the organisation, and also to enhance the communication between the employees and the management. This, in turn, creates a more supportive work environment which sustains continued participation by employees and encourages the growth of small group activity. The small group of employees is led by a leader, who may either be a volunteer, or one assigned to lead the group. Each group may also have a facilitator, who typically is from the management. The facilitator assists the group leader and the group in identification of the problem, data acquisition and analysis, use of problem-solving tools, conduct of meetings and sometimes even in the implementation of the improvement ideas. He is not a member of the circle or group and generally acts as technical advisor or consultant to the group. As an employee participation technique, small group activity is much more effective than the use of task forces. Since task forces have a limited life, they do not necessarily foster a sense of belonging to the organisation. Moreover, in task forces, employee participation is not as enthusiastic or spontaneous as in circles or groups.

Herein an important point to remember is that the use of one technique does not necessarily mean the abrogation of a lower-order involvement technique. As an example, the reader will appreciate that information sharing by the management with the employees must be a most basic feature of all employee involvement efforts. Lack of information about the performance of the organisation one serves and about decisions which affect one's livelihood not only alienates the person but also results in a feeling of uncertainty and insecurity. Thus, whatever strategy of employee participation is used, an information sharing scheme must exist side-by-side. Another important point is the efficacy of progressing from a lower-order technique to a higher-order technique as opposed to starting off with a higher-order technique. This turns out to be much more effective in a majority of cases since it affords the time to tie up loose ends and to fine tune a lower-order technique thereby creating an environment which will be able to support a higher-order strategy. There are many organisations, for example, which start off with information sharing and employee suggestion schemes and move over to small group activity, in the form of quality circles and/or PM groups, only after two or three years of successful operation of the suggestion system. In this regard, one must appreciate that as a strategy of employee participation, small group activity has the potential of being much more effective than the employee suggestion system. This is due to the fact that only the individualistic and talented employees are attracted to the suggestion system. Thus, only a handful of employees take part in a suggestion scheme. The other employees feel left out and this, over a period of time, may usher in a sense of alienation. Small group activity, on the other hand, enables the participation of a larger number of employees. This, in turn, brings in a sense of togetherness — a sense of belonging to the group and the organisation — in the workforce. Dey explains this phenomenon and presents the comparative advantage of the small group activity over the suggestion scheme in the following words [6]:

> "Suggestion schemes are usually preferred by employees who are individualistic, highly creative and hardworking. In any typical organisation, individuals belonging to this category constitute only a small percentage of the total workforce. (Moreover) the usual practice in a suggestion scheme is to reward the employee whenever his suggestion is found feasible. Normally, he is not responsible for implementation of his suggestion ... Most of the employees in an organisation are not highly creative. They do not have the temperament to invest a great deal of energy and time in preparing individual suggestions. Collectively, they have the potential to share the load of solving problems. A few quality circle members are required to be directly involved in implementation of quality circle suggestions. The chance of successful implementation of a suggestion is, therefore, higher when it is routed through quality circles rather than suggestion schemes."

Out of those organisations who have seriously taken up employee participation, most are in the middle-order stage and make extensive use of small group activity [1]. In India as well, many organisations are using small group activity and many more, who have been successfully using information sharing and suggestion schemes, are considering its use. In this regard, an obvious question is - why is it taking companies so long to progress to higher-order techniques, such as empowered teams? The use of empowered teams is a very sophisticated technique. It not only requires extensive and radical organisational restructuring and work redesign, but also calls for a very high level of maturity in the employees [1] who will always work for the team and place the team and organisational goals at a much higher level than personal goals, recognition and advancement. To ensure this, a very extensive recruitment method is necessitated to screen job aspirants to make sure that their character traits are consistent with the ideals espoused by the company. This requirement somehow seems to preclude this strategy of employee participation as far as larger manufacturing organisations are concerned. This brings us to a basic characteristic of human behaviour; and the fact that this basic human drive is best satisfied by participation in small group activity. Peter and

Waterman, in the introduction to their famous book, quote psychologist Ernest Becker to point out that "man is driven by an essential dualism; he needs both to be a part of something and to stick out" [19]. A man wants to belong to a winning team and at the same time, he wants recognition of his individual abilities and knowledge - "he wants to be a star in his own right" [19]. Small group activity affords him an opportunity to satisfy this basic dualism. He can belong to a high performance group and at the same time, he has the opportunity of being recognised by his co-members and by the management for his knowledge, improvement ideas and problem-solving skills.

We have, through our discussion in the preceding paragraphs, shown that small group activity is the most effective and most practical strategy, or scheme, of employee participation. Another important point about the use of small group activity is that this technique of employee participation requires a formal structure to ensure its effective functioning, and this is usually in the form of overlapping small groups starting from the top of the organisational structure right down to the grassroot employees. At the top, the group is much larger and it takes the form of the TPM promotion committee, or quality circle steering committee, and as we go down, we have departmental/divisional committees, through shop PM groups/ circles, down to circles and groups for each shift. Such a formal structure is very useful for the promotion of TPM, or TQM related activities, or in other words, for enabling and ensuring the involvement of all departments and all levels in improvement activities. In this manner, the use of small group activity not only enables the participation of the grassroot employees in work-related problem-solving and improvement activities, but also makes possible the involvement of all employees — in all other departments/functions and at higher levels in the organisation. We will discuss TPM promotion later in this chapter, but here we may conclude by noting that small group activity enables the promotion of TPM, or TQM related activities much more effectively than the other available approaches, or strategies, of employee participation.

We have used the term 'autonomous' in the title of this section, but till now, we have avoided its use and instead referred to the strategy, or technique, as the use of small groups activity. In Chapter Three, we have discussed the points of difference between quality circles and PM groups. From this discussion and from Table 3.1, the reader would have noted that there exists some difference in the perceived level of autonomy available to employees in quality circles as compared to PM groups.[2] We will return to this difference in autonomy and the other points of difference later in this section when we take up the characteristics of PM groups and circles. However, before we do that, we must enlist and discuss the so-called principles of participation. These principles are essentially in the form of guidelines which assist in enabling the successful implementation of small group activity.

PRINCIPLES OF PARTICIPATION

Certain guidelines, or principles, have emerged from experiences of companies and research studies conducted by behavioural scientists. These guidelines are useful for establishing and sustaining employee participation schemes, or strategies. There are ten guidelines in all; and whereas some of these guidelines apply to all known approaches, or strategies/methods, of employee involvement, all ten given below, are more pertinent to the initiation, operation and sustenance of small group activity in a manufacturing organisation.

1. Successful schemes call for genuine, and not superficial involvement of the top and senior managers of the company. Moreover, there must be full understanding at all levels of management of the multifaceted objectives of the scheme and its various purposes.
2. Employee contributions and ideas must receive serious consideration and the suggestions, or ideas, which are found to be sound and relevant, must be implemented.
3. It must be realised by and clearly explained to all employees that the scheme is not only meant for operators and tradesmen in the shops and that it is equally important for office employees.
4. The organisation and administration of the scheme must be kept clear and simple. This implies that successful schemes require to be initially planned and prepared very carefully.
5. It is essential that the members of the circles and groups not only find the meetings and involvement sessions interesting and meaningful, but also are able to actively participate in them. This calls for adequate training for the employees not only in identification and analysis of problems, but also in group participation and group dynamics.
6. It should be ensured that the themes/topics and problems selected for the meetings and involvement sessions are fresh, up-to-date and relevant to factory and organisational issues and concerns. This requires moving on the other problems and activities if the ones on hand have been gone into for a long time (lest they become stale and uninteresting).

7. As an extension of the sixth guideline the contents of the scheme should have long-term continuity and contribution to plant and company operations. Short-term activity in which interest and value quickly fade should be avoided.
8. At the beginning of the scheme, the members and leadership of the circles and groups may be nominated, or otherwise selected by the management. However, subsequently attempts should be made to achieve voluntary participation of employees with a minimum of imposition of the scheme.
9. The leadership of the circles and groups should be from and directed to line operations in the factory and offices of the company. This is to ensure direct participation of the operating personnel rather than the management.
10. Employee involvement schemes are an important ingredient to, but not a substitute for, the companywide and plantwide quality assurance and productive maintenance programmes demanding work in the areas of marketing, design, production and service functions. Some of these activities, in turn, can provide inputs to the activities of involvement schemes and also benefit from some of their outputs.

CHARACTERISTICS OF PM GROUPS AND CIRCLES

In Chapter One, we had noted that T in TPM stands essentially for total involvement, or involvement of all employees at all levels, and also that for this purpose, right at the beginning of its development at the Nippondenso Company, taking a cue from quality circle (or QC circle) activities, TPM was evolved as 'PM with all employees participating (in it) through small group activities' [16]. In Chapter Three, we have noted the similarity of TPM with TQM in this regard and have used the definitions of TQC and TPM given by Suzaki to stress that the use of small group activity is critical to establishment and promotion of TPM. We will discuss TPM promotion in the next section, and herein, in the following paragraphs, we will discuss the basic characteristics of PM groups and circles.[3]

PM groups and circles are also set up with the twin objectives of (i) tapping the knowledge and abilities/skill of the employees for solving work-related problems and for generating improvement ideas and suggestions, and (ii) developing a motivated workforce and improving communication between the employees and management through employee participation. PM groups are also small groups and similar in size as quality circles. But beyond this there are few similarities. The two characteristic features of PM groups and circles are the two basic roles of small groups in TPM, which, in turn, are as follows:

1. Harmonising group goals with the company, or corporate goals.
2. Implementation of the five Ss and autonomous maintenance.

In TPM, group goals coincide with the company goals [18]. We have noted earlier that PM groups have evolved from ZD groups and ZD groups must choose goals which are consistent with the annual goals, or targets, of the company because ultimately zero defects 'is aimed at the elimination of defects and promotes the attainment of all related goals' [18]. Thus, in TPM, the small groups must choose themes and goals which are consistent with the goals of the organisation, and problems taken up by the groups are usually those which are of concern to the management as well. Some of the proponents of quality circles, particularly the traditionalists, may argue that this goes against the principle of autonomy in as much as the autonomy in the selection of work-related problems is taken away from the circle members, and this would, therefore, tend to diminish the motivation derived by the members from participation. This argument is not quite justified since autonomy in the selection of problems to be discussed, and themes and goals, is only important in situations where the necessary understanding and trust between the management and the employees does not exist. In his book on the concepts and practices of quality circles, Dey says that this autonomy in the selection of problems or themes, is 'essential in the early stages of the quality circles experiment and when mutual trust is established between the management and the workforce, the former may suggest some of the problems to the quality circle members' [6]. This is what is actually done in successfully operating schemes, wherein the members of the steering committee suggest the themes and goals, and sometimes even the specific problems which are of concern to the management. In this regard, one must also consider that in most organisations, a participative scheme involving the use of quality circles, or small group autonomous activity for quality and productivity improvement, precedes the formation of PM groups and circles, or in other words, TPM is implemented in an environment of (adequate) trust between the management and the workforce. Thus, the autonomy in the selection of themes and goals is not very important to the employees any more. In this context, Suzuki stresses the importance of harmony of group goals with the company goals by adding that [21]:

> "The autonomy of small groups must be respected, but middle managers have the vital role of ensuring that small-group goals are compatible with top management goals and policies. TPM is a top-down rather than a bottom-up process."

The TPM promotion structure of overlapping small groups helps ensure this, as we had noted at the beginning of this chapter. To ensure this harmony, in the TPM promotion structure, group leaders at every level are part of the company management structure, right from supervisors, through middle managers upto the top management. As for example, PM group and circles at the shop floor level are led by supervisors. The leaders of these circles form a group under the leadership of the shift superintendent, who, in turn, works in a group under a departmental manager. These managers participate in a group led by the Works Manager, who is, in turn, part of the TPM promotion committee [10}. This structure implies that the leadership role is assumed by the management personnel and at the lowest, or the grassroot level, the leadership is assumed by supervisors. This is another major point of difference of the PM groups from the quality circles, as noted earlier in Chapter Three and shown in Table 3.1. Herein, as well, a case of loss of autonomy may be put forward by the traditionalists. A closer scrutiny will reveal that this is also only a perceived loss of autonomy. In reality, leadership by supervisors is not only quite in conformance with the ninth principle of participation, namely 'leadership of the circles and groups should be from and directed to line operations,' but also is better since supervisors are more suited for the leadership role than equipment operators and maintenance tradesmen. On leadership of quality circles, Dey opines that 'a person is expected to be a successful leader when he has good interpersonal relationship and is perceived as a competent individual' by the circle members [6]. A supervisor is normally expected to be more competent and also to have better interpersonal skills than operators and tradesmen.

The second characteristic of PM groups and circles is derived from their role in the implementation of autonomous maintenance and the five Ss. In Chapters One and Two, we have noted the importance and vital need of autonomous maintenance in TPM, and later in Chapter Five, we have also noted that the implementation of autonomous maintenance is both difficult and time consuming. PM groups and circles have a major role to play in this regard. Small groups have two distinct roles, namely social and problem-solving. The social aspect of small group activity holds the group together and brings about the necessary cohesion. Assisting in the implementation of autonomous maintenance and the five Ss is part of its social role. Autonomous maintenance requires skilled, highly motivated and disciplined operators. Moreover, all operators must realise that autonomous maintenance activities are vital for their machines/equipment and form a necessary part of their daily work. It must be brought home to them that autonomous maintenance is not a voluntary activity — it is essential and mandatory. This requirement and need has to be viewed in the context of existing conditions and ground realities. In most organisations, the implementation of autonomous maintenance is impeded and otherwise affected by the fact that most operators have scant regard for maintenance of their machines and equipment and many of them feel that this activity is not a part of their job and has been forced on them. This attitude is aggravated by the human tendency of resisting change. Such an attitude has to be changed and this can be brought about through peer pressure and counselling. Moreover, weaknesses pointed out by colleagues and coworkers are readily acknowledged. Therefore, co-members of circles and groups can help in the correction of weaknesses so that unnecessary lapses are avoided.

In Chapters Four and Five, we have noted the importance of maintenance of operating procedures and standards and training of equipment operators in proper operation of their equipment/machines. Maloperation is the most important cause of machine and equipment breakdowns. Improper operation of machines, poor maintenance of operating procedures and standards, and equipment breakdowns caused by inattention and lack of adherence to standards are the results of operator attitudes and habits. The five Ss — *seiri, seiton, seiso, seiketsu* and *shitsuke* — assist in the inculcation of the right work habits, namely, of clearing and sorting out, systematic arrangement of items and things, cleanliness and neatness, tidiness and orderliness, and self discipline. These habits, in turn, create a mindset, or attitude, of perfection. These habits have to be ingrained into the individual and if that is done, then adherence to operating procedures, practices and standards is ensured. The explanations of the five Ss are given below:

1. SEIRI (sorting out and clearing)
   Separate accepted, reworkable and rejected parts/products, rework the reworkable parts, sort out unnecessary items and rejected parts and discard them.

2. SEITON (systematic arrangement)
   Arrange necessary items in predecided locations and in good order, so that they are easily accessible and can be easily picked up for use — a place for every necessary thing and everything in its place.

3. SEISO (cleanliness and neatness — spic and span)
   Clean your workplace and machine properly and completely, so that there is no dirt or dust on the floor, workbench and the machine/equipment.

4. SEIKETSU (tidiness and orderliness)
   Practice SEIRI, SEITON and SEISO to ensure a high standard of housekeeping and workplace organisation at all times.

5. SHITSUKE (self discipline)
   Ensure self discipline and train others to follows rules strictly and maintain prescribed operating standards and procedures.

The enforcement of the five Ss enables the ushering in of an environment which is supportive of quality, efficient and high output work in a neat, clean, orderly and disciplined workplace. The following advantages can be derived by ensuring the practice of the five Ss by the workforce:

1. Improvement of product quality, since operations can be performed without error, proceeding in the prescribed and well-regulated manner, resulting in fewer defective parts and products.
2. Greater safety since operations can be performed safely, comfortably and conveniently reducing the chances of accidents.
3. Significant reduction in the number of machine/equipment breakdowns.
4. Higher productivity and reduction/elimination of waste since operations can be performed efficiently and without errors and defects.

Thus, the enforcement, or more correctly the practice, of five Ss by the workforce not only ensures adherence to operating procedures and standards, but also enables a significant reduction of the six big losses. Is that not what the TPM programme is all about? However, consider that the five Ss have to be fully assimilated by the employees so much so that these good habits come naturally to them and become part of their ordinary behaviour. PM groups and circles, through friendly persuasion and peer pressure, can bring about such a drastic change of habits and attitude.

The Japanese call the five Ss the five guiding policies. Many in India already recognise the importance of imbibing the five Ss by employees at all levels and many industries are having their employees trained in the five Ss. However, there are many in our industries who think that the hype with regard to the five Ss is unnecessary and meaningless. They find the whole thing frivolous and consider the entire exercise of training in the five Ss farcical and ritualistic. But consider for a moment the breakdowns, accidents, defects and defectives, poor house-keeping, disorganised workplace, lack of attention and carelessness, and you will appreciate the importance of these five good work habits. Before we close our discussion of the characteristic features of PM groups and circles and with it, of small group autonomous activity, we must discuss the following two points:

(i) the remaining differences between PM groups and quality circles, and

(ii) some lessons learnt from the Indian experience in employee participation through the use of small group autonomous activity.

However, before we do this, we must resolve the matter of autonomy in PM groups and circles. There is a lot of autonomy available to members of PM groups in as much as they get an opportunity of voicing their opinions about work-related problems, proffering their suggestions and taking part in problem-solving and implementation of improvement ideas and improved methods and procedures.

In this chapter, we have already discussed the basic difference in the structure of PM groups and quality circles and noted the justification for formation of PM groups within the existing organisational structure, as opposed to quality circles, which are formed by workers independent of the organisational structure and assumption of leadership of PM groups and circles by supervisors (also see Chapter Three and Table 3.1). We have also discussed the difference between the two as far as selection of themes, goals and problems is concerned. Now we come to the other two areas of differences, namely, the mode of participation and period of conduct of meetings and payment of overtime if conducted outside the working hours. In Chapter Three, we have already noted that the participation in PM groups and circles is mandatory whereas in quality circles, it is supposed to be voluntary. We have also noted that PM group and circle meetings are usually conducted during the working hours and if for some reasons, some meetings need to be conducted outside the working hours, then overtime is paid to the members in contrast with quality circle meetings which are usually held outside (or after) working hours and no overtime is paid for attending these meetings.

Small group autonomous activity, in the form of quality circles, is not new in India and has been used for 15-20 years already, and the Indian experience is quite revealing. In India, in many organisations, the quality circle movement has not been very successful, whereas in some other organisations, the movement has caught the fancy of the grassroot employees and is prospering and growing. During discussions with some primemovers[4] of successful experiments, the author has noted the following important points:

(i) In India, if participation is made voluntary as proposed by the traditionalists, then the employees do not normally come forward to enroll as members and take part in the meetings. However, if participation is mandatory, then employee participation is enthusiastic. The reason behind this is probably that the employees feel that the management is not serious about the whole thing if they feel that employee participation should be made voluntary.

(ii) Successful companies hold quality circle meetings during the working hours, such as the first hour (in the respective shifts) every Monday or Wednesday, and also pay overtime for any time that is spent in meetings(s) beyond the working hours. The reason for this is obviously because the workers question management's commitment to participation if they feel that this is not important enough to be considered as a part of their job and held during the working hours. Moreover, if the managements think that it is important, then they should be prepared to pay employees for the time spent after working hours, in meetings and for training.

(iii) Continued and repeated references to Japan, Japanese management principles, the Japanese quality circles movement and the practice of quality circles in the Japanese industries has been found to be distracting and obstructive. Many employees feel that what is good for Japan may not necessarily be good for India. They also find such repeated references distasteful. Instead they ask for a 'made in India' scheme. In a particular case (a large corporation engaged in mining operations and related activities), use of the Indian translation of quality circles for the scheme, using Indian names for the circles and overhauling the scheme and recastings its rules and procedures made the difference — a dying experiment turned into a flourishing scheme. Instead of quality circle, the Hindi translation, namely '*Kaushal Chakra*' was used. In the same vein, the author proposes the use of '*sanrakshan gosthi/mandali*' for PM groups and circles.

TPM Promotion

To promote is to 'help to organise and start,' or 'help the progress of' [11]. Thus, TPM promotion should include activities aimed at helping to organise and start TPM and also helping its progress in the organisation. In this context, we should remember that the objective of productive maintenance is not just the maximisation of equipment availability; it is the maximisation of equipment effectiveness, which is the product of (and which includes in itself) equipment availability, equipment, or more correctly, man-machine productivity, and product and process quality. Quite obviously, this objective of maximisation of overall equipment effectiveness cannot be attained just by efforts of the maintenance, production/operations and quality control departments. The attainment of this objective requires coordinated efforts by all functions of the organisation and not just the efforts of these three functions without the supporting activities by other functions. Moreover, T in TPM stands for total involvement which signifies the involvement of all employees in all functions and at all levels. We have also noted that for this, the departmental boundaries have to be transcended and employees in the various departments have to work together. Thus TPM, by definition, requires cross-functional management of efforts of various functions of the organisation. But TPM is 'productive maintenance, through total employee participation' [17], and the strategy of employee participation used is small group autonomous activity, in the form of PM groups. Thus, organising, starting and helping the progress of TPM calls for cross-functional management of the activities of the small groups in various departments and functions and at different levels of the organisation. But what exactly is cross-functional management? Clark and Wheelwright, in their recent book on the management of new product and process development, point out that unfortunately it is 'often limited to communication and coordination activity, with little or no impact on working level activities' [4]. They suggest cross-functional integration instead. This is also what TPM promotion should aim for — conduct of the activities of small groups in the various functions and at different levels of the organisations in a well-coordinated and integrated manner. This calls for a formal structure and accordingly, for this purpose, a promotional structure of overlapping small groups is used. In this section, we will discuss various aspects of TPM promotion and we will divide our discussion into five parts and these five parts are as follows:

1. Concept of TPM promotion.
2. Organisational structure used for TPM promotion, or the TPM promotional structure.
3. Steps involved in TPM promotion.
4. Role of management in TPM promotion.
5. Developing small group activity and evaluating the progress of small groups.

CONCEPT OF TPM PROMOTION

In TPM, harmonising the goals and themes of the small groups with the company, or corporate goals is very important. We have already discussed this and noted the overriding justification of this requirement. The company, or corporate goals are set by the top and senior management personnel. They set the organisational goals and they also determine the companywide PM policies.[5] These goals and policies have then to be transmitted down the organisational structure, through departments and departmental managers, to the shops and sections, and these goals and policies form the basis for the determination of the departmental PM goals and policies. The departmental PM goals are, in turn, used for setting of goals for the PM groups and circles in the shops and sections and further down, the PM subcircles, if necessary. This is the first ingredient of the concept of TPM promotion, namely 'top down' goal setting and direction of activities, as shown in Fig. 6.2.

The goals of the PM groups and circles, so set, have in turn, to be achieved by the respective PM groups and circles. For the achievement of the goals, the improvement ideas and suggestions have to be implemented. The implementation of improvement ideas and suggestions requires the involvement, active support and assistance of higher level groups right through departmental PM committee, upto the companywide, or central TPM promotion committee. Implementation of ideas and suggestions of the groups is essential for the sustenance and growth of motivation in the members, and motivated employees participate spontaneously and enthusiastically in the activities of the PM groups and help in the progress of TPM in the organisation. This brings us to the second ingredient of the concept of TPM promotion, namely, 'bottom up' (or bottom-to-top) small group activities and implementation of improvement ideas and suggestions of the groups, as shown in Fig. 6.2.

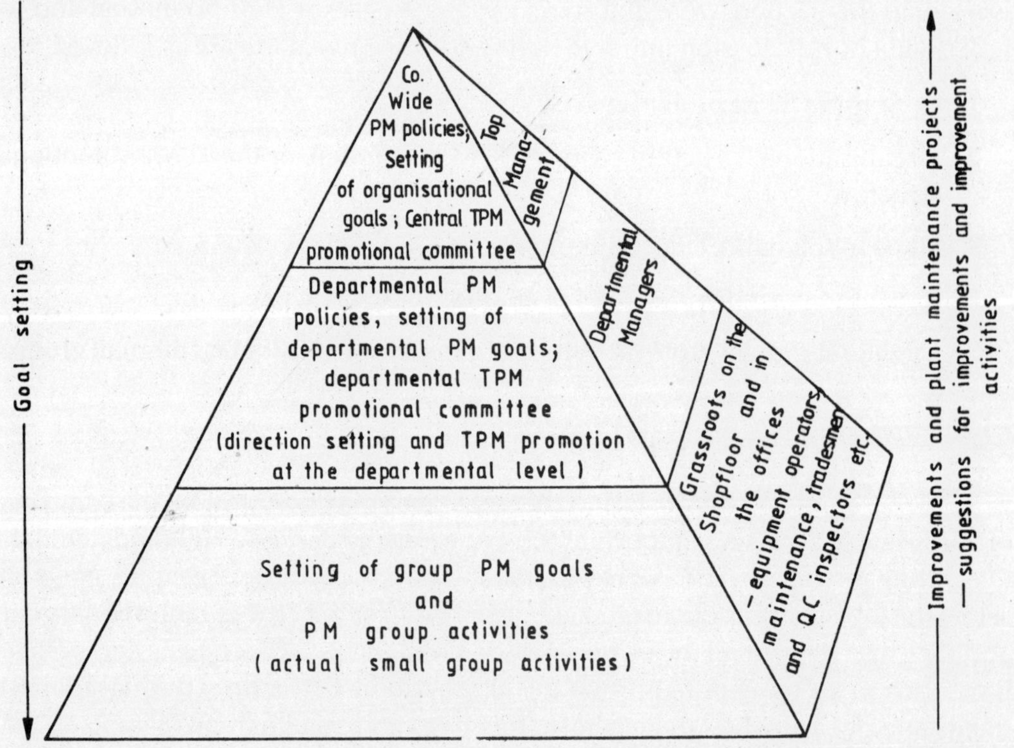

Fig. 6.2. Concept of TPM Promotion —'Top Down' Goal Setting and Direction and 'Bottom Up' Improvement Activities

These two ingredients of the concept of TPM promotion, namely 'top down' goal setting and 'bottom up' improvement activities, ensure that the activities of the PM groups and circles, at every level of the organisational structure, complement and enhance the organisational activities [18]. This way they help in the achievement of the organisational goals. For this, it is necessary that the PM groups should be integrated into the corporate, or company, organisational structure [18]. This, in turn, calls for the integration of an organisational structure used for TPM promotion, or the TPM promotional structure, with the organisational structure of the company, as shown in Fig. 6.2.

TPM PROMOTIONAL STRUCTURE

The effective administration of the scheme of small group autonomous activity, thus, requires a formal structure, that is, TPM promotion requires an organisational structure. The TPM promotional structure of overlapping small groups is shown in Fig. 6.3. This organisational structure is based on the concept of TPM promotion and it ensures that the activities of the small groups in the various functions, like production, design and development, purchasing etc., and at various levels in the organisation are properly directed, coordinated and linked. The TPM promotional structure enables cross-functional integration.

The TPM promotional structure is based on the following three important principles:

1. Use of overlapping small groups.
2. Use of committee and subcommittees.
3. Fanning out from the production/operations department to the entire company.

The small groups function at every level of the company, starting from the top and senior management levels to the production shops and production lines. The two ingredients of the concept of TPM promotion call for proper linking of the small groups at different hierarchical levels, and this is done through the use of overlapping small groups. The leaders of the PM circles at the lowest, or the first level are members of the small group at the next higher, or the second level, and so on right upto the top. This ensures linking of different groups, and enhances vertical (both top to bottom and bottom to top) and horizontal (between shops, departments and functions) communication. This is illustrated in Fig. 6.3.[6] The reader will notice that the promotional structure, shown in the figure, has a TPM promotion

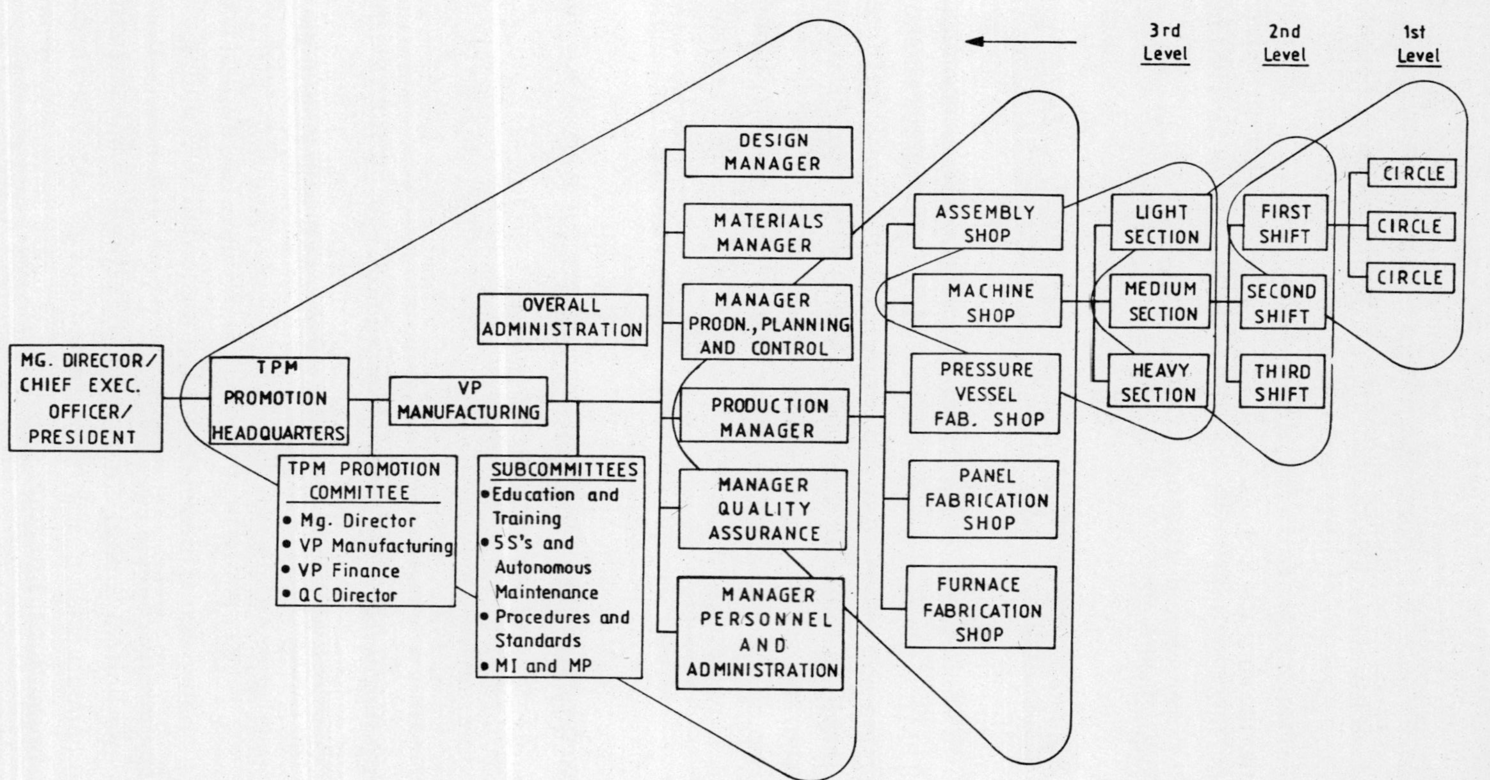

Fig. 6.3. TPM Promotional Structure — Overlapping Small Groups

committee, four subcommittees (they can as well be called committees), and a TPM promotion office for overall administration of the scheme of small group autonomous activity. The TPM Promotion Committee is the apex body under the chairmanship of the Managing Director, or the Chief Executive Officer, of the organisation. It is responsible for directing the TPM activity of the entire company. It sets the TPM policy for the company and it also sets the TPM goals and activities for the company as a whole. It coordinates the TPM efforts of the various functions, or divisions and departments, to enable the achievement of corporate goals. Under the TPM Promotion Committee, there are a number of committees/ subcommittees, with each committee/subcommittee being responsible for a particular topic, such as education and training, implementation of five Ss and autonomous maintenance, development of procedures and standards, and MI and MP. The number of committees/subcommittees will differ from one organisation to another.

Although TPM efforts are essentially directed at line activities, and the equipment operators, maintenance tradesmen, and the quality control inspectors and technicians are still the leading players [18], the TPM effort should spread to the other departments and functions of the company. Only when this happens, will the total involvement, as enunciated in the definition of TPM, be achieved. In this regard, one alternative is to take up the job of TPM promotion in two phases, with phase I concentrating on the production shops and departments and in phase II, fanning out to the other departments such as design/engineering, sales and service, purchasing and general administration. In this context, Suzuki states that although, in most organisations, PM groups are still concentrated in the production shops/departments, TPM has recently begun to spread out to other departments [21].

STEPS FOR TPM PROMOTION

The TPM promotional structure, just by itself, is not enough. We have noted earlier that the basic enablers of employee participation are a motivated workforce, availability of participative approaches, and training of circle and group members and leaders in participation, group dynamics, problem-solving, facilitation and leadership. We have also noted that the attainment of skill and competence in own job/trade and provision of a conducive work environment are essential for development of a motivated workforce. Therefore, in addition to instituting a scheme of employee participation, for its success, an organisation has to ensure:

(i) training for all its employees so that they are not only competent in their trades and fields of specialisation, but also have learnt about participation, groups dynamics and techniques of identification and analysis of problems (the seven tools) to effectively participate and contribute in meetings and implementation projects, and

(ii) sustenance and growth of motivation of its employees through reinforcement, and this reinforcement of motivation is achieved through recognition, implementation of improvement ideas and rewards.

Therefore, effective TPM promotion not only requires a promotional structure, but also calls for (i) education and training for all employees, (ii) enunciation of policy, goals and plans, and (iii) reinforcement of motivation through evaluation and feedback, implementation, recognition and rewards. Based on this, now we are in a position to define the four steps of implementation of the scheme of employee participation through small group activity, or steps of TPM promotion. The four steps of TPM promotion are as follows:

Step 1: Education and training for all employees.

Step 2: Enunciation of TPM policy, goals and plans.

Step 3: Development and implementation of the TPM promotional structure.

Step 4: Development of methods and procedures for evaluation of suggestions, implementation of improvement ideas, recognition and rewards.

The objective of TPM is maximisation of equipment effectiveness and for this, TPM involves the entire workforce in raising standards continuously through improvements in equipment availability, product and process quality and productivity. But improvement ideas do not come easy. Improvement ideas are results of competence, practice and reinforcement. Small group activity provides an opportunity to employees to practice what they have learnt and imbibed, and as we have already noted, reinforcement is provided by the last step of evaluation, implementation, recognition and rewards. The most important input required for improvement ideas is competence, which, in turn, is derived from education and training. Both kinds of training are required, namely, training in job-related skills and knowledge, and training in participation and problem-solving. We have already noted the importance of the TPM policy and goals in TPM promotion. The step of enunciation of policy, goals and plans gives the necessary direction to small group activity and the PM groups and circles cannot operate without them. This step includes the definition of the company TPM policy and the company-wide TPM goals. As a part of this step, the management should also develop the TPM plans for the company, which, in addition to the goals, must include the targets, or benchmarks, time scales and budgets. The TPM topics and the TPM goals are selected based on the characteristics of the manufacturing organisation, namely, its products, processes, the type and condition of plant(s), its employees and productive maintenance problems. Thus, each company has its unique TPM policy, improvement topics and TPM goals [21]. Each small group must have its own TPM goals (please see Fig. 6.2 and recollect the first ingredient of the concept of TPM promotion,namely 'topdown' goal setting) and what is more important, each PM group and circle must understand that achieving these goals will lead to the achievement of the company TPM goals. We have already discussed the third step, which is the TPM promotional structure and its implementation. Herein we will only add that the number of committees/subcommittees should be as few as possible and we will reiterate that the inclusion of other departments is important and this should be kept in mind and planned for. The fourth step is one that ensures that the scheme of small group activity lives and grows. The suggestions of PM groups and cirlces must receive due consideration. They should be evaluated promptly, and the good improvement ideas—ones which are practical and implementable—should be taken up for implementation. The results of implementation should be recognised and adequately rewarded. The most important thing to remember is that the procedures for evaluation of improvement ideas, selection, trial implementation and monitoring of results should be kept as simple as possible since the more complex a system, more difficult it is to administer and such systems tend to sink under the weight of their rules and procedures.

ROLE OF MANAGEMENT IN TPM PROMOTION

Management has to play a very large role in TPM promotion. The role of management in the promotion of small group activity should appropriately be discussed under the following two heads:

1. The role of top and senior management.
2. The line manager's role in promoting small groups.

We have already discussed the need for a motivated workforce, ability and competence in the workforce, and a conducive work environment. The success of any small group activity depends on these three conditions. The top and senior management of a company (as a group) has to take the responsibility of providing these three primary conditions. They have to involve themselves personally in the following four tasks:

1. Developing a competent and motivated workforce through education and training, as discussed by us earlier.
2. Creating a conductive work environment which is clean, tidy, well lighted and well ventilated and also free from insecurity and fear of loss of jobs.
3. Creating an environment of mutual trust and enthusiastic participation through clear instructions and procedures, fairness and transparency in dealings and human interactions, small group activity, feedback of performance, recognition and reward.
4. Providing a physical environment which provides challenging work and encourages high standards and providing the necessary equipment, tools, fixtures and accessories.

These tasks cannot be delegated. The top and senior management can take the assistance of middle level managers to ensure the fullfillment of these tasks and maintenance of the three conditions, but their personal commitment to these four tasks is essential.

The role of line managers can be sub-classified under the following four headings:

1. Helping the PM groups and circles in the tasks of setting and achieving goals and plans.
2. Recognising the importance of work done by PM groups and circles through advice, suggestions and encouragement, and continually encouraging ingenuity and fresh ideas.
3. Ensuring speedy action on suggestions of PM groups and circles and enabling the implementation of creative and cost-effective improvement ideas.
4. Rewarding the efforts of individuals and groups.

Whereas, all these four tasks are important, the primary role of line managers lies in goal setting, facilitating group activity and helping groups to achieve the goals set, and evaluation and implementation of group suggestions and projects. As noted earlier, goal setting also includes planning and similarly for PM groups, goal setting exercise must include the actual targets to be met and time scales, or time frames, for achievement of the defined goals. Most PM groups need the help of line managers in the task of goal setting. Moreover, particularly in the initial periods, most PM group leaders also require the help of facilitators, and middle managers,in both line and staff functions, can fulfill this role very well. Accordingly, the staff managers must be roped into the small group activity scheme and their personal involvement should be sought and obtained.

DEVELOPING SMALL GROUP ACTIVITY AND EVALUATING THE PROGRESS OF SMALL GROUPS

Many attempts at employee participation through small group activity have failed primarily because of the lack of management commitment. The top management must be sincere about its intentions and must be wholly committed to the four tasks mentioned earlier. Without the commitment of the top and senior management, no scheme can ever succeed. Moreover, the planning of the scheme of small group activity is very important. All the four steps of TPM promotion are equally important and all of them have to be planned out in detail. Every aspect should be considered and accounted for, including the infrastructure and support required for the conduct of meetings of PM groups, circles and sub-circles, and the procedures for the evaluation of group suggestions, and nothing should be left to chance. Finally, top management must appreciate that the development of small group activity is both difficult and time consuming. The management must also be prepared to encounter initial difficulties and failures, and should set up contingent plans to meet such hurdles and problems. Moreover, it is best to attempt the implementation of small group activity in phases, as discussed earlier.

As noted above, the development of small group activity takes time. It is comparatively a slow process and management must have the necessary patience and forbearance. It is best to give each stage of development enough time so that the PM groups can move with competence and confidence from one stage to the next. The four stages of development of small group activity are as follows:

Stage 1: Learning and self development.

Stage 2: Proposing and implementing improvement activities through group involvement.

Stage 3: Taking up and solving problems of concern to the organisation.

Stage 4: Performing goal setting, problem-solving and improvement activities through self management.

The first stage is one of learning to interact with others and participate in groups. In this stage, the management should permit members to take up problems of their own interest. These problems may have no relationship with organisational problems, and the emphasis, at this stage, is on learning to work as a group. In the second stage, the group proposes improvement projects and works together on the task of implementing these projects. Herein as well, the project may not always be in conformity with the organisational TPM goals. The emphasis, at this stage, is to develop teamwork and leadership. The group learns to set its own targets and to plan improvement activities. In this stage, planning and implementation of group projects is most important. By the third stage, the group has matured to do goal-setting and problem-solving. In this stage, the group develops goals and targets in conformance with the organisational goals and solves them through group activity within its planned time frame. The emphasis, at this stage, is on problem-solving. This stage also provides a trial, or test, of group teamwork and leadership. The fourth and final stage is one of self management. By this stage, the groups have matured to a state wherein the group goals and targets always match and complement the organisational goals, and group activities are in consonance with the improvement activities identified by the organisation. Moreover, the group shows superior teamwork and leadership and can sustain its own activities and projects without facilitation and with minimal help from management.

The evaluation of the progress of small groups and of small group activity in the organisation is dependent on the ability to recognize the state of development of the groups and the stages they are in. This requires an understanding of the four stages of development of small group activity, or the four stages of TPM promotion, enumerated and discussed in the preceding paragraphs.

In conclusion, it should be reiterated that if there is no commitment from top management, then TPM promotion will not succeed. Therefore, if top and senior management commitment is not available, then do not undertake TPM promotion.

References

1. Belcher, J.G. Jr. (of the American Productivity Center, Houston, Texas—a non-profit organization), *Productivity Plus +*, Universal Book Stall, New Delhi, 1991, pp 67, 69, 77, 85-96 and 97-105.

2. Bhadury, B., 'Work Culture : An Exposition in the Indian Context,' *Vikalpa* (the journal of the Indian Institute of Management, Ahmedabad), Vol. 16, No. 4, October-December, 1991, pp 33-42.

3. Bhadury, B., 'Employees Must Share a Common Goal of Growth', *Vikalpa* (the journal of the Indian Institute of Management, Ahmedabad), Vol. 17, No. 3, July-September, 1992, pp 67-69.

4. Clark, K.B. and Wheelwright, S.C., *Managing New Product and Process Development*, The Free Press (a division of Macmillan, Inc.), New York, 1993, p 457.

5. Cohen-Rosenthal, E., 'On Arrogance and Participation', in *The Quality Yearbook* 1995 (Cortada, J.W. and Woods, J.A., Editors), McGraw-Hill, New York, 1995, pp 287-298.

6. Dey, B.R., 'Quality Circles', presented at the Tata Personnel Managers' Conference on 'A Human Resource Approach to the Management of Industrial Relations', Tata Management Training Centre, Pune, India, 1984.

7. Fiegenbanm, A.V., *Total Quality Control*, McGraw-Hill Book Company, New York, 1986, p 207.

8. Goetsch, D.L. and Davis, S., *Implementing Total Quality*, Prentice Hall, Englewood Cliffs, New Jersey, 1995, pp 39-42.

9. Gondhalekar, S., 'Employee Participation Through Kaizen,' *The TMTC Journal of Management*, Vol. V, No. 1, June 1995, pp 3-11.

10. Goto, F., 'Autonomous Maintenance'. Chapter 4 in the *TPM Development Program: Implementing Total Productive Maintenance* (Nakajima, S., Editor), Productivity Press, Cambridge, Massachusetts, U.S.A., 1989, pp 165-217.

11. Hornby, A.S. *Oxford Advanced Learner's Dictionary of Current English*, Oxford University Press, Delhi, Third Edition, 1974, p 668.

12. Juran, J.M., *Juran on Leadership for Quality: An Executive Handbook*, The Free Press (a division of Macmillan, Inc.). New York, 1989, pp 72-75 and 287-294.

13. Kelly, A., 'Topics in Terotechnology: An Introduction Series—10, Motivation of the Maintenance Tradeforce,' *Maintenance Management International*, Vol. 4, 1984, pp 71-81.

14. Mizuno, S., *Company-wide Quality Control,* Asian Productivity Organisaiton, Tokyo, Japan, 1988, pp 23-24.

15. Moolgaokar, S., 'Acceptance Speech' on being presented the Sir Jehangir Ghandy Medal for Industrial Peace, Xavier Labour Institute, Jamshedpur, India, 1984.

16. Nakajima, S., 'TPM—Challenge to the Improvement of Productivity by Small Group Activities,' *Maintenance Management International*, Vol. 6, 1986, pp 73-83.

17. Nakajima, S.,'An Introduction to TPM,' *Chapter 1 of TPM Development Program: Implementing Total Productive Maintenance* (Nakajima, S., Editor), Productivity Press, Cambridge, Massachusetts, U.S.A., 1989, pp 1-26.

18. Nakajima, S., 'TPM Small Group Activities,' *Chapter 8 of TPM Development Program: Implementing Total Productive Maintenance* (Nakajima, S., Editor), Productivity Press, Cambridge, Massachusetts, U.S.A., 1989, pp 349-363.

19. Peter, T.J. and Waterman, R.H. Jr., *In Search of Excellence: Lessons from America's Best-run Companies,* Harper & Row Publishers, New York (and India Book Distributors, Mumbai), 1982, pp XX-XXII (part of the introduction).

20. Sheth, N.R. Misra, S. and Mookherjee, S., 'Oh Manager!' (a case study published in the diagnositc section of the Journal), *Vikalpa* (the journal of the Indian Institute of Management, Ahmedabad), Vol. 17, No. 3, July-September, 1992, pp 59-61.

21. Suzuki, T., *New Directions for TPM,* Productivity Press, Cambridge, Massachusetts, U.S.A., 1992, pp 31, 40 and 41.

22. Tamaki, A., 'Total Productive Maintenance and Its Impact on the Japanese Industry,' *Guest Editorial, Terotechnica,* Vol. 2, 1981, pp 3-4.

23. Tosti, D. and Jackson, S., 'Cultural Transformation', in *The Quality Yearbook 1995* (Cortada, J.W. and Woods, J.A., Editors), McGraw-Hill Inc., New York, 1995, pp 299-306.

24. Webster's Third New International Dictionary, Encyclopaedia Britannica, Inc., Chicago/London, 1966, Vol. II, p 1646.

Endnotes

1. Vision is a dream or picture of what the organisation would like to ultimately achieve. It provides both direction and focus and it enables the formation of a mental image of the future to which the employees can align. Mission statements, on the other hand, describe the missions of the organisation—the current and future business areas in terms of products/product ranges, customers/consumer segments and sometimes even market sizes and market price.

2. This is, however, more a matter of perception as we will note later during our discussion of the characteristics of PM groups.

3. A small group in TPM can either be called a PM group or PM circle depending on its size and its position in the TPM promotion structure (please see Fig. 6.3). Usually groups lower down in the organisational structure are often called circles, as for example, machine shop medium section, first shift circle and the higher PM group may be called machine ship medium section circle leaders group, or committee.

4. Men behind the movements—the senior managers who have taken it upon themselves to make the movement successful.

5. An example of TPM policy is given on page 14, as Fig. 1-5, of Nakajima's book entitled TPM Development Program: Implementing Total Productive Maintenance [17]. At the company, or top management level these policies are in the form of mission statements.

6. In Fig. 6.3, the tree uses the production department, machine shop, medium machine section and the first shift for the purpose of illustration. The reader will appreciate that the same kind of overlapping structure will be incorporated for the other two shifts, for the other sections of the machine shop, and for the other shops.

Measuring Maintenance Effectiveness

Measurement of maintenance effectiveness is the measurement of the effectiveness of performance of the maintenance function, or in other words, the effectiveness of maintenance activities, decisions and efforts directed at the maximisation of plant and equipment availability and effectiveness. But why, in the first place, do we measure performance? A measure of performance of a function, or department, is necessary for the purposes of control. To be able to control a function, one must be able to assess how much has been achieved and how well a course of action, or courses of action undertaken, achieve a particular objective. Thus, the performance of a function must be measured against stated objectives or goals. This brings us to the difference between efficiency and effectiveness. Whereas efficiency is the ratio of output and input, or, in other words, the output achieved as a percentage of the input to the function (in terms of the resources consumed), effectiveness of a function is the measure of its actual performance against the planned performance. This implies that initially a 'goal' or an objective (or goals/objectives) is set, and at the end of the period under consideration, the extent to which the goal is achieved is also measurable. Therefore, it is quite clear that measures of efficiency, by themselves, will not be sufficient for the purposes of control and measures of effectiveness are also required. This is particularly true for the maintenance function, wherein, not only is it necessary to be able to assess the efficiency with which the maintenance activities are performed, but also one must be able to assess the effectiveness of the maintenance decisions and the productive maintenance efforts. However, it is necessary to remember that employing a measure of effectiveness requires the prior definition of a goal, or an objective, to be achieved. Measures of maintenance effectiveness should, therefore, reflect the performance of the maintenance function against the overall objectives of the organisation.

Now that we have defined a measure of effectiveness, let us turn our attention to maintenance and see why we need to measure maintenance effectiveness. In a manufacturing organisation, plant, equipment and machines are used to convert raw materials, into value-added products. In a majority of cases, the product output depends entirely on the availability of plant and equipment, and the unavailability of plant, equipment and machines has a direct bearing on the quantity, or volume, of output produced. Thus, equipment availability is of primary concern to manufacturing organisations and the effectiveness of the maintenance function has a direct bearing on equipment availability and also on equipment effectiveness. Another important point to bear in mind is the fact that maintenance of plant and equipment and operating costs are related, in as much as, if maintenance is not carried out effectively and condition of plant and equipment is allowed to deteriorate, then the operating costs, or the cost of operation or use, goes up. Thus, the performance of the maintenance function has an effect on the operating costs as well. This brings us to an interesting point. On the one hand, the cost of maintaining plant and equipment is significant and this maintenance cost gets added to the total production cost pointing to the need to keep the maintenance cost under control. Such control, in turn, calls for measures of efficiency of maintenance activities. On the other hand, declining maintenance costs and inadequate plant maintenance result in higher operating costs pointing to the need for measures of maintenance effectiveness, particularly those dealing with equipment availability and effectiveness.

In this chapter, we will discuss the various measures of efficiency and effectiveness used for the control of the maintenance function. These measures are required for control at different levels in the organisation. The maintenance manager is more concerned with the performance of essential maintenance tasks and accordingly, he requires measures pertaining to the efficiency of performance of maintenance tasks and activities and also about completion of preventive maintenance jobs. The works manager, on the other hand, requires measures which deal with equipment effectiveness, effective use of the maintenance labour force, energy conservation and safety. The various facets and aspects of measurement of maintenance performance will be discussed in this chapter. Before we take up the discussion of the various measures of maintenance performance, we must first discuss the characteristic features of control of maintenance.

CONTROL OF MAINTENANCE FUNCTION

The effective control of the maintenance function is a particularly difficult problem. There are two complimentary but distinct aspects of control—the control of the maintenance activity by the chief of the maintenance function and the overall control of the maintenance function as exercised by the works, or the process plant, management. Whereas the former, that is, the control by the maintenance manager, is a point-to-point and a day-to-day job, the plant, or works management requires measures to enable an audit of the performance of the maintenance function in the light of the ultimate objectives of the company. Therefore, as we have already noted earlier, whereas the maintenance manager requires measures of efficiency, at the level of plant management, measures of maintenance effectiveness are required. The task of control of the maintenance function is further complicated by the fact that maintenance, as a function, is both difficult and complex. For the continuous process industry, in particular, maintenance is a high-technology, important and demanding function [4]. The fact that it is an essential function is rather easy to see, in as much as, inadequate maintenance of plant and equipment has a direct effect on equipment availability and, in turn, on production and revenues. However, it is not a function which is independent in itself and therefore, cannot be controlled independently of other functions. For effective control, one must understand the inter-relationship of maintenance with production and basis of maintenance decisions. The maintenance cost structure is also different, in as much as, in maintenance, the direct costs are much less than the costs of lost production due to equipment breakdowns and stoppages and also due to degradation/deterioration of equipment caused by inadequate/inferior maintenance.

In this section, therefore, we will study the various aspects of the maintenance function. We will initially study the maintenance cost structure and then discuss the factors which affect maintenance. Thereafter, we will discuss the maintenance decision process and identify the decision variables. The detailed discussion of the various aspects of maintenance will, in turn, provide us a basis to develop the indicators of maintenance performance.

COSTS ASSOCIATED WITH MAINTENANCE

There are four fundamental costs associated with the maintenance function and these are as follows:

1. Direct cost of maintenance labour/manpower.
2. Direct cost of equipment spares and incidental material required for maintenance.
3. Function loss cost, or the cost of lost production due to breakdowns and stoppages.
4. Function reduction cost, or the cost of lost production due to degradation, or deterioration of equipment.

The reader should note that the function loss and function reduction costs are incurred on account of inadequate, or inferior maintenance of plant and equipment. These are costs of poor maintenance and these two add up to the total cost of lost production due to maintenance reasons. In maintenance, this cost of lost production is much more than the total direct cost of maintenance, which, in turn, is obtained by adding the direct costs of maintenance manpower and materials and spares. Wireman estimates that the ratio of these two types of costs, that is, the total cost of lost production and the total direct cost of maintenance, ranges from 2:1 to as high as 15:1 [11]. This implies that in any time period, if the direct costs of maintenance add up to Rs. 100,000, then the total cost of maintenance can be as high as Rs. 300,000-Rs. 1,600,000. Thus, 'the savings or benefits from maintenance revolve around cost avoidance' [11]. This means that although it is necessary to keep a check on the direct costs of maintenance, it is best to remember that spending money on maintenance activities and jobs avoids incurring an additional and much greater cost of lost production.

The direct cost of maintenance labour must include the cost of salaries, wages, and other staff costs, including welfare expenses, for the manpower directly involved in the maintenance of plant, equipment and machinery in any given time period. It should also include any overtime and incentive payments actually made. In case, this cost is to be evaluated for a given equipment, or asset class, then it should only consider direct costs of manpower, as defined above, employed for the maintenance of that particular equipment, or class of equipment. Similarly, the direct cost of maintenance material must include the total cost of spares and incidental material, including lubricating oil, grease, felting/webbing, gaskets, seals, spring washers and cotton waste, used for the repair and preventive maintenance activities in any given time period. Herein as well, if this cost has to be evaluated for a given piece of equipment, or class of equipment, then the direct material cost elements pertaining to the particular equipment, or class of equipment, should only be considered. The direct costs of maintenance labour and material are easy to obtain from the maintenance job card entries and wages and stores records. However, the two costs of lost production due to maintenance reasons are not so easily obtained. The function loss cost, or the cost of lost production due to equipment breakdown and stoppages, in any given time period is obtained by first multiplying the hours lost on any equipment/machine by its machine hour cost (or the cost per hour), and then adding these for all the production equipment. The number of hours lost on account of equipment breakdowns can usually be obtained from breakdown slips and the maintenance department and shop log books, but the record, or notings, of the time lost on an equipment on account of stoppages are not usually kept. As we had noted in Chapter Four, the function loss cost caused by equipment stoppages and the function reduction cost are usually the hidden costs. However, these two add up to a significant amount. In Chapter Four, we had also noted that equipment stoppages account for a large percentage of loss of production capacity particularly in continuous process plants, and the first case study of Chapter Eight will help to bring this out more clearly. The function reduction cost details are also difficult to obtain. This is the cost of lost production due to low capacity utilisation of plant and equipment, or due to speed losses. These details are usually available in production records, such as job cards and shop log books. The data required for the calculation of the function reduction cost can also be used for the calculation of the performance rate of the equipment (recall that, overall equipment effectiveness = availability × performance rate x quality rate).

FACTORS AFFECTING MAINTENANCE

For plant and machinery to work with sustained value and high precision in performance level and reliability in operation, an integrated approach to maintenance management is required which, while following the overall objectives of the organisation, must be based on a proper understanding of the nature of maintenance, its relationship with production and the dynamic nature of the maintenance-production system.

The factors which affect maintenance decisions fall into three groups which are as follows:

(i) *Plant factors*—these are possible alternatives to spending money on repairs, such as consequences of modifications to components and machines prone to recurrent failure, duplication or redundancy etc. to reduce the effects of a failure on system performance.

(ii) *Production factors*—these factors are not under the control of the maintenance department but affect maintenance planning and control. Examples include changes in operating rate and in production schedules, frequency and length of production delays, level of in-process inventory and characteristics of raw material feed which sometimes result in equipment failures. The maintenance department should be able to make proper use of production windows and this requires flexibility and adequate control procedures.

(iii) *Maintenance factors*—unlike production factors, these come under the control of maintenance and include the organisation of the maintenance department, the total number of men employed for maintenance and the mix of the necessary trades, the level of training of maintenance personnel, the level of preventive maintenance used and the level of stocks of spares available.

MAINTENANCE DECISIONS AND DECISION VARIABLES

A decision situation is characterised by three things and these are as follows:

1. A desired outcome, or objective/goal.
2. Two or more courses of action which will enable the achievement of the desired outcome.
3. An environment, which, in turn, consists of all the factors which can affect the outcome, and all these factors may not necessarily be under the decision maker's control.

A decision maker recognises the existence of a decision situation only when these three conditions are present. He then has to choose the 'best,' or optimal course of action. In a decision situation, there also exists a state of ambiguity in the decision maker's mind with regard to the best alternative, or course of action, and accordingly, the identification of the best course of action requires the use of a suitably defined decision criterion. We have, in this chapter and earlier, noted the need for the identification of an objective, or goal, as the foremost requirement of a decision process. For maintenance decisions as well, the objective has to be defined first.

Moreover, in the context of maintenance, the decision environment consists of the factors which we have discussed in the preceding paragraphs. Now we are ready to discuss the stages of the decision making process which consists of the following four steps:

1. Recognition of a decision situation and definition of the desired objective/objectives, or goals.
2. Identification of the possible courses of action, or alternatives.
3. The choice and definition of a decision criterion, which when invoked will distinguish among the set of alternatives and help find the best alternative.
4. Decision making, or the identification of the best course of action among all the possible courses of action by using the decision criterion.

From the above, it is obvious that the choice of the decision criterion is of primary importance. The definition and use of the decision criterion must take due account of the existing problem environment, or the factors which can affect the outcome. Control is exercised for the purpose of achieving a desired objective/objectives. Control of the maintenance function involves decision making and the measures of maintenance performance are used as decision criteria in this process.

Now, how is the decision criterion defined? For this, we must identify the different types of decision variables and study the relationship between them. There are the following three types of decision variables:

(i) Control variables,
(ii) Uncontrolled variables, and
(iii) Consequence variables.

Whereas control variables are the alternative courses of action, uncontrolled variables are the events, or states of nature. A consequence variable is a decision variable in terms of which the effects of the alternative courses of action can be evaluated [1]. It is a function of the control and uncontrolled variables, in as much as, it is derived from a detailed study and clear understanding of the control variables and must take due account of the uncontrolled variables. The decision criterion, in turn, is a function of the consequence variables. From this discussion, it follows that of the three different types of decision variables, particular attention must be paid to the role of consequence variables in the context of measurement of maintenance performance. Moreover, since the measure is to be used to gauge the effectiveness of the maintenance function in the light of the overall goals defined by the company management, it follows that the consequence variables to be used therein should be the constituents of the total maintenance cost, namely, the direct costs of maintenance manpower and spares and incidental material and also the costs of lost production due to maintenance reasons.

INDICATORS OF MAINTENANCE PERFORMANCE

We have already noted that measures of performance can either be used to measure efficiency or effectiveness. We have also noted that the performance of the maintenance function can best be evaluated through a measure of its effectiveness since the measure should reflect its performance in the context of the overall objectives of the organisation. This does not mean that measures of efficiency are not necessary. In maintenance also, we have measures which basically are measures of efficiency rather than effectiveness. Measures of efficiency are generally useful at the departmental level, that is, by the maintenance manager to better organise the department and for timely actions. As matter of fact, even the cost-based measures, or financial indicators, are technically also measures of efficiency. However, once a goal, or an objective, is set and the indicator provides a measure of the extent to which the objective has been achieved, it becomes, a measure of effectiveness. In nearly all areas of performance, in maintenance, such targets or goals should be set to enable continual improvement. Therefore, we will not waste any more time and space on semantics and split hair about efficiency and effectiveness. Instead we will discuss the various indicators of maintenance performance.

There are essentially three basic kinds of indicators of performance of the maintenance function, and these are activity based indicators, equipment effectiveness indicators, and maintenance cost-based or financial indicators. The activity-based, or maintenance performance indicators can either be measures of completion of planned activities, utilisation of maintenance resources, or effectiveness of maintenance actions taken. Equipment effectiveness indicators are measures of equipment availability, performance rate and quality rate, as discussed earlier in Chapters Two and Four. These indicators are of interest to the plant, or works management and are used for the overall control of the maintenance function. The financial indicators are of two types, namely, ones which are based on individual elements of maintenance cost, such as the direct costs of maintenance labour or maintenance material, and others which are based on the total maintenance cost. The former are used by maintenance managers and supervisors for control of maintenance performance at the departmental level, whereas the latter are of interest to the works management. Examples of total maintenance cost indicators are total maintenance costs incurred on an asset, on a class of assets, as a percentage of its purchase price or its estimated replacement value, and total maintenance cost as a percentage of the total production cost or total sales. Thus, we may conclude that the total cost and the equipment effectiveness indicators located at the top of the pyramid are used by the works, or plant management, and the maintenance performance, or activity-based indicators at the base of the pyramid are used for control at the departmental level. This is shown in Fig. 7.1. From Fig. 7.1, we find that the maintenance performance indicators can be further broken down into daily, weekly, monthly and annual indicators. These include a wide variety of

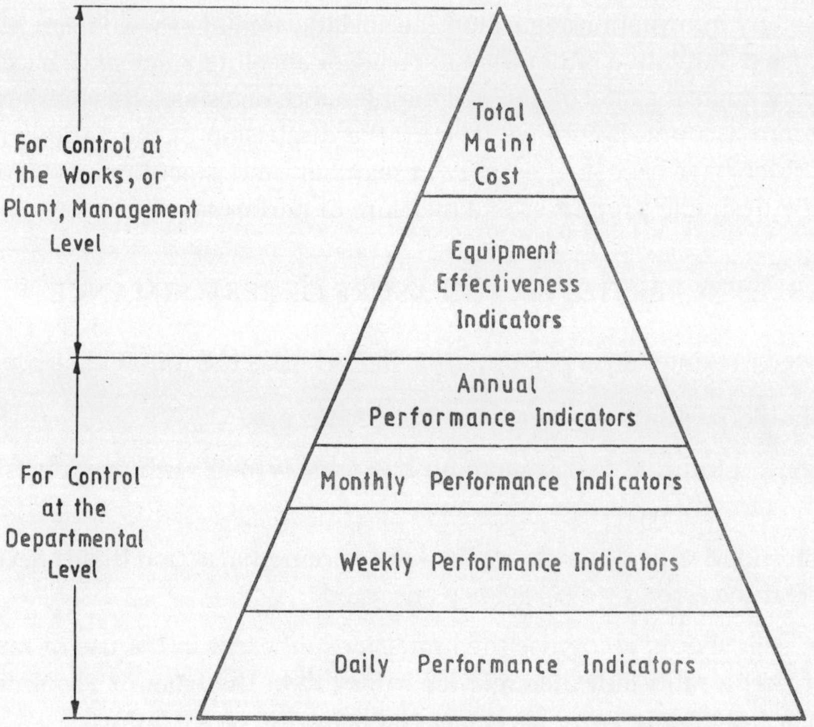

Fig. 7.1 Hierarchy of Measures of Maintenance Performance

indicators, starting from indicators of essential maintenance tasks completed, preventive maintenance and predictive maintenance backlog hours and craftwise backlogs on a weekly and monthly basis, to emergency maintenance work as a percentage of total maintenance hours, downtime hours caused by equipment breakdowns as a percentage of total downtime hours, and maintenance labour costs as a percentage of total manpower cost.

Use of Indices and Properties of an Indicator

The measure of effectiveness of the maintenance function must indicate the actual performance against the planned or budgeted performance. This brings to mind a ratio and indices have accordingly been recommended as aids to decision-making in maintenance [2]. These indices use decision variables, which as we have noted are also known as consequence variables. Indices are used for all kinds of indicators irrespective of whether they are measures of efficiency or effectiveness. An index or ratio is also very practical since not only is it easy to understand but also it clearly indicates the trend in performance. However, a ratio has an inherent defect in as much as it only gives an indication of the trend of performance but does not, by itself, give any information regarding the specific area(s) of weakness. Moreover, a ratio gives us a relative rather than the true, or absolute value and in case a ratio is used to evaluate the effectiveness of maintenance decisions, this limitation must be taken into account. Before we take up the discussion of the various ratios, or indices, which have been suggested by researchers and practitioners, let us briefly discuss the desirable properties of a measure of performance.

DESIRABLE PROPERTIES OF A MEASURE OF PERFORMANCE

A measure of maintenance performance should have the following properties:

1. It should be relatively easy to calculate and use.
2. It should indicate that something has gone wrong with past decisions and some remedial action is necessary.
3. It should ideally also indicate the kind of remedial action that is necessary to correct the error, or discrepancy observed.
4. The user should recognise the limitations inherent in the use of ratios—the fact that a ratio indicates relative rather than the true, or absolute, consequence of maintenance decisions and actions.
5. The measure should accurately reflect management's subjective notion of what constitutes, or should constitute maintenance performance especially with respect to the organisational objectives as a whole. This is the property of compatibility of maintenance performance objectives with the overall objectives of the organisation.
6. The measure of the overall performance of the maintenance function should not be difficult to interpret. This is particularly important when a single index

of performance of the maintenance function is used. This property implies that the information provided by the index of overall performance should not give rise to more than one interpretation.

7. The measure(s), if possible, should reflect all relevant consequences which affect performance. Where this is not practical due to the large number of such consequence variables, the measure should atleast include those consequence variables, which are considered by the management to contribute a great deal to the resulting consequence of any particular action, or decision.

Older Measures of Performance

In this section, we will discuss the measures of maintenance performance suggested by Corder, Priel, Luck and Kapoor. Corder, Priel and Luck's measures of maintenance performance were postulated in the 1950s and 1960s, and in that sense, these were the earliest published attempts at measurement of maintenance effectiveness. Moreover, these measures, or indices were published before the advent of TPM.

CORDER'S INDEX [5]

Corder recommended the use of a single index for the assessment of the relative performance of the maintenance function in an organisation, on a year-to-year basis. Corder, in his index uses the relevant information, in the form of the actual values of three consequence variables, of a base year (selected for the purpose of measurement) such that the index in the base year equals 100. By comparing the value of the index each year, one can discern whether the performance of the maintenance function has improved or worsened over the previous year's performance.

Corder's performance index E is given by

$$E = \frac{k}{xC + yL + zW}, \text{ where}$$

C = total maintenance cost, expressed as a percentage of replacement value of plant and equipment,

L = lost time due to maintenance causes expressed as a percentage of scheduled production hours,

W = waste of material due to maintenance causes expressed as a percentage of total output at the appropriate stage of the process, x = total cost of maintenance in the base year,

y = total cost of lost time due to maintenance causes in the base year,

z = total cost of waste produced due to maintenance causes in the base year, and

k = a constant such that the efficiency index equals 100 in the base year.

The reader will notice that Corder has used only three consequence variables in his measure of maintenance performance and these three consequence variables are as follows:

(i) the total maintenance cost expressed as a percentage of the replacement value of plant and equipment,

(ii) lost time due to maintenance causes expressed as a percentage of the scheduled production hours, and

(iii) wastage of material due to maintenance causes expressed as a percentage of the total output at the appropriate stage of the process.

Although Corder's index is relatively easy to calculate and presents no difficulty or ambiguity in interpretation, the number of consequence variables used may be considered too few to represent the actual conditions. The advantages of Corder's single index are as follows:

1. It is relatively easy to calculate and it presents no difficulty in interpretation.
2. If the decision maker is satisfied that the three consequence variables used are the only ones of interest in all maintenance decision situations, then this index would reflect the trend in performance from one year to the next.

However, the single index proposed by Corder has a number of disadvantages and these are as follows:

1. It is unlikely that the decision maker will be prepared to accept that these three consequence variables are by far the only ones that need to be considered. In a majority of practical situations, the number of consequence variables, which should be taken into account, is much larger.
2. It is also unlikely that the decision maker will accept the method of aggregating the three consequence variables. The use of a linear relation may also not be universally acceptable.
3. The measure has disadvantages of a ratio, which we have noted in the preceding section.

PRIEL'S INDICES [9]

To counteract the main disadvantages of Corder's index, namely disadvantages one and two discussed above, Priel postulated a large number of indices. This is to be viewed in the context of a single index proposed by Corder. Priel proposed the use of a total of twenty indices and these twenty indices are further classified under three main groups, which are maintenance efforts, or department operation, maintenance effects, or service assessment (effects of the service provided), and overall effectiveness, which he calls expense justification. The twenty indices proposed by Priel are as follows:

a) Department Operation

Manpower

(1) Manpower Efficiency $= \dfrac{\text{Total manhours allowed on jobs}}{\text{Total manhours worked on same jobs}}$

(2) Incentive Coverage $= \dfrac{\text{Manhours on bonus}}{\text{Total direct hours available}}$

(3) Craft Hours Utilisation $= \dfrac{\text{Total crafts hours worked}}{\text{Total crafts hours docked}}$

Workorder

(4) Workorder Turnover $= \dfrac{\text{Number of jobs completed}}{\text{Total number of jobs handled}}$

(5) Completion Delays $= \dfrac{\text{Number of jobs delayed}}{\text{Number of jobs handled}}$

Economy

(6) Cost of Maintenance Hours $= \dfrac{\text{Total maintenance costs}^{1}}{\text{Total direct maint. hours applied}}$

(7) Departmental Overhead $= \dfrac{\text{Total overhead cost}}{\text{Total maintenance expenditure}}$

b) Service Assessment

Plant and Equipment Performance

(8) Downtime due to Maintenance $= \dfrac{\text{Total downtime for service}}{\text{Total shift hours worked}}$

(9) Breakdown Frequency $= \dfrac{\text{Units produced or hours worked}}{\text{Number of breakdowns}}$

Degree of Planning

(10) Routine Service Workload $= \dfrac{\text{Total hours of regular service}}{\text{Total direct applied maintenance hours}}$

(11) Breakdown Workload $= \dfrac{\text{Total hours spent on breakdowns}}{\text{Total clocked maintenance hours}}$

Amount of Service

(12) Maint. to Prod. Ratio $= \dfrac{\text{Total direct maintenance hours}}{\text{Total direct production hours}}$

(13) Maintenance of Mechanisation $= \dfrac{\text{Total clocked maintenance hours}}{\text{Total connected horsepower (of machines)}}$

Cost of Service Provided

(14) Maint. Cost Component $= \dfrac{\text{Total maintenance expenditure}}{\text{Number of units produced}}$

(15) Cost of Scheduled Service $= \dfrac{\text{Cost of scheduled services}}{\text{Total production costs}}$

(16) Cost of Supplies and Spares $= \dfrac{\text{Total cost of supplies and spares}}{\text{Total maintenance expenditure}}$

(17) Ratio of Maint. Cost and Investment $= \dfrac{\text{Total maintenance expenditure}}{\text{Total value of investment}}$

c) Expense Justification

(18) Cost Reduction Effects $= \dfrac{\text{Index 10}}{\text{Index 6}} = \dfrac{\text{Routine services workload}}{\text{Cost of maintenance hour}}$

(19) Maintenance Intensity $= \dfrac{\text{Index 12}}{\text{No. of Prod. workers}} = \dfrac{\text{Maint./prod. ratio}}{\text{No. of production workers}}$

(20) Overall rate of expenditure (on maintenance) $= \dfrac{\text{Index 14}}{\text{Index 13}} = \dfrac{\text{Maint. cost component}}{\text{Maint. of mechanisation}}$

Now we are ready to compare Priel's indices with Corder's index and discuss the advantages and disadvantages of Priel's measures of maintenance performance. By proposing a large number of indices as opposed to a single index, Priel has been able to overcome the first limitation of Corder's index and ensure that some account is taken of all relevant consequence variables. However, having a number of indices creates the problem of interpretation of the measures and assessment of the performance of the maintenance function, in as much as some indices may indicate improvement whereas others may indicate a deterioration, or worsening of performance; that is, it is very likely that some of the indices will indicate a favourable trend of performance, whereas the others will not. This possibility has been duly recognised and an attempt has been made to resolve the problem of interpretation by suggesting three indices under the overall effectiveness (expense justification) group after suggesting seventeen indices under two main groups of maintenance efforts (department operation) and maintenance effects (service assessment). However, the difficulty in interpreting the overall performance due to the large number of indices involved still remains. In this context, it must also be pointed out that more information is better, if and only if, the resulting increase in benefits obtained outweigh the necessary increase in efforts and costs. Moreover, an increase in the number of indices implies that Priel's measures are more difficult to calculate and use, as compared to Corder's index. Finally, inherent disadvantages of using a ratio/ratios remain. In conclusion, we may note that Priel has attempted to include a greater number of consequence variables and thereby also cover all facets of maintenance activity.

KAPOOR'S INDICES [6]

Kapoor, in his discussion of the various facets of control of the maintenance function, has also recommended the use of a number of indices for evaluating the performance of the maintenance function. However, as compared to Priel, he has postulated a much smaller number of indices. Moreover, he has multiplied each ratio by 100 to get the measure as a percentage. Kapoor's measures of maintenance performance are as follows:

1) Frequency of Breakdown $= \dfrac{\text{Total hrs. spent on maint. last month}}{\text{Total hrs. spent on maint. current month}} \times 100$

2) Breakdown Maint. Index $= \dfrac{\text{Total hrs. spent on breakdowns}}{\text{Total man-hours available}} \times 100$

3) Level of Maintenance $= \dfrac{\text{Total hrs. spent on scheduled maint.}}{\text{Total man-hours available}} \times 100$

4) Equipment Availability Index $= \dfrac{\text{Actual running time of equipment}}{\text{Total running time available}} \times 100$

5) Manpower Index $= \dfrac{\text{Manpower strength during last year}}{\text{Manpower strength during current year}} \times 100$

6) Maint. Cost Index $= \dfrac{\text{Total cost of maintenance}}{\text{Total cost of production}} \times 100$

7) Yearly Maint. Cost Index $= \dfrac{\text{Total maintenance cost for last year}}{\text{Total maintenance cost for current year}} \times 100$

A comparison of Kapoor's indices with Priel's first seventeen indices reveals that Kapoor, quite obviously, has not been able to include as many consequence variables. Use of a much smaller number of indices is probably due to his concern about the possibility of creating a larger problem of interpretation giving rise to ambiguity by recommending a larger number of indices. Moreover, since Kapoor has postulated only seven measures, he has not made any attempt at defining indices which combine two other indices like Priel's measures 18, 19 and 20. In conclusion, one must also point out that Kapoor has, in a manner, been taken in by Corder's index and has accordingly defined three indices, namely index numbers 1, 5 and 7, which give comparison on a month-to-month and year-to-year basis (no. 1 for monthly comparison and numbers 5 and 7 for annual comparison). Of particular interest is Kapoor's last index, in as much as it seems totally unnecessary since a comparison of index no. 6 for the current year with the one calculated at the end of the previous year will indicate the trend in maintenance cost. Instead of this, Kapoor could have included another consequence variable of relevance.

LUCK'S MULTIFACTOR GRAPHS [7]

Luck uses a number of indices involving a large number of consequence variables and then combines these indices to provide the manager with a single measure of maintenance performance. In this manner, he is able to take into account a large number of consequence variables which he considers important and at the same time, avoid the difficulty in interpreting the overall effect of the indices. The amount of calculations required by his method is not much more than that associated with Priel's method, but he requires the determination of the present value of the indices and also a subjective estimate of the future value of the indices which would represent a reasonable objective. Luck has defined 16 indices under four heads, or groups, namely planning, workload, cost and productivity. Luck also proposes an ingenious, and controversial way of combining these indices using a graphical method for the purpose. The use of the graphical technique results initially in four graphs for the four groups, and thereafter the information from these four graphs is used to construct another graph which gives a composite measure of maintenance effectiveness. As noted earlier, in addition to determining the sixteen indices, or measures of performance for the present period, Luck's method also calls for a subjective estimate of the future values of these indices, which would represent a reasonable objective, or target. This is shown in Table 7.1 for the sixteen indices. Moreover, using the present values of the indicators and the

Table 7.1: Luck's Indices with Representative Present and Targeted Values

Group of Indicators	*Index/Indicator of Performance*	*Value for Present Period*	*Goal for Next Period*
Planning	1. Labour effectiveness	65%	80%
	2. Work planned and forecast weekly / Total maintenance manhours	50%	85%
	3. Emergency work done per month / Total maintenance manhours	15%	14%
	4. Overtime hours worked per month / Total maintenance manhours	8%	2%
Workload	5. Crew weeks of current backlog	5	3
	6. Crew weeks of total backlog	85	25
	7. Preventive maintenance hours per month / Total maintenance manhours	10%	25%
	8. Daily maintenance work hours per month / Total maintenance manhours	90%	75%
Cost	9. Maintenance cost / Plant investment	10.5%	6%
	10. Increase/decrease in maintenance cost / Unit of product	+15%	- 10%
	Note: This is over the base period		
	11. Direct and general maintenance cost / Total maintenance cost	65%	85%
	12. Indirect maintenance cost / Total maintenance cost	35%	15%
Productivity	13. Maintenance activity / Manpower engaged	55%	75%
	14. Forecasting effectiveness	40%	75%
	15. Operating time lost for maint. reasons	12%	3%
	16. Increase/decrease in number of units produced	+12%	+17%
	Note: This is also over the base period		

targets set, Luck's graphical method enables the display of the present and targeted levels of performance under the four heads of planning, workload, cost and productivity as shown in Fig. 7.2 (a). Thereafter, these group performance indicators are used to show the present and targeted values of maintenance effectiveness (or overall maintenance performance) as shown in Fig. 7.2. (b).

Luck has proposed a methodology which is a combination of the methods proposed by Corder and Priel. Like Priel, he uses a number of indices thereby using a large number of consequence variables. However, like Corder, he wants to provide the manager with a single measure of maintenance performance, and for this purpose, he uses a method of combining these indices in two stages as shown in Fig. 7.2 and discussed above. In this manner, he is able to take into account a large number of consequence variables which he considers to be important and at the same time, avoid the difficulty in interpretation. Luck's graphical method, however, raises many questions. Not only does he give equal weight to all indices within a group (which may lead to the neglect of some important consequence variables), but also the use of a square to derive the overall group indicator is rather novel and difficult to substantiate.

DU PONT METHOD OF MEASURING MAINTENANCE PERFORMANCE [10]

Before we conclude our discussion of the older measures of maintenance performance and move on to a discussion of contemporary approaches, it will be worthwhile to briefly discuss a method proposed by Takahashi and Osada, which, in turn, is based on the method used by Du Pont to measure maintenance performance. This method also calls for the calculation of sixteen indices under four heads, or groups of planning, amount of work, or workload, costs and productivity. The sixteen indices, or indicators, which have been proposed are as follows:

1. Planning Characteristics :
- 1.1 Planned activities
- 1.2 Unplanned activities
- 1.3 Labour effectiveness
- 1.4 Overtime labour

2. Amount of Work :
- 2.1 Current volume of work
- 2.2 Total volume of work
- 2.3 Preventive maintenance

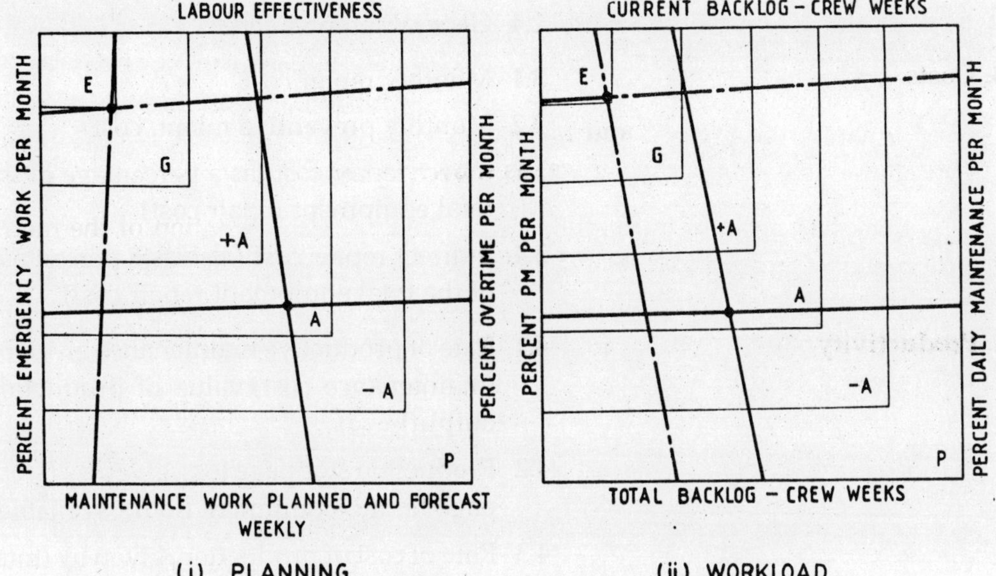

(a) GRAPHS FOR GROUPS OF INDICATORS
(—— Present Values , ——-—— Targets)

Note : Similar graphs are required to be drawn for Cost and Productivity

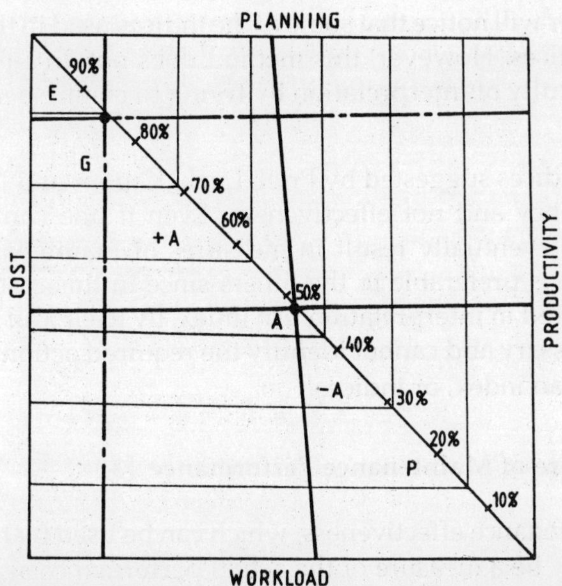

(b) GRAPHS FOR COMPOSITE OF INDICATORS
(—— Present Values , ——-—— Targets)

Fig. 7.2 Luck's Multifactor Graphs

2.4 General maintenance

3. Costs :
3.1 Monthly repair cost
3.2 Monthly preventive maint. cost
3.3 Direct repair cost (as a percentage of the total equipment repair cost)
3.4 Indirect repair cost (also as a percentage of the total equipment repair cost)

4. Productivity :
4.1 Rate of productive maintenance given by (maintenance cost/value of production output)
4.2 Production stoppage loss, given by (stoppage hours/equipment hours available)
4.3 Rate of cost of production, given by (total maintenance departmental cost/value of production output)
4.4 Rate of actual operation time, and this is efficiency of work of maintenance

An observant reader will notice that some of the indices used in this method are the same as Luck's indices. However, this method does not, in any way, attempt to overcome the difficulty of interpretation by trying to combine indices as done by Luck.

Some of the indices suggested by Priel, Luck, Kapoor and Du Pont are really measures of efficiency and not effectiveness. Even if one contends that all the methods proposed eventually result in measures of maintenance effectiveness, Corder's one index is preferable to the others since in this case there will be no problems encountered in interpretation. An index, by itself, can only indicate that some action is necessary and cannot identify the required action. This is the major limitation of using an index, or indices.

A Proposed Measure of Maintenance Performance [3]

A measure of maintenance effectiveness, which can be used by the plant management, must not only be a measure of the actual performance against the planned performance, but must also give an indication of the efficiency of the maintenance activity. An index or a set of indices used to measure performance should have the following characteristics:

(i) The index should only call for such data which are easy to obtain. Also the index or the measure should be easy to calculate.

(ii) The measure should be easy to interpret and must not be such that more than one interpretation is possible regarding the trend.

(iii) The measure should provide a comparison of performance in any given time period with the performance in the time period immediately preceding it. In this way, corrective action can be taken before it is too late.

(iv) The measure should embrace as many of the relevant consequence variables as possible. At the same time, only such consequence variables should be considered which the management believes to be really significant in decision-making, that is, in deciding on the alternative course of action.

(v) The measure of performance should not only give the trend of performance and results of past decisions, but also in some manner indicate the corrective course of action. This is an obvious and inherent shortcoming of a ratio or an index. Whereas having too many ratios or indices with a large number of consequence variables is not at all desirable, at the same time the management should have the means of using the ratio or the index as an aid to decide upon a course of corrective action after discerning an undesirable trend in performance.

The limitations inherent in the use of a single ratio, as proposed by Corder, have been recognised and the evaluation of the performance of the maintenance department in two stages has been proposed.

STAGE I — EVALUATION OF THE TREND

This is the primary function of the ratio. Only after the management knows the trend in performance, can it discern the need for corrective action. For the performance index, the following five consequence variables have been defined:

1.M — Cost of salaries, wages and other staff costs for the manpower directly employed for maintenance of plant and machinery in any given time period, or the direct cost of maintenance labour/manpower as explained earlier under costs associated with maintenance.

2. S — Total cost of spares and incidental materials used in any given time period, or the direct cost of maintenance material as explained earlier.

3. L — Cost of lost time due to maintenance reasons in any time period. This is obtained by multiplying the hours lost on any particular cost centre by the

cost per hour and adding these for all the production cost centres in the plant.

4. R — Cost of rejections due to maintenance causes for any given time period. This is of significant importance in engineering industries where, in most cases the rejects have to be totally scrapped and cannot be recycled into the next run or another product.

5. B — Backlog work of maintenance carried over from any given time period to the next time period. This should include preventive maintenance work which could not be attended to for any reasons. This is obtained by multiplying the estimated backlog hours of work carried over to the next time period by the average manhour cost of the maintenance department.

Then P_j, performance index for time period j,

$$= \frac{Mi + Si + Li + Ri + Bi}{Mj + Sj + Lj + Rj + Bj} \times 100,$$

where period i immediately precedes period j.

The index obtained will be an integer and for an improving trend should be greater than 100. The multiplier has been used as in the case of Corder's index to facilitate comparison using the base of 100. However, in contrast to Corder's index, this index provides a comparison of shorter spans, thus allowing corrective actions to be taken before it is too late rather than a comparison with a base year in the past far removed from the time period under study.

STAGE II — CHECKS TO DECIDE ON NECESSARY CORRECTIVE ACTIONS

As a next step, four ratios have been defined. They cover the first four consequence variables which have been used earlier to obtain the maintenance performance index.

$$m = \frac{M_j \text{ (as defined earlier)}}{\text{Total cost of salaries/wages and other staff costs (including that of maintenance) for the entire factory/plant for the given time period.}} \times 100$$

$$s = \frac{S_j \text{ (as defined earlier)}}{\text{Total replacement value of plant and equipment}} \times 100$$

$$1 = \frac{L_j \text{ (as defined earlier)}}{\text{Cost of total production planned for the given time period.}} \times 100$$

and

$$r = \frac{R_j \text{ (as defined earlier)}}{\text{Cost of total production achieved during the given time period}} \times 100$$

Once these ratios are calculated, they should be checked against:

(i) budgeted figures. Since these are ratios, they lend themselves to comparison with ratios similarly obtained from the annual budget (of the profit centre of the company) for the year of which the time period under study forms a part.

(ii) corresponding ratios obtained in the industry (like industry, otherwise the comparison will be erroneous), ratios brought out by the ministries, government agencies, productivity councils etc.

Once ratios m, s, 1 and r for the profit-centre are compared against those planned for (as per the budget) as well as the average industry figures and with the trend given by the performance index, the management will have sufficient indication with regard to the nature of the problem and will be in a position to carry out further investigations, as necessary, to arrive at the corrective action required.

DISCUSSION

The proposed measure was prompted by two basic concerns, namely the difficulty of interpretation posed by a number of indices, as suggested by Priel, Luck and Kapoor, and the lack of information provided by an index with regard to the specific areas(s) of weakness. The first concern led to the definition of a single measure of trend of maintenance performance and the second to the enunciation of four more indices to enable the identification of specific area/areas of weakness, which, in this case, will be limited to maintenance manpower cost, maintenance material and spares cost, cost of lost production due to maintenance, or cost of rejections due to maintenance. The proposed method only considers five consequence variables, which, in turn, include the four cost elements noted earlier and the backlog hours of maintenance work carried over from one period to the next. There was also another underlying concern—the third concern which led to this measure, and this was the fact that the use of Corder's index may result in a situation wherein an unfavourable trend in performance would go undetected for as long as one year, since Corder uses a base year for comparison and his index can, therefore, be only used for year-to-year comparisons. This concern was prompted by the fact that the analysis of data obtained from two case studies conducted in two types of manufacturing environments, namely the moulding department of a plastics and metals factory and the heavy machine shop of a heavy engineering factory, clearly showed that the total cost of maintenance in general and the cost of lost time due to maintenance reasons in particular varied on a month-to-month basis [3]. Accordingly, it has been suggested that even quarterly comparisons are inadequate and the time period for comparison should be one month.

Before moving on, the author needs to make an important point. The proposed method of measurement of maintenance performance presented and discussed in this section was developed in 1982 and at that time, the author was oblivious of TPM and till that time had not come across any literature on TPM. As a matter of fact, TPM came about six years later to India. The author was, therefore, unduly concerned about the need for a single index, and that too based primarily on the maintenance cost elements. Corder's single index, Priel's and Luck's multiple indices and their attempt at developing composite, or overall measure(s) of performance led to this concern in the mind of the author. This, in turn, led to the need to identify the important consequence variables and the two case studies were undertaken with this basic aim. However, now the author feels that the concern about the difficulty of interpretation resulting from the use of multiple indices is unfounded. As a matter of fact, a single index cannot measure the performance of the maintenance department, or function, because maintenance is a complex and multi-faceted function and its adequate control must consider a large number of consequence variables. For this reason, a number of activity-based and cost-based weekly and monthly indicators, or measures are required for control at the departmental level, or at the lower levels in the hierarchy, and a measure of effectiveness is required for control at the level of the plant, or works management, as we have noted earlier in this chapter. The lower level measures of efficiency can be indices of maintenance labour productivity, overtime hours worked, or overtime cost, preventive maintenance worked, work load of emergency repair or breakdown maintenance, maintenance cost etc. as formulated by various authors in the past and some of whose work we have discussed in the preceding section. The lower level measures are related to productivity, quality, cost, delivery, safety and morale. These indices are called the PQCDSM indices in the TPM literature [8]. For control at the level of works management, the best possible measure is the equipment effectiveness measure, as defined under TPM and as discussed in detail in Chapter Four. In the following section, we will discuss the measures of maintenance performance which can and should be used under TPM.

Measures of Maintenance Effectiveness under TPM

TPM has given a very different perspective to maintenance and consequently to measurement of maintenance effectiveness. As we have discussed in Chapter Two, maintenance initially consisted only of breakdown maintenance, or emergency repairs. The prime responsibility of the maintenance department then was one of prompt and efficient repairs and the measures of performance of the maintenance function were downtime caused by equipment breakdowns and equipment availability (wherein loss of availability caused by equipment breakdowns was only considered). Then came preventive maintenance and with the coming of preventive maintenance came the realisation that equipment breakdowns could possibly be prevented (frequency of failures significantly reduced) by proper care of the equipment. However, with the coming of preventive maintenance, for the maintenance department, the workload and the planning and execution of scheduled maintenance activities became matters of concern. Also as far as the plant, or works management was concerned, the cost of maintaining plant and equipment was one of the elements which needed to be monitored (earlier maintenance had been a necessary evil and accordingly, maintenance cost was not a matter of concern since the machines(s) having broken down had to be repaired quickly). The measures of performance of the maintenance function, thus had to include indices which evaluated the level and effectiveness of planning, maintenance workload and backlog, cost, manpower utilisation and productivity (see Priel's, Luck's, Kapoor's and Du Pont indices). With the coming of productive maintenance, the picture has changed drastically. It has brought with it the realisation that maintenance is a most basic and important function, since it not only affects breakdowns and equipment availability, but also non-productive times, or losses, caused by adjustments, minor stoppages, low capacity utilisation or operation at lower than specified speeds, and product quality defects. Thus, with productive maintenance has come the realisation that maintenance not only affects equipment availability, or the operating rate of plant and equipment (as it is referred to by some Japanese authors), but also its performance rate and quality rate. To take this into account, productive maintenance and TPM have defined the equipment effectiveness measure (please see Chapter Four), and this is an important measure of effectiveness of the maintenance function [11]. Moreover, with the advent of productive maintenance, the importance of the following activities have been realised:

(i) maintainability improvement efforts as discussed in Chapter Two,

(ii) energy conservation efforts, particularly in continuous process industries, and

(iii) efforts directed at reduction of in-process quality defects and improvement of process and machine capability.

These consequence variables must also be given adequate visibility and should be considered during the development of measures of maintenance performance. Finally, TPM has brought with it the need for employee involvement in the improvement efforts, and the measures of effectiveness of the maintenance function must also, therefore, take into account measures of safety, and employee morale.

In this section, we will discuss the measurement of maintenance effectiveness under TPM. We will initially break up our discussion in two parts. In the first part, we will discuss the effectiveness measures which will be of interest to the works, or plant management. Thereafter, we will discuss the measures which can be used for control at the departmental level. After this, we will present our case for an integrated system of measurement of maintenance effectiveness.

MEASURES FOR THE WORKS MANAGEMENT

The top management requires indicators, which are measures of the overall performance of the maintenance function. We have already noted earlier in this chapter that these measures of overall performance include financial indicators based on total maintenance cost, and the equipment effectiveness indicator. The total maintenance cost based financial indicators are required at the highest level in the organisational structure and the equipment effectiveness indicator is required for control to be exercised at the second level in the company hierarchy, namely the works, or plant management level[2] [11]. In addition to these two kinds of indicators, there are some measures of performance which are of interest at the level of plant, or works management. This class of indicators may include measures of energy conservation, claims and customer returns, safety and employee morale. We will, accordingly, discuss the top level indicators in three parts, in the following sequence:

1. Equipment effectiveness indicator.
2. Total maintenance cost indicators.
3. Other performance indicators of interest to top management.

Equipment Effectiveness Indicator

We have defined the equipment effectiveness measure in Chapter Four (please see Fig. 4.1). We will briefly go over it again to enable discussion of the measure and also the identification of the second stage indicators which will direct attention to the possible problem areas and enable corrective action. The overall equipment effectiveness measure has three components, namely equipment availability, performance rate, and the quality rate, and it is obtained from the product of these three components as follows:

$$\text{Equipment effectiveness} = \text{equipment availability} \times \text{performance rate} \times \text{quality rate:}$$

where,

$$\text{Equipment availability} = \frac{\text{Operating time}}{\text{Loading time}}$$

$$= \frac{\text{Loading time} - \text{downtime due to breakdowns, setup, and adjustments}}{\text{Loading time}}$$

and loading time = net available time, as explained in Chapter Four;

$$\text{Performance rate} = \frac{\text{Net operating time}}{\text{Operating time}}$$

$$= \frac{\text{Ideal cycle time x output}}{\text{Operating time}}\text{, or}$$

$$= \frac{\text{Operating time} - \text{time lost due to idling, minor stoppages, and low capacity/low speed operation}}{\text{Operating time}}\text{; and}$$

$$\text{Quality rate} = \frac{\text{Value -added operating time}}{\text{Net operating time}}$$

$$= \frac{\text{Input} - \text{volume of quality defects}}{\text{Input}}, \text{ or}$$

$$= \frac{\text{Net operating time} - \text{time lost due to quality defects, and defectives produced during startup/restart.}}{\text{Net operating time}}$$

From the above, it is obvious that for determining the equipment effectiveness measure for a given time period, whether it be a particular week, or a month, or a quarter, the equipment availability, performance rate, and the quality rate have to be determined for that time period. Moreover, the equipment effectiveness measure, and consequently the equipment availability, performance rate, and the quality rate, can be determined for a particular machine, or equipment, a class of machines, a line consisting of a number of equipment or machines (like the urea line in a fertilizer plant), a manufacturing section, or shop, or for the entire factory, plant, or the manufacturing division. The determination of the equipment effectiveness measure also implies that for the calculation of equipment availability, the downtime losses due to equipment breakdowns, setups, and adjustments have to be separately evaluated for the given time period. Similarly, for the performance rate, the productive time lost on account of idling and minor stoppages, and due to low capacity utilisation, or operation at lower speeds than specified, have also to be separately determined. Also for the quality rate, in-process quality defects, and yield losses/quality losses in the form of production of nonconforming, or defective product at the time of startup and restarting of the equipment have to be separately determined. This implies that for the determination of the equipment effectiveness measure, the productive time or capacity lost due to (i) breakdowns, (ii) setup and adjustments, (iii) idling and minor stoppages, (iv) reduced capacity utilisation/operation at reduced speeds, (v) in-process quality defects, and (vi) quality/yield loss at startup and restart have to be determined. Thus, the equipment effective measure takes into account six major equipment losses discussed in Chapter Four. Although the equipment effectiveness measure is a number between 0 and 1 and obtained as a product of three indices, this particular property of the measure can be utilised to overcome the inherent weakness of an index. Not only does the measure provide an indication of the trend of performance by comparing it with the values of the measure for immediately preceding and earlier time periods (weeks, or months), but also through its use the trends of the three components, namely equipment availability, performance rate and quality rate, are obtained and the specific areas(s) of weakness can also be identified by comparing performance with regard to the six major equipment losses as discussed earlier.

The use of the equipment effectiveness measure requires the setting of targets on a rolling basis. Based on actual achievements and the planned improvement projects already taken up for implementation, targets for the three components are set for the succeeding two time periods as shown in Table 7.2. As soon as the current period gets over, the measures for the current period become the achieved values and based on a review, targets for the next two periods are set. The target setting is done in a review meeting chaired by the works manager in consultation with the production/operations and maintenance departments. The targets set should be difficult (and mildly challenging) but not impossible since setting of impossible objectives is counter productive and results in frustration and apathy. This target setting exercise also gives rise to targets/goals for the activity-based performance indicators for the six major equipment losses. These are lower level indicators used for control by the maintenance manager. All the six losses will rarely be found to

Table 7.2. Using the Equipment Effectiveness Measure

Measure/Performance Indicator	*Achievement - last period*	*Target - current period*	*Target - next period*
Equipment availability	0.85	0.91	0.95
* equipment breakdowns * setup and adjustments	similar targets to be set for control at the departmental level.		
Performance rate	0.90	0.93	0.95
* idling and minor stoppages * low capacity/low speed operation	similar targets to be set for control at the departmental level		
Quality rate	0.92	0.95	0.97
* in-process quality defects * quality losses at start and / or restart	similar targets to be set for control at the departmental level		
Equipment effectiveness	0.7038, or 70.4%	0.8040, or 80.4%	0.8754, or 87.5%

be significant in all manufacturing situations. In a continuous process plant engaged in the production of bulk materials, for example, breakdowns, stoppages (called minor stoppages in TPM literature), low capacity/low speed operation, and in process quality defects due to maintenance reasons usually are the significant contributors to the loss of production capacity. The first case study of Chapter Eight shows that stoppages are a major contributor of loss of production capacity in a continuous process plant. In some cases, idling, adjustments, and/or startup/restart losses may also have important contributions. On the other hand, in the manufacturing industry engaged in the production of discrete engineered products, setup, breakdowns, and in process quality defects are the major contributors, whereas idling and minor stoppages, adjustments and startup/restart losses do not generally account for a significant share of loss of production capacity. This must be borne in mind and lower level, or downstream activity-based indicators should be used only for the losses which apply in a given manufacturing situation.

Total Maintenance Cost Indicators

The works, or plant management will tend to use total maintenance cost indicators which relate it to the value of fixed assets, replacement value of plant and equipment, total manufacturing cost, or the value or amount of production output. Thus, the various financial indicators which are used at the highest level for the purpose of control include one or more of the following:

1. $$\frac{\text{Total maintenance cost}}{\text{Total value of fixed assets, or plant investment}}$$

   (Priel's index 17 and Luck's index 9)

2. $$\frac{\text{Total maintenance cost}}{\text{Replacement value of plant and equipment}}$$

   (a component of Corder's single index)

3. $$\frac{\text{Total maintenance cost}}{\text{Total manufacturing cost}}$$

   (Kapoor's index 6)

4. $$\frac{\text{Total maintenance cost}}{\text{Total value of production output}}$$

   (Du Pont indices 4.1 and 4.3)

5. $$\frac{\text{Total maintenance cost}}{\text{Units of production, or tonnes of output}}$$

   (Priel's index 14)

Moreover, Luck's index 10 measures the increase/decrease in the fifth indicator, and Kapoor has an additional measure (his index 7) which compares the total maintenance cost for the current year with that of the past year. We have, in this context, already noted that yearly comparisons, or annual indicators, are not appropriate for control of maintenance costs and the time period should be much smaller, even for control at the level of works management. Accordingly, this measure should be appropriately modified for comparison of the total maintenance cost for the current period with that of the preceding period.

An important point emerges with regard to what should be included in the total maintenance cost. This is all the more important since Priel, in his indices, desists from using total maintenance cost and uses total maintenance expenditure instead. Should the cost of lost production, or cost of lost production capacity due to maintenance reasons, which incidentally includes both the function loss and function reduction costs, be included in the total maintenance cost? This is a controversial point. However, leaving out these two elements of the maintenance cost goes against the philosophy espoused by terotechnology and TPM. Before we move on, it should also be pointed out that (i) all the five indices given above will not be used in any given organisation, and (ii) these total maintenance cost indicators also give rise to lower level financial indicators which are needed for control at the departmental level.

Other Maintenance Performance Indicators for Top Management

As we have noted earlier, there are some other indicators of performance which are of special interest at works, or plant management level. These generally deal with the following:

(i) reduction of use of energy/energy conservation/energy cost reduction,

(ii) safety/accidents,

(iii) reduction of external quality failures/customer satisfaction, and

(iv) implementation of employee participation/employee morale.

The reader will notice that whereas these losses are, to some extent, caused by inadequacy, or ineffectiveness of the maintenance function, improvements in these areas require a high level of involvement of top management. This class of indicators includes the following indices and measures:

1. $\dfrac{\text{Kcalories or Kwh of energy}}{\text{Kgm, or tonne of product}}$

2. $\dfrac{\text{Total energy cost}}{\text{Units of production, or Kgm, or tonne of output}}$

3. $\frac{\text{Total energy cost}}{\text{Total manufacturing cost}}$
4. Increase/decrease of Kwh of energy, or total energy cost.
5. Number of accidents
6. Number of accidents requiring shutdown of equipment
7. Number of claims
8. Number of customer returns
9. Number of small group meetings
10. Number of improvement suggestions
11. Increase/decrease in the number of autonomous small groups (this measure is particularly useful during the initial stages of the implementation of a scheme of employee participation).

Herein as well, the reader will notice that in any given organisation all the indices and measures given above will never be used. All possible variations of a particular indicator, that is, all possible measures in any one of the four areas, have been included since different variants apply to different organisations. Accordingly, in a given manufacturing organisation, four to six of these indicators will suffice.

The use of PQCDSM indicators is quite common in Japanese companies [8]. PQCDSM indicators measure performance in the areas of production/productivity, quality, cost, delivery, safety and morale. We have till now not included any indicators in the area of delivery. The measures in the area of delivery of product/output to customers, or against customer orders, include number/frequency of delivery delays, stock turnover rate and inventory warehousing time [8]. In the opinion of the author, the use of these performance indicators for measurement of maintenance effectiveness is not universally justified. These indicators should be used only in cases, or situations, where the delivery delay is caused by inadequate/ineffective maintenance of plant and equipment, such as loss of equipment availability, and poor performance rate of plant and equipment.

MEASURES FOR CONTROL AT THE DEPARTMENTAL LEVEL

The measures which are required for control by the supervisors and managers of maintenance departments should be directed at the following issues:

i) Fulfilment of plans, that is, the measures must indicate whether the work in the department is proceeding according to plans.

ii) Effectiveness of the activities undertaken, that is, the measures must bring out the extent to which the work of the department is helping to raise the operating standards and the product quality.

iii) Efficiency of the jobs and activities, that is, whether the work is being done efficiently and in the most economical manner.

These measures are derived from the higher-level measures and include both activity-based and financial indicators. The activity-based measures are usually derivatives of the equipment effectiveness indicators and include measures for the following:

1. Breakdown maintenance/emergency repairs—workload, rate, frequency, and downtime as a percentage of the loading time, or the net available time.
2. Preventive maintenance and predictive/condition based maintenance—workload, achievement/completion rate, and backlog.
3. Stoppages (called minor stoppages in the TPM literature) and adjustments—number, frequency, and downtime, or downtime loss incurred as a percentage of the net available time.
4. Maintainability improvement (MI)—number, workload, trend of MI jobs undertaken, and completion rate, or number of MI jobs completed during the period.
5. Low capacity operation, or speed loss—loss incurred in hours, and as a percentage of the operating time (where operating time = net available time—downtime due to breakdowns and setup and adjustments), increase/decrease in the loss due to low capacity/low speed operation.
6. Product quality—defect rate or percent defectives (for the plant and also for critical operations/machines), rework rate, backlog of rework jobs, increase/decrease in quality defects, or per cent defectives, and process capability, or process capability index, for critical processes/machines.
7. Setups and setup times, wherever important (particularly in manufacturing industries)—unit setup time, which is the ratio of total setup time and total number of setup operations, downtime due to setups as a percentage of the loading time, or the net available time, increase/decrease in the number of internal setups (or the number of internal setups which have been externalised).
8. Startup and restart loss, if and where applicable (that is, in industries where such losses are significant) — loss as a percentage of the total loss due to

maintenance reasons (or, as a percentage of the total equipment - related loss), increase/decrease in this loss.

9. Breakup of the maintenance jobs, since the total maintenance jobs undertaken is the sum of the breakdown maintenance/emergency repair jobs, planned/preventive and predictive maintenance jobs, and the maintainability improvement jobs. The intention is to spend more time and effort on preventive maintenance (PM) and maintainability improvement (MI) jobs, so that the incidence of breakdowns and also the time and manhours required to be spent on breakdown maintenance jobs are brought down significantly and continuously. This results in a proportional, significant and continuous improvement in equipment availability[3].

The financial measures which are used at the departmental level are primarily measures of efficiency, although targets are usually set for them as well. Most of these financial indicators have been discussed earlier since they find a place in the older measures of performance, namely, Priel's, Luck's and the Du Pont measures. These measures generally emphasise the followings areas/issues:

1. The breakup of the total maintenance expenditure in a particular time period into direct and overhead expenses. This is done primarily to draw attention to the percentage contribution of overheads to the total maintenance expenditure.

2. The breakup of the total maintenance cost, or the total maintenance expenditure, in a particular time period into breakdown maintenance/repair costs, and scheduled/preventive maintenance costs.

3. The breakup of the breakdown maintenance cost into the direct and indirect cost elements, wherein the direct costs include the costs of maintenance manpower and of spares and incidental materials, and the indirect cost is the loss of productive capacity caused by breakdowns. The indirect cost is the function loss cost.

4. The overtime cost incurred in a particular time period or the cost of overtime labour employed for maintenance of plant and equipment. This measure is used to draw attention to the need to reduce the use of overtime labour, which, in turn, brings up the need to reduce the incidence of breakdowns, and the importance of planning.

The author feels that proper attempts should also be made to highlight the function reduction cost (function loss cost having been included under the indirect cost of breakdowns). This is particularly necessary for continuous process industries. Towards this end, the low capacity, or low speed operation caused by inadequate, or ineffective maintenance should be identified and reported to the maintenance manager and the works manager regularly, as for example, on a monthly basis.

NEED FOR AN INTEGRATED SYSTEM

Our preceding discussion in this section has clearly brought out the need for an integrated system of measurement of maintenance effectiveness. Measures of performance are used to highlight deficiencies and deviations from plans and the use of these measures must enable corrective actions. Due to the diverse nature of maintenance activities, different types of measures are required, namely, measures of efficiency and effectiveness on the one hand and financial, equipment effectiveness and activity-based indicators on the other. At the same time, since top management cannot go into the daily nitty gritty and is, thus, interested in overall indicators of performance, we have broken up the full set of performance measures into two parts. However, we have also shown the direct link between the two parts, and also the two-way interaction between them. Whereas the lower level indicators are derived from the overall indicators of performance which are of interest to the top and works/plant management, the attainment of the targeted levels for the higher level measures depends on the levels of achievement of targets for the associated lower level measures. Also the causes for nonattainment of higher level indicators are provided by examining the lower level indicators [11]. Thus, an integrated system of measurement of maintenance effectiveness should be developed. This will also facilitate planning and allocation of necessary resources for the reliability and maintainability improvement activities and project.

References

1. Armitage, W. 'Maintenance Effectiveness', in *Operational Research in Maintenance* [A.K.S. Jardine, Editor], Manchester University Press, 1970, pp 196-223.
2. Armitage, W. and Jardine, A.K.S., 'Maintenance Performance — A Decision Problem', *The International Journal of Production Research,* Vol. 7, No.1, 1968, pp 15-22.
3. Bhadury, B. and Basu, S.K., 'Measuring Maintenance Performance' in Proceedings— Seminar on Systems Engineering, Indian Institute of Technology, Kharagpur, July 6-7, 1982, pp 68-76, and Chapter 6 of Some Applications of System Analysis in Terotechnology [B. Bhadury] Unpublished Ph.D. Thesis, University of Burdwan, (W.B., India), 1985.

4. Blegen, H.M. and Nylehn, B., 'Organising the Maintenance Function—An Analytical Approach', *The International Journal of Production Research*, Vol, 7, No. 1, 1968, pp 23-32.

5. Corder, G.G., 'Maintenance—Techniques and Outlook,' Seminar Publication by the British Productivity Council, Sect. 6, 1967, pp 73-77.

6. Kapoor, V.K., 'Control and Measurement of Maintenance Effectiveness,' *Productivity* (New Delhi, India), Vol.XV, No. 3, Oct.-Dec. 1974, pp 305-315.

7. Luck, W.S., 'Now You Can Really Measure Maintenance Performance,' *Factory Management and Maintenance*, Vol. 114, No.1, 1956, pp 81-86.

8. Nakajima, S., 'Measuring Maintenance Effectiveness,' Chapter 9 of Nakajima, S. (Editor), *TPM Development Program: Implementing Total Productive Maintenance*, Productivity Press Cambridge, Massachusetts (U.S.A), 1989, pp 365-375.

9. Priel, V.Z., 'The Case for Multi-aspect Performance Measurement,' Maintenance Engineering, Vol. 8, No. 4, 1964.

10. Takahashi, Y. and Osada, T., *Total Productive Maintenance, Asian Productivity Organisation*, Tokyo, Japan, 1990, p 311 (Table 8.2).

11. Wiremen, T., *Total Productive Maintenance: An American Approach*, Industrial Press, Inc., New York, 1991, pp 156-167 and 178-183.

Endnotes

1. This is the sum of the direct costs of maintenance manpower of various jobs undertaken and completed during the given time period.

2. This does not imply that the works management does not need the total maintenance cost based indicators. In addition to these indicators, for effective control, the works management needs the other two classes of indicators.

3. Stoppages also call for preventive actions but most of such preventive actions are in the form of autonomous maintenance of equipment. Maintainability improvement activities can also be instrumental in reducing the loss caused by stoppages. Therefore, PM, autonomous maintenance and MI efforts also help in improving the performance rate. The first case study of Chapter Eight will illustrate the significance of stoppages and downtime caused by them.

Implementing TPM - Discussion of Real-Life Case Studies

Having discussed the various facets of TPM, we are now ready to discuss the implementation of TPM. The various aspects of TPM implementation will be presented through the discussion of two real-life case studies. The two case studies were carried out in large tyre manufacturing plants, located in India. A tyre manufacturing plant is a good representation of a continuous process industry. The reader will recollect that TPM evolved on the shop floors of the Japanese manufacturing industry, engaged in the production of discrete engineered products and not in the continuous process industry as was the case with terotechnology. For this particular reason, many maintenance practitioners believe that TPM finds applications in the manufacturing industry. These two case studies help to bring out two important facts, which are (i) the applicability of TPM in the continuous process industry has been incorrectly doubted, and (ii) the TPM, as a practice, can probably make a much greater impact in the continuous process industry.

The two case studies will be discussed in some detail in this chapter. The first application, though a smaller and limited of productive maintenance (the reader will notice that total from TPM has been left out) has been discussed first since, in addition to being small and thus, allowing progressive development of the subject matter, it presents a state of affairs pointing to the need for productive maintenance, or a case for the application of productive maintenance. The analysis of downtime data clearly brings out the set of circumstances calling for the application of autonomous maintenance and maintainability improvements, in addition to properly planned and scheduled preventive maintenance. This application was carried out in the mixing and rubber preparation section of a tyre manufacturing plant in 1995. As noted earlier, the second case study was also carried out in a tyre manufacturing plant, but it was carried out much earlier (in 1991) in a different (and larger) tyre producing factory. This case study describes a much larger and more involved application and it will be used to discuss the various stages and ten important and sequential steps of TPM implementation.

An Application of Productive Maintenance to the Banbury Section [1]

The objective of terotechnology is the pursuit of economic life cycle cost of plant and equipment, and this is achieved by maximising equipment availability coupled with increasing the useful life of the equipment. Productive maintenance is a Japanese term. They took preventive maintenance and expanded its application to include preventive actions directed at losses due to setup and adjustments, idling and minor stoppages, startup and restart etc., since they also cause loss of equipment availability. This is what differentiates productive maintenance from preventive maintenance. As a matter of fact, productive maintenance and total productive maintenance (TPM) are the applications of the concept of terotechnology.

The project of application of productive maintenance was undertaken for the mixing and rubber preparation section of a tyre manufacturing plant, known as the Banbury section. This section had been plagued with poor equipment availability, and this was affecting production of tyres. The management of the company was, therefore, interested in improving the equipment availability of this section as the first stage of tyre production is carried out here. In this section, the rubber compound is prepared in the form of sheets for the rest of the tyre plant. The section has four units (and each unit is also called a Banbury and given a number, namely, 1, 2, 3 and 4). Each unit, in turn, consists of the following subsystems:

1. Carbon weighing and feeding system.
2. Polymer weighing and feeding system.
3. Oil weighing and feeding system.
4. Internal mixer.
5. Extruder with R/D calender (for Banburys 1 and 3), and DC and AC mills (for Banburys 2 and 4).
6. Batch - off unit.

The outline diagram of a unit showing the different subsystems and equipment is given as Fig. 8.1.

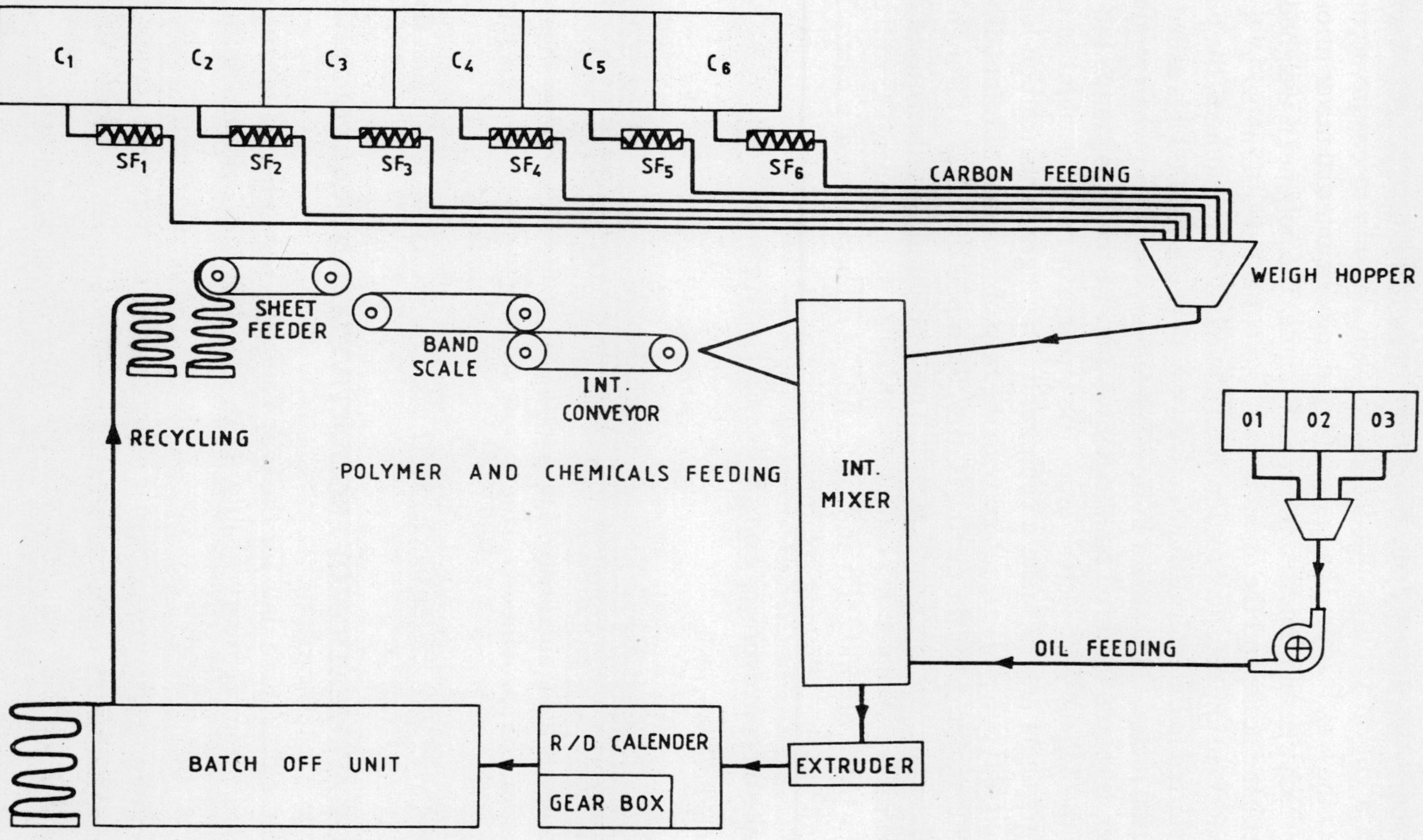

Fig. 8.1. Outline Diagram of Banbury Unit (Banburys 1&3)

The carbon black is loaded into the six day storage bins $C_1, C_2, ..., C_6$. A screw feeder with a cut-off valve is fitted beneath each day bin to ensure accurate feeding onto the weigh scale. The material is fed into the internal mixer through the flexible discharge and fluidised mixer entry chute. The polymer is weighed on the polymer band scale, and the operator can load either bales of rubber by hand or rubber sheets using the sheet feeder. After the required weighment, the polymer is transferred to the intermediate conveyor, where it is held till it is called for by the internal mixer. Oil is stored in three heated day tanks and when required by the mixer, is routed to the oil scale. After weighment, the oil is pumped to the mixer with the help of the injector pump. The purpose of the internal mixer is to mix the ingredients and to make a compound. The ingredients (carbon black, chemicals, oil and polymer) are mixed with the help of two flanged rotors driven by a 1500 H.P. motor. After the mixing is over, the mix is discharged through the discharge door onto the extruder/DC mill. The compound is further mixed and formed into rubber sheets in the extruder with roller die calender/DC mill and AC mill. The batch-off unit cools and stacks up the rubber sheets of a batch. The batch-off unit has the following subunits:

1. The take-off conveyor.
2. The inclined conveyor.
3. The cooling rack.
4. The spray unit used to spray soap slurry onto the rubber sheet.
5. An automatic take-out device to take the leading edge of the rubber sheet off, the suspension bar at the end of the cooling rack and to deposit it on the stacker carriage.
6. The wig-wag to stack the batch, which requires recycling, on the first floor.

A CASE FOR APPLICATION OF PRODUCTIVE MAINTENANCE

The equipment downtime data for the four Banburys was collected for the six-month period—from February to July, 1995. The data was collected from the following registers/log books:

(i) The monthly delay time register maintained by the industrial engineering department, and

(ii) The shift log book maintained by the maintenance department.

It was found that the data regarding setup and adjustment loss was not available. Moreover, from the description of the equipment and process, it is obvious that losses due to poor product quality, low capacity utilisation (also known as speed loss in TPM literature), and low yield/productivity at startup and restart do not apply to the mixing and rubber compounding section. Therefore, the equipment and component failures which resulted in equipment downtime were classified under two heads, namely, breakdowns and stoppages. A failure is classified as a breakdown when the equipment/subsystem is not in an operating condition and this state is caused by a component, or an equipment, breakdown or defect. Breakdowns require some kind of repair, or replacement, to restore the equipment to the normal operating condition. Equipment and subsystem stoppages are failures caused by jamming/sticking of material (e.g., carbon black, rubber) in chutes and racks, malfunctioning of components such as limit switches, valves and air cylinders, and loss of signal resulting in the operation of interlocks stopping the equipment/subsystem.

The causes of downtime were divided into the following four classes:

1. Downtime due to breakdowns.
2. Downtime due to stoppages.
3. Downtime due to preventive maintenance (PM) jobs.
4. Downtime due to other causes.

A list of other causes is as follows:

(i) Late start time.
(ii) Loading stopped by workmen due to personal reasons.
(iii) Power failure.
(iv) Material shortage.
(v) Empty skid not available.
(vi) Absenteeism.
(vii) Chemical not ready
(viii) Change of power supply.
(ix) Work stopped due to technical follow-up.
(x) Unmixed batch dumped.
(xi) Compound change-over.
(xii) R.P.M. change.

The analysis of the downtime data was carried out for the entire section (all the four units together) and also for the four units separately. The downtime in the Banbury section during the six-month period was found to be a significant fraction of the total available time. For the entire section the downtime was found to be 36 per cent of the total time. From the unit-wise analysis of data, it was found that downtime for the four units varied from 34.3 to 37.4 percent. Thereafter, further analysis was carried out with the data classed under the four heads as noted earlier. The distribution of downtime for the Banbury section during the six-month period is shown in Fig. 8.2 and the unit-wise distribution is given in Table 8.1.

Table 8.1. Downtime Distribution for the Four Units (February to July, 1995)

Unit	*Total downtime in per cent*	*Breakup of downtime under four heads*			
		Breakdown (%)	*Stoppage* (%)	*P.M.* (%)	*Other* (%)
Banbury 1	37.4	8	25	22	45
Banbury 2	36.7	3	26	22	49
Banbury 3	34.3	8	31	09	52
Banbury 4	36.7	4	25	35	37
Banbury Section	36	6	26	22	46

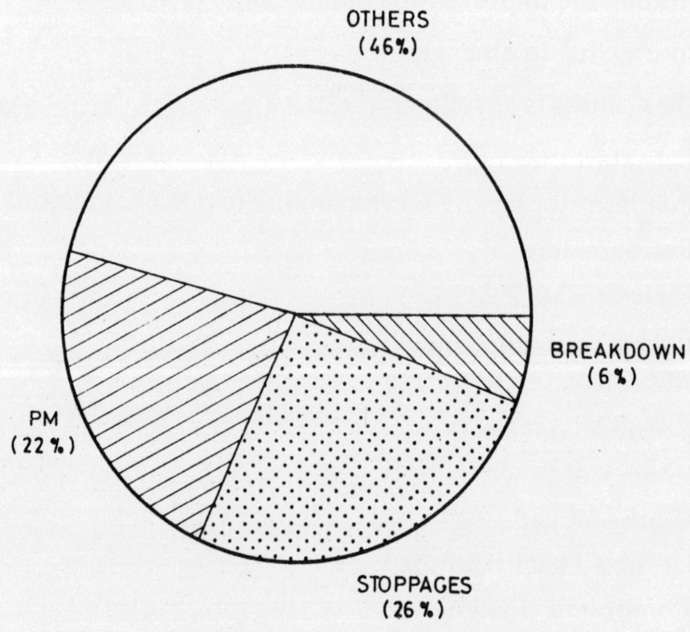

Fig. 8.2. Downtime Distribution of Banbury Section for the Period Feb. to July, 1995

From this analysis, the following conclusions can be drawn:

1. The availability of the section is poor—just about 64 percent. Thus, there is need to improve its availability by taking appropriate measures to reduce downtime.
2. The downtimes on account of stoppages, preventive maintenance and other causes are significantly higher than that due to breakdowns. For the section as a whole, the downtime due to breakdowns constitutes just 6 per cent of the total downtime, as compared to 26 per cent for stoppages, 22 per cent for preventive maintenance and 46 per cent for other causes.
3. The loss of availability due to other causes is very high and needs to be brought down. These causes are not under the control of the maintenance department. The plant management should take steps to minimise this loss. However, the loss due to nonavailability of power is beyond the control of even the plant management.
4. Some amount of time has to be spent on preventive maintenance jobs, that is some amount of downtime for PM is unavoidable. However, from the analysis, it is found that the downtime due to PM is on the high side and needs to be brought down. This can be done by proper planning and scheduling of the PM jobs. It is necessary, therefore, to develop a computerised maintenance management information system for scheduling and control of PM.
5. Stoppages account for as much as 26 per cent of the total downtime and nearly four and a half times of that for breakdowns. Moreover, stoppages are very large in number and the downtime for each stoppage is comparatively smaller. This points to the need for productive maintenance, particularly the application of autonomous maintenance.

PARETO ANALYSIS OF STOPPAGES AND BREAKDOWNS

From the downtime analysis, it was found that stoppages and breakdowns together account for about one-third (26+6=32 per cent) of the loss of equipment availability. The incidence of breakdowns and stoppages can be reduced by taking appropriate preventive actions, in the form of autonomous maintenance, preventive inspections and preventive replacements. A detailed analysis of all the breakdowns and stoppages was carried out to identify the vital few stoppages and breakdowns. This would enable management by exception and also a phased attack on the problems. Accordingly, a Pareto analysis of all equipment failures due to breakdowns and stoppages was carried out. The necessary data for this was obtained from the shift log books and data for one month, namely July, 1995, was used. From this analysis, it was found that out of a total number of 163 failures, the first 60 failures accounted for 80 per cent of the downtime. The remaining 103 failures accounted for only 20 per cent of the total downtime and the frequency (number of occurrences per month) of these failures was not more than two. Most of them occurred only once during the month and the downtime did not exceed 30 minutes for any of these failures. The details of the first 60 failures which accounted for 80 per cent of the downtime are given in Table 8.2. From Table 8.2, it is found that these 60 failures consisted of only 9 breakdowns, whereas 51 out of the 60 failures were stoppages.

From this analysis, one may surmise that by exception, the maintenance department may concentrate on these 60 failures rather than trying to take up all 163 of them. Concentrating the efforts on these 60 will pay much greater dividends.

Table 8.2. 60 Failures Which Accounts for 80 Per Cent of Downtime

Sl. No.	*Problem Description*	*Breakdown/ Stoppage*	*Frequency (Occurrence per month)*	*Avg. Down-time in minutes*	*Total Down-time per month in minutes*	*%*	*Cum. %*
01.	Discharge door latch going back	S	9	68	615	6.97	6.97
02.	Ram rope cut off	B	6	83	500	5.67	12.64
03.	Rubber stuck up in cooling rack	S	19	25	475	5.38	18.02
04.	Slurry pump jammed	S	11	28	308	3.49	21.51
05.	Rubber stuck in discharge door	S	14	21.4	300	3.40	24.91
06.	Double loop problem	S	12	22.8	273	3.09	28.01
07.	Discharge door limit switch problem	S	11	23.2	255	2.89	30.90
08.	Lube oil master block problem	S	1	220	220	2.49	33.39
09.	Mixer oil pump out of order	B	1	180	180	2.04	35.43
10.	Band scale error	S	10	16.5	165	1.87	37.30
11.	Carbon accumulation in chute	S	3	53.3	160	1.81	39.12
12.	Ram air pipe problem	S	1	155	155	1.76	40.88
13.	Extruder lube pump out of order	B	1	145	145	1.64	42.52
14.	Carriage rubber stuck up	S	1	140	140	1.59	44.11
15.	Dust stop jammed	S	1	136	136	1.54	45.65
16.	D/d problem, less oil in tank	S	1	125	125	1.42	47.06

Sl. No.	*Problem Description*	*Breakdown/ Stoppage*	*Frequency (Occurrence per month)*	*Avg. Down-time in minutes*	*Total Down-time per month in minutes*	*%*	*Cum. %*
17.	Charging conveyor belt off centre	S	6	20.8	125	1.42	48.48
18.	Hugger roll jack bolt problem	S	3	41.7	125	1.42	49.90
19.	Lube oil low flow	S	1	120	120	1.36	51.26
20.	Carbon scale error	S	8	13.9	110	1.25	52.51
21.	Cooling rack imbalance	S	4	27.5	110	1.25	53.75
22.	T.C.U. motor electrical problem	S	3	36.7	110	1.25	55.00
23.	D.C. mill isolator problem	S	1	100	100	1.13	56.13
24.	Slurry pump burnt	B	1	100	100	1.13	57.26
25.	Cooling rack RSU due to slurry spray	S	1	95	95	1.08	58.34
26.	Cooling rack hugger chain broken	B	6	15.8	95	1.08	59.42
27.	H.T.M. electrical problem	S	2	45	90	1.02	60.44
28.	Wig-wag small belt drive roll got shifted	B	2	42.5	85	0.96	61.40
29.	Rubber stuck up in sheet feeder	S	2	42.7	85	0.96	62.36
30.	Rubber stuck up in inter-mill conveyor	S	4	21.2	85	0.96	63.32
31.	Rubber stuck in hopper door	S	3	26.7	80	0.91	64.23
32.	Hydraulic powerpack accumulator bottom collector oil leakage	S	1	75	75	0.85	65.08
33.	Excessive spray on inclined belt	S	1	75	75	0.85	65.93
34.	Cooling rack bar got bent	S	1	70	70	0.79	66.72
35.	Charging conveyor belt off centre	S	4	17.5	70	0.79	67.51
36.	Carbon over weight problem	S	1	65	65	0.74	68.25
37.	Rubber stuck up in vertical conveyor	S	1	65	65	0.74	68.99
38.	Gripper read switch out of position	S	6	10	60	0.68	69.67
39.	Band scale conveyor roller out of order	B	1	60	60	0.68	70.35

Sl. No.	Problem Description	Breakdown/ Stoppage	Frequency (Occurrence per month)	Avg. Down-time in minutes	Total Down-time per month in minutes	%	Cum. %
40.	Oil leakage from oil injector	S	4	13.8	55	0.62	70.97
41.	Chute butterfly valve problem	S	1	55	55	0.62	71.59
42.	Process oil problem	S	2	27.5	55	0.62	72.21
43.	Carbon not flowing from bin to screw	S	1	45	45	0.51	72.72
44.	Air line filter broken	B	1	45	45	0.51	73.23
45.	Discharge door closing problem	S	1	45	45	0.51	73.74
46.	Sheet feeder drive roll got shfited	B	1	45	45	0.51	74.25
47.	Pusher line jammed	S	1	45	45	0.51	74.76
48.	Rubber stuck up in laydown	S	1	45	45	0.51	75.27
49.	Cooling rack problem, circulation `ON' push button not `ON'	S	4	10	40	0.45	75.72
50.	Carbon cleared from H/D area	S	1	40	40	0.45	76.17
51.	Hopper door air pipe leakage	S	1	40	40	0.45	76.62
52.	Pusher problem, oily compound dropped	S	1	35	35	0.40	77.02
53.	Pusher limit switch problem	S	1	35	35	0.40	77.42
54.	Carbon jamming in bin	S	1	35	35	0.40	77.82
55.	Sheet feeder trip due to rubber stuck up	S	1	35	35	0.40	78.22
56.	Indexing cylinder yoke not in position	S	1	35	35	0.40	78.62
57.	Oil feeding problem due to solenoid valve	S	1	35	35	0.40	79.02
58.	Butterfly valve closing signals L/S base loose	S	2	15	30	0.34	79.36
59.	Carriage not running due to high pressure solution not coming	S	1	30	30	0.34	79.70
60.	C/R timer problem, giving continuous signal	S	2	15	30	0.34	80.04

Taking up 60 problems at one time is a difficult proposition and it would be worthwhile to do this task in two phases—concentration on a smaller number of problems in the first phase and a larger number undertaken, after the successful completion of the first phase, in the second phase. A closer study of Table 8.2 reveals that the first 18 failures accounted for 50 percent of the downtime (due to breakdowns and stoppages) and the remaining 42 failures accounted for the remaining 30 per cent. Accordingly, it was suggested to the management that in phase I, the first 18 problems should be taken up and after successful completion of phase I, the remaining 42 problems should be taken up in phase II. This would be more practicable and also better for morale.

Coming next to the first phase of implementation of productive maintenance for the Banbury section, closer observation of Table 8.2 reveals that the first 18 failures consist of 15 stoppages and 3 breakdowns. The incidence of these breakdowns and stoppages can be reduced by taking certain preventive actions. The preventive actions can be in the form of maintainability improvements, autonomous maintenance, or preventive maintenance, which could, in turn, either be periodic (not daily) preventive inspections, or preventive replacement (these replacements are preceded by inspections). Maintainability improvements, in turn, can be either in the form of modifications to plant and equipment, or incorporation of improved operating procedures. Three out of the 18 problems (or out of the 15 stoppage problems) were identified for maintainability improvement efforts. These three problems are as follows (serial nos. from Table 8.2):

Sl. No.	*Problem Description*	*Frequency*	*Average downtime*	*Total downtime per month*
4.	Slurry pump jamming	11	28 mins.	308 mins.
10.	Band scale problem	10	16.5 mins.	165 mins.
11.	Carbon jamming in chute and screw feeder	3	53 mins.	160 mins.

These three maintainability improvement exercises are briefly described in the following section. For the remaining 15 problems, each problem was taken up and for each problem:

(i) the necessary preventive action was determined, and

(ii) the frequency of the preventive action, either preventive inspection/check (in most cases) or preventive replacement, was decided upon.

Moreover, if the preventive action necessary is in the form of daily cleaning, lubrication and bolt tightening, or simply daily or routine checking/inspection, then it was proposed for inclusion under autonomous maintenance to be carried out by the equipment operators.

IMPLEMENTATION OF SUGGESTIONS FOR MI

As noted earlier, three suggestions were made for maintainability improvements for three stoppages out of the 15 taken up in the first phase. The first suggestion was for a minor modification to the plant consisting of incorporation of a small filter to the end of the suction pipe dipped in the slurry tank. The other two suggestions were for improvement of the operating procedures. Brief discussions of these three maintainability improvement suggestions are as follows:

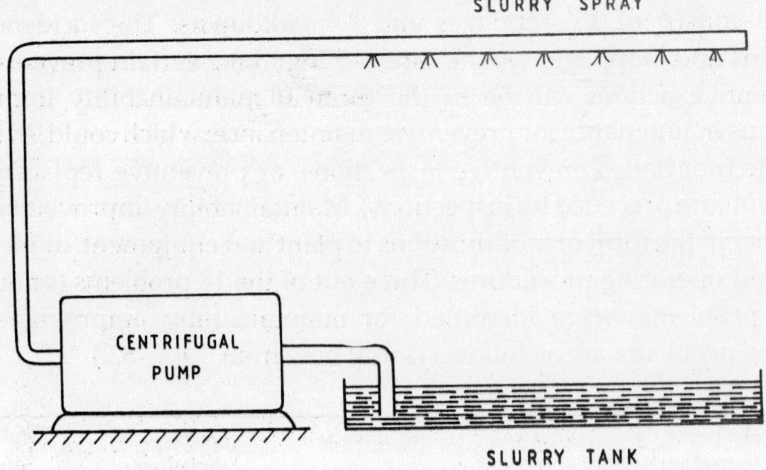

(a) SLURRY PUMP ARRANGEMENT

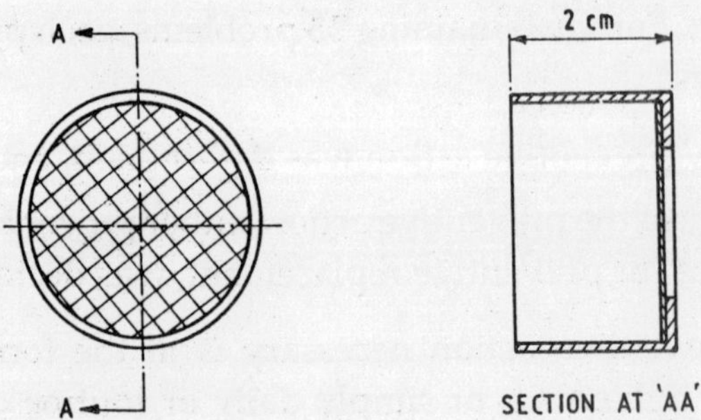

(b) FILTER FOR SLURRY PUMP SUCTION PIPE

Fig. 8.3. Suggestions for Modification — Slurry Pump Jamming Problem

Stoppages on Account of Slurry Pump Jamming

Slurry pump is part of the batch-off unit and is used for spraying soap solution on the rubber sheet to reduce the stickiness and also to cool it. The arrangement used for slurry spraying is shown in Fig. 8.3(a). Slurry pump jamming problem is caused by the clogging of rubber pieces and other materials in the suction pipe of the pump. The incidence of this problem can be greatly reduced by attaching a filter, shown in Fig. 8.3(b), to the end of the suction pipe. 20 mesh sieve can be used for the filter. The filter should be cleaned every 15 days and replaced, if necessary. This job can be attended to by the equipment operator.

Stoppages Due to Band Scale Error

As explained earlier, band scale is part of the polymer feeding system. It is used to weigh natural rubber bales, synthetic rubber and rubber sheets. The band scale arrangement is shown in Fig. 8.4. At present, there are stoppages because sometimes the band scale gives wrong readings. Wrong readings are obtained when rubber bales are thrown by the operator from a distance on the band scale. This problem can be greatly reduced by ensuring that the distance between the rubber bale container and the band scale does not exceed one meter.

Problems of Carbon Leakage and Carbon Jamming in Chute and Screw Feeder

These two problems are related. The carbon feeding system is shown in Fig. 8.5. The internal mixer has a dust extraction system to collect the carbon leaking through the clearance between the ram and the housing and also to keep the dust away during the emptying of sacks into the day-bins. It is mounted on top of the carbon day-bins. As the door of the day-bins are kept open, the effectiveness of the dust extraction system is reduced. This, in turn, results in carbon leakage.

Sometimes carbon gets jammed inside the screw feeder and the chute, which stops the feeding of carbon to the internal mixer and results in subsystem stoppage. Such jamming occurs because the carbon in the day-bins absorbs moisture from the outside atmosphere. This problem can be greatly reduced by closing the door provided at the top of the day-bins. As the carbon loading is done for one bin at a time, the doors of the other bins can be kept closed. The operator, who loads the carbon, should be made responsible for ensuring that the other doors are firmly closed.

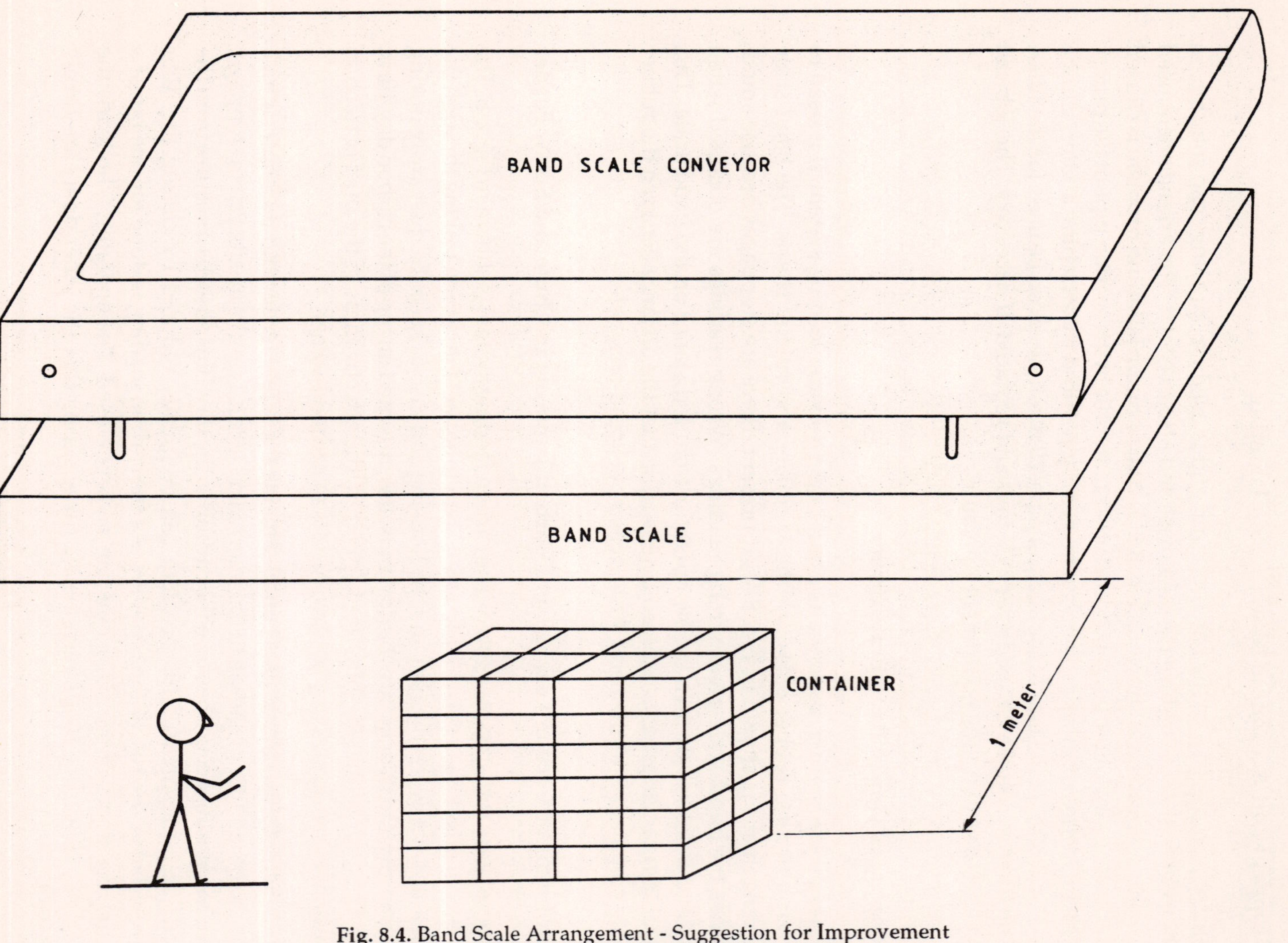

Fig. 8.4. Band Scale Arrangement - Suggestion for Improvement of Operating Procedure

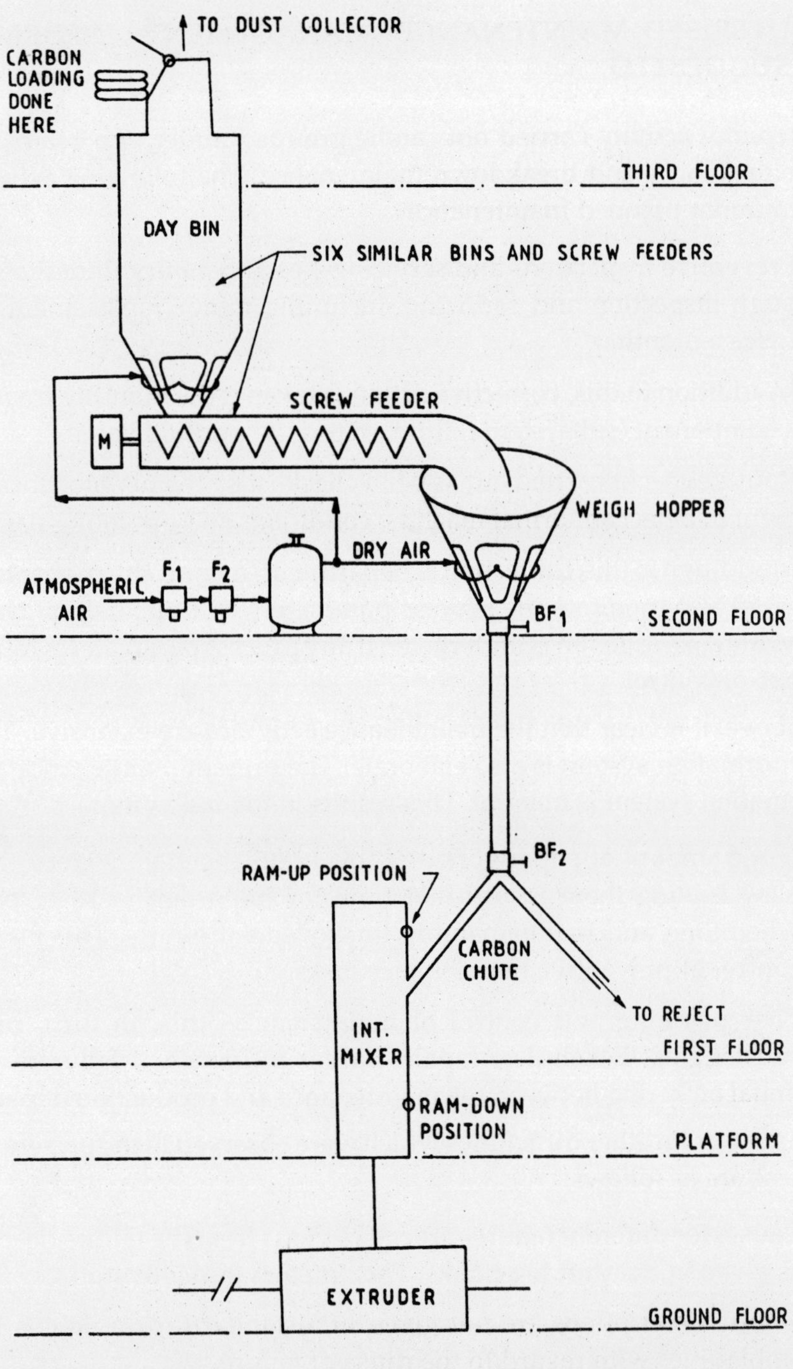

Fig. 8.5. Carbon Feeding System

A COMPUTERISED MAINTENANCE MANAGEMENT INFORMATION SYSTEM SUGGESTED

The maintenance activity carried out can be grouped under two heads, namely, planned maintenance and breakdown maintenance. The following activities are undertaken under planned maintenance:

(i) Preventive inspections and servicing—each Banbury undergoes a thorough inspection and servicing, including minor replacement, usually twice a month.

(ii) In addition to this, corrective action is taken if the monthly frequency of a component/subsystem failure exceeds a specified value.

(iii) Routine checks carried out as per a checklist by the maintenance department to detect abnormal machine conditions and operating parameters.

(iv) In addition to this, the technical department (manned by rubber technologists) also monitors the process parameters with the help of checklists. Maintenance action is undertaken if any process parameter is found to be out-of-control.

From the above, it is clear that the maintenance activities are extensive. Thus, the required information system is also elaborate. The present maintenance management information system is manual. This results in the following:

(i) Large amount of paperwork and this keeps the maintenance engineers busy leaving them insufficient time for important tasks of planning, scheduling and maintainability improvement efforts. This also affects control of preventive maintenance tasks.

(ii) Poor planning and control of maintenance—this, in turn, results in backlogging, incomplete repairs, larger incidence of failures and continual bickering between the maintenance and production departments.

There are certain other difficulties which were observed in the present system. Some of these are as follows:

(i) Causes for different failures are not obvious from the failure descriptions as given in the shift log-books. This impairs in-depth study of failures.

(ii) Failure descriptions are not given in a standard form, which leads to ambiguities with regard to the cause of failure.

(iii) There appears to be a significant amount of redundancy in data entry.

(iv) The system is not favourable for conduct of studies on downtime distributions, availability, trend analysis and reliability and critical analysis (of components).

(v) The system does not provide information regarding the manpower, tools and spares required and also the estimated repair/maintenance times.

A computerised maintenance management information system has been proposed. The proposed system is user-friendly and also has the query facility. It also has the following desirable features:

(i) It is based on a comprehensive data base.

(ii) It permits detailed and varied types of analysis

(iii) It can be used not only to produce different types of regular and special reports to support managerial decisions, but also can serve as a decision support system for planning of maintenance activities, both preventive and corrective in nature.

CLOSING REMARKS

Intuitively it seems that the practice of productive maintenance would have a greater impact in a continuous process industry setting since productive maintenance calls for preventive actions directed at the minimisation of six major equipment - related losses as opposed to preventive maintenance which considers preventive actions directed at only one of the six losses, namely loss due to breakdown of equipment. This was the primary motivation for undertaking projects of implementation of productive maintenance and TPM in tyre manufacturing plants. The application of productive maintenance described in this case study was undertaken for the Banbury section, since, in addition to being the feeder department on which the subsequent processes/departments depended, it had the worst record as far as downtime losses were concerned. This was a matter of concern and the minimisation of the downtime loss had become an important objective.

We have stated earlier that this case study is a description of a limited application. Its scope is limited in two respects, which are as follows:

(i) Downtime analysis, implementation of maintainability improvement ideas, and the proposed maintenance management information system apply to only one section of the plant.

(ii) It is an application of productive maintenance and not total productive maintenance, in as much as the aspects of education and training to enable total involvement, creation of an organisational structure for TPM promotion, and implementation of employee participation have not been addressed.

What has been done for the Banbury section has to be done in stages for the entire plant. However, before this is done, it is imperative that the first two steps of TPM implementation (which will be discussed in the next section), namely announcing top management's decision to implement TPM and the launch of an educational campaign, should be implemented. During the conduct of the case study, it was observed that the actual conditions in the plant were not conducive for the implementation of autonomous maintenance.

This is an important point and it needs to be investigated further. The downtime analysis for the section showed that other causes accounted for as much as 46 per cent of the total downtime loss (please see Table 8.1). This implies that 0.46 of 36 per cent, or 16.6 per cent of the equipment availability, or the productive capacity of the Banbury section, was lost for non-maintenance reasons. The list of other causes also shows that only two of the twelve causes, namely power failure and change of power supply, are external and beyond the control of the organisation. The list also includes late start time, loading stopped by the workmen due to personal reasons and absenteeism. These three causes accounted for a fairly significant share of the loss. As an example, during the study it was observed that in a number of shifts the work was started as much as 30 minutes late which means that 6.25 per cent of the available productive capacity was lost just because the operators did not start work on time. This shows an attitude of total indifference to the work and the organisation. The operators who do not have a sense of belonging to the organisation cannot be expected to display a sense of ownership of the equipment they operate. This explains the 'I operate, you fix' attitude which predominates in the plant. The list of other causes also brings out lack of material control (material shortage), supervision, or shop controls (empty skid not available, chemical not ready, and compound change over) and process controls and technical support (work stopped due to technical follow up, RPM change, and unmixed batch dumped). These reasons bring out a lack of commitment from shop supervision, middle management and staff specialists. This is not an isolated case, in as much as the state of affairs in this section is not very much worse than that in similar shops and sections in other continuous process plants.

Although it is a limited application, this case study has brought out a number of important points. These are as follows:

1. Preventive maintenance activity is directed at breakdowns. This assumes that component failures and equipment breakdowns are the only causes of downtime. This study brings out the fallacy of this assumption and shows that in a continuous process plant, stoppages account for a large (and significant) share of loss of equipment availability. In this case study, it was found that stoppages alone accounted for 26 per cent of the total downtime as opposed to only 6 per cent caused by breakdowns. Moreover, breakdowns were comparatively much fewer in number (than stoppages) and also less frequent. Stoppages needed greater attention as compared to breakdowns.
2. Stoppages are caused by jamming and/or sticking of materials in chutes and material handling devices, malfunctioning of components and loss of signals resulting in loss of interlocks etc. Prevention of stoppages requires greater attention to daily tasks of cleaning, lubrication and tightening of bolts and fasteners and certain simple (but important) periodic equipment checks/ inspections. These activities have to be carried out by equipment operators as otherwise they would never be done since maintenance department personnel would not find the time to attend to them. This brings out the importance of autonomous maintenance and also the pressing need to implement autonomous maintenance, particularly in a continuous process industry setting.
3. Some of the stoppages can be prevented by the implementation of maintainability improvement ideas and suggestions given by employees. Moreover, maintainability improvement does not necessarily mean a design change or a modification to the plant or the equipment. Some stoppages can be prevented by improved operating procedures. This also brings out the importance of operator training in proper operation of the equipment and plant.
4. The importance of education and training aimed at bringing about a change of attitude in the equipment operators and employees in general and also greater involvement of supervisors, middle management personnel and staff specialists has also been brought out adequately by this case study.

IMPLEMENTATION OF TPM IN A TYRE MANUFACTURING COMPANY [2]

This study was undertaken in a large tyre manufacturing company. The company is the second largest tyre manufacturer in the country, and second only to the market leader, both in terms of sales and profits. In recent years, however, competition, both domestic and foreign, had been threatening its position in the marketplace, and the competition had threatened to take away some of its share of the market with similar high quality products at lower costs. It had become necessary, therefore, to further improve the product quality and simultaneously reduce the manufacturing costs to be able to take on the competition on its own terms. To further improve its quality image and increase its exports, the management of the company had also recently decided to work towards obtaining an ISO 9000 certification.

The manufacturing unit of the company was headed by a Vice President and employed over 3,000 persons. The technology used by the company was state-of-art and the production shops were also well laid out. Moreover, since quite a few years the unit had been following the traditional system of preventive maintenance and also 100 per cent inspection of the product at various stages throughout the manufacturing process. Certain drawbacks of the existing system had recently come to light and these drawbacks were found to be as follows:

(i) only preventive maintenance had not been useful in correcting recurring defects,

(ii) 100 per cent inspection had not been 100 per cent effective, and

(iii) 100 per cent inspection had essentially been a process of sorting good products from bad and had been far from cost-effective.

In addition to this, the operators had little responsibility for quality and no apparent incentive for building a tyre right the first time. The quality control department acted as a "police force" trying to enforce corrective action after a defective item was found and thus, inspection by the quality control department had been directed only at defect detection and no attempt had been made at defect removal. The quality and productivity performance had not been upto the expectations of the management. Equipment availability, in some critical processes such as curing, had also been a nagging problem. Any attempt at improving product quality and reducing the number of breakdowns had always been met with a call to increase the number of inspectors, and the resulting increase in the number of inspectors and maintenance tradesmen had not always borne fruit.

THE PROCESSES/MANUFACTURING DEPARTMENTS

Mainly heavy duty tyres, such as truck tyres and tyres for tractors and earth movers etc., are produced by the company. A tyre is a resilient air container designed to perform the following essential functions:

1. Provide load carrying capacity.
2. Provide abrasion resistance (greater mileage).
3. Facilitate transient driving, braking and torque.
4. Provide dimensional stability.

A tyre is a composite of rubber, fabric, bead wire, carbon black and chemicals. All these components are mixed and processed together in the raw stage to form a green tyre. To get the required properties, a green tyre is cured by a process called vulcanisation, or curing. The various processes used in the production of a tyre, and accordingly, the production departments are as follows:

1. *Mixing*. This is the first operation. In the mixing department, rubber and other ingredients are mixed together to form a rubber compound.
2. *Calendering*. Nylon/rayon cord has very poor affinity for rubber compounds. Hence, the cord surface is coated with RF resin to improve the bond strength between the fibre and rubber compound interface. This RF resin is well dispersed in rubber latex and the coating of the RFL solution onto the fibre surface is done by dipping the fabric in RFL solution. Dipped fabric is then coated on either side with rubber films on 4-roll calender machines.
3. *Bias Cutting*. Calendered fabric rolls of length 300-350 metres are cut into plies. Passed calendered rolls are brought to the bias cutting machines and loaded in such a way that the stamping on the calendered fabric faces the top to enable proper fabric identification. The calendered roll is bias cut as per specifications and cut pieces of calendered roll are called plies.
4. *Band Building*. The bias rolls with proper identification are brought to the band building department for converting into bands. Bands are preassembled set of plies and are made of 2, 3, or 4 plies depending upon the size of which bands are being made.
5. *Extruding*. Extruding is a process by which unvulcanised rubber is shaped through a particular die opening under pressure and temperature. During the process of extrusion, both the tread and the bead are formed. Tread is a rubber compound that comes in contact with the road, whereas bead is a very hard and strong part of the tyre whose function is to anchor the tyre firmly onto the rim.
6. *Truck Tyre Building*. In this department, different components of tyres are assembled on tyre building machines in a compact form. The various compo-

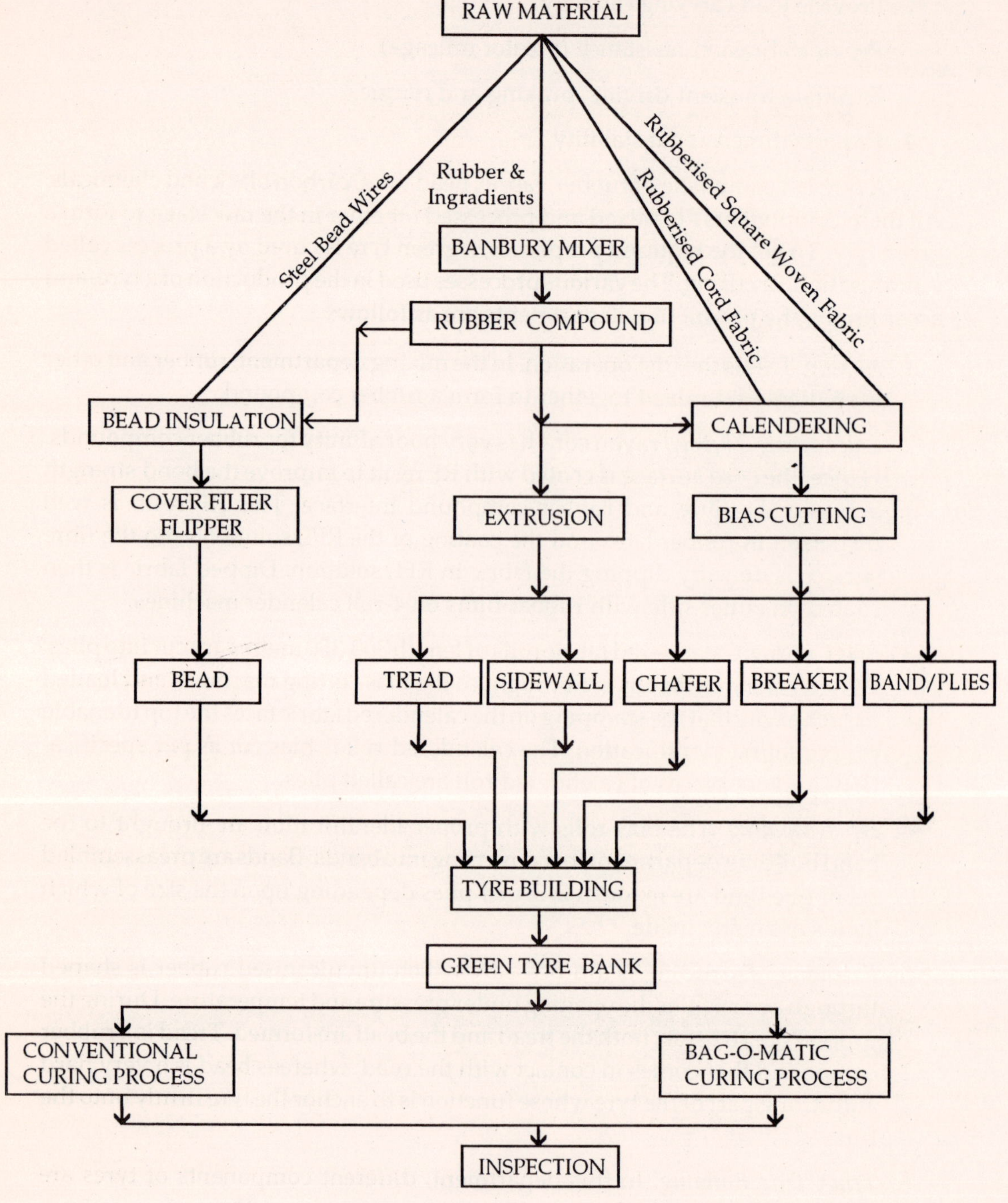

Fig. 8.6 Flow Chart - Production of a Tyre

nents are bands, beads, chafer, sidewall and tread. All these components are identified by the code marking depending on the size. This compact assembly of components is called a "green tyre."

7. *Curing.* In this process, an unvulcanised tyre is moulded to its proper size and shape and vulcanised in a curing press under high temperature and pressure. Two types of presses are basically used, namely, the conventional, or the air bag type, and bag-o-matics wherein bladders are used in place of air bags. Bag-o-matic presses are most modern and are widely used. The bag-o-matic presses have the following inherent advantages:
   - (i) lower curing cycles, and
   - (ii) they do not involve additional operations, bagging/debagging and thus save time and labour.

The manufacturing unit has various sizes of presses to suit various tyre sizes. The flowchart showing the various processes used in the production of a tyre is given as Fig. 8.6.

WHERE TO START?

The long and extensive process of manufacture of the tyre demands constant coordination between departments since otherwise delay at any intermediate stage would show up in the end, either on account of the loss of green tyre (LOGT), or due to sporadic breakdowns. The adverse effect of LOGT can be minimised by ensuring that a particular tyre, which is either low in inventory or has an immediate demand, is built. This can also be done when there is either a shortage of personnel in a particular shift, or a breakdown on one, or a couple, of the tyre building machines. The only place where the timings, or production, cannot be so adjusted is the curing department, because the cycle time of curing for a particular type of tyre is fixed. Thus, delay, or loss of production, on account of LOGT is not expected, and has in fact been rarely observed. However, curing is the last stage of the manufacturing process, and the product obtained after curing directly affects the "output."

In the curing department, it was further observed that one of the bag-o-matic presses - the E-2 press - was scheduled for overhauling and during overhauling, the following problems had to be attended to:

1. Right side inner bull gear bushes had moved resulting in the lubricating oil not reaching the seal.

2. The hydraulics of the press was in bad shape and had a lot of problems.
3. The valves of the press, besides the pipelines, had a number of leakage problems.

Moreover, the performance of the E-2 press had been far from satisfactory and in the last six months, its overall effectiveness had never crossed 60 per cent. As an illustration, the weekly performance figures of the E-2 press (for a period of one week—on a daily basis—as submitted to the management) is given in the following table.

Table 8.3. E-2 Press Performance
(Period April 24 to April 30, 1991)

Day	*Number of tyres cured*	*Availa-bility*	*Perfor-mance Rate*	*Quality Rate*	*Effectiveness (per cent)*
1	24	0.777	0.75	0.875	50.99
2	30	0. 87	0.833	0.867	62.75
3	28	0.836	0.813	0.712	48.39
4	32	0.892	0.871	0.812	63.08
5	8*	0.667	0.602	0. 75	30.09
6	24	0.739	0.788	0.833	48.52
7	30	0.833	0.875	0.833	60.71
1-7	176	0.801	0.79	0.811	51.32

* Sunday/Holiday

Based on the above and also since curing was the last stage of the manufacturing process and the performance of the curing department affected both quality and quantity of output, it was decided that TPM implementation should start from this department. Also it was decided to take the E-2 bag-o-matic press for the implementation of TPM.

IDENTIFYING AREAS OF IMPLEMENTATION OF IMPROVEMENT PROJECTS

For the effective implementation of TPM, not only should one know which particular area of the plant is experiencing problems, but also be able to identify these problems and their solutions. The first task was thus to preferably get all employees from the top management to the operators on the production line for discussion on a common platform and to get their views and suggestions on improvements. From this point onwards, a series of brainstorming sessions on specific areas of the problems were held with a view to pinpoint the optimal solutions of these problems. A large and extended team comprising of the top management, managers of different functions, such as production, engineering maintenance, electrical maintenance, technology (rubber technology, as in the preceding case) and R & D, and supervisors and shop floor workers, both from maintenance and production, was formed for this purpose. Close monitoring of parameters and performance at all levels assisted in the understanding of the equipment and development of effective countermeasures.

After many such brainstorming sessions, a number of improvements were identified for the E-2 press. These improvements were classified under three heads, namely engineering and technical, production, and energy conservation. The improvements which were identified, classified under these three heads, are as follows:

Engineering and Technical Improvements

1. Sinclair Colin diaphragm valves should be used for increased reliability and easier maintenance.
2. The hydraulic unit should be raised on a platform and should be improved by the provision of rupture discs.
3. In addition to rubber cup washers, brass piston rings should be used.
4. Grease - based lubrication system should be used for improved lubrication and better monitoring.
5. Better quality teflon gaskets should be used for the main cylinder and dome to reduce leakages.
6. Both the dome grooves should be repaired.
7. For greater reliability, the pressure switches should be relocated, the diameter of the copper tubes should be increased and bleeding points should be provided (in the copper tubes).
8. Strain gauges should be provided on both arms.
9. The valves and pipelines should be standardised as per the L & T presses.
10. The solenoid valves should be relocated for easier access.
11. All bends and fittings should be of the forged socket weld type.
12. The diameter of the dome steam condensate pipe should be increased (for the improvement of water removal).
13. Bottom dome opening provided for removal of water should be made bigger.

14. In place of convectional timer, PLC should be used.
15. Leslie valve should be provided for better and individual shaping control.

Production Improvements

1. Two separate hydraulic valves should be provided for individual cylinders to avoid delay in cylinder movement.
2. The near and front arms should be adjusted for the convenience of unloading of tyres.
3. Signal blinker lamps should be provided for indicating cure malfunctioning.
4. Provision of bladder stripping during shaping of tyres.
5. Mould lighting should be improved.
6. Cylinder ejection should be preponed.

Energy Conservation

1. Calcium silicate insulation should be used for the presses.
2. For improving the reliability of steam traps, strainers should be used on the dome condensate line.
3. For improved flushing, an additional half inch line should be provided for the internal drain.

IMPLEMENTING TOTAL PRODUCTIVE MAINTENANCE

An integral part of any successful implementation project is the active and continuous support of top and senior management. The positive attitude and active involvement of top and senior management personnel fosters a dynamic, team-oriented environment, which transcends all working levels. The first stage of implementation of TPM is called the preparation stage. Herein one tries and creates a suitable environment by establishing a plan for the introduction of TPM. The ten basic steps which were carried out and which will be discussed in the succeeding paragraphs are as follows:

1. Announcing top management's decision to introduce TPM.
2. Launching of educational campaign.

3. Creation of an organisation to promote TPM.
4. Establishment of basic TPM policies and goals.
5. Formulation of a master plan for TPM development.
6. Improvement of equipment effectiveness.
7. Establishment of an autonomous maintenance programme for operators.
8. Setting up of scheduled maintenance programme for the maintenance department.
9. Conducting training to improve operation and maintenance skills.
10. Development of new (initial) equipment management programme.

Step 1: Announce Top Management's Decision to Introduce TPM

The first step is the official announcement to introduce TPM. The official announcement is made during a formal presentation, during which the concepts, goals and the expected benefits are explained. During this presentation, top management explains the reasons behind the company's decision to implement and also conveys to the employees its enthusiasm for this project of TPM implementation. This presentation is immediately followed by printing this announcement in the company's bulletin, newsletter and house magazine, and also displaying it on the company's bulletin boards. At this point, it is essential that the top management must have a strong commitment to TPM since a firm foundation has to be laid during this period. Immediately after this announcement, it becomes the task of the senior managers and middle management personnel to train the employees to deal with the equipment and equipment problems on their own by improving their operation and maintenance skills and promoting autonomous maintenance. This is primarily done on a day-to-day and one-to-one basis during the daily rounds and visits to the shops (basically through the practice of management by walking around).

In the tyre manufacturing plant, the formal presentation was made by the Director of the Production Division in a meeting with all employees chaired by the Vice-President. During the presentation, the Director of Production Division was assisted by the Director of the Engineering Division. Also in the plant, the task of convincing and training was taken up seriously by the managers of the maintenance and tyre production departments and the middle management personnel. Even then, it took a considerable amount of time to change people's attitude and habits. However, as the shop floor environment improved, the employees started finding their work satisfying.

Step 2: Launch Educational Campaign

The second step was TPM training and promotion and this was launched soon after the introduction announcement. The objective of TPM education was not only to explain concepts, goals, benefits and the practice of TPM, but also to raise employee morale and soften their resistance to change. It was found that the resistance to TPM came from both equipment operators and maintenance tradesmen. Workers seem to prefer the conventional division of labour, namely that operators run the equipment while the maintenance tradesmen repair it. This is due to the fact that the workers on the production line fear that TPM will increase their workload, while the maintenance mechanics etc. are skeptical about the operators' ability to carry out maintenance of their equipment. TPM education should be designed to eliminate this resistance and raise the morale of the workmen. In the tyre factory, TPM education of workmen included slide presentations and used other visual aids. Supervisors and middle management personnel were invited to address sessions in which they explained their expectations and related their experiences.

TPM training was more specific. It dealt with the specifics of participation and problem-solving in PM groups and circles. The training module used for the supervisors also included group dynamics, facilitation and leadership.

Step 3: Create TPM Promotion Organisation

After the completion of the introductory education (to create an awareness of TPM) of the employees at different levels, the task of forming an organisational structure for the promotion of TPM was taken up. This structure should consist of committees to oversee different facets of TPM and also small groups at each level of the organisation. The reader will recollect the concept of TPM promotion which stresses the integration of top-down goal-oriented management with the activities of autonomous small groups on the shop floors. Based on this, it was suggested that a network of overlapping small groups be organised covering all levels from top management to the workers on the shop floor, wherein each group leader participates as a member in a small group at the next higher level (please see Fig. 6.3). This way, the group leader would serve as a link between levels facilitating vertical as well as horizontal communication within the company.

In Chapter Six under concept of TPM promotion, we had noted that it is essential to integrate the organisational structure used for TPM promotion with the organisational structure of the company. Towards this end, it became necessary to modify the company's organisational structure. The first modification, shown in Fig. 8.7(b), was not found to be entirely satisfactory, and accordingly, the modification had to be carried out in two steps. The original organisational structure, the first modification and the final structure are shown in Fig. 8.7. With the modified organisational structure in place, the organisational structure for TPM promotion was created. The TPM promotion organisation which was developed is shown in Fig. 8.8.

Step 4: Establish Basic TPM Policies and Goals

The fourth and fifth steps are very important and they precede the actual work of implementation of TPM, which are taken up in steps 6 to 10. The fourth step is one in which the basic TPM policies and goals of the company are established. This was the first major task undertaken by the management of the tyre manufacturing plant. It was recognised that although the policies may be abstract, written, or verbal statements, the goals should be quantifiable and precise, specifying the what (objective/goal), how much (the targeted quantity) and when (time frame/plan period). For example, a basic management policy may be as follows:

> "To reduce losses by eliminating breakdowns, stoppages, defects and accidents, while enhancing the profitability of the company and creating a favourable work environment for all employees."

In this statement, the objectives of the management are clear, and at the same time, the basic policy can be stated in concrete figures, such as the goals given in quantitative units. However, since the total elimination of breakdowns, stoppages and defects may not be possible, the management must set intermediate goals.

At this stage, it was decided that the annual goals should be determined by the managers and supervisors, who should, in turn, ensure that the improvement themes and goals set by the small groups at the shop floor workers' level were consistent with the overall goals of the company. Meetings were held to determine the target areas and to set goals. The following points were discussed before the formulation of the policy, specification of target areas and statement of the goals:

External Demands

1. Timely and effective production of new products.
2. Flexible response to fluctuations in demand.

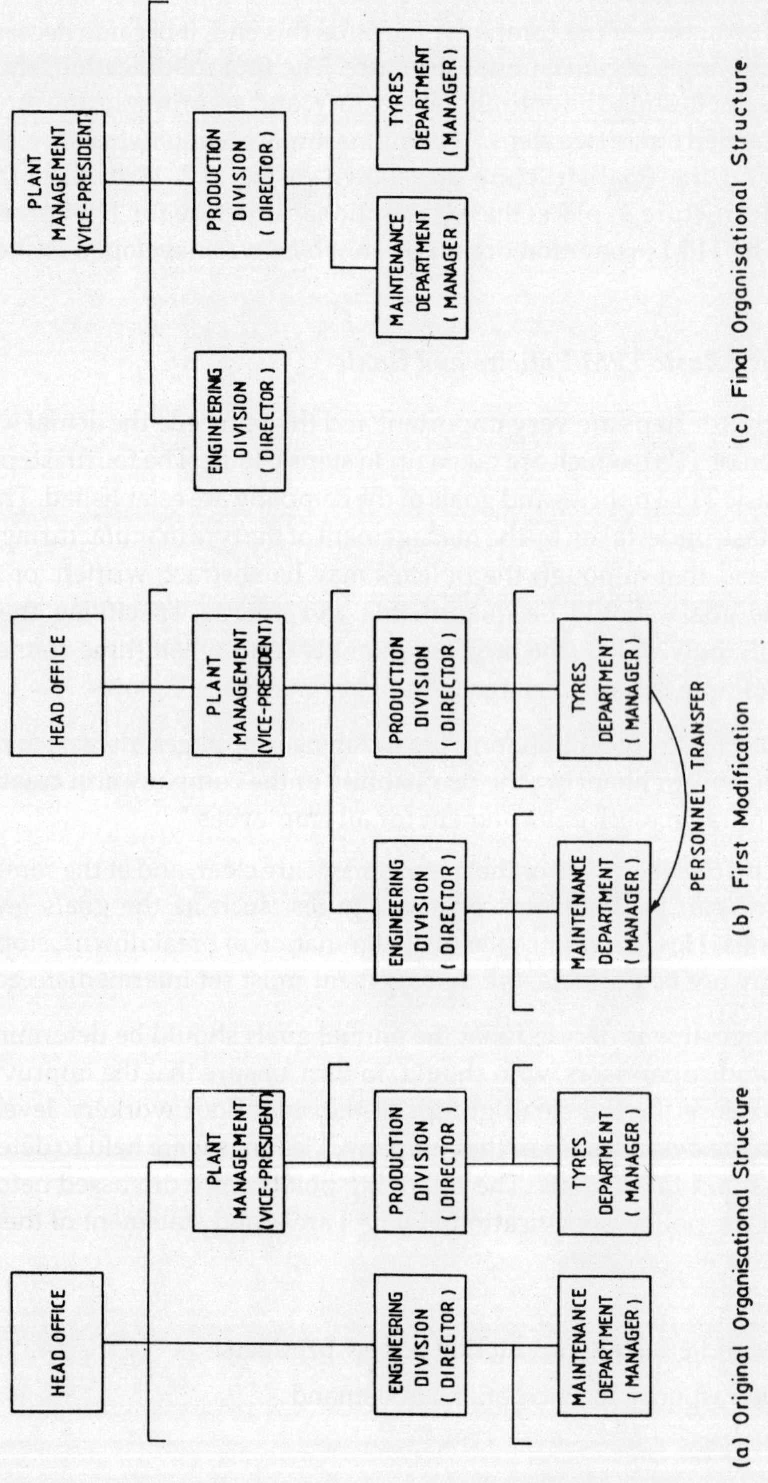

Fig. 8.7. Modification of Structure to Carry Out TPM

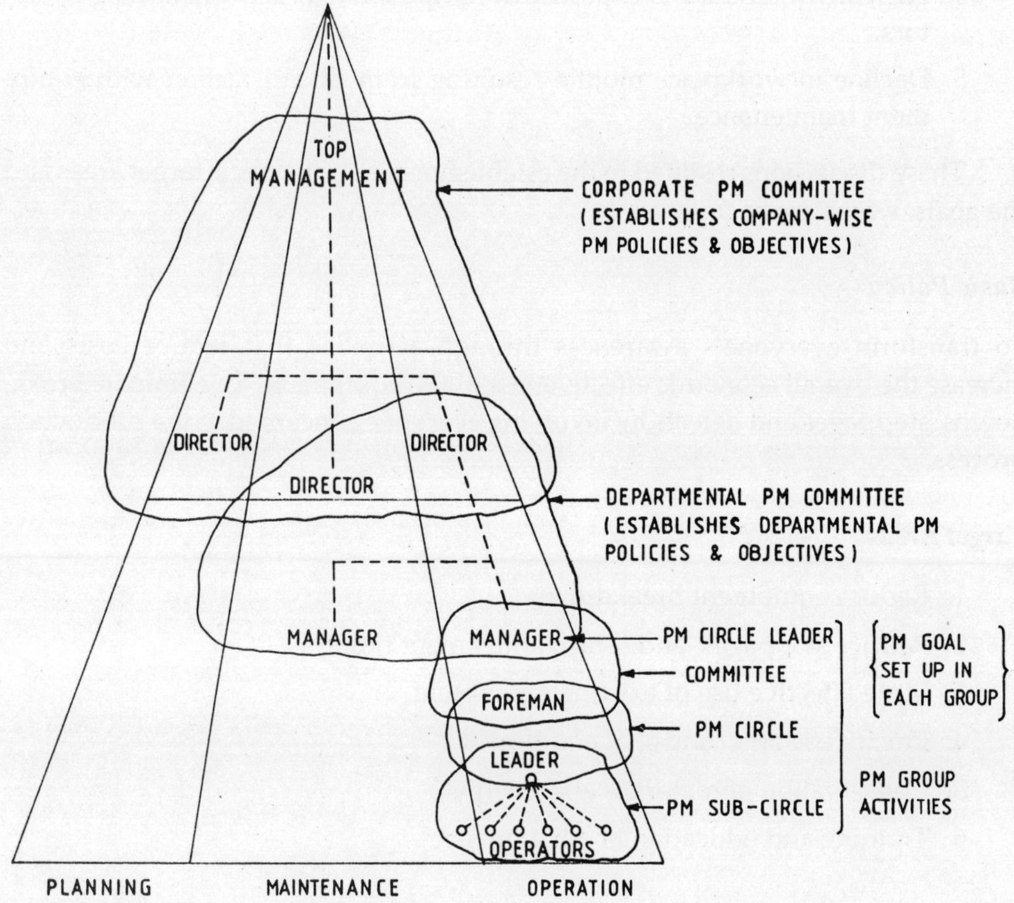

Fig. 8.8. TPM Promotion Organisation

3. Reduction in price of product.
4. Guaranteed high level of product quality.

Internal Problems (within the plant)

1. Increasing production and quality problems resulting from frequent equipment failures.
2. Deteriorating condition of equipment caused by continuous high-load operation.

3. Increase in the number of equipment with design weaknesses.
4. Lack of awareness and expertise in equipment maintenance among operators.
5. Decline in workplace morale resulting from dissatisfaction with equipment maintenance.

These discussions resulted in the establishment of the policy, target areas and the goals, which are as follows:

Basic Policy

To transform everyone's awareness through activities that reduce costs and increase the overall economic effectiveness of the equipment. To eliminate breakdowns, stoppages and defects by involving everyone concerned in the production process.

Target Areas

1. Reduce equipment breakdowns.
2. Reduce stoppages, and setup/adjustment time.
3. More effective use of existing equipment.
4. Precise use and control of equipment.
5. Conservation of materials and energy.
6. Training and education of personnel.

Goals

1. Reduce failures and equipment downtime.
2. Reduce equipment failure rate.
3. Reduce incidents of serious equipment failure.
4. Reduce non-operation time.
5. Reduce defects in process.
6. Conserve energy.
7. Increase in the number of improvement suggestions.
8. Reduce accidents.

Step 5: Formulate a Master Plan for TPM Development

In this step, after the formulation of the basic policy and definition of the goals, a master plan for TPM development was established. This master plan concentrated on the following five basic activities:

1. Improving equipment effectiveness through the minimisation of the six major losses. This activity would build the foundation for the implementation of autonomous maintenance.
2. Establishing an autonomous maintenance programme for equipment operators.
3. Ensuring a reasonable level of product quality and concentrating on activities directed at improvement of quality.
4. Establishing a schedule for periodic preventive maintenance of equipment to be carried out by the maintenance department.
5. Education and training of personnel to improve their knowledge/abilities and skills.

It was also decided that this master plan should be reviewed and revised, if necessary periodically, to ensure that the projects do not fall behind schedule.

The first five steps discussed above were the preparatory steps. The actual implementation of TPM had yet to start, and as noted above, it had to begin with the battle against six major equipment - related losses. This can only happen if the individual workers are made to move away from their traditional daily work routines and begin to practice TPM. Every employee has to participate in this effort. The start of actual implementation was the holding of the TPM 'kickoff.' The kickoff should help to usher in an atmosphere that increases worker morale and commitment. At the tyre manufacturing factory, the kickoff took the form of a meeting which was attended by all employees and in which the top management:

(i) announced the kickoff,

(ii) gave a report of the plans developed and also the work done during the preparation stage,

(iii) presented and explained the basic TPM policy and the TPM goals, and

(iv) presented the master plan for TPM development.

Step 6: Improve Equipment Effectiveness

As noted earlier, the E-2 bag-o-matic press and the curing department had been selected as the starting points for the implementation of TPM. Moreover, the areas of improvement and the improvement projects for the E-2 press had also been identified. It was realised that the fate of the TPM implementation programme depended on the success of this step — the ability to improve the equipment effectiveness of the E-2 bag-o-matic press. Therefore, the work was taken up with all seriousness, and engineering and maintenance personnel, production supervisors and members of PM circles and sub-circles were organised into project teams. Each team concentrated on a few of the identified improvement projects.

Since a number of persons express doubts about TPM and its potential to produce results, it is essential that these doubts be removed and the effectiveness of TPM be clearly demonstrated to build confidence in the employees. For this, teams should be formed and team efforts should be focussed on equipment which suffer from chronic losses. This way, through focussed team efforts, marked improvements can be demonstrated after a period of three or four months. The managers should also remember and explain to the team and group/circle members that they should not hesitate to apply any technique; particularly cause-and-effect analysis and P-M analysis, which can be very useful in these equipment efectiveness improvement projects.

This is what was done on the E-2 bag-o-matic press. The efforts of the teams were crowned with unprecedented and unexpected success. After the implementation of TPM and through the implementation of the improvement projects, the equipment effectiveness of the E-2 press went up from around (below) 60 per cent to more than 90 per cent. During the first week after the implementation itself (that is, during the seven day period from October 1 to October 7, 1991), the equipment effectiveness went up to 89.5 per cent. There was further improvement in the following week with the effectiveness going up to 96.1 per cent. This impact could be maintained and thereafter, equipment effectiveness had been kept at a figure above 90 per cent. The details of the performance of E-2 press are given in Table 8.4 and 8.5. The daily performance figures for the first eighteen days after the implementation of TPM (that is, from October 1 to October 18, 1991) are given in Table 8.4. The weekly performance figures for the first 7 weeks (including the first 18 days for which details are given in Table 8.4) are given in Table 8.5. The before TPM entries in the two tables are the daily performance figures for the seventh day or April 30 and the weekly performance figures (as given in Table 8.3) respectively.

Table 8.4. E-2 Press Performance After TPM
(October 1 to October 18, 1991)

Day	*Number of tyres cured*	*Availa-bility*	*Perfor-mance Rate*	*Quality Rate*	*Effectiveness (per cent)*
Before TPM	*30*	*0.833*	*0.875*	*0.833*	*60.71*
1	34	0.854	0.967	0.941	77.70
2	40	1.000	0.972	1.000	97.20
3	36	0.924	0.947	1.000	87.50
4	38	1.000	0.924	1.000	92.40
5	40	1.000	0.972	1.000	97.20
6	12*	1.000	0.875	1.000	87.50
7	38	0.965	0.957	1.000	87.50
8	40	1.000	0.972	1.000	97.20
9	40	1.000	0.972	1.000	97.20
10	40	1.000	0.972	1.000	97.20
11	40	1.000	0.972	1.000	97.20
12	42	1.000	1.021	0.952	97.10
13	12*	1.000	0.875	1.000	87.50
14	42	1.000	1.021	0.976	99.60
15	40	1.000	0.972	1.000	97.20
16	42	1.000	1.021	1.000	102.10
17	12*	1.000	0.875	1.000	87.50
18	40	1.000	0.972	1.000	97.20
1-7	238	0.963	0.944	0.984	89.50
8-14	256	1.000	0.972	0.989	96.10

* Sunday/Holiday

Table 8.5. E-2 Press Weekly Performance

Week	*Number of tyres cured*	*Availa-bility*	*Perfor-mance Rate*	*Quality Rate*	*Effectiveness (per cent)*
Before TPM	*176*	*0.801*	*0.790*	*0.811*	*51.32*
1	238	0.963	0.944	0.984	89.50
2	256	1.000	0.972	0.989	96.10
3	230	0.997	0.960	1.000	95.71
4	248	0.978	0.972	0.987	93.82
5	222	0.980	0.960	1.000	94.08
6	260	1.000	0.972	0.993	96.51
7	254	0.983	0.953	1.000	93.67

Step 7: Establish Autonomous Maintenance Programme for Equipment Operators

The second basic activity of the master plan was establishing an autonomous maintenance programme for equipment operators. Regarding this step, there was a realisation at all levels of the management that its implementation would take time. This is primarily because it takes time to change deep-seated attitudes and habits. For implementation of autonomous maintenance, everyone in the organisation, from the top to the bottom, must sincerely believe that it is feasible for the operators to perform autonomous maintenance activities (in addition to their job of operating the equipment), and also that individuals should be responsible for their own equipment. The management must realise the need to inculcate a sense of ownership in the equipment operators. This understanding and belief in the workers and realisation in the management come gradually over a period of time. Moreover, each and every operator has to be trained in the skills necessary to perform autonomous maintenance. With this, training in the 5 Ss is also necessary. The training in the 5 Ss and in autonomous maintenance skills also take time.

At the tyre factory, this step was taken up pretty early in the TPM implementation programme. The work of implementation of autonomous maintenance was taken up in the curing department in the month of August, 1991 and accordingly, there was an overlap as far as the implementation of steps 5 and 6 were concerned. Right at the beginning, it was decided that in addition to training in autonomous maintenance skills, the equipment operators must start the practice of autonomous maintenance and this, in turn, must start with cleaning of their equipment and then they must develop their own cleaning and lubrication standards. Based on this, it was decided that the following programme should be adopted for the production line workers initially in the curing department and later in the remaining manufacturing departments:

1. Initial cleaning.
2. Developing countermeasures for the causes and effects of dirt and dust.
3. Developing cleaning and lubricating standards.
4. General inspection.
5. Developing inspection standards.
6. Organisation and tidiness.
7. Full implementation of autonomous maintenance.

This programme was very effective as will be noticed from the description of actual experiences given in the following paragraphs.

Through initial cleaning, operators developed an interest and concern for their machines. The operators also realised that cleaning is inspection. They also learnt basic lubrication and bolting techniques and became fairly skilled at detecting problems and sometimes even repairing them. During the programme, it was noticed that the more difficult it is for the individual to perform initial cleaning, the stronger will be his/her desire to keep the equipment clean, and thus reduce the cleaning time. This heralded the beginning of the efforts aimed at developing countermeasures. Various measures were adopted, including covers and shields, to eliminate the accumulation of dust, dirt, chips etc. In fact, if the cause could not be removed, the problem was taken up by the PM circle/subcircle and suggestions for more efficient cleaning and inspection procedures were sought and designed for these problem areas. Although a group of operators were held responsible for keeping their work area clean and improving the housekeeping, the engineering and maintenance staff were asked to cooperate with them, as and where needed, and support their efforts. The first two steps of the programme helped the operators to identify the basic conditions that should apply to their equipment. Based on this, they developed their own cleaning and lubrication standards. They also realised that the time available for cleaning, lubricating, bolting and detecting minor defects is limited. The supervisors gave them ten minutes every shift at the beginning of the shift and this was the only time available besides the time available during the curing cycle. This brought out the need to improve cleaning and lubrication practices wherever the standards set could not be maintained within the targeted time. This was accompanied by investigating innovative ideas, such as visual control to show limits on oiler level gauges, along with better positioning of oilers and more efficient lubricating methods.

The first three steps were carried out to prevent deterioration and maintain the basic conditions of the equipment through cleaning, lubrication and tightening of bolts and fasteners. The fourth step was aimed at detecting and measuring deterioration through general inspection of the equipment. This step was carried out in two phases, one after the other. Initially PM circle leaders were trained in these inspection procedures (taking up one category of inspection at a time) using a general inspection manual prepared by supervisors, and maintenance and engineering staff. These leaders then shared what they had learnt with the circle members. Thereafter, the circle members worked together on problem areas discovered during general inspection of their equipment. In this effort, they got the assistance of the maintenance personnel, and with their help they took action to correct deterioration and improve the affected area of the equipment. It is necessary to remember that this step takes a long time because all operators are required to develop the ability to detect abnormalities. This step was not rushed and enough time was given since this is the best way of producing equipment-competent operators. After the completion of the fourth step, the cleaning and lubrication standards and the tentative inspection standards were reviewed and re-evaluated to eliminate any inconsistencies and to ensure that the autonomous maintenance activities could be carried out within the established time frames. This step resulted in the development of general inspection standards.

At the end of the fifth step, it was decided that in addition to maintaining basic conditions and carrying out general inspection of their equipment, the operators were also to be responsible for the following:

(i) correct operation and setup (setting conditions and checking product quality),

(ii) detection and treatment of abnormal conditions,

(iii) recording data on operation, quality and processing conditions, and also

(iv) minor servicing of their equipment.

With this, the programme for the production department was finalised. It consisted of the following elements:

1. Prevention of deterioration and for this, the operators must
   (a) operate their equipment correctly,
   (b) maintain basic equipment conditions,
   (c) make necessary adjustments (during set up and operation),
   (d) record data on breakdowns and other malfunctions, and
   (e) collaborate with the maintenance department to develop and implement improvements.
2. Detection and measurement of deterioration and for this, the operators must
   (a) conduct daily inspections, and also
   (b) conduct certain periodic inspections.
3. Restoration of equipment and for this, the operators must
   (a) make minor repairs (simple repairs and replacement of parts),
   (b) report promptly and correctly about breakdowns and other malfunctions, and
   (c) help maintenance tradesmen in the repair of sporadic breakdowns.

The equipment operators gradually developed greater morale and competence through PM circle activities led by supervisors.

Step 8: Set Up Scheduled Maintenance Programme (for Maintenance Department)

Scheduled maintenance carried out by the maintenance department must be coordinated with the autonomous maintenance activities of the operations/production department so that the two departments can function together like the two wheels of a car. Until general inspection becomes an integral part of the routine of the equipment operators, the assistance of the maintenance department will be required more often. Moreover, breakdowns, while gradually decreasing, will continue to demand attention. Thus, the work load of the maintenance department could be high initially. This temporary excess workload has to be handled promptly either through overtime or sub-contracting in order to support the commitment of the equipment operators. Otherwise, the operators will lose their enthusiasm for autonomous maintenance.

This is what was done at the tyre factory. The development of a scheduled maintenance programme actually began before the setting up of the general inspection procedure by the operators. The maintenance department developed the equipment inspection standards independently, so that these were available for comparison with the standards set by the operators during the autonomous inspection stage. It must be remembered that a clear division of the responsibilities of the two departments is the key to thorough and effective inspection and effective equipment inspection can only be accomplished when the two sets of standards are combined.

Step 9: Conduct Training to Improve Operation and Maintenance Skills

Education and training are investments in people. A company implementing TPM must make this investment to enable employees to manage their equipment properly. In addition to training in maintenance techniques, the equipment operators must sharpen their operational skills. Whereas the content and organisation of the introductory training materials may not vary much from company to company since the objective is technical education and training for operation and maintenance of plant and equipment, the education and training programme for both operators and maintenance tradesmen must be tailored to the requirements of the workplace. The competence of the maintenance personnel is essential for the success of the TPM implementation programme and in the tyre factory, considerable effort was made for upgrading the 'know-how' of the maintenance tradesmen. At the end of this step, the operators were also able to operate their equipment safely and as per the set standards, in addition to being able to maintain the basic equipment conditions.

At the end of this step, the TPM Promotion Committee gave its recommendations on the new maintenance policy. These recommendations are as follows:

1. Autonomous maintenance - enforce daily and weekly inspections by equipment operators.
2. Improve corrective maintenance techniques through the upgradation of skills of the maintenance personnel.
3. Identification and correction of plant abnormalities which cause low equipment availability, high maintenance costs, or poor quality. Also ensure the feedback of such information to maintenance planning section and design for plant and equipment modifications and maintainability improvements.

Step 10: Develop New (Initial) Equipment Management Programme

New equipment management is a very difficult task. Problems often show up during test running and start up even though the design, manufacture and installation appear to have gone smoothly. Design, process and maintenance engineers may have to make many improvements before normal operations can begin. Even then, startup period repairs, adjustments, inspections and also the initial lubrication and cleaning needed to prevent deterioration and breakdowns may be so difficult to carry out that one tends to get discouraged. Initial equipment management has to be performed mainly by production/operations and maintenance personnel (with help from design/engineering and process/technical departments). The objectives of the programme are improving equipment reliability and increasing the ease of maintenance.

At the factory, it was decided to work towards these objectives through improvement activities by ensuring the following:

(i) Proper attention to reliability and maintainability features, safety and economy of life cycle costs during the equipment investment planning and specification development stages of the life cycle.

(ii) Setting up a team which will be entrusted with the task of developing the equipment specifications, installation plans and commissioning trials. This team should include representatives from design/engineering, process/technical, operations/production and maintenance departments.

(iii) Working with the equipment manufacturer to ensure that the equipment is actually manufactured according to specifications developed by the team and has the desired features.

(iv) Reducing the period from acquisition to stable operation by proper execution of installation plans and commissioning trials and debugging.

Moreover, by working together with the design engineers during the start up phase to eliminate problems at their source, the technical and maintenance staff could absorb and apply knowledge about maintenance prevention (MP) design.

With the completion of the tenth step, the work of TPM implementation in the curing department had been completed. This, however, was in no way the end of the TPM implementation programme. On the other hand, it was just the beginning since TPM had to be implemented in other departments for other processes. Moreover, there were still a number of loose ends and therefore, the work of refining and perfecting TPM implementation had to be taken up. Higher goals of equipment effectiveness in the curing and other departments had to be set. However, the programme of TPM implementation in the curing department had given the necessary impetus and the employees were ready to take up the task of implementing TPM fully and aiming for higher goals.

CLOSING REMARKS

As compared to the first case study, this case study was a much more extensive application of TPM. It was carried out on a much larger scale and was also more complete, particularly in as much as it did not fight shy of education and training, employee involvement, development of a participative approach and TPM promotion. The lessons learnt and experiences gained from this case study are too numerous to recount. In the final remarks, we will highlight the most important lessons, or the most important points brought out by this case study. These are as follows:

1. The need and importance of carrying out the implementation programme in phases and first identifying a particular equipment and starting from a department shop/section wherein the improvement efforts will have the maximum, and also the most visible, effect.
2. For the selected equipment and/or department, the need to identify improvement projects and implementing these improvement projects and suggestions as an essential part of the TPM implementation programme.
3. The importance of the preparation stage and the first five steps of the TPM implementation programme. All the five steps are important but of these, the

second and third steps, namely, launching and conduct of the educational campaign and creation of the TPM promotion organisation, are probably the most important.

4. The role of the PM groups in the implementation of autonomous maintenance. This case study brought out the crucial role of PM groups in the promotion and absorption of autonomous maintenance. It has shown, through practice, that the most effective method of training operators in detection and measurement of deterioration through general inspection of the equipment is by first training the PM circle leaders and having them train the equipment operators.
5. The importance of the training programme for the equipment operators and maintenance tradesmen and the fact that the skills and competence of the maintenance personnel is crucial to the success of the TPM implementation programme.
6. The fact that proper implementation of TPM calls for measurement of maintenance effectiveness. The case study also brought out clearly that the equipment effectiveness measure is the best yardstick not only for assessing the effectiveness but also for setting targets and benchmarks.

References

1. Bhadury, B., 'Application of Productive Maintenance: A Case Study' in Proceedings (Technical Volume) of the All India Seminar on Terotechnology and Condition Based Maintenance, The Institution of Engineers (India), Pune (Maharashtra, India), February 3 and 4, 1996, pp. 160-180.
2. Singh, S., Implementing Total Productive Maintenance in a Continuous Process Plant, Unpublished M. Tech thesis (research carried out under the supervision of Dr. Bikash Bhadury), Department of Industrial Engineering and Management, Indian Institute of Technology, Kharagpur (West Bengal, India), December, 1991.

Subject Index